CHOICE OF FORCE

Special Operations for Canada

CHOICE OF FORCE

Special Operations for Canada

Edited By

David Last and Bernd Horn

Published for the School of Policy Studies, Queen's University
by McGill-Queen's University Press
Montreal and Kingston • London • Ithaca

Library and Archives Canada Cataloguing in Publication

Choice of force : special operations for Canada / edited by David Last and Bernd Horn.

Includes bibliographical references.
ISBN 1-55339-045-8 (bound).—ISBN 1-55339-044-X (pbk.)

1. Special operations (Military science)—Canada. 2. Canada—Military policy. I. Last, David M. II. Horn, Bernd, 1959- III. Queen's University (Kingston, Ont.). School of Policy Studies

U262.C48 2005 355.4'22'0971 C2004-907234-X

CONTENTS

PREFACE

As this volume is written, an American-led coalition still has over 100,000 troops in Iraq. A NATO force occupies parts of Afghanistan. Sudan is experiencing ethnic cleansing and genocide. Armed First Nations activists again defy police on reserves. Immigration combines with organized crime in Italy to impinge on national politics. Islamic separatists attack Thai police stations to seize weapons. India and Pakistan continue nuclear posturing. One could go on. This is our security environment. Battleships, jet fighters, and main battle tanks cannot win on these slippery fields, although they may be part of the team. How do we invest in security?

The purpose of this volume is to explore concepts that will be helpful in developing a Canadian approach to special operations. Useful concepts might find their way into Canadian doctrine. Doctrine is not a substitute for thinking problems through; it is not a catalogue of how we do things, or what we should think about things. Rather, sound doctrine can give us a philosophy and a common approach that enable us to solve problems collectively.

Business leaders go to business schools so they can work together to solve business problems. Military leaders go to staff colleges so that they can work together to solve military problems. But today's security problems transcend borders, have political, economic, and social dimensions, and involve dozens of government departments and agencies. Without a federal-provincial, civil-military, public-private "Security College", how will we develop the next generation of security concepts? How can we get beyond the still-difficult problem of forcing army, navy, and air force tribes to work together and achieve a balance of police and military, intelligence, and commercial resources, while preserving civil liberties at home and rule of law among nations? At the instigation of the Asymmetric Threat Working Group of the Department of National Defence, we brought together academics and practitioners to discuss these ideas in two roundtables at the Royal Military College of Canada, the country's only national university.

The terms Special Operations (SO), Special Forces (SF), and Special Operations Forces (SOF) have specific meanings that are rooted in the history and practice of special operations as they have been employed by major powers, particularly the United States and the United Kingdom. It may not be useful for countries like Canada to limit their exploration of special operations according to the needs and experience of major powers. Indeed, it may be useful for other countries to re-examine their ideas about special operations in the light of the constraints faced by Canada. Canada is an active player in the international community, a beneficiary of the liberal world order underwritten by American military power, and an ally in the war on terror – albeit perhaps with some reservations about the campaign strategy. Any country in this situation faces similar challenges. The challenges extend to all branches of government, security organizations, and the academic community that examines and supports them through research and public debate. Above all, the policy and doctrine communities, including politicians and civil servants, have an interest in understanding special operations and taking a stand on their role in the pursuit of national and human security.

Special Operations, Special Forces, and Special Operations Forces (as proper nouns) are taken to have the meanings assigned by the Department of Defence Dictionary or NATO lexicon. Special Operations, for example, are:

> ...military activities conducted by specially designated, organized, trained and equipped forces using operational techniques and modes of employment *not standard to conventional forces*. These activities are conducted across the spectrum of military operations, independently or in co-ordination with operations of conventional forces to achieve military, political, economic and psychological objectives. Political-military considerations may require clandestine, covert or discreet techniques and the acceptance of a degree of physical and political risk not associated with conventional operations.[1]

The previous book in this series, *Force of Choice: Perspectives on Special Operations*, explores some of the missions associated with special operations, including direct action, support for unconventional warfare or counter-insurgency, counter-terrorism and hostage-rescue operations, civil affairs, and psychological operations.[2] Whether or not a particular operation is considered "special" in the doctrinal sense usually hinges on whether it is a mission that might normally be assigned to Special Forces (such as US Army Special Forces or the UK Special Air Service) or to Special Operations Forces (such as the US Army Rangers or perhaps a parachute battalion). But for countries like Canada, which do not have this organizational constraint, "special operations" can be used in the policy debate to imply a broader range of possibilities. Because Canada does not have Special Forces, we can leave force structure as an open question. In these books, we generally avoid discussion of Special Forces and SOF and instead use the term special operations (without capitals) to imply operations outside the scope of conventional army, navy, and air force missions that may be conducted by specially trained, equipped, and organized forces and that may include non-military assets.

THE FUTURE SECURITY ENVIRONMENT

This book is organized in four parts. The first explores aspects of the future security environment and their implications for special operations that Canada might have to conduct. The common theme of these chapters is that security is not a matter for defence departments alone, if ever it was. The new security environment is going to require more sophisticated combinations of security professionals, in uniform and out of it.

In Chapter One, historians Michael Hennessy and Bernd Horn describe the origins of Canadian special operations capability and some alternative futures that Canada might face. We suggest what this might imply for Canada's national counter-terrorist force, Joint Task Force 2 (JTF2).

Professor Nicole Schwarz-Morgan applies her knowledge of philosophy, psychology, and education in Chapter Two to the changing psychological and physiological landscape within which special operations must be conducted. The minds of our special operatives might be the most important battleground of the future, and education might be our most important defence.

In Chapter Three, political scientist Todd Hataley considers the problems posed by Canada's border with the U.S. Defending this vital economic lifeline against increasingly sophisticated attacks will require special task forces and new military-police combinations if we are to make it the "security membrane" that it needs to become.

Political scientist Christian Leuprecht suggests in Chapter Four that our demographic diversity might represent a comparative advantage in the shrinking global community. To take advantage of it, we must find more effective ways of bringing ethnic minorities into security organizations, particularly the armed forces.

In Chapter Five, Professor Christopher Spearin of the Canadian Forces College considers issues that are raised by private security companies in the emerging environment for special operations. Private security is a historical reality. States need to be prepared to regulate private security companies, to prevent loss of skilled personnel, and to take advantage of the capabilities they may offer.

THE CANADIAN POLICY ENVIRONMENT

The second part of the book surveys the Canadian policy environment. What kinds of operations are permitted, desired, or required by Canadian policymakers, and how is the conduct of these operations constrained? All four chapters in this section have a common starting point in a list of potential missions or tasks. This list, summarized in Table 1, might be grouped in four categories –

kinetic and non-kinetic missions, at home and abroad. Task 1, for example, is a non-kinetic domestic mission, while Task 12 is a kinetic foreign operation. The label "kinetic" implies speed and violence, while "non-kinetic" implies patience and cooperation.

TABLE 1
Sample Mission Descriptions

1. Help civilians deal with a chemical, biological, or radiological attack on a major Canadian city
2. Evacuate Canadian citizens from dangerous situations, with the consent of the country involved
3. Free hostages anywhere in Canada, for example by storming a building where they may be held
4. Evacuate Canadian citizens from dangerous situations, without the effective cooperation of the country involved
5. Seize or free a Canadian commercial ship or aircraft taken hostage by criminals or terrorists on the high seas
6. Free Canadian hostages in a foreign country, with the cooperation of that country's government
7. Deploy to war-torn regions multidisciplinary teams including medical people, aid experts, and security specialists
8. Enhance the security of Canadian civilians working in war-affected or unstable countries by providing security advice, training, or oversight
9. Free Canadian hostages in a war-affected foreign country, without local assistance
10. Provide humanitarian assistance in the case of natural disasters outside North America
11. Work with a multilateral force to destroy a weapons facility in a hostile country
12. Work with a multilateral team to disable or destroy large facilities such as a military headquarters in countries that are a threat to Canada or other democratic countries
13. Gain covert entry to a computer installation as part of information warfare
14. Capture and extract vital information without the knowledge or consent of a country hostile to Canada
15. Capture and extract an individual such as an indicted war criminal from a hostile region at the request or with the cooperation of the country's own government
16. Capture and extract a person without the knowledge or consent of a country hostile to Canada

The list was developed by serving officers and academics, including several of the authors. We drew on work by the Canadian Forces Directorate of Land Strategic Concepts (DLSC) Special Operations Capabilities Working Group but also consulted widely with other government departments to identify the sort of tasks that might be contemplated for military or civilian forces in light of the emerging security environment. Work by the Australian Defence Forces to develop special operations capabilities was also considered.[3] Most mission types described in the previous volume are encompassed within the list.[4] Technical mission descriptions and conjecture about capabilities that might be required were then reduced to common language that made sense to civilian respondents. The resulting list of 16 mission descriptions in Table 1 was the starting point for all four chapters, although it was used in slightly different ways for each.

In Chapter Six, Dr. Susan Breau, a Canadian lawyer and senior research fellow with the British International Institute of Comparative Law in London, England, explores the framework of international law that would affect such missions. Can special operations support a rules-based international order, or do current interpretations of international law and international humanitarian law limit the scope for special operations? Although international law is evolving, particularly through the report of the International Commission on Intervention and State Sovereignty, *Responsibility to Protect*, there are still significant legal constraints on the use of force by states, even when this purports to be in support of an international regime. States like Canada, which benefit from a rules-based international order that constrains the use of force, are unlikely to transgress against these laws and norms of state behaviour.

Chapters Seven and Eight draw on a common survey instrument about attitudes towards special operations of the sort listed in Table 1. Stephanie Mullen, who has considerable experience conducting research with parliamentarians, conducted interviews in person with senators and members of parliament, allowing both structured and open-ended answers to the survey. Combined with the framework of international law explored in Chapter Six, these insights serve to narrow the scope of Canadian special operations. Parliamentarians across the political spectrum have a preference for special operations that help and protect Canadians, as opposed to operations that might be considered offensive. Offensive operations are more acceptable when framed as part of a strategy of prevention.

Chapter Eight reports on the results of an exploratory elite survey conducted by Dr. Conrad Winn and his colleagues at COMPAS, a leader in opinion and market research. The results of more than 170 interviews with opinion leaders and decision makers reveal patterns about the preferences of Canada's policy elites, and a surprising acceptance of assertive special operations when these are framed as part of preventive action. Taken together, Chapters Six, Seven, and Eight suggest that all four types of special operations are important but that a national strategy would emphasize non-kinetic and domestic special operations, with kinetic operations undertaken defensively within the limited framework of international law.

Chapter Nine explores the process by which Canada makes decisions that might lead to the execution of special operations. Here we took a key-informer approach to describing the way in which national security decisions have been made and how decision-making structures have evolved. We conclude that any national special operations plan should include liaison and advisors within central agencies such as the Privy Council Office in order to combine the efforts of government departments.

CONTEMPORARY SPECIAL OPERATIONS

The third part of the book explores both continuity and change in special operations as they are conducted in today's strategic environment. Three of these chapters were commissioned to fill gaps identified by the authors and the sponsor of the study in roundtables conducted at the Royal Military College.

Kosovo and Afghanistan have served in many ways as crucibles for testing new concepts for the employment of special operations. Since both campaigns involve large conventional forces, we might be tempted to see these as cases of special operations supporting conventional forces. Dr. Sean Maloney has extensive experience investigating field operations on the ground, and he demonstrates that the leading edge in both campaigns consists of special operations, supported by the stabilizing influence of the conventional forces. Conventional forces hold the ring, while crucial steps forward can be achieved only through "special operations", whoever actually conducts them. The same argument can be made for the difficult business of post-conflict reconstruction. Provincial Reconstruction Teams (PRTs) are being developed in Afghanistan as an alternative to using conventional security forces, which have a large footprint and contribute comparatively little to the reconstruction efforts that (it is hoped) will eventually permit withdrawal of international forces.

Chapters Thirteen, Fourteen, and Fifteen address technical aspects of support for special operations. Signals officer Major Sylvain Leblanc and Dr. Scott Knight explore the contribution of information operations to each stage in the conduct of special operations. Major Andrew Godefroy, PhD, has served with both the Directorate of Space Development and the Canadian Forces Joint Operations Group in developing space-support concepts and procedures. In Chapter Fourteen he explores the benefits space power can confer upon special operations, as well as the potential hazards of relying on use of space power against them. In Chapter Fifteen, historian and science-fiction author Jason Ridler examines the relationship between forces configured for special operations and the technology that is required to support them. The vaunted Revolution in Military Affairs has created new opportunities to substitute quality for quantity, putting more combat power and more information into the hands of small, specialized teams.

DOCTRINE FOR SPECIAL OPERATIONS?

The final part of the book addresses the problem of doctrine. One of the central problems is interoperability – between agencies and across organizational lines and between carefully crafted special teams and the outside specialists with whom they may have to work on particular tasks. We asked Dr. Tom Dececchi, an organizational theorist, and Ms. Berndadette Dececchi, a doctoral candidate in education, to consider the problems of combining experts to produce teams for specific missions. The problem is not trivial, because the precise nature of the tasks and conditions of work are seldom known in advance, and the time for producing effective teams may be very short. Dececchi and Dececchi apply a systems approach to the team-building problem and arrive at practical conclusions to overcome barriers to effective teambuilding.

Teambuilding across national boundaries can be even more daunting. Few countries have the resources of the U.S. Should they develop independent capabilities, work with a leading power, or plan to deploy within a multinational framework for special operations? Working out of Washington, James Kiras explores the ongoing transformation of the American military and particularly of US Special Operations Forces following the September 2001 attacks in New York and Washington. What can Canada learn from this for the development of Canadian doctrine? German doctoral candidate Benjamin Zyla has conducted interviews in NATO headquarters to explore the extent of a common NATO approach to special operations and its potential for multinational collaboration.

The conclusion poses questions about the way forward for the development of Canadian concepts and doctrine for special operations and the forces that might conduct them.

ACKNOWLEDGEMENTS

This project began with funds made available to the Royal Military College by the Asymmetrical Threat Working Group, through the efforts of Tony Hunt, Bob Gemmell, and Clive Russell. Its intellectual debts, however, go back further. As the researcher responsible for assembling the contributors, I am indebted to Dan Holt, Ed Czank, Barry McLeod, Mark De Smedt, and Paul Taillon for an early introduction to the arcane world of special operations and counter-terrorism in its unique Canadian form. RMC officer cadets Jamie Green, Michael St. Pierre, Daniel Arsenault, Karla Lyster, Jaime Phillips, Alexandre Dumulon-Perrault, Caleb Walker, and Nicholas Wheeler helped to bring fresh ideas into the project.

Several significant pieces of research related to future special operations are not included in this volume, but their authors have contributed to this discourse. Lawrence McDonough's work on cost-benefit analysis of alternative force structures, with the assistance of Tara Nordick, is reported in an occasional paper of the Institute for Defence Resources Management. Kerim Ousman has begun important work on terrorism in sub-Saharan Africa, and Fahim Youssofzai continues innovative work on assessing operational effectiveness. Paul Taillon helped to bring together the expertise reflected in both volumes of this series. As director of the War Studies Program at the Royal Military College, Brian McKercher has provided leadership, support, and funding for international conferences that have contributed to the stock of knowledge reported on here. Larry Jenkins, Ruth Taronno, Karla Lyster, and Stefan Dordrechter have helped assemble ideas for new thinking about civil-military cooperation and Provincial Reconstruction Teams. In addition to providing a chapter, Christian Leuprecht managed the research assistants at Queen's University: Gabrielle Tree, Alex Dissette, Sheilagh Wilson, Natasha Kanerva, and John Murray.

Managing the budget and a large number of academic contributors, contracts, and claims was made easy by Aline Larose, Gisele LaBrie, Lucie Lefebvre, Bernadette Scott, and Liz McIlwaine. Many thanks. Moira Jackson provided not only technical editing but useful substantive comments and a common-sense check on jargon and abbreviations. The product is much more readable thanks to her efforts. Val Jarus and Mark Howes, as usual, have done stalwart work on putting the book together. Responsibility for the finished product rests with the authors and editors and does not necessarily represent the views of any of the organizations or other individuals who helped with the project.

David Last
Bernd Horn

Kingston, 2004

NOTES

1. AAP – 6(V) Mod 1 (13 Dec 99).
2. Bernd Horn, J. Paul de B. Taillon, and David Last, eds., *Force of Choice: Perspectives on Special Operations* (Montreal and Kingston: McGill-Queen's University Press for Queen's School of Policy Studies, 2004).
3. Headquarters Special Operations, "The ADF Commando Capability". Unpublished paper. Canberra, 1998, *inter alia*.
4. Civil affairs and support to humanitarian missions are encompassed within task numbers 7, 8, and 10, while training assistance such as that provided to Sierra Leone falls under task number 7.

PART I

THE FUTURE SECURITY ENVIRONMENT

CHAPTER ONE

FUTURE SECURITY ENVIRONMENTS

IMPLICATIONS FOR CANADIAN SPECIAL OPERATIONS

Michael A. Hennessy, Bernd Horn, and David Last

This chapter considers the evolution and current state of special capabilities in the Canadian Forces, the impact of possible future security environments, and the implications for future configurations of special operations. It serves as prelude and background to the following chapters, which address specific aspects of the environment that will affect special operations and Canada's pursuit of security.

CANADA'S SPECIAL OPERATIONS LEGACY

There were no special forces in Canada until the Second World War. During that war Canada produced a large number of individuals who operated in special commando, airborne, and elite forces. Drawing from diverse ethnic communities, Canada was able to provide individuals for covert operations in enemy territories. Canadian agents operated in Asia, across the Mediterranean, and throughout Europe. A combined Canadian-American unit, The Devil's Brigade or First Special Service Force, was employed in high-risk, high-value missions that foreshadowed the employment of American Ranger battalions. This was the largest contribution made by the Canadian Army to a special commando force during the War.

Following the Second World War, the Army eschewed special forces. Efforts to create a formation like the British Special Air Service (SAS) faltered as post-war budgets declined. The Chiefs of Staff decided that the force was too small for a specialist commando force and instead opted to ensure that the small regular-force infantry formations were highly trained and capable across a range of potential specialist missions. This tradition of excellence is still the custom today, and standard Canadian infantry battalions remain among the best-trained and most versatile infantry in the world.

While highly capable by the 1960s, the regular battalions were optimized for mechanized warfare in Europe. After the 1964 White Paper, the government created a separate airborne regiment, with battalions drawn from the ranks of the three regular-force infantry regiments. It was to serve as a highly mobile rapid-reaction force but had little opportunity to demonstrate its prowess. It remained a force-in-being waiting for high-risk operations that never materialized.

A similar fate befell the Emergency Response Team established by the Royal Canadian Mounted Police (RCMP) as Canada's first national counter-terrorist and hostage-rescue unit. Following the dramatic hostage-taking at the 1972 Olympics, most western nations developed hostage-rescue forces. As a domestic security problem, this task fell to the RCMP, but the limited number of potential recruits within its ranks made maintaining the force difficult. It was also costly because of overtime pay and allowances required under police contracts. Responsibility for counter-terrorism and hostage rescue was transferred to the Canadian Forces in 1993, although the mandate was strictly domestic and the capability was to be deployed under the authority of the Solicitor General, not the Minister of National Defence.

To fulfil its new mandate, the Canadian Forces established Joint Task Force 2 (JTF 2). The disbandment of the Airborne Regiment in 1995, following several failures of discipline and command, left JTF 2 as the only CF formation with special capabilities related to the precise application of violence, although it was not structured for international operations.

SPECIAL OPERATIONS IN TRANSITION

As domestic and international missions evolved in the 1990s, demand arose for new capabilities. Internal security tasks at Oka, Akwasasne, and elsewhere called for close cooperation with national, provincial, and local police forces. Electronic warfare sections were sent to support peacekeeping missions. Language and culture specialists were sought out. A Military Information Support Team (MIST) was established for Haiti in 1995. A Nuclear, Biological and Chemical Response Team (NBCRT) was formed in 1997. Network Vulnerability Assessment Teams were established to prepare for the anticipated millennium threat to information infrastructure. Civil affairs and civil-military cooperation became more salient in both domestic and overseas missions, and a reserve Civil Affairs structure was established in 2001. Foreign training teams were assembled for Burundi, Sierra Leone, and Kosovo, and both the CF and the RCMP contributed to international training assistance missions in unstable states. These initiatives represented special selection and training for tasks beyond the scope of conventional operations. But they did not represent a commitment to special operations or to special forces by a conventional force that was stretched too far for comfort in many conventional tasks, let alone allow for commitment to new organizations.

The current composition, tasking and training of JTF 2 qualifies it as a member of the international Special Forces community – a community that includes units like the German GSG 9, the British SAS, and American Delta force and SEAL teams. However, JTF 2 is too small and too task-specific to conduct all the potential special roles defined by our major allies. American doctrine, for example, includes the following missions and roles for Special Operations Forces: foreign internal defence (combatting insurgencies), civil affairs, direct action, combatting terrorism, strategic reconnaissance, psychological operations, unconventional warfare (fostering insurgencies), information warfare, and counter-proliferation of weapons of mass destruction.[1] We could add to this list such tasks as close personal protection, non-combattant evacuation operations (NEO), Combat Search and Rescue (CSAR), and information operations. Each of the future security environments considered below suggests new potential missions, and it is unrealistic to expect any single unit to fulfil them all. On the other hand, a task force or formation embodying a range of skills may be a realistic approach for a medium power to conduct special operations.

Although our purpose here is not to explore force structure, the alternatives considered by Canadian planning staffs to develop special operations capabilities illustrate some of the dilemmas that constrain a small force like Canada's. Of interest here is the relationship between so-called black, green, brown, support, and blue forces.

JTF 2 was established as a counter-terrorism and hostage-rescue unit (dubbed "black" because troops wear low-visibility black clothing like police SWAT teams). Fitness and skill at arms fit individual members and small teams equally well for strategic reconnaissance and other small-team tasks in support of combat operations (dubbed "green"). But for strategic raids, establishing bridgeheads, and other large-scale acts of special combat, small teams of four (the SAS model) or a dozen (the American "A" team) are inadequate. Several hundred specially trained troops may be necessary (like an American Ranger Battalion). They may require special insertion skills, such as parachuting or mountain climbing. These "green" operations bridge the gap between the small-team "black" operations, and larger, conventional ("brown") operations conducted by brigades and divisions (involving thousands rather than hundreds of troops). With the demise of the Airborne Regiment, Canada has no such capability, yet these may be precisely what we will need to operate in future environments. It can take decades to develop and perfect difficult collective skills.[2]

Staff discussions have considered augmenting JTF 2 for green roles. They have also discussed re-assigning troops from conventional Light Infantry Battalions to more specialized roles, perhaps rotating these roles between green and brown forces over time.[3] Shifting resources among black, green, and brown roles may entail trading quality for quantity; it is easier to recruit and train soldiers for routine duties than for more demanding military tasks, which typically have lower rates of acceptance and success.[4] Table 1-1 illustrates the problem. If 4,000 mature soldiers are ready for new challenges and a difficult life-style, most of them would be able to get into the infantry, but only about 500 might be capable of passing JTF 2 selection. Table 1-1 illustrates the problem of increasing barriers to entry as we move from infantry recruits to recruits for elite counter-terrorist forces. Basic fitness standards required for infantry are a baseline from which fitness standards rise, and to which initiative, independence, reflex speed, intellect, and psychological suitability are added.

TABLE 1-1
Quality-Quantity Trade-offs[5]

Type of Unit	*Typical Volunteer Success Rate*	*Potential Recruits (from a pool of 4,000)*
Infantry ("brown")	90%	3,600
Airborne	75%	3,000
Rangers ("green")	50%	2,000
Special Forces, e.g., SAS ("green")	25%	1,000
Elite hostage-rescue, e.g., JTF 2 ("black")	10-15%	400-600

Special support functions such as intelligence, surveillance, psychological operations, information support, civil affairs, language assistance, and strategic transport become more important as the green operations become more ambitious and as forces operate in less stable environments. Green forces cannot always count on operating in the same theatre as conventional forces, and supporting different equipment and different missions may have unique requirements that are critical to their success. In cases of stabilization or post-conflict reconstruction, the support functions, working with non-governmental organizations and local authorities, may actually become the leading edge of the mission. Establishing these functions in *ad hoc* part-time units cobbled together at short notice may undermine the effectiveness of scarce and expensive forces assigned to black or green operations.

Finally, military operations with civilian police, under constrained rules of engagement, are dubbed "blue" operations. These may be for internal security, domestic counter-terrorism, or international law enforcement. In a domestic hostage-rescue situation, JTF 2 soldiers act as special constables under Canadian criminal law; they are responsible for preservation of evidence and legal conduct as any police officer would be. As we turn to alternative future security environments, we will develop an appreciation of the relative importance of different types of special operations, which will help us evaluate some of the alternative combinations of black, green, brown, blue, and support operations.

FUTURE SECURITY ENVIRONMENTS

Many of today's violent conflicts appear to be protracted problems not susceptible to amelioration or remedy. We expect larger wars to be confined within a region, and unstable regions today are likely to remain unstable over the next two decades. There will be no shortage of opportunities for Canadian military deployments. Climate change, communicable diseases, armed conflict, malnutrition and hunger, population growth and migration, resource constraints, international crime, and governmental corruption will not disappear.[6] The domestic front could continue to be comparatively benign, or it might deteriorate significantly.

We begin with a point 15 to 20 years from now. Getting there encompasses the careers of recruits entering today's forces, and they may have to adjust to these environments. The Future Operations Study of Canada's Vice Chief of Defence Staff in 1999 envisioned a ten- to fifteen-year strategic lull during which there would be no major non-discretionary war.[7] This remains plausible despite the war in Iraq and is congruent with the US Quadrennial Defence Review[8] and with other mainstream views of the future. What does the world look like in 2020? We offer here brief encapsulations of eleven scenarios that depict alternative futures. Each contains plausible elements or issues that may prompt special operations. Five are from the Proteus project, an American government-industry exercise,[9] which focused on North America. Five are from an Australian Defence Force study, which aimed to generate capabilities required by Australian Special Forces.[10] The last is a product of the US Naval War College.[11] Some liberties have been taken to present the scenarios succinctly.

"Camelot" is the best of worlds. Globalization, strong and effective American leadership, a cheap energy breakthrough and environmental clean-up, and a renaissance in ethical government and public leadership all leave the world more secure. Security and defence burdens are spread more evenly. Global corporations have regional and national representation on their boards, and well-oiled international organizations and NGOs help to counterbalance dysfunctional nationalism. Political affinity groups that transcend borders and digital democracy help with global governance. There are still some losers, but globalization is working for most people, most of the time.

In contrast to "Camelot" the next three scenarios envision serious domestic disorder. "Amazon-dot-plague" is a bleak world swept by recurrent deadly viruses, exacerbated by environmental deterioration and climate change.

Fearful and isolated communities try to keep themselves healthy, communicating primarily by Internet technology. States fail, and personal security from disease and climate change is more pressing than national security from human enemies.

"The Enemy Within" sees western liberal-democratic society unravelling. By 2020 it is characterized by endemic and unpredictable violence, both criminal and political. Separatists and local militias with no faith in the federal government beset the United States. Anti-intellectualism, a debased popular culture, youth violence, recreational drug use, vigilante violence in response to riots and looting, and a brain drain to Europe and Asia are combined with suspected foreign funding of terrorists who conduct symbolic attacks. Unable to recruit enough police or soldiers, the U.S. pulls its troops home to maintain order as Europe and China re-arm. "Home Brew" is an Australian vision of this domestic meltdown. There is a crisis in governance. Drug-crime syndicates, eco-cyber terrorists, and white-supremacy movements bring violence home. Unable to cope, government loses legitimacy. Such collapse is not unknown in the Western hemisphere. Peru, Colombia, and Argentina have experienced related phenomena.

Next we have five scenarios that paint images of irregular warfare crossing national and regional boundaries. Violence is generally outside the control of states. This seems to be the most common vision for the future of conflict. It comes in many variations but implies a wide range of military and police operations to deal with its security threats, particularly criminal, commercial, and non-state networked organizations.

In "Militant Shangri-La", the U.S. and other market democracies continue to live with a prosperous, information-driven global economy, but there are worrisome anonymous attacks and instability. An alliance of anti-liberal states is increasingly powerful, using criminal and commercial alliances to manipulate crises for profit and waging information warfare against forces that oppose them. These states function both as a legitimate international bloc and as a base for less visible cartels of criminal non-state interests.

The "Yankee Going Home" scenario posits an American withdrawal from the world after several disastrous debacles. Powerful non-traditional actors, such as corporate alliances, criminal groups, and mercenary organizations, compete for influence. Without a hegemonic power shaping the security environment, national allegiances are up for grabs and rules of international conduct are fluid. There are hybrid commercial-states and mercenary local governments serving special interests.

"Yankee Going Home" is congruent with the Australian scenario, "Cast Adrift", in which waves of migration, consolidation of Islamic forces, climatic chaos in Oceania, and Australian policies combine to isolate Australia in a hostile and dangerous region. Two other Australian scenarios suggest similar patterns of regional and global violence. "Argy Bharji" envisions anarchy in South East Asia, multinational piracy, a scramble for resources in the China

Sea, and challenges to assert control over Antarctica. "Trouble Elsewhere" leaves South East Asia relatively stable, but it looks like the beginning of the next major systemic war as meltdown in the Middle East combines with Ebola in Africa and a resource crunch for the developed market economies. The U.S. stumbles in trying to maintain order and to preserve trade and stable financial regimes.

This brings us to two scenarios for major systemic war. The Australian scenario "Everybody's Brawling" envisions overt conflict for the role of global hegemon – probably between China and the U.S. but possibly involving competition between regional blocs such as Europe, North America, and Asia. The conviction that there can be only one hegemonic power drives increasingly desperate competition, exacerbated by disease, climate change, and economic instability. The conflict might look like a surreptitious and unconventional war without boundaries, or it might entail weapons of mass destruction and major conventional battles. Whither Canada in such a conflict?

The final scenario for systemic warfare within the next generation, "Asian War" is suggested by energy demands in Asia and casts light on several of the other scenarios discussed above. American military power is the "leviathan" that provides security, underwriting a single set of global rules on which the international economy is based. As long as the global economy functions effectively, it produces the investment and infrastructure that permit distribution of resources and growth. A functioning global system, it is hoped, will accommodate a doubling of energy consumption by China and India by 2020,[12] most of it through increased oil consumption. Since only the Middle East and South West Asia have the oil reserves that will be needed, 2020 could see the next major oil war waged between rising Asian powers and declining European/American powers.

IMPLICATIONS FOR CANADIAN SPECIAL OPERATIONS

These future scenarios share important characteristics that are already part of our security environment. How these alternative worlds materialize will depend partly on our policies and responses as they evolve. Intrastate wars and irregular, low-intensity conflicts, for example, have been the dominant forms of war since the Second World War.[13] Commercial non-state actors like the East India Company and the Ottoman Trading Company were important as vehicles for breaking down sovereignty in the interests of profit, and they are increasingly important today. Criminal non-state actors like the Barbary pirates have their contemporary analogues in drug cartels and insurgencies, and the same observations can be made about the social construction of criminality for both corporate and criminal actors.[14] This is why our understanding of security and how to achieve it is so important in shaping instruments for national security.

Canada's national security policy, published in April 2004, describes three spheres of security: personal safety, human security, and national security. It is striking that national security begins at home, with obvious roles for policing, border security, and domestic disaster management. Roles for deployed military forces are less evident. The spectrum of conflict broadly accepted by NATO countries and incorporated in Canadian doctrine picks up security in the international community and extends into domestic operations. Special operations might be conducted to support different kinds of security at different points in the spectrum of conflict and domestic operations. Interstate wars for national security demand a leading role for robust military forces; special operations play a supporting role. Intrastate wars imply various forms of policing, including the international policing arrangements we describe as peacekeeping. Special operations of various sorts, typically combined with conventional military and police operations, play a major role in these conflicts. Finally, the new (or re-emerging) non-state conflicts described in scenarios like "Enemy Within", "Militant Shangri-La", and "Yankee Going Home" may put a premium on novel types of special operations to manage trust and to maintain or restore stability. Multiethnic, trade-dependent states like Canada are vulnerable in the face of non-state wars, aggressive non-state actors, and overlapping intrastate wars, which break down the state system and fuel violence in unregulated international space. Managing personal safety, human security, and national security in the face of these threats will take more than conventional policing and military solutions.

Building on future security scenarios, we can describe some of the types of special operations that might be required. In a major war, specialized teams to coordinate and deliver firepower using covert and perhaps clandestine techniques would be important. Covert operations entail soldiers avoiding detection. Clandestine operations entail agents pretending to be non-threatening. One of the Proteus insights is that there is an increasing tendency to hide high-value assets in plain sight – clandestine operations are the tactic of the weak, and we can expect them to be used increasingly, particularly in urban operations, which may make up much of any future war.

ALTERNATIVE FUTURES FOR CANADIAN SPECIAL FORCES

We can conceive four scenarios in response to these futures that test the limits of special force developments. These scenarios range from the minimal time and effort of JTF 2 in stasis to the greatest time and effort required for major structural and operational change. The first scenario, "JTF 2 in Stasis", entails a force little changed from the present. "From Black to Green" examines what is involved in preparing the existing covert strike/rescue force to undertake more overseas army operations. "Total SOF Brigade" looks at expanding the force into a full-spectrum, brigade-level formation fleshed out for the full range of "special" operations, including capacity for civil affairs, psychological operations, human intelligence collection, and training for local forces. The final scenario, "Black and Blue Hybrid", examines development of the current force into one better integrated with the Canadian Security and Intelligence Service (CSIS) and national police forces. This would entail policing and security roles ranging well beyond JTF 2's current focus, which is primarily on domestic SWAT-type operations.

There can be no certainty about what might prompt the Canadian government to conduct special operations outside Canada. Emerging technology and doctrine surrounding "force transformation", however, are starting to become clear. New doctrines include harnessing information technology to manage battlefield resources, coordinating fire from multiple sources, and accelerating the operational cycle from sensor to shooter. Miniaturization, long-range precision weapons, and secure communications will permit small groups of highly trained individuals to accomplish results out of proportion to their size across the spectrum of conflict from minor irregular conflicts to full-scale war.[15] In American doctrine, managing disparate forces to achieve the desired operational and strategic effect is termed effects-based operations (EBO),[16] but whether this is new jargon for an old concept remains to be established. Planning for such operations should increase the effectiveness of joint air, land, and sea operations and allow them to work more closely with Special Operations Forces, which are inherently joint.

In the future environments described in the previous section, EBO will have to extend beyond military forces to encompass police, information, special support, and other operations not routinely undertaken by conventional military forces. The level of force, numbers of troops, and types of capabilities may be discretionary; a contribution to a multinational expedition in "militant Shangri-La", for example, might elicit a token contribution. On the other hand, significant military contributions might be necessary to demonstrate solidarity of an alliance or to contribute to defeat of adversaries in major systemic wars, like those described in the last three scenarios above. At the same time, a Black and Blue Hybrid force might be essential for the five scenarios involving irregular war. The right kind of mix is vital for alliance confidence, on which intelligence-sharing and collaboration will depend. The irony of many of the future scenarios is that international trust will decline at the very time that it is increasingly necessary to defeat ever-more-complex transnational trends. Getting the balance right will be important.

Scenario One: JTF 2 in Stasis

JTF 2 is designated the national counter-terrorist and hostage-rescue unit, with domestic operations as its primary mission. For practical and bureaucratic reasons its role and strength may remain largely unchanged. When opportunities arise for foreign deployment, the first staff question is whether deployment will affect response to a domestic incident. In its current configuration, it has been deployed to support operations in Afghanistan and to help evacuate noncombattants from Haiti. More ambitious operations will require a larger force that can both maintain a domestic response capability and a deployed unit, and still permit continuous training. We can envision one element deployed, one on standby for domestic response, one in training, and one preparing to deploy. As with Canada's hard-pressed infantry battalions and brigade groups, breaking the cycle or increasing the numbers deployed will affect collective training, sustainability, and retention. But in addition, any diminution or dilution of individual training could put JTF 2 soldiers at risk or compromise missions that have no margin for error. Faced with stasis, JTF 2 could be always deployed (and consequently run down), or an expensive resource-in-waiting, always held in reserve.

Units (or task forces) like JTF 2 are populated by self-selected and highly motivated individuals who may feel constrained by regular military employment. They have a code of cooperation and respect for each other's skill at arms and spirit of teamwork. The high standards and barriers to entry make such organizations elite groups, which are not easily entered or expanded. Any effort to expand rapidly risks dilution of training and selection standards, which may be set subjectively but must be achieved objectively for entry. Such groups also resist institutional change and may have unhealthy subcultures that resist authority, although this can also contribute to their unorthodox utility. Despite these potential obstacles, the U.S. provides examples of successful expansion of Special Operations Forces.[17]

Scenario Two: From Black to Green

Developing JTF 2 into a larger special formation to handle both overseas green roles and domestic black roles raises difficult questions about how much is enough, about organizational dynamics, and about where the demarcation line is between conventional and special roles. Can we manage the combination of a highly trained special force in a formation with largely conventional units? The seams between special and conventional assets can cause disasters, like the failed American hostage-rescue attempt (Operation Eagle Claw) in the Iranian desert in 1980. Critics of the SAS success at raiding in the Falklands argued that a company of the Parachute Regiment or Royal Marines could have achieved the same.[18] Questions of organization, training, and tasking would have to be addressed, and the capacity of conventional units to conduct special operations would have to be reviewed.[19] Hasty augmentation of special forces has been a recipe for disaster for some countries, and Canada's experience at Dieppe in 1942 illustrates the problems of sending regular troops to do special tasks when the risk is high. Raids and deep-strike operations are among the most difficult to mount, and problems in the past have been made worse by *ad hoc* structures and lack of thorough testing.

Scenario Three: Total SOF Brigade

To match the range of missions performed by US Special Operations Forces, Canadian forces would need significant reorientation and restructuring, including equipment, communications, transport, intelligence, and weapons systems. This would require a political decision to reallocate resources from the three existing brigade groups and from Maritime and Air elements to a new joint special forces formation that would recruit from the widest base possible.

What is now JTF 2 would be only part of a formation capable of balanced and sustained operations. Additional units necessary for sustained special operations might be created. Various proposals for a special forces brigade revolve around resurrecting the Airborne Regiment (or the First Special Service Force), combining JTF 2 and the Disaster Assistance Response Team (DART) in a single formation capable of civil affairs and psychological operations. More ambitious proposals suggest more elaborate combinations of specialized elements useful in particular circumstances: nuclear, biological, and chemical response teams; information operations specialists; development assistance officers; and so on.

The idea that a brigade-sized formation might include a number of possible task force configurations is not alien to our military traditions – combat teams and battle groups have been our post-Second World War stock in trade. But diversity of special capabilities and their different needs for development and sustainment would make this a particularly difficult formation to establish. Creating a large special operations force drawing on all elements of the current force structure would demand active political leadership because it would entail significant reorganization of forces. The United States and Australia have undertaken similar projects in the last decade, and both cases illustrate that attention and direction from the highest levels of government had been essential for the changes to take hold.[20] In Canada's case, the problems of overcoming institutional resistance cannot be overstated.

Scenario Four: Black and Blue Hybrid

Most discussion of restructuring or expanding the CF's special operations capability focuses on international operations. But JTF 2 was founded to address domestic security concerns and has been optimized for hostage rescue. Fitness, physical speed, psychological screening, and superior shooting and mobility skills are used in selection for these high-end policing tasks. If transnational threats of terrorism, organized crime, and social breakdown become dominant themes in national security (in scenarios like "Home Brew", "Enemy Within", and "Militant Shangri-La"), then the distinction between domestic and international policing will blur. Units like JTF 2, structured to take on high-risk policing roles at home, might make vital contributions to international law and order. In these scenarios, the future of special operations is more blue than green.

Finding the right legal framework within which to employ skilled individuals may be the central organizational question. We currently designate soldiers as special constables when they undertake domestic missions for the Solicitor General, but this is short-term and situational. Might we ask individual soldiers, police, and intelligence operators to assign "power of attorney" to the Solicitor General, who might then employ them at will as soldiers, police, or CSIS agents? If it no longer makes sense to distinguish between soldiers and sailors in a joint force, will it make sense in the future to distinguish between soldiers and police, or between covert intelligence-gathering and covert weapons-delivery? International and domestic laws restrict such cross-employment, but considerable latitude might be achieved with minimal changes.

Employment of JTF 2 in international policing, or development of a covert force to cooperate with allied agencies like CIA field forces, would entail what might be seen as espionage roles. It would mean closer cooperation and cross-postings of personnel with other government departments and agencies like the RCMP and CSIS. This might be a useful step if Canada chooses to join America's "Global War on Terror" more enthusiastically. The war on terror shares important characteristics with several of the transnational threat scenarios described above: they are unconventional, they use human resources intensively, and they may continue for generations. It may well make sense to tailor new forces for this sort of threat.

FORWARD

Future scenarios range from domestic turmoil and transnational threats to general warfare. The four scenarios for future development of Canadian special forces to address these threats diverge on details but suggest several common concerns.

First, human resources are critical. Even with a clear mandate to expand, the Canadian Forces can provide only a limited number of recruits for units with standards as high as those of JTF 2. Expanding the recruiting base and regularizing career paths to improve retention might help to keep people with special skills where they are needed. Tapping Canada's diverse population will be important to provide the diversity needed for future special operations, particularly in their green and blue variants.

Second, barriers to change are difficult to overcome. Expanding JTF 2 or creating new units and formations will require consistent political leadership and vision to preserve and balance or to sweep away old interests and bureaucratic considerations. But foot-dragging on the road to the future should not be despised; it may be essential to prevent the "flavour of the month" from spoiling the palate![21]

Third, new capabilities and structures will be costly. Specialized equipment, secure communications, robust command and control, strategic covert insertion and extraction, and precision-guided munitions take us well beyond our present capabilities. Our allies, particularly the U.S., are making rapid strides in technology and doctrine. If we wish to be considered reliable allies in joint and combined operations with them, we face considerable costs for training and infrastructure on top of the development of new capabilities.

Fourth, the scenarios imply two capabilities. Properly conceived and executed, special forces can provide both for obligatory domestic responses and for discretionary international responses to the wide variety of new threats that may confront us in the future. At home they offer a quick response to terrorist violence. Abroad they offer flexible and precise application of violence with a small footprint. As a valuable contribution to any coalition, they bring access to the highest level of intelligence-sharing, communications, and command decisions. Keeping a low profile or conducting covert or clandestine operations, special forces can minimize the impact of media and fickle public opinion when vital national interests are at stake.

Whatever future Canada faces, special forces will be needed to conduct special operations, at home and abroad. It is time to consider how we will provide them.

NOTES

1. Modified list extracted from General Peter J. Schoomaker, "CINCUSSOCOM *Special Operations Forces: The Way Ahead*," USSOCOM, 2000.
2. Major Tony Balasevicius, "A Ranger Capability For The Canadian Army: Can It Lead The Way?" forthcoming in *Army Training and Doctrine Bulletin*, 2004.
3. Interviews with members of the Special Operations Capabilities Working Group and Directorate of Land Strategic Concepts at Kingston, September 2003.
4. See, for example, Anna Simons, "The Evolution of the SOF Soldier: An Anthropological Perspective" in *Force of Choice: Perspectives on Special Operations*, Bernd Horn, J. Paul de B. Taillon, and David Last, eds. (Montreal and Kingston: McGill-Queen's University Press, 2004).
5. Belasavicius, "Ranger Capability."
6. See www.copenhagen-consensus.com. "The Future Security Environment," Directorate-Land Strategic Concepts, Fort Frontenac, Kingston, Ontario, June 1999; Ann M. Florini and P.Simmons, "The New Security Thinking: A Review of the North American Literature," Project on World Security, Rockefeller Brother Fund (New York: Rockefeller Foundation, 1998); Joan M. Nelson, "Poverty, Inequality, and Conflict in Developing Countries," Project on World Security, Rockefeller Brothers Fund, (New York, Rockefeller Foundation, 1998); Warren Rudman, "New World

Coming: American Security in the 21st Century, Supporting Research and Analysis. The Phase I Report on the Emerging Global Security Environment for the First Quarter of the 21st Century," The United States Commission on National Security (Washington, 1999); QDR 2001 Working Group, *All Possible Wars? Toward a Consensus View of the Future Security Environment 2001-2025,* McNair Paper #63 (Washington, DC: US National Defense University, 2001). Eli Berman, "Hamas, Taliban and the Jewish Underground: An Economist's View of Radical Religious Militias," NBER Working Paper 10004, www.nber.org/papers/w10004.

7. Vice Chief of Defense Staff, *Future Operations Study* (Ottawa: National Defence Headquarters, 2000)
8. United States Department of Defense, *Quadrennial Defense Review*, (Washington, DC: Department of Defense, 2000).
9. Pamela Krause, Michel S. Loescher, Chris Schoreder, and Charles W. Thomas, "Proteus: Insights from 2020," based on research conducted for the National Reconnaissance Office (Washington, DC: Copernicus Institute Press, 2000).
10. Dr. Joanne Nicholson and Captain Guy Duczynski, "Defining Future Scenarios for the Special Forces After Next," Presentation by Directorate of Scientific and Technical Operations. Land Operations Division, Headquarters Special Operations, Australian Department of Defence, Canberra, 21 October 2003.
11. For readers unfamiliar with scenario-development techniques, suffice it to say that all three sources – Proteus, ADF, and Naval War College – used credible panels of experts and scenario-generation techniques.
12. Thomas P.M. Barnett, "New Rule Sets Project Summary, Roadshow Brief" and "Asia: The Military-Market Link" (Annapolis, MD: US Naval Institute, January 2002): slides 53-56.
13. Peter Wallensteen, *Understanding Conflict Resolution: War Peace and the Global System* (London: Sage, 2000), 29.
14. R.T. Naylor, *Wages of Crime: Black Markets, Illegal Finance, and the Underworld Economy* (Montreal: McGill-Queen's University Press, 2002); see particularly Chapter Two, "The Insurgent Economy: Black Market Operations of Guerrilla Groups," 44-87. See also Ivelaw L. Griffith, "Organized Crime in the Western Hemisphere: Content, context, consequences and countermeasures," *Low Intensity Conflict and Law Enforcement*, Volume 8, Number 1 (Spring, 1999): 1-33.
15. On the emerging non-linearity, network essential, and more joint operational environment, see US DOD, *Knowledge and Speed: The Annual Report of the Army After Next Project* (Washington, DC, July 1997). See also Stephan Herrera, "Soldiers and Nanotechnology," *Acumen Journal of Life Sciences*, V1. No.IV (December 2003): 40-51.
16. Lieutenant Colonel Douglas Neill, "Effects Based Operations: Not Simple but necessary" (Toronto: Canadian Forces College, October 2002).

17. See, Susan L. Marquis, *Unconventional Warfare: Building US Special Operations Forces* (Brooking Institution: Washington, DC, 1997).
18. Alan Bell, "Successes and Failures of Special Forces Operations During the Falklands War", in *Force of Choice*, eds. Horn, *et al.*
19. For an expanded view of reorganizing the present brigade structures, see Michael A. Hennessy, *"Sharpening the DART"*, presentation to the DCDS staff retreat, Chateau Montebello, February 2002.
20. The Australian SAS and rapid reaction commando forces received concerted national attention, as has the strategic intelligence function of the state. See various issues of the *Australian Army Journal* and comments, "The Re-structure of the Australian Forces," Mgen. A. J. Molan, Australian Defence College, 21st Century Strategic Environment Symposium, Ottawa, January 2003. On the US case, see Marquis, *Unconventional Warfare.*
21. On bureaucratic foot-dragging, see the various reports by the MND's Monitoring Committee for Change, various dates, Hon. John Fraser, Chairman.

CHAPTER TWO

LOOSE CANNONS IN CYBERSPACE

SOCIETY AND PSYCHOLOGICAL CHANGE

Nicole Schwartz-Morgan

> "A ghost is stalking the corridors of general staffs and defense departments all over the 'developed' world—the fear of military impotence, even irrelevance."
>
> Martin van Creveld, *The Transformation of War*

This chapter challenges the model that suggests humanity remains stable while technology changes. It explores the impact of technology and culture on the people and social structures involved in the next generation of special operations. Despite the unprecedented impact of technology and interconnections among technology, society, and the natural world, we continue to assume that human thinking is stable. But the human mind is evolving. Stress, shock, "cybershock", and breakdowns in organizational cohesion attest to the instability and change we all confront. Partly as a result of exposure to computers and information technology at early ages, younger generations internalize knowledge and emotions in new ways. These changes are neither individual nor cultural and, therefore, are not temporary. There is potential for these changes to be integrated genetically and to affect sociability. They therefore have implications for loyalty, esprit, respect, training, and education. Chaos and instability may emerge as the most important "enemies". It is particularly important for strategic units addressing complex threats to understand pioneering research in human ecology. This chapter is part of ongoing research in human ecology and touches no more than the surface of these complex issues.

NEW WORLD, OLD ASSUMPTIONS

For several decades, recognition has been growing of the unprecedented impact of technologies on the natural world,[1] of the speed and irreversibility of these changes,[2] of their complex interconnections in a whole system,[3] and of the impossibility of addressing these issues in isolation.[4] Attention is now turning increasingly to impacts of change on the human body as its integrity is threatened by chemicals, by viruses new and old, and by changes in the biosphere.[5]

Paradoxically, but understandably, we have difficulty looking at human behaviour in the detached way we observe nature.[6] Beliefs, judgments, moralistic undertones, or genetically coded optimism make it especially difficult to address the notion of a human ecology on the move.[7] Whether we define humanity as just another animal product of evolution,[8] the possessor of a special human nature,[9] or a blank slate free from determinism,[10] we take for granted that human thinking, emotional process, and socialization have been stable for several millennia, although we readily accept that factors such as height and weight have changed radically over time. This generalization embraces most evolutionists.[11] The mind of *Sapiens homo sapiens*, so anthropologists tell us, has not changed since our ancestors roamed glaciers. Should her frozen embryo be revived, should she be brought up in the third millennium, dressed at Harrods and educated at Harvard, nobody would ever guess her humble origin.[12]

An entire industry of human behaviour, including military training, has been built on the premises that behaviour is predictable (if we get enough data), that behaviour is replicable, and that behaviour changes slowly, if at all.[13] So far the development of military strategy and tactics, and the training to support them, has relied on these premises with some success.[14] Indeed, the stability of the "political animal" as defined by Aristotle some 2,500 years ago[15] has made Nicolas Machiavelli and Carl von Clausewitz relevant to modern scholars and useful to computerized strategies. Both Machiavelli and Clausewitz depended on historic regularities as guides to their strategy manuals. A similar presumption that Abraham Maslow's hierarchy of human needs is immutable seems to explain its immense popularity in military circles.[16]

Rigid schemas like those above make it difficult to understand how the human mind and body have evolved. Only a handful of thinkers, such as Stephen Jay Gould, Lewis Mumford, and V. Gordon Childe, have addressed the complexity of the evolving web of human ecology.[17] A fixation on stasis makes it impossible to understand the unprecedented mutation humanity is currently undergoing. We are at a loss to find the words to describe new types of behaviours appearing in new generations.

The pace and impact of technological change have vastly exceeded what earlier observers described as the change of perception and values that identify a "generation" (Ortega y Gasset). Robert Wright speaks of "transitional instability",[18] while Neil Postman laments the surrender of humanity to technology, joining a crowd of sociologists and philosophers who announce "the end" of this or that world.[19] More pragmatically, psychologists describe new behaviours as pathological within normality as we know it. Mainstream psychology is no longer using ill-defined terms from psychoanalysis (neurosis, psychosis), but instead uses metaphors borrowed from mechanical engineering and military psychology, such as "stress", "breakdown", "shock", "post-traumatic stress disorder",[20] and "cybershock". The latter term is understood in special operations to describe the paralysis induced by new information technology.[21]

HYPOTHESIS: HOMO SAPIENS NO MORE

In this chapter, I seek to challenge our faith in stability and normality. Technology is changing us. The body of humanity, the body of the state, the social body, the body of organizations, and the individual body and mind are less stable than we would like to believe. My challenge is based on the following conjectures, familiar in some research circles but not common in public discourse. The first conjecture is that extensive use of new technologies and new chemical compounds is radically changing the way humans process knowledge, emotions, and relationships. The second conjecture is that these changes are not individual or cultural, which would make them temporary. They are universal and, given time, have the potential to be integrated into the genetic code through the evolution of propensity genes. The third conjecture is that these changes challenge the very basis of humanity as we have come to understand it through studying history and anthropology, because they will affect the way we relate to one another in society. For thousands of years, our social relations have featured hierarchy, family, conflicts, wars, and negotiations. Can we continue to take these patterns for granted?

And what does this mean for special operations? It suggests that strategies of chaos might be used to attack our management of vital information. Worse, our enemy might be within. The chaos of disordered minds and the disembodiment of technological society can undermine traditional military prowess, perhaps making it a thing of the past.

THINKING THE UNTHINKABLE

My challenge to our belief in stability is based on the conjecture that the human mind is being rewired. New technologies and new chemical/pharmaceutical composites are radically changing our cognitive process. Because the definition of cognitive process would require a dissertation in itself, it is narrowed here to its simplest components: "the process of thinking" and "the act of remembering".[22] (These are complicated enough, encompassing all mind-body processes from perception to kinaesthesia.)

The process of thinking starts with selection on a grand scale. Thanks to new technology, we begin to be able to observe the process. The brain scan, for example, provides new empirical evidence about the way humans incorporate knowledge, habits, and culture. We can actually see how neurons entangle themselves and how sensory chaos can be transformed into a learned and cultural structure, through eliminating and ordering sensory inputs.

The Human Mind Is Being Rewired

A baby does not come into the world as a genetically pre-programmed automaton, nor is she totally determined by the environment. Cognitive development is a more exciting process. There is an inherited genetic structure, which is partly determining, but within this structure there is some flexibility. The potential is not a destiny, although it is inclination. A baby is the product of heredity but is also receptive to environment, and by communicating with it, he learns. That is also the way we evolve as a species, each individual being a part of a chain, adding to it through adaptation to new conditions, bit by bit. This means that every man registers in the structure of his brain his own unique experience, bringing flexibility and suppleness to the determinism of the genetic structure. Neurons and their connections follow the order of a genetic program while environment screens the outcome. In this process repetitions actually become structures, literally imprinted in the individual circuits we inherit. We are the same and different.

There is a caveat! This elegant dance between nature and nurture has a time limit. It closes down in early infancy for we age much more quickly than any of us want to acknowledge. Neurologists explain how learning stabilizes pre-established synaptic combinations while eliminating others by a process called epigenesis. By a very early age the major synaptic avenues are traced and fixed, and the only change possible is to add a few streets. But we also know that the richer and more varied the early experience, the richer and more varied the cerebral structure. This doesn't mean it is impossible to go beyond heredity, but it is easier during a limited period of time and within certain parameters. Experts have named this early learning period a "window of opportunity" – a whiff of liberty or the source of evolution within determinism.

More importantly, this learning process explains how shared experiences can eventually alter genetic material. Nothing is ever truly stable, but the genetic structure aims at stability. The issue of our times is a radical change in the way the "window of opportunity" is used: on the one hand, information has never been so abundant, complex, and interrelated; on the other hand, the intellectual tools used to process information have never been so inadequate, as educators have abandoned structure.

Super-abundance of information has fostered the term "infoglut". In a recent book, the authors invite us to think about

> all the text in those 60,000 new books that spew out of U.S. presses every year, or the more than 300,000 books published worldwide,...about the more than 18,000 magazines published in the United States alone – up almost 600 from the year before – with more than 225 billion pages of editorial content. There were more than 20 billion pages of magazine editorial content about food and nutrition alone! Consider the 1.6 trillion pieces of paper that circulate through U.S. offices each year. Try scanning the 400,000 scholarly journals published annually around the world. If you prefer lighter reading, peruse some of the 15 billion catalogues delivered to U.S. homes in 1999, or the 87.2 billion pieces of direct mail that reached U.S. mailboxes in 1998. ...If you believe that print media are obsolete, consider the more than 2 billion Web pages in the world, a large chunk of which can't even be found with the best search engine. A U.S. government study estimates that the amount of Internet traffic doubles about every hundred days. And online information is not restricted to the Internet. A 2000 University of Illinois study revealed that there are 11,339 distinct electronic databases on the market (up from 301 in 1975). If you like to sit in front of larger screens, you have 80 percent more feature films to watch today than were released in 1990. [23]

Paradoxically, the technical tools designed to process and communicate the interrelated and sophisticated mass of data are part of the glut. Search engines, for example, simply give us more information to wade through.

The abandonment of structure and repetition has created a problem for the way we manage information. Repetition is essential for structuring a young brain. In this process, reactive behaviours become actual structures, literally imprinted in the individual circuits.[24] It might be seen as a restrictive exercise. Yes, it is (habits and prejudices are formed), and no, it is not (without this process, no information can "stick").

For the last thirty years, hoping to help young minds become better adapted to a complex world, we have abandoned rules (like grammar and spelling) and repetition (learning by rote). We have emphasized creativity and free association of ideas. We may have done more harm than good, not understanding how crucial it is in early years to structure the brain around patterns and cognitive associations, thereby adding to the difficulty of putting some order in the infoglut. In his book *Data Smog*, David Shenk describes the oppressive aspect of accessing information.[25] The stress caused by information overload suggests that the increase in non-hereditary Attention Deficit Disorder (ADD) is linked to the information revolution. Research by neuropsychiatrist Gabor Maté supports the hypothesis.[26]

For the true causes of ADD we have to look at the social and psychological conditions that shape the brains of children in late-twentieth-century and early-twenty-first-century Western societies. "In attention deficit disorder the chief physiological problem appears to be located in the frontal lobe of the brain, in the area of the cortex where attention is allocated and emotions and impulses are regulated."[27] The circuits of attention and emotion control need an appropriate input of stability and repetition; without it they malfunction.

Another major change in brain structure is illustrated by the influence of images in the modern learning process. Interactive screens replace books, and we revert to the pre-alphabet of iconic images. Students are saturated with visual images, and those designing educational materials are advised to vie for their attention in a rich visual environment. From traditional textbooks to the educational software, we find a wealth of pictorial representations.[28] But a picture is not worth a thousand words. The visually rich technical environment is actually changing the way we think. Images do not "speak" to us as books do. Techniques such as magnetic resonance imaging (MRI) have made it possible to demonstrate that images do not stimulate the same cerebral circuits. They are more emotive and passive, speaking directly to collective images, requiring less logic, no grammatical structure, and no semantics. What we gain in universality, we lose in cultural diversity and sophistication. Some would argue that this makes us less effective, if not actually "dumb". PowerPoint presentations epitomize this process.[29]

The way we store knowledge has also changed. The effects of our image-laden environment are especially dramatic when they are combined with our reliance on "external memory". Queen's University professor Merlin Donald explains how "a gradual externalization of human memory" has changed the way we think, remember, and communicate:

> External storage has dwarfed and overwhelmed individual memory. Methods of external memory retrieval are gaining ever-greater dominance, in relative terms, over the speed and accuracy of biological memory retrieval. The new technology of imagination – virtual reality, television, and cinema – threatens to outweigh individual imagination, and programmed corporate agendas already outstrip the individual thought process in many kinds of work.[30]

Everywhere we see technology that is beyond our impoverished human capacity to synthesize, metabolize, and control. This inhibits our ability to use knowledge intelligently, in ways that are not self-destructive. In a recent book, *The Human Factor*, Kim Vincente points out that "when it comes to safety-critical sectors… the consequences are worrisome."[31]

Changes Are Not Temporary

The fabric of society has been irreversibly affected by these changes. They challenge the very basis of humanity as we have come to understand it through our study of history and anthropology, because they affect the way we relate with one another in society. The hierarchies, family relationships, and emotional deals embedded in complex cultures that have adapted to circumstances are changing as a result of the processes described above. There are implications for the managers of violence.

It is increasingly difficult to draw lines between virtual killing and real slaughter, between truth and lies, right and wrong, justice and injustice, information and propaganda, plagiarism and creation. All forms of social interaction are affected.[32] Without these standards, which have held our world together since the decline of universal religion, the ethical structure of our society is less cohesive. Looking into the future, dystopian academics emphasize the rapid erosion of the social fabric in speeches, books, journals, and paradoxically, web sites.[33] Utopians argue that "electronic space" can lead to the betterment of society, by creating "Smart Mobs," like the near-instant gatherings orchestrated by supporters of US presidential candidate Howard Dean. These have the function of using technology to mobilize rather than isolate individuals.[34]

For now we should admit that we just do not know what new epistemological tools, criteria, and standards will be created to accommodate the new reality. We are in the throes of passage, shooting the rapids, as described by writers like Robert Kaplan and Thomas Homer-Dixon.[35] However, we can expect that opportunistic "viruses" will invade any weakened organism. In organizations, these viruses might manifest as organized crime, fascism, or terrorism. In individuals, we see new forms of disorder and abhorrent behaviour, some of which no longer fit into psychiatric terminology.

Changes Will Affect Sociability

Changes in ways of processing knowledge and building emotions are neither individual nor cultural. If they rested exclusively in either the individual or the collective, they would be temporary changes, lasting only as long as the individual lived or the organization functioned. They are not temporary. I believe these changes are universal and, given time, have the potential to be integrated in the genetic code through the evolution of propensity genes.

Recent research, especially in Europe, is reinforcing the credibility of Lamarck's theory about the inheritance of acquired characteristics. It is now believed that changes in the genetic material occur faster than can be accounted for by a Darwinian approach. This can be seen in the contemporary epidemic of obesity, which is partly explained by the awakening of an atavistic fat-propensity gene. This epidemic is so striking that it has attracted attention, but there is now a field of research on possible changes in the brain structure, which must be taken into consideration in studies of human metabolism, whether of food, knowledge, or emotions.

PRACTICAL ISSUES: VIRTUAL BATTLEFIELDS AND REAL SOLDIERS

Changes in the building blocks of thought are bound to have a dramatic impact on military life in general and on special operations in particular. Successful strategy depends on a clear, accurate understanding of the environment and perpetuation of traditional military ethos: discipline of the body, order of the mind, and the deep emotion of *esprit de corps*.

I will not expand here on the challenge of understanding increasingly complex environments and weaponry. It is addressed elsewhere. The changes attracting the most attention today are technological developments. New terms have been added to discussions of present and future military operations: smart weapons, brilliant weapons, digitized battlefield, virtual theatre of war, cybermanoeuvre, dominant battlespace awareness, psychotechnology, narcotechnology, nanotechnology, and so on. John Arquilla and David Ronfeldt envision "Cyberwar – a comprehensive information-oriented approach to battle that may be to the information age what Blitzkrieg was to the industrial age."[36] Robert J. Bunker tells us, "The goal of the Army in future war, beyond that of securing assigned politico-military objectives, will be that of total cyberspace dominance not just digital battlespace dominance."[37] Armies seek to operate in the mind, as well as on the battlefield.

Consider the implications of this thinking. Everything has become hidden and blurry. Old concepts such as "frontiers", "enemy", "civilians", or "strategies" do not hold much reality. Fourth-Generation Warfare, dispersed, undefined, and manipulated by "chaos strategists...pits nations against non-national organizations and networks of organizations – including oppressed ethnic groups, mafias, narco-traffickers and extremist quasi-religious cults..."[38]

If psychological operations represent the genesis of special operations, we should consider carefully the impact on their next generation:

> Psychological operations may become the dominant operational and strategic weapon in the form of media/information intervention. Logic bombs and computer viruses, including latent viruses, may be used to disrupt civilian as well as military operations. Fourth generation adversaries will be adept at manipulating the media to alter domestic and world opinion to the point where skillful use of psychological operations will sometimes preclude the commitment of combat forces. A major target will be the enemy population's support of its government and the war. Television news may become a more powerful operational weapon than armored divisions.[39]

But in addition to thinking about the use of psychological operations by the next generation of military and political adversaries, we should consider the new vulnerabilities of complex military systems that have become cybernetically complex.[40] These complex organizations are

> creating a whole new pattern of defeat, placing cybershock and paralysis on par with attrition and annihilation and manoeuvre and exhaustion. The cybershock-paralysis-defeat pattern does not replace or compete with the other two, however. Instead, cybershock supplements and complements attrition and manoeuvre. Cybershock induces deep systemic paralysis throughout a complex military system, culminating the transformation in warfare first wrought by the Industrial Revolution more than 100 years ago.[41]

My purpose is to draw some attention to new kinds of "internal disorders" faced by soldiers and leaders, which are not a simple mirror image of external disorders but possess a dynamic of their own and have the potential to jeopardize an already difficult process of adaptation to an environment that is changing quickly and continuously.[42] This challenges the unspoken but persistent assumption that psychic and organizational structures are stable and will re-establish themselves after the individual human actors have recovered – that is, when stupor and disorganization have passed.

When we challenge our assumptions of stability and normality, we step into uncharted territory for military strategy, where the scope is immense and the research scant.[43] Two concepts that provide a sample of changes to come, and subjects for further research, are chaos of the mind and disembodied *esprit de corps*.

Chaos in the Mind

We pay lip service to the "human component" of the modern army. Lieutenant-Colonel Tim Thomas points out that the American obsession with systems and information leads them to neglect the human factor in their theories of information warfare. Terminology, he argues, leads them towards hardware and software, when it is the humans in the data-management business who are really vital. How will we prevent terrorists or other adversaries from disrupting the people in our information systems?[44]

But disorder does not originate only with adversaries – the so-called "chaos strategists".[45] One could argue that the enemy is already inside, or rather, the objectives of the enemy may be substantially assisted by the weaknesses of a modern mind that is in chaos. What do we do to ourselves as leaders and managers that makes us vulnerable to single-minded fanatics? We insist on multitasking to the point that we find it impossible to focus.[46] We specialize to the point that we lose the capacity to synthesize. We rely on external memory to the point of losing the capacity to memorize. We rely on technology in general to the point that we are unable to "read" a foreign environment and adapt to it.

The last point is all the more worrisome in the context of special operations, where the possibility of being stranded far from technological help is ever-present. Will special operators be like science fiction starship crews, looking for life with sensors but unable to see it in front of them?

Disembodied Esprit de Corps?

We understand how important the emotional dimension is for training and motivating soldiers. In special operations, we may tend to focus only on the fact that the enemy do not have uniforms, drill, salutes, or, for the most part, ranks. We pay scant attention to the question of how troops can remain cohesive in a new military order that relies less and less on traditional order. New technologies are affecting the entire social and emotional spectrum of human life, and military life is no exception. We could even advance the hypothesis that these changes will be more dramatic for the military than for civilian professions. This is a profession whose entire ethos is linked to strong social emotions and interactions, from hand-to-hand combat to loyalty to one's country. In a borderless world, with corporate warriors for hire, this ethos will be challenged beyond our capacity to imagine.[47]

Hand-to-hand combat illustrates the problem. New technologies, such as videogames and simulators for training and precision munitions in operations, have changed the ethos of violence. They make it remote and virtual. It is safer for us but more deadly for them. We are beginning to understand that immersion in virtual violence can make people more fearful, numb to violence, hungry for more, and even more aggressive in the real world.[48] The remoteness of warriors from actual casualties, cries of agony, decaying bodies, and the smell of death helps to situate the individual in a virtual world, cutting him off from the root of ethics, because empathy is the basis for laws of war that require humane treatment of prisoners, civilians, and the wounded.

Esprit de corps presents another problem. In military organizations, it is an indispensable commodity that cannot be bought, sold, bartered, or commanded.[49] It was born of the revolutionary military advances in close-order drill, introduced to mercenaries in the service of the Netherlands by Maurice of Nassau in 1580. Close-order drill for the handling of firearms dramatically increased military effectiveness and had the added effect of creating social bonds and *esprit de corps* among a disparate group of soldiers for hire.[50] The model has been the basis for professional armies ever since, and it has been emulated by industry.[51] But distance education, computerized work places, and the information society have made inroads on the synchronized group-in-motion pioneered by Maurice of Nassau. Military organizations have been forced to ask themselves whether "*esprit de corps* and the joint team perspective and mind-set so critical to military operations could be replicated in a 'virtual' PME (Professional Military Education) environment."[52] Despite these misgivings, the virtual environment is a more prevalent experience than the parade ground. As early as 1970, one of the doyens of military sociology was pointing to changes that this technology would force:

> Technological trends in war-making have necessitated extensive common modification in the military profession....The changes in the military reflect organizational requirements which force the permanent military establishment

> to parallel other large-scale civilian organizations. As a result, the military takes on more and more the common characteristics of a government or business organization. Thus the differentiation between the military and the civilian is seriously weakened. In all these trends the model of the professional soldier is being changed by 'civilianizing' the military elite to a greater extent than the 'militarizing' of the civilian elite.[53]

If this trend to civilianizing the military elite continues, *esprit de corps* will not survive. Will soldiers bond emotionally to their distant and invisible staff? Loyalty may become as irrelevant in military life as it has become in the corporate world. Yet highly skilled special operators may be approached frequently by those trying to recruit them for private jobs or foreign armies. What will keep them on our team?

Respect for hierarchy will be another casualty of the changes. When technology creates virtual staffs, the amount of information available to commanders in a digital battlespace is multiplied. Defence analyst David Lutz asks troubling questions about these staff officers. If civilians in the digital loop exercise judgement in combat situations, what responsibility do they have for the outcomes?[54] There has always been a gulf between those who fight at the front and those who direct from the rear. When military and civilian staff officers are ensconced in air-conditioned comfort in Florida, will special operators at the front accept instructions that lead to their own loss of life and limb?

CONCLUSION

Do we face military irrelevance? Military thinkers must do more than talk about technological change and revolutions in military affairs. They must strive to understand both the philosophy underlying them, and the physiology and neuroscience that are driven by broad currents of social evolution. For example, how many budding strategists understand that the military technical revolution, from which the more holistic revolution in military affairs is derived, is itself grounded in Marxist philosophy? Soviet Marshal Nikolai V. Ogarkov pointed to the radical changes in operations that would be brought about by automation, search-and-destroy complexes, and long-range precision-guided weapons.[55] Americans have built on Thomas Kuhn's ideas about scientific revolution and the Tofflers' futuristic visions,[56] but they have not begun to think about the fundamental instability of the human mind. Our vision of the future is built on images of a historical and anthropological past, and these images are changing. Our minds are being re-wired by technological change. The minds of the future will not behave in the same ways as those of the past. These changes will become part of the genetic code that we carry forward with us. The wars of the future may be fought with strategies of chaos that take advantage of the chaos of the mind, and unless we understand these phenomena, our soldiers will be loose cannons in cyberspace.

NOTES

1. Colin Mason, *The 2030 Spike: Countdown to Global Catastrophe* (London: Earthscan publications, 2003).
2. Thomas Homer-Dixon, *The Ingenuity Gap* (New York: Alfred A. Knopf, 2000).
3. Fritjof Capra, *The Web of Life: A New Scientific Understanding of Living Systems* (New York: Anchor Books, 1997).
4. John L. Casti, *Complexification* (New York: HarperCollins, 1994). Also see M. Mitchell Waldrop, *Complexity* (New York: Simon and Schuster, 1992).
5. Intergovernmental Panel on Climate Change (IPCC) Third Assessment Report - Climate Change 2001 (Geneva: United Nations, 2001).
6. Freud called it "cultural narcissism". See Sigmund Freud, *Civilization and Its Discontents.* Translated from the German and edited by James Strachey (New York: W. W. Norton, 1961).
7. Lionel Tiger, *Optimism: The Biology of Hope* (New York: Simon and Schuster, 1980).
8. Merlin Donald, *Origins of the Modern Mind: Three Stages in the Evolution of Culture and Cognition* (Cambridge, MA: Harvard University Press, 1991). Robert Wright, *The Moral Animal. Why we are the way we are: The new science of evolutionary psychology* (New York: Random House, 1994).
9. Steven Pinker, *The Blank Slate: The Modern Denial of Human Nature* (New York: Viking, 2002).
10. An important ideology, the basis of our concept of modern democracy, developed by John Locke and to some extent Jean-Jacques Rousseau and Jean Paul Sartre.
11. Robert Wright, *Nonzero: The Logic of Human Destiny* (New York: Vintage Books, 2000), claims that there is a human nature and that technological innovation is chaotic "and only after a Darwinian survival-of-the-fittest process of testing and elimination do successful new technologies become established...The number of possible technologies is infinite, and only a few pass this test of affinity with human nature." See also Kim Vincente, *The Human Factor: Revolutionizing the Way We Live with Technology* (Toronto: Routledge, 2004), 41.
12. V. Gordon Childe, *Man Makes Himself* (London: Watts & Co., 1941).
13. Michael Butz and Linda Chamberlain, eds., *Clinical Chaos: A Therapist's Guide to Nonlinear Dynamics and Therapeutic Change* (Philadelphia: Brunner/Mazel, 1998).
14. J. E. diGenova, "Terrorism, Intelligence, and the Law," in *Proceedings of the Annual Symposium on the Role of Behavioral Science in Physical Security (9th)*, Symmetry and Asymmetry of Global Adversary Behavior, Springfield, VA, 3-4 April 1984, AD-A152 459 (Washington, DC: Department of Defense, 4 April 1984): 53-59.

15. Aristotle, *The Politics*, Book 1.
16. Abraham Maslow, *The Farther Reaches of Human Nature* (New York: Viking, 1971; Harmondworth, U.K.: Penguin Books, 1973).
17. Lewis Mumford, *Technics and Civilization* (New York: Harcourt, Brace & World, 1963). As V. Gordon Childe explains, man very quickly became

    > inadequately adapted for survival in any particular environment. His bodily equipment for coping with any special set of conditions is inferior to that of most animals. He has not, and probably never had, a furry coat like the polar bear's for keeping in the body's heat under cold conditions. His body is not particularly well adapted for escape, self-defence, or hunting. He is not, for instance, exceptionally fleet of foot, and would be left behind in a race with a hare or an ostrich. He has no protective colouring like the tiger or the snow leopard, nor bodily armour like the tortoise or crab...He lacks the beak and talons of the hawk and its keenness of vision. For catching his prey and defending himself, his muscular strength, and nails are incomparably inferior to those of the tiger.

    See Childe, *Man Makes Himself*, 41-42. Man's body has become a *techné that* depends mainly on external technologies; that is, on human communities producing and managing them. We leave here forever the word of biology and zoology, for this knowledge is transmitted "artificially" through cultures.
18. Wright, *Nonzero*, 2000.
19. Neil Postman, *Technology: The Surrender of Culture to Technology* (New York: Vintage, 1992).
20. Eric T. Dean Jr., *Shook Over Hell: Post Traumatic Stress, Vietnam, and the Civil War* (Cambridge, MA: Harvard University Press, 1997); A. Gabriel Richard, *The Painful Field: The Psychiatric Dimension of Modern War* (Westport, CT: Greenwood Press, 1988).
21. James J. Schneider, *The Structure of Strategic Revolution: Total War and the Roots of the Soviet Warfare State* (New York: Ballantine, 1994).
22. J. Michael Jaffe, "Media Interactivity, Cognitive Flexibility, and Self-efficacy," doctoral dissertation (Communication), The University of Michigan, 1995; http://research.haifa.ac.il/~jmjaffe/Dissert
23. "Does your company suffer from organizational ADD? When there is contention for attention, those who seek it turn to the most reliable attention getters". See Thomas H. Davenport and John C. Beck, *The Attention Economy: Understanding the New Currency of Business* (Cambridge, MA: Harvard Business School Press, April 2001).
24. E. Jensen, *Learning Smarter: The New Science of Teaching* (San Diego: The Brainstore, Inc. 2000); R. Rupp, *How We Remember and Why We Forget* (New York: Three River Press, 1988).
25. His research involved collecting numerous books and articles from journals, magazines, and newspapers, recording many hours of interviews, and accumulating over twenty thousand pages of text by performing

NEXIS searches and downloading information from the Internet. David Shenk described his grievance with this process in *Data Smog: Surviving the Information Glut* (San Francisco: Harper Edge, 1997).

26. Gabor Maté, *Scattered Minds: A New Look at the Origins and Healing of Attention Deficit Disorder* (Toronto: Vintage Canada, 2000).
27. Ibid.
28. R. K. Lowe, *Successful Instructional Diagrams* (London: Kogan Page,1993).
29. Edward Tufte makes the point clear in a provocative essay, "PowerPoint Is Evil," *Wired,* September 2003.

> Rather than learning to write a report using sentences, children are being taught how to formulate client pitches and infomercials. Elementary school PowerPoint exercises (as seen in teacher guides and in student work posted on the Internet) typically consist of 10 to 20 words and a piece of clip art on each slide in a presentation of three to six slides – a total of perhaps 80 words (15 seconds of silent reading) for a week of work. Students would be better off if the schools simply closed down on those days and everyone went to the Exploratorium or wrote an illustrated essay explaining something....In a business setting, a PowerPoint slide typically shows 40 words, which is about eight seconds' worth of silent reading material. With so little information per slide, many, many slides are needed. Audiences consequently endure a relentless sequentiality, one damn slide after another. When information is stacked in time, it is difficult to understand context and evaluate relationships. Visual reasoning usually works more effectively when relevant information is shown side by side. Often, the more intense the detail, the greater the clarity and understanding. This is especially so for statistical data, where the fundamental analytical act is to make comparisons.

30. Acquisition of these skills is difficult, explains Queen's University professor Merlin Donald, because they have put significant new demands on the human brain in the form of new cognitive "architectures" that must be imposed by extensive education. Furthermore, "a gradual externalization of human memory" has changed the way we think, remember, and communicate. See Merlin Donald, *Origins of the Modern Mind: Three Stages in the Evolution of Culture and Cognition* (Cambridge, MA: Harvard University Press, 1991).
31. Vincente, *The Human Factor: Revolutionizing the Way We Live with Technology* (Toronto: Routledge, 2004).
32. This is true whether we apply a Jungian model or the framework used by Craig Calhoun, to name only two alternatives. The latter has identified four basic types of social integration: primary relations are based on friendship and caring; secondary relations are interaction with strangers; tertiary relations involve communication through a medium such as a computer or telephone. Finally, Calhoun describes the concept of the quaternary relationship, in which individuals may not be aware that they

are in contact with another party. All these relationships have been affected by new computer technologies.

33. John P. Robinson, Norman H. Nie, Editors, *IT and Society, a web journal* (Stanford University: SIQSS, 2002) http://www.stanford.edu/group/siqss/itandsociety/v01i02.html
34. Howard Rheingold, *Smart Mobs: The Next Social Revolution* (New York: Basic Books, 2002).
35. Robert D.Kaplan, *The Coming Anarchy: Shattering the Dreams of the Post Cold War* (New York: Vintage Books, 2001); and Homer-Dixon, *The Ingenuity Gap.*
36. John Arquilla and David Ronfeldt, "A New Epoch and Spectrum of Conflict," in *Athena's Camp: Preparing for Conflict in the Information Age*, eds. Arquilla and Ronfeldt (Washington, DC: RAND, 1997). http://www.rand.org/publications/MR/MR880/
37. Robert J. Bunker, "Advanced Battlespace and Cybermaneuver Concepts: Implications for Force XXI," *Parameters*, 26 (1996): 112; http://carlisle-www.army.mil/usawc/Parameters/96autumn/bunker.htm. See also David W. Lutz, "Unit Cohesion and Organizational Change," presentation to the Joint Services Conference on Professional Ethics XX, National Defense University, Fort McNair, Washington, D.C., 29-30 January 1998.
38. Harold A. Gould and Franklin C. Spinney, "Fourth-Generation Warfare Is Here," The RMA Debate, 15 October 2001; http://www.comw.org/rma/fulltext/asymmetric.html. See also William S. Lind, Colonel Keith Nightengale (USA), Captain John F. Schmitt (USMC), Colonel Joseph W. Sutton (USA), and Lieutenant-Colonel Gary I. Wilson (USMCR), "The Changing Face of War: Into the Fourth Generation," *Marine Corps Gazette,* October 1989: 22-26; and Steven Metz, "Strategic Asymmetry," *Military Review,* July-August 2001.
39. Lind *et al.*, "The Changing Face of War".
40. James J. Schneider, *The Structure of Strategic Revolution. Total War and the Roots of the Soviet Warfare State* (New York: National Book Network, 1994).
41. Ibid.
42. Lind *et al.,* "The Changing Face of War".
43. "Recurring proposals to substitute advanced technology for conventional military capabilities reflect a peculiarly American faith in science's ability to engineer simple solutions to complex human problems..." See Paul Van Riper and Robert H. Scales, Jr., "Preparing for War in the 21st Century," *Parameters*, 27 (1997): 4; http://carlisle-www.army.mil/usawc/Parameters/97autumn/scales.htm; originally published in *Strategic Review*, Summer 1997.
44. Lieutenant-Colonel Timothy L. Thomas, "US Military Publication," *Parameters*, Spring 1998: 84-92.
45. P. H. Liotta, "Chaos as Strategy," *Parameters*, Summer 2002: 47-56.

46. Craig Brod, *Technostress: The Human Cost of the Computer Revolution* (Reading, MA: Addison-Wesley, 1984).
47. P. M. Singer, *Corporate Warriors. The Rise and Ramifications of the Privatized Military Industry* (Ithaca, NY: Cornell University Press, 2003). See also Eugene B. Smith, "The New Condottieri and US Policy: The Privatization of Conflict and Its Implications," *Parameters*, Winter 2002-03.
48. Sissela Bok, *Mayhem: Violence as Public Entertainment* (Reading, MA: Addison-Wesley, 1999).
49. Major-General Russel L. Honoré, "Battle Command," *Military Review*, September-October 2002 (English edition).
50. Emily O. Goldman and Richard B. Andres, *Systemic Effects of Military Innovation and Diffusion.*(Davis, CA: Joint Centre for International and Security Studies, University of California, 2000).
51. Maury D. Feld, *The Structure of Violence: Armed Forces as Social Systems* (London: Sage, 1977),169.
52. Steven H. Kenney, "Professional Military Education and the Emerging Revolution in Military Affairs," *Airpower Journal*, Fall 1996.
53. Morris Janowitz, *Political Conflict: Essays in Political Sociology* (Chicago: Quadrangle Books, 1970).
54. David W. Lutz, "Unit Cohesion and Organizational Change," presentation to the Joint Services Conference on Professional Ethics XX, National Defense University, Fort McNair, Washington, D.C., 29-30 January 1998.
55. Mary C. FitzGerald, "The Soviet Military and the New Air War in the Persian Gulf," *Airpower Journal*, 5 (1991), http://www.cdsar.af.mil/apj/fitzg.html.
56. Lutz, "Unit Cohesion". See Thomas S. Kuhn, *The Structure of Scientific Revolutions* (Chicago: University of Chicago Press, 1968).

CHAPTER THREE

GUARDING THE CANADA-UNITED STATES BORDER

THE NEED TO CHALLENGE TRADITION

T. S. Hataley

"Any member of the Canadian Parliament or American Congress who offered now a bill appropriating money to fortify the border would be regarded as mildly insane."

S. Whittemore Boggs – 1940

"Not only do we have a hundred years of peace at our borders, but we think in terms of peace.....We live in a fireproof house, far from inflammable materials."

Senator Raoul Dandurand – 1925

The border between Canada and the United States is a primary line of defence for valuable political, social, economic, and material resources. Traditionally Canada has not expended significant material resources on guarding or fortifying the border because it was rarely considered politically or strategically necessary. This chapter contends that it is essential to challenge the convention of the "longest undefended border in the world", that land border crossings are a critical component of Canada's modern trade routes, representing a vital strategic link to its economic viability. Given such importance, the Canada-U.S. border should have the infrastructure required to safeguard north-south trade routes. Secondly, there are political reasons for Canada to do more to guard the border region with the U.S. The shifting discourse in the U.S. has begun to compare this border to the U.S.-Mexico border: might we see the "Mexicanization" of the Canada-U.S. border? The third section examines the role played in border security by the US military's Joint Task Force Six and suggests a similar role for Canadian special operations forces. The chapter concludes by drawing the link between border security and a role for Canada's military. It challenges Canadian policy-makers to take a proactive stance on border security by initiating a role for the Canadian military in the security and management of the Canada-U.S. border region.

STRATEGIC AND POLITICAL VALUE OF THE CANADA-U.S. BORDER

Canada and the U.S. share a border that is 8,895 kilometers long, with 133 land ports of entry, most of which are in underpopulated or wilderness areas. Each year approximately 200 million people cross the border. The value of product that crosses each day is almost $2 billion, most of it carried by the 45,000 trucks that cross daily.[1] One third of all truck traffic entering and leaving Canada crosses the Ambassador Bridge between Detroit and Windsor. Two thirds of all traffic flows across four international bridges in southern Ontario. Furthermore, eight of the ten busiest border crossings with the U.S. are either bridges or tunnels.[2]

A number of observations can be made from this brief list of statistics. First, the great length of the Canada-U.S. border makes intensive management and policing difficult. The job of guarding the border is complicated by the large expanses of wilderness or water surrounding it. At certain points on the St. Lawrence River, for example, it is possible to cross from Canada to the U.S. in less than twenty seconds by speedboat.[3] It is difficult, therefore, for law enforcement officials to apprehend even a minority of offenders who choose to cross this border outside legal ports of entry. On the other hand, the volume of traffic at legal ports of entry creates its own problems.

The second point is the importance of the border to Canada's economy: 82 per cent of all Canadian exports are destined for the U.S., and 22 per cent of US exports are destined for Canada, making the two countries the world's largest and most integrated bilateral trading partnership.[4] More important is the fact that 35.2 per cent of Canada's gross domestic product is a direct result of the trade in goods and services with the U.S. Under these conditions Canada's economic prosperity depends on trade with the U.S., and that trade depends on maintaining a secure cross-border flow of goods and services.

The third point is the importance of key border crossings. The vast majority of trade between Canada and the U.S. crosses through a minority of border points. As noted above, one third of all Canada-U.S. trade moves through the Detroit-Windsor corridor, including an estimated 9,000 trucks per day each way across the Ambassador Bridge.[5] Maintaining the integrity of these important crossings is critical as an economic "life line" for the Canadian economy, a problem compounded by the physical structure of key border crossings. That eight of the ten busiest crossings between Canada and the U.S. are either bridges or tunnels reflects the fact that much of the boundary between

Canada and the U.S. is defined by water, which must be passed over or under. The consequence of this type of infrastructure is that these passage routes are potential targets for disrupting the important trade routes.

To regulate traffic crossing on legitimate routes between Canada and the U.S. with borders that are secure and efficient is a primary goal of the Canadian government. To that end, the governments of Canada and the U.S. have entered into a series of bilateral arrangements to create more effective and secure transborder movement. Despite these programs, Canadian customs officials can inspect only a very small proportion of vehicles crossing the border. Although they have increased in recent years, inspection rates are only about 4.5 per cent.[6]

Efforts to secure the border are not restricted to legitimate crossing points. There are thousands of kilometers that are surveyed only minimally, if at all. American officials are convinced that the Canadian border has become a favoured route for illegal immigrants (many of them economic refugees), drug smugglers, and potential terrorists.[7] As the demand for high-potency Canadian marijuana has increased in the U.S., so too has the sophistication of smugglers, making it increasingly difficult to intercept drugs moving across the border. Evidence along the U.S.-Mexico border clearly illustrates that smugglers are interested in transporting anything or anyone that pays. Success in shutting down the Caribbean/Florida drug route had the net result of increasing the smuggling of drugs and illegal immigrants through Mexico. As American officials achieve increasing success in blocking Mexican trade routes, Canada has the potential to become the next best alternative.[8]

There is a real concern that Canada may be a target of a terrorist attack, but US security officials believe that Canada is home to terrorist "sleeper cells" waiting for a chance to cross the border and attack the U.S.[9] More central to this chapter is the claim by American officials that the Canadian immigration and refugee system is overly lax in keeping track of refugees and immigrants who enter Canada.[10] Indeed, some people believe that Canada's refugee system is "dysfunctional".[11] Moreover, officials have pointed to strong international ties between Canadian ethnic communities and their respective home nations as a potential source of support for terrorist activities in North America.[12]

The political case to be made for border security is linked to the strategic. For many years the Canada-U.S. border was outside of Washington's political radar, eclipsed by concerns over the southern American border. Despite a considerable amount of illegal activity, the U.S. was content to leave the border alone.[13] In the aftermath of September 11, the focus on the Canada-U.S. border has been dominated by a new security discourse that has continued to hold the attention of American policy-makers. Canada has been labelled a "haven for terrorists", and the border, as Andreas notes, is perceived and treated as a source of American vulnerability.[14] A problematical image of the border has been repeated in the media and in political debates,[15] and President Bush has pointed to illegal cross-border movement of drugs from Canada to the

U.S. as further evidence of a border "out of control".[16] Canada has also been singled out as a staging point for illegal immigrants wishing to cross over into the U.S.[17]

The altered American image of the Canada-U.S. border has been matched with shifting agency mandates and increases in material resources for guarding the northern entrance to the U.S. In the 2003 fiscal year, President Bush allocated an additional US$2.1 billion for border security.[18] According to Robert Bonner, commissioner of the Bureau of Customs and Border Protection, the immediate goal is to "substantially increase our control of the border, which is essential, given the real and ongoing threat of international terrorism".[19] To fulfil that mandate a variety of new technologies have been introduced at border inspection points, including:

- VACIS, the Vehicle and Cargo Inspection System, which searches vehicles using gamma rays;
- radiation detectors to scan for WMD;
- video surveillance known as "smart camera" to detect unusual movements along the border.[20]

Given the current American discourse on the Canada-U.S. border, it should not be surprising that comparisons are made between the evolving image of the Canadian border and the established image of the Mexican border. According to Andreas, "Remove the word 'terrorism' and put in the words 'drug trafficking' or 'illegal immigration' and the new discourse of border security is strikingly familiar, mimicking the old discourse that has characterized U.S. border relations with Mexico."[21]

Before September 11, however, the image of the Canada-U.S. border was much more positive. Both Canadian and American officials were well aware of security problems along the border, however. In 1988, US Customs officials arrested three members of a Syrian terrorist group linked to al-Qaeda attempting to enter the U.S. with explosives. Some of the bombers of the 1993 attack on the World Trade Center entered the U.S. from Canada and were planning to use Canada as an escape route. In December 1999, Ahmed Ressam was arrested crossing into the U.S. in possession of bomb-making materials and plans to carry out a terrorist attack.[22] As well as security concerns, the initial Free Trade Agreement and NAFTA have led to a substantial increase in the cross-border movement of goods and services, putting greater pressure on the border infrastructure.

It was in the context of increased trade and security problems that the U.S. and Canada launched the *Canada-United States Accord on Our Shared Border* in February 1995. The language of the Accord suggests an assured and cooperative spirit, to the extent that it brought together five agencies to focus resources on areas of shared concern, such as security.[23] Although the Accord acknowledged the need to improve protection against drugs, smuggling, and the illegal movement of people, it is largely directed towards making cross-border movement more efficient.[24] The 1995 Accord was followed in 1999 by the *Canada-U.S. Partnership Forum*, which created a mechanism for the two governments, border communities, and other stakeholders to discuss issues of border management. Finally in 2002 the two governments signed the *Smart Border Declaration*, which included a thirty-point plan to secure the border and facilitate the movement of legitimate goods and persons.

Why then should an image of the Canada-U.S. border that is constructed and reconstructed in American political and policy-making circles be of concern to Canadian policy-makers? Perception and understanding have the potential to determine how a given object is treated. If American policy-makers believe the border to be problematic, it will be treated as such. The fallout from a fortified border was made evident in the immediate aftermath of September 11, when trucks waited in line for days to cross the border. More recently, the upgraded security alert during the 2003-2004 Christmas period caused border backups as long as ten kilometres in some cities,[25] playing havoc with "just in time" deliveries. Indeed, this led the President of the Ontario Trucking Association to claim that the border is the most serious economic issue facing Canada.[26] This position is echoed by the Coalition for Secure and Trade-Efficient Borders, an organization formed by Canadian businesses to help the government deal with border issues.[27]

LESSONS FROM THE U.S.-MEXICO BORDER

In order to understand the current conditions along the U.S.-Mexico border, it is necessary to realize that, like the Canada-U.S. border, it was not for many years seen as a problem. As Andreas notes, the call to regain control of the southern border ignores the fact that there was never a time when the border was actually under control, and only recently had national attention even been paid to it.[28] That noted, however, the fundamental motivations for increased efforts on the part of the Americans to police the Mexican border were immigration and drug control.

Although immigration issues have been significant, particularly in regional settings, it is the war on drugs that has had the greatest policy impact. In contrast to the immigration issue, the scope of the war on drugs involves a large number of agencies. Although drug enforcement along the U.S.-Mexico border has a hundred-year history, the 1990s saw rapid increases in funding and material resources to combat drug smuggling along that border.[29] In part, these increased efforts were a response to alliances formed by South American drug cartels and Mexican smugglers. Success in disrupting the Florida-Caribbean smuggling routes had the unwanted effect of moving drug-smuggling efforts to the southwest border region. Smugglers operating along the southwest border quickly retooled and became substantially more sophisticated, thanks in great part to large sums of money received for their services.[30]

The politicization of immigration and drugs along the U.S-Mexico border has quickly moved them from being separate and distinct issues to a point where they are considered linked. The Border Patrol became more preoccupied with drug enforcement during the Reagan administration, starting with the passing of the *Immigration Reform and Control Act* in 1986. In that context, the Immigration and Naturalization Service deputized Border Patrol agents as Drug Enforcement and Customs agents to fight drug smuggling.[31] This transition has accelerated the construction of an image that defines illegal aliens not simply as economic threats but as national security threats. As Durch explains, illegal aliens have become associated with criminal gangs, failed states, and drug traffickers, resulting in the belief that illegal aliens are transnational threats to American interests, rather than individuals or groups of people in need of assistance.[32]

Increased force along the U.S.-Mexico border is evident not only in the manpower levels[33] on the border but also in the expanded infrastructure and the development and application of technology. This includes over forty-five miles of fences and walls, seismic sensors, infrared detectors, encrypted radio sets, infrared scopes, watchtowers, surveillance cameras,[34] and air surveillance support. Much of the technology being applied at the border was initially used by the military, including some that was developed for the war in Vietnam. Technologies previously off-limits to law enforcement are now being deployed along the border. Moreover, in March 1995 a Border Research and Technology Center was opened in San Diego to aid in the conversion of military technology for use in border enforcement.[35]

Increased efforts at border control have not been accomplished in the absence of a military contribution. Legally, the *Posse Comitatus Act* of 1879 has limited military involvement in domestic law enforcement tasks. However, the 1982 *Department of Defense Authorization Act* substantially broadened the guidelines under which the military was allowed to assist civilian police agencies. These powers were further enhanced by a series of new legislative measures between 1986 and 1992.[36] The new guidelines allow the military to operate and maintain equipment on loan to police agencies, to transfer surplus supplies to federal and state agencies, to conduct military reconnaissance activities at or near the border, and to train law enforcement agencies. A further shift in operational conduct was affirmed in September 2003, when support for counter-drug operations was redefined and expanded to include counter-narco-terrorism operations.[37]

The military component of counter-narco-terrorism is Joint Task Force Six (JTF-6). Created in 1989, JTF-6 was initially used only for counter-drug operations along the southwest border,[38] although evidence shows that its current operational area has expanded to the Canada-U.S. border. From 1990 to 1992, JTF-6 conducted 384 missions,[39] an average of 128 a year. This increased to 320 missions in 2003 alone, including at least 25 along the Canada-U.S. border.[40] JTF-6 provides a variety of operational support capabilities to the Bureau of Customs and Border Protection; for example, Forward Looking

Infrared Radar is used to provide real-time intelligence to border agents working in the field. In addition, JTF-6 provides aviation reconnaissance, aviation refuelling, engineer support, unattended ground sensors, controlled delivery, intelligence analysis, drug-trafficking assessment, tunnel detection, topographic imagery, ground surveillance radar, and mobile training teams.[41] In addition to JTF-6, the Defence Intelligence Agency has contributed a database, the Migration Defense Intelligence Threat Data System, designed to support military missions of combatting terrorism and force protection.[42]

Although the military do not have powers of arrest, US military doctrine of Low Intensity Conflict (LIC) defines their role along the U.S.-Mexico border. As the American analyst Dunn states, "the essence of LIC doctrine is the establishment and maintenance of social control over targeted civilian populations through the implementation of a broad range of sophisticated measures via the coordinated and integrated efforts of police, paramilitary and military forces".[43] In consultation with the Department of Defense Center for Low Intensity Conflict, the Immigration and Naturalization Service developed a comprehensive plan of "prevention through deterrence" as a means of being more proactive than reactive to illegal border crossings.

Although military relations between the U.S. and Mexico have traditionally been very limited, the war on drugs has made bilateral military arrangements more commonplace. These include a working group for military issues, military assistance, and training, including CIA instruction, resources, and operational support for Mexican army intelligence.[44]

An assessment of the U.S.-Mexico border present two important lessons. First, small problems can become large problems when they are politicized. By most accounts, the Mexican border did not become a serious concern until very recently. Initially the problem was not even the border itself, but rather illegal immigrants working in the U.S. The border became the tangible "line in the sand", the identifiable objective that needed to be brought under control. This shift from an economic to a security discourse has proved to be a rallying point on which American political leaders can attempt to dispel certain fears held by their domestic constituents. Moreover, the border represents a tangible good to which material resources can be applied in order to further American goals.

Second, small problems can become large problems through faulty policy choices. The shifting of drug-smuggling operations from Florida did little to cut the flow of drugs into the U.S.; rather, it provided the means and motivation for smugglers along the U.S.-Mexico border to become more sophisticated and much wealthier. Furthermore, increased efforts to block the border have had the net effect of forcing more illegal aliens to use the services of professional smugglers, who in some cases exploit their human cargo as a means of transporting narcotics.

Illegal immigrants and drugs have driven the increased policing and, according to some observers, the outright militarization of the U.S.-Mexico border over the last twenty years. The policy response on the American side has been one of largely unilateral action to tighten transborder movement, through greater use of manpower and technology. These efforts, we must recall, have been primarily focused on drug interdiction, with a more recent shift to counter-narco-terrorism. What, then, should Canada take from the evolution of the U.S.-Mexico border, given the suggestion by some American policy-makers that Canada is a primary source of some illegal drugs and a potential source of terrorists? Change in how the border is managed is inevitable. However, to avoid the "Mexicanization" of the Canada-U.S. border, Canada must appear committed and proactive in border security.

THE CANADA-U.S. BORDER AS A FILTER

Efforts to theorize borders have given rise to a number of border metaphors. For the purpose of this chapter, conceptualizing the Canada-U.S. border as a filter may prove useful for thinking about border security.[45] This metaphor conceives of the border as a semi-permeable membrane, separating legitimate from illegitimate transboundary traffic. The value of the border is less about demarcating sovereign territory and more about proactive defence.

The challenge, then, for Canadian policy-makers is to design and implement proactive policies that are compatible with those of the U.S. As the U.S. rapidly increases its attention to transnational threats and the need to coordinate security efforts for homeland and regional security purposes, the net result is the development of a Joint Interagency Task Force North (JIATF-North). Although it is too early to determine who will be lead agency, the hope is that JIATF-North will bring a multitude of American federal agencies under one roof to combat transnational threats. More important for Canada is that JIATF-North proposes to extend the geographic playing field to the North American continent.[46] Canada must be prepared to work with JIATF-North or risk being left on the sidelines of a major North American security initiative.

A close look at the task of guarding the Canada-U.S. border points up four apparent hurdles for Canadian policy-makers. The first is the physical enormity of the border itself. CSIS has noted that Canada's long borders and coastlines offer many points of entry that facilitate movements to and from various sites around the world, particularly the U.S.[47] Securing the vast wilderness of the Canada-U.S. border will undoubtedly require more manpower and more technology. The U.S. has opted for both options along its borders, increasing the number of agencies and the number of agents and using military technology to aid in surveillance, intelligence gathering, and law enforcement. Given the capabilities and resources available, it is reasonable that Canada could follow much the same course on a smaller, less aggressive scale, including use of military resources for training border officials and for border surveillance and intelligence gathering.

The second challenge will be the crossover effect of unrelated policies on border management and security, most notably Canada's immigration and refugee system and the pending decriminalization of marijuana. Approximately 30,000 refugees are admitted into Canada each year, through a system that critics claim does a poor job of separating legitimate refugees from potential terrorists. Moreover, CSIS maintains that a variety of terrorist groups are operating in Canada and that some cell members have entered Canada by claiming refugee status. A CSIS report to the Special Senate Committee on Security and Intelligence in January 1999 made clear that the large volume of refugees accepted into Canada provides a stream through which terrorists could gain entry.[48] Canada's refugee system does not go unnoticed south of the border, either: US lawmakers were quick to point fingers at Canada after the September 11 attacks.[49] Relatively easy access to Canada, ease of internal and external movement, and the large number of refugees and immigrants accepted each year make Canada's refugee system difficult to manage. As a result, Canada is a very real access point for terrorists and criminals trying to enter North America.[50]

The third issue will be the compatibility of domestic agencies as well as the interoperability of Canada-U.S. agencies. Different departments have different mandates as well as different capabilities. The way in which the RCMP, CSIS, and Citizenship and Immigration Canada (CIC) share information has been criticized as one of the problems in the screening process of new arrivals to Canada.[51] In terms of transborder communication, under the terms of the *Accord on Our Shared Border*, a number of agencies were to be brought together to rationalize the use of resources, streamline communications, and share capabilities, all in the effort to enhance security. The development of JIATF-North, however, poses even more challenges for Canadian officials intent on regional cooperation to combat transnational threats. The current structure of JIATF-North does not include a role for Canada, despite the fact that its operational area is all of North America.

The fourth challenge will be overcoming traditional conceptions of what the border between Canada and the U.S. represents. The image of the border has a real effect in terms of material resources that are applied, or not applied, to create a border infrastructure. The notions that Canada is a "fire proof house" and that it shares an undefended border with its neighbor to the south have clearly influenced the development of border policy and continue to do so. Perhaps this is most clearly illustrated by the fact that Canadian frontline border workers – customs officers – are seen more as a revenue collection agency than a law enforcement agency. Ron Moran, national president of the Customs and Excise Union, has commented that "the agency that has the job of protecting the border should be run by an organization that is fundamentally about law enforcement and public security rather than a revenue-generating organization".[52]

This is not to say that Canada has been completely lax in its response to largely foreign concerns over how the border is managed. The development of the Integrated Border Enforcement Teams (IBETs) and the purchase and employment of some new technologies are examples of Canadian changes aimed at making the border less permeable. Whether or not these changes have made a positive impact is not yet clear. According to one Canada Customs and Revenue Agency officer, recently acquired equipment that uses gamma rays to search for contraband is rarely used on the Canadian side, in contrast to American border officials at the same crossing, who use the technology much more frequently.[53] IBETs, by contrast, have been promoted by the government as an example of policy success within a cooperative framework.[54] However, it remains unclear if the increased seizure of assets is due to an increased level of smuggling or if it is the direct result of a policy shift in how the border is policed.

Reconceptualizing the border as a filter, rather than simply as a point of territorial demarcation or a point of contact, forces a change in policy direction and material resources applied in border management. With the exception of internal EU borders, most borders must act both as bridges to interstate communication and as barriers to contraband. Since the border exists at the junction of two sovereign territories, managing transborder movement involves two sovereign actors. In the case of the Canada-U.S. border, it is imperative for the economic security of Canada that the transborder flow of legitimate goods, services, and people be efficient and secure. This, it seems, is a simple matter of strategy. The other side of the argument is much more political: if the Canadian border is perceived as being insecure, then ease of transboundary movement will be degraded. That is, guarding the Canada-U.S. border is an essential component to successful political, social, and economic interaction between Canada and the U.S.

NOTES

1. Canada, Department of Foreign Affairs and International Trade, "Canada-U.S. Border Summit: Background Information," 2 September 2002, 9.
2. Canada, Transport Canada, unpublished data.
3. Miro Cernetig, "Hole in the border," *Toronto Star*, 11 October 2003, H1, H3.
4. Canada, "Canada-U.S. border summit," 9.
5. Unpublished data from Transport Canada based on numbers of truck crossings for 2002.
6. Canada. Canada Customs and Revenue Agency, "CCRA Performance Report 2001-2002 Annual Report to Parliament"; www.ccra-adrc.gc.ca/agency/annual/2001-2002/performance-e/mainpoints_customs-e.pdf, 1-71.
7. Jerry Seper, "Guarding America's border," *The Washington Times,* 8 December 2003; www.washingtontimes.com/functions/print.php?StoryID=2003208-123627-333r.htm
8. See National Drug Intelligence Center, "United States-Canada border: Drug threat assessment," December 2001.

9. Jerry Seper, "Terrorist cells too close for comfort," *The Washington Times,* 10 December 2003; www.washingtontimes.com/national/20031209-114319-3699r.htm
10. Ibid.
11. Stephen Gallagher, "Canada's dysfunctional refugee policy: A realist case for reform," *Behind the Headlines* 58(4), Summer 2001; and Charles M. Campbell, *Betrayal and Deceit: The Politics of Canadian Immigration* (West Vancouver: Jasmine Books, 2000).
12. Canada, Canadian Security and Intelligence Service, "International terrorism: The threat to Canada," *Perspectives,* 3 May 2000; www.csis-scrs.gc.ca/eng/miscdocs/200004_e.htm
13. Peter Andreas, "A Tale of Two Borders: The U.S.-Canada and U.S.-Mexico lines after 9-11," in *The Rebordering of North America: Integration and Exclusion in a New Security Context,* eds. Peter Andreas and Thomas J. Biersteker (New York: Routledge, 2003), 8.
14. Ibid.
15. See, for example, Andreas, "A Tale of Two Borders"; Graham Fraser, "Border not a problem, Manley says: Wary of charging into commitment to U.S. perimeter," *Toronto Star,* 5 October 2001; Tim Harper, "Tightening the Canada-U.S. border: Will we sacrifice our sovereignty for security?" *Toronto Star,* 8 October 2001; Steve Miller, "Canadian border patrol extended," *The Washington Times,* 5 November 2001; Allan Thompson, "Is Canada really the weak link? Rush to judgement fuels distortions on immigration," *Toronto Star,* 6 October 2001.
16. A December 2001 report by the National Drug Intelligence Center recognizes Canada as a major source and transportation route for high-grade marijuana, heroin, and precursor chemicals in the production of synthetic drugs (United States-Canada Border Drug Threat Assessment, 2001).
17. Chris Bury, "Miles to go: Feds increase attention on U.S.-Canada border after Sept. 11," ABC News Detroit, 10 May 2002; www.printerfriendly.abcnews.com/printerfriendly/Print?fetchFromGLUE=true&GLUEe
18. United States, The White House, Office of the Press Secretary, "Fact sheet: Border security," 25 January 2002; www.whitehouse.gov/news/releases/2002/01/print/20020125.html
19. Quoted in Seper, "Guarding America's border"
20. Ibid., p.2.
21. Andreas, "A Tale of Two Borders," 9.
22. Christopher Sands, "Canada and the war on terrorism: The U.S. challenge on the North American front," *Canada Focus* 2(3) October 2001; www.csis.org/americas/canada/focus/Focus0110.htm
23. Those agencies are Citizenship and Immigration Canada, Canada Customs and Revenue Agency, Royal Canadian Mounted Policy, Immigration and Naturalization Service, and U.S. Customs Service.

24. Canada, Citizenship and Immigration Canada, "Canada-United States Accord on Our Shared Border" (Ottawa: Minister of Public Works and Government Service, 2000).
25. Kevin McGran, "Windsor suffers border woes," *Toronto Star,* 13 January 2004: A4.
26. Ibid.
27. See Coalition for Secure and Trade-Efficient Borders, "Rethinking our borders: A plan for action," www.cme-mec.ca/coalition
28. Peter Andreas, *Border Games: Policing the U.S.-Mexico Divide* (Ithaca, NY: Cornell University Press, 2000), 8.
29. For a brief summary of increased spending on drug enforcement along the U.S.-Mexico border, see Andreas, *Border Games*, 51.
30. Ibid., 51-64.
31. Joseph Nevins, *Operation Gatekeeper: The Rise of the "Illegal Alien" and the Making of the U.S.-Mexico Boundary* (New York: Routledge, 2003), 68.
32. William J. Durch, "Keepers of the Gate: National militaries in an age of international populations movement," in *Demography and National Security,* eds. Myron Weiner and Sharon Stanton Russell (New York: Berghahn Books, 2001), 125.
33. Determining an exact number of agents working along the U.S.-Mexico border is difficult, since there are several agencies, including the border patrol, state and local police, Drug Enforcement Agency, FBI, and the US military.
34. Nevins, *Operation Gatekeeper,* 4.
35. Peter Andreas, "The escalation of immigration control in the post-NAFTA era," *Political Science Quarterly* 13(4) 1998-99: 597.
36. Durch, "Keepers of the Gate," 125.
37. Author interview, 1 February 2004.
38. Andreas, *Border Games*, 56.
39. Josiah McC. Heyman, "Why interdiction? Immigration control at the United States-Mexico border," *Regional Studies* 33(7) 1999: 626.
40. Author interview, 1 February 2004.
41. Author interview, 28 January 2004.
42. Durch, "Keepers of the Gate," 125.
43. Timothy Dunn, *The Militarization of the U.S.-Mexico Border: Low Intensity Conflict Doctrine Comes Home* (Austin: University of Texas Press, 1996), 4.
44. Andreas, *Border Games*, 66.
45. Ilidio do Amaral describes the border as "a zone of contact with sufficient permeability". He contends that national boundaries can be compared to cell membranes that are both separating and permeable. Ilidio do Amaral, "New reflections on the theme of international boundaries," in *World Boundaries Volume 1: Global Boundaries,* ed. Clive H. Schofield (London: Routledge, 1994), 17.

46. Author interview, 18 February 2004.
47. Canada, Canadian Security and Intelligence Service, "Trends in terrorism," *Perspectives,* 18 December 1999; www.csis.gc.ca/eng/miscdocs/20001_e.html
48. Canada, "The report of the Special Committee on Security and Intelligence," www.parl/gc.ca/36/1/parlbus/senate/com-e/secu-e/repsecintjan99part2/e.html 12/05/01, 8
49. John Geddes, "The terrorists next door," *Maclean's* 144(39), 24 September 2001: 24.
50. For a complete discussion on the shortcomings of Canada's refugee system, see Gallagher, "Canada's dysfunctional refugee policy".
51. Geddes, "The terrorists next door," 24.
52. Adrian Humphreys, "Border duties trump taxes, union says," T*he National Post,* 1 February 2003: A9.
53. Author interview, 15 November 2003.
54. Canada, Royal Canadian Mounted Police, "The central St. Lawrence integrated border enforcement team – Seven million in seized assets in one year," www.rcmp-grc.gc.ca/on/press/2003/2003_feb_06_e.htm 1/22/04

CHAPTER FOUR

THE ETHNIC DEMOGRAPHY ADVANTAGE

CANADA'S FORCE MULTIPLIER[1]

Christian Leuprecht

The most valuable asset Canada contributed to the recent naval deployment in the Persian Gulf may have been neither material nor technology, but human resources. An ordinary sailor made a unique contribution to the campaign – not because of his training, position, or skill – but because he spoke Farsi, the language of Iran. This unassuming Canadian sailor served as the front man whenever the armada stopped Iranian ships or communicated with Iranian authorities.

Ethnic diversity and multiculturalism are distinguishing characteristics of Canada. Scholars of immigration and multiculturalism often point to a range of instrumental benefits flowing from such policies in a shrinking global community. This chapter hypothesizes that the military stands to benefit from harnessing both trends. It advances three propositions in support of the argument, each of which posits demographics as the independent variable.

The first contention is that greater diversity is good for the military. Ethnic under-representation – or non-representation – is causing Canada to forsake its potential comparative advantage over virtually any other Western military. Canada has the most diverse pool of potential recruits of almost any liberal democracy. It also maintains comparatively good relations with its ethnic minorities, which should make it easier to recruit them, preserve their language and culture, and employ these in the service of the state.

The second contention is that ethno-cultural diversity within the military serves as a nation-building tool. Building trust, community, and a sense of belonging co-opts members of diasporas into the Canadian state. As members of the Canadian Forces, they serve Canada's national interests, thus integrating immigrants into the state and legitimizing national interests in the eyes of the group represented.

The third contention is that greater ethno-cultural diversity in the military is good for Canadian sovereignty. If integrated into the CF, Canada's immigrant population will bolster Canada's relations with the United States and other NATO allies by making Canada the force of choice in a coalition. The Canadian Forces' position as the foremost peacekeeping, peace-making, and peacebuilding force would thus be reasserted.[2]

Canada's comparatively good relations with the country's resident ethnic diasporas represents a unique human resource. It can be leveraged to contribute to public information, civil affairs and psychological operations, command and control warfare, and information operations. In effect, Canada's ethno-demographic advantage facilitates the use of civil affairs and psychological operations as a Canadian force multiplier in support of today's asymmetrical operations.

Civil affairs units have emerged as some of the busiest troops in the US military. Their activities establish, maintain, influence, or exploit relations among military forces, civil authorities, and the civilian population in support of military operations. Their expertise in bridging military and civil affairs has been in demand in virtually every recent military operation: Somalia, Haiti, Bosnia, Kosovo, Afghanistan, and Iraq. Since they lead civil reconstruction efforts, demand for their capabilities is bound to remain high for both security and humanitarian reasons.[3]

Psychological operations are used to convey selected information to foreign audiences to induce or reinforce attitudes and behaviours favourable to the originator's objectives. Like civil affairs units, psychological operations units are similarly sought after for peacekeeping and humanitarian missions. Their public-diplomacy and public-safety activities have been integral parts of US operations in Somalia, Haiti, Kurdistan, the Balkans, Afghanistan, and Iraq. They have extensive language and cultural training and experience.[4]

In JTF 2, Canada currently possesses a capability for direct-action special operations with its own special-reconnaissance and counter-terrorism capabilities. Yet, direct action is the special capability least in need of cultural affinity because it is the least likely to carry out culturally dependent missions. JTF 2 garners great respect for its people, equipment, and training and for its ability to carry out missions. A force, however, is only as effective as its ability to deploy. This is where JTF 2 falls short. Special operations "lift" comes in the form of two strategic assets: maritime and air. The CF possesses neither capability in the forms used by US SOF (a strategic submarine fleet and long-range cargo aircraft like the C17). Canada thus maintains a small, effective, and costly unit whose instrumental value is diminished severely by its inability to conduct strategic moves.

Future theatres of deployment for a direct-action counter-terrorist unit will probably be concentrated in Asia, including the Middle East, and Africa, particularly in countries with Muslim majorities or substantial Muslim minorities. A cursory survey of groups declared illegal by the Canadian government since September 11 pursuant to Part II.1 of the *Criminal Code* substantiates this claim. Of the groups that have since been banned (see Appendix for the complete list), sixteen are associated with the Middle East (47 percent), eleven are based in Asia (32 percent), two in North Africa (6 percent), one in the rest of Africa (3 percent), three in South America (9 percent), and one in Europe.[5] Although fairly short, the list is significant because it represents Canadian interests; these groups were banned because their activities are believed to conflict with Canada's national interest. It follows that Canada might participate in international action directed against some of these groups in the future. Canada's contribution to the campaign in Afghanistan to oust the Taliban regime (in league with al-Qaeda) illustrates the point. In other words, Asia, particularly the Middle East, is by far the most probable theatre of operations for special operations.

Yet, the countries capable of mounting effective special operations in this theatre are constrained by phenotype, culture, and language. Their phenotypic markers, as well as their unfamiliarity with the language and customs and the inadequacy of their subversive networks of internal support for inserted troops, present formidable obstacles to effective operations. This phenotypic, cultural, and linguistic disjuncture impinges on their mobility, efficacy, and versatility. They cannot blend into the local population, which makes it difficult for them to hide, especially for extended periods of time. They can communicate with locals on only a very limited basis, making it difficult to build trust or collect intelligence through conversations. Even the need to procure supplies from outside the area further limits the scope of a mission.

DEMOGRAPHY AND DIVERSITY

Canada is well positioned to find people familiar with the indigenous population of many regions in conflict, where knowledge of language and culture confers advantage. The diaspora communities of other countries notwithstanding, Canada is particularly well positioned demographically within the G8. But in addition to meeting the socio-demographic precondition, Canada's state apparatus has earned the trust of its immigrant and refugee communities. Without trust in the state, members of diasporas are unlikely to be induced to join the military in any capacity.

Only three liberal democracies have a migrant stock larger than Canada's: the United States (with almost 35 million), Germany (7.3 million), and France (6.3 million). Canada's migrant stock stands at 5.8 million.[6] About three percent of the world's population, some 175 million people, currently reside outside their country of birth. The proportion of Canada's foreign-born population, however, is more than five times that: 18.9 percent. Among large and mid-sized liberal democracies, only Australia (at about 24 percent) has a greater proportion of immigrants among its population. The U.S., France, Germany, the U.K., and Italy fall between 12 to about 3 percent.[7] In so far as the total number of migrants as well as their proportion of the population is concerned, Canada is favourably situated.

The rate at which new immigrants are arriving, added to the existing stock of immigrants, is also a factor in demographic diversity. Sixty percent of the world's migrants reside in industrialized countries, 56 million in Europe and 41 million in North America. Almost one person in ten living in more developed regions is a migrant. Between 1995 and 2000, the world's more developed regions gained over 12 million migrants. For the year 2002 alone, the figure stood at 2.3 million. Over half of the total was absorbed by North America. While the U.S. accounts for 1.25 million of them, Canada still had a higher annual average rate of net migration per thousand. Among liberal democracies, Canada's rate of net migration is second only to Australia's.[8]

Economic "push-pull" theories of migration suggest that migrants end up where they can maximize their economic benefit.[9] The socio-geographical evidence, however, suggests otherwise.[10] Migrants settle where they already have family or ethnic kin – with both variables usually coinciding.[11] This accounts for differentials in immigrant stock among countries. For example, the top ten countries of origin for foreign-born Canadians in the 2001 census were England, France, Scotland, Ireland, Germany, Italy, China, Ukraine, Netherlands, and Poland. For the United States in the 2000 census, they were Mexico, China, Philippines, India, Cuba, Vietnam, El Salvador, Korea, the Dominican Republic, and Canada.[12] The differences reflect historic settlement patterns and networks of immigrant communities, which facilitate subsequent settlement.

In light of the differential in total population between the two countries, Canada turns out to have a far greater proportion of immigrants from India, the Philippines, and Vietnam, for instance, than the United States, where the disproportionately large number of Hispanics and African-Americans dwarfs other ethnic groups. In Canada, by contrast, no single ethnic group of non-Caucasian origin clearly outweighs all others.

Pakistan and Iran have emerged as important sources of immigration to Canada (in third and fifth place). By contrast, in 2001, Pakistani and Iranian immigration (as a proportion of immigrants received) ranked 23rd and 25th in the United States. Currently, about 1.5 million immigrants from the Middle East live in the United States, less than half of one percent of America's total population. According to the 1996 census, the figure for Canada stands at 210,000, or almost one percent. The proportion of Middle-Eastern immigrants is thus marginally higher in Canada than it is in the U.S.

Yet, Canada's comparative advantage is bolstered by numbers that imply Middle-Eastern immigrants prefer Canada to the United States – with the notable exception of Jewish Israelis. About 700,000 Jewish-Israeli expatriates (most with Israeli-US dual citizenship) reside in the United States. This suggests that the figures for the Middle-Eastern population residing in the U.S. may be skewed. On the one hand, then, the disaggregated numbers indicate that Arabs make up a greater proportion of Canada's foreign-born population.

On the other hand, both that proportion and the discrepancy between the U.S. and Canada are likely to rise in the wake of September 11. It follows that the pool of potential special-operations links with, say, the Arab community in Canada is *relatively* more plentiful than the potential pool of Arab recruits for US special operations, although the total number of potential Arab recruits in the U.S. is certainly larger. Whether the Canadian Forces can harness this latent advantage hinges on the community's internal dynamics and its relationship with the Canadian state.

Irrespective of the positive correlations between multiculturalism and immigration, government policy towards immigrants represents the other side of Canada's comparative advantage. Canada's multiculturalism policy has created a wide range of ethnic organizations, including youth groups, which have been co-opted into the Canadian state and whose mandates are congruent with Canada's national interests. Nevertheless, these organizations enjoy legitimacy within their own communities. As a consequence, the Canadian state enjoys better relations with communities of recent immigrants than do many other liberal democracies.[13] Survey results confirm the positive attitude Canadians have towards interethnic relations.[14]

POLITICAL DEMOGRAPHY OF ETHNIC-DIASPORA LINKAGES

Political and ethnic dynamics make Canada a fruitful ground for strategic linkages with select ethnic diasporas. What is more, data available to us through census results and Statistics Canada actually facilitate this strategy. The census tracks immigrants not only by ethnic group and province but also by division. Like most immigrants to Canada, Iranian immigrants, for instance, tend to settle in Ontario and British Columbia. The 2001 census shows about 42,000 immigrants from Iran in Ontario, about 18,000 in B.C., and about 8,000 in Québec. The figures for the remaining provinces are negligible.[15] This pattern reflects the kin networks already in place.

Census data allow us to go further to identify significant regions. In Ontario, for example, Iranians choose to settle predominantly in Toronto and York region over any other census division. It is relatively easy to determine how many immigrants from a selected place of birth have settled in particular census divisions.[16] Concentration in large cities facilitates strategic recruitment of Canada's ethnic diasporas.[17]

OPERATIONALIZING CANADA'S DEMOGRAPHIC ADVANTAGE

Canada's demographic and political advantage notwithstanding, the argument as presented so far merits caution. An immediate concern is the historic difficulty in recruiting minorities. But that is precisely why it makes sense for the CF's special operations to develop civil-affairs and psychological-operations capabilities. While immigrants may be reluctant to join traditional military units, they might be more receptive if recruited specifically for their language and area expertise. There would be comfort for some in knowing that future dealings with their homeland or its neighbours would be undertaken with the advantage of a Canadian uniform and government passport. More problematic for my argument are concerns about trust and sociological research into the ways by which immigrants integrate into a host population.

Some critics argue that targetting a specific pool of potential recruits may reduce the quality of acceptable recruits. Would federally equalized recruitment patterns – regional origin and first official language have long been variables in CF recruitment – not have the same effect? Targetted recruitment helps to ensure the social balance dictated by policy, including germane regional and linguistic representation. This balance makes it easier to maintain public support for operations and provides local knowledge in the case of aid to civil authorities, as in the 1997 ice storm or the 1999 Winnipeg flood. In these operations, and in the internal security operations at Oka, Akwesasne, and Kanasetake in 1990, both official languages were important. Targetting other language groups for international operations can have the same positive impact, increasing both representation and operational effectiveness.[18]

Recruits for physically demanding direct-action forces like parachute units or counter-terrorist forces should be drawn from the widest possible pool because the success rate is quite low.[19] It would be inappropriate to search for these qualities in ethnically or linguistically defined groups. Civil affairs and psychological operations, on the other hand, suggest different types of training and different qualities. Physical fitness and reflexes are less important here than maturity, intellect, patience, and linguistic and cultural knowledge.[20]

Concerns with recruitment may also reflect a myopic attitude towards the role that diasporas can play. Members of immigrant communities in Canada need not be recruited into special operations units or even into the CF in order to play an instrumental role. It may be sufficient to identify individuals among specific immigrant groups with knowledge or skills that may prove useful in future missions. For example, recent immigrants may have local knowledge of urban geography around a target for hostage rescue or direct action. Being able to identify these individuals and gain their cooperation does not necessitate them being recruited, selected, and trained.

Trust and confidence are built over time and are affected by experience. Migrants often leave their countries of origin because of conflict with organs of the state, particularly the police and the military. In other words, they migrate because they have lost confidence in their own states. It may take them some time to regain confidence, to realize that the state is not intrinsically to be feared but rather that the Canadian state, and the values it embodies and defends, warrants their support and collaboration. Building confidence within immigrant communities, followed by active recruitment, could develop a valuable human resource.

Canada would be well served by a pool of trusted members among strategic diasporas. A teacher, for instance, might be called in at short notice to provide language or cultural-sensitivity courses to troops prior to deployment. The CF could draw on the expertise of the Canadian Foreign Service Institute (CFSI), which offers instruction in 42 languages. More importantly, the CFSI's Centre for Intercultural Learning (CIL) specializes in making the country's diplomatic corps proficient in the skills and knowledge required to live, work, and negotiate in a foreign setting. If special forces are to be "global diplomats", this is the sort of expertise that must be added to their skill set. Organizations such as the CFSI and CIL are well positioned to teach soldiers and police as well as diplomats.[21]

A translation service run by a native speaker may serve as a stand-by source for timely translation of open-source documentation before, during, or after a mission. Through Internet and satellite connections, some translators might even work in Toronto or Vancouver, supporting civil affairs or other special operations in distant theatres. Reliable translators for potential theatres of operation may be few, and in a crisis, the translation capacities in CSIS or the Communications Security Establishment (CSE) are likely to be stretched or overwhelmed. When units cannot overcome language barriers, they cannot understand their environment, gather intelligence, or even protect themselves effectively. Timely communication can be vital to mission success. Be it a military unit, intelligence service, development agency, or international policing, any agency operating in the global village needs language services and would benefit from a network of reliable translators who can be available on short notice.

The Toronto Police Service, for instance, has translators for 140 languages, on standby around the clock every day of the year. They can be brought into the field with community liaison officers or regular constables or patched into a three-way call between a 911 operator and a caller. By incorporating recent immigrant populations, the Toronto Police can interact with them and serve them effectively.

CANADEM provides another model for incorporating multicultural expertise. Funded by the Department of Foreign Affairs, it maintains a national roster of more than five thousand Canadian civilians with a broad range of knowledge and skills, including human rights monitoring, conduct of elections, democratization, administration and logistics, security, and post-conflict reconstruction. CANPOL is an affiliated agency that maintains a roster of policing expertise for international deployment. Both of these government-sponsored non-governmental organizations serve as vehicles for rapid, nationally directed response to international crises. They allow Canada to provide appropriately qualified people to international missions sponsored by bodies such as the UN. They can also be tapped by other non-governmental organizations. CANADEM, or another agency modelled on it, could mobilize and catalogue immigrant expertise to serve the national interest.

Immigrants from a potential theatre may be a source of vital intelligence through contacts they still have in their places of origin. They may also have topographical and geostrategic insights. Despite all the cartographical information and intelligence available, arguably there is no better source of guidance than someone with intimate, first-hand knowledge of the area, either accompanying the troops or available for consultation through radio contact. Since those who have left a conflict zone most recently may be the least forthcoming, Citizenship and Immigration Canada might offer incentives to individuals with urgently needed knowledge or skills.[22]

Through their contacts, immigrants may also be able to enhance the success of a mission in other ways. Trusted family members abroad might be recruited to harbour operatives, to assist in communications, or to supply food or information. MI6's Special Operations Executive pioneered such tactics during the Second World War.[23] Friendly locals can extend strategic reach beyond the limits of military logistics, increase the longevity of missions, and provide for backup in case other arrangements fail. This makes it possible for special operations to be conducted prior to any armed intervention, or even in its absence. Detailed local knowledge and friendly forces in location may pay significant dividends, for development and diplomacy no less than for invasions such as those of the Second World War. Family ties to immigrants back in Canada will help to increase the reliability of such help.

Reliability will always be a concern in working with immigrant communities. As Canada acts in concert with allies, and as special operations affect highly classified intelligence, technology, or sensitive national interests, both Canadian and allied decision-makers might question the wisdom of involving recent immigrant communities. The U.S., for example, has a high proportion of blacks and Hispanics and a representative proportion of various other ethnic groups, but minorities are vastly under-represented in Special Operations Forces, particularly in the officer ranks.[24] Americans view minority members of their own forces as "American", but Canadians recruited from ethnic minorities may not necessarily be viewed as such.[25] Two Muslim members of the US forces stationed at Guantanamo Bay, for example, have been charged with various trust- and loyalty-related offences. Ethnies in the military invariably raise the question of loyalty and trust.

For purposes of recruitment, the relationship between identity (be it ascriptive or descriptive) and culture – the patterns of behaviour associated with a particular group – is important. It might be posited that immigrants from cultures that put a premium on familial, local, and tribal relationships would prove difficult to recruit, if only because recruitment would break that nuclear bond. In a country as big as Canada, military moves are almost inevitable. Ethnic recruits might be separated from their families for training, garrisoned far away from their kin, deployed overseas for extended periods, and so forth. Research suggests that if familial, local, and tribal attributes are related to culture rather than identity, they will dissipate fairly rapidly upon separation.

Under Canada's "mosaic" model, immigrants are thought to retain a strong sense of ethnic identity, but this is not to be confused with the retention of elements of the culture of origin. A strong identity does not necessarily mean immigrants are more conversant in their original language, well-versed in their original religion, more likely to marry within the group, or more likely to want to live within an ethnic neighbourhood. On the contrary, on many of these criteria immigrants to Canada quickly relinquish links with their ancestral culture.[26] It follows that the relationship between identity and culture is probably inverse rather than direct.

A weak sense of culture but a strong sense of identity may be the prerequisite combination to recruit individuals from more "traditional" cultures in the first place. A strong sense of ethnic identity, however, may cause problems when ethnic recruits are mixed.[27] Can we expect to send a Canadian unit made up of personnel from different ethnic groups to a region where those same groups are in conflict? Members of all groups may have better knowledge of the geography and cultures, but they may sympathize with one faction or the other.[28] The experience with recruiting and employing mixed ethnic teams is limited.[29]

Targetted recruitment of ethnic minorities is fraught with contradictions. To be useful, immigrants have to have maintained ties with their countries of origin and retained a good deal of the kin culture. But to serve Canada, they have to place Canadian interests ahead of the interests of their former homeland or kin group. To this end, immigrants need to be supportive of Canada's political culture. In cases where the Canadian interest coincides with the interest of the country (or group) Canada is trying to help, any tension between them is not a problem. But the more closely ethnic recruits identify with the country or people where they are deployed, the less they will be able to serve Canadian interests when there is a clash with those of the kin community or state. Such is the historic dilemma of ethnic armies.[30]

Despite residual attachments to their homelands, involvement of immigrants in homeland affairs is often instrumental in adaptation to the norms of their new country of residence.[31] Multiculturalism policies support this adaptation by nurturing diffusion of norms within countries and across international boundaries. Multiculturalism as a principle of government relations with diasporas, therefore, stands to serve Canada's goals with respect to foreign policy and nation-building.

IMPLICATIONS FOR SPECIAL OPERATIONS

The ethnic composition of Canada's population pyramid is changing rapidly. As the population ages, the proportion of Caucasians diminishes. In 2001, the proportion of visible minorities in Canada (not counting 1.4 million aboriginals) stood at 13.4 percent, a 43 percent increase since 1991 (Table 4-1). Increases were greatest in British Columbia (52 percent), followed by Ontario (47 percent).

TABLE 4-1
Proportion of Visible Minorities, 1991-2001

	1991	*1996*	*2001*
Canada	9.4	11.2	13.4
Newfoundland and Labrador	0.8	0.7	0.8
Prince Edward Island	1.0	1.1	0.9
Nova Scotia	3.4	3.5	3.8
New Brunswick	1.2	1.1	1.3
Québec	5.6	6.2	7.0
Ontario	13.0	15.8	19.1
Manitoba	6.9	7.0	7.9
Saskatchewan	2.6	2.8	2.9
Alberta	9.4	10.1	11.2
British Columbia	14.2	17.9	21.6
Yukon Territory	2.7	3.3	3.6
Northwest Territories	3.5	3.8	4.2
Nunavut	0.9	0.6	0.8

Source: Statistics Canada

Current recruiting patterns present a problem. The recruitment-age cohort (15-29) is shrinking along with the pool of traditional Caucasian recruits. But the pool of young ethnic recruits is growing because immigrants tend to have more children than the Canadian average. In fact, the total fertility rate is inversely proportional to the amount of time spent in Canada: the longer immigrants remain in Canada, the closer their fertility rate approximates the national average. If we were to plot effort required to recruit on a vertical axis and useful knowledge of a foreign homeland on a horizontal axis, the result would probably be a curve like a normal distribution. The horizontal axis would also correspond to time spent in Canada. At the low left side of the curve, we would find recent immigrants who have not yet adopted Canadian ways or allegiance to the Canadian state. Their experiences may lead to apprehension about any connection with state security apparatus, and they may deter their children from joining. At the low right side of the curve, we would find assimilated Canadians with low fertility rates, requiring relatively higher effort to recruit. At the high centre of the curve, we find second- and third-generation immigrants whom we might still expect to have useful knowledge of or contacts in a foreign homeland.

The proportion of visible minorities in the population is growing while the proportion of Caucasians is waning. By 2011, 39 percent of Canada's population is projected to identify as non-anglophone, non-francophone, and non-Canadian. A force in which ethnic recruits are under-represented is not optimizing its labour pool. I have made the argument above that greater diaspora involvement in special operations enhances capacity in a global community by harnessing Canada's demographic edge. This is complemented by the utilitarian argument that recruiting amongst the largest pool of available youth will optimize return on recruiting investment.

Is the CF constraining its potential through its recruiting strategy? At 54,000, the CF falls short of its authorized troop strength of 60,000. Using the American figure of two percent suggests about 1,200 troops engaged in special operations – more if reserve civil affairs units are included. This is all the more problematic, given the difficulties in keeping elite units up to strength. Delta Force in the U.S., for example, has never exceeded 82 percent of its authorized strength. To optimize special operations recruitment, Canadian Forces must first optimize recruitment, and greater diversity is the key to achieving this end. Research into structural and perceived barriers responsible for low rates of ethnic-minority representation among US special operations may offer some helpful insights into the Canadian ethnic-recruitment predicament.[32] This research shows that equality of opportunity for minorities in special operations can be improved.

Greater integration of immigrant communities (in national institutions generally and in the Canadian Forces and special operations in particular) will enhance social cohesion in Canada. It can enhance the allegiance of future immigrants to the Canadian state by demonstrating mutual benefits from commitment and by providing role models and focal points for identity. This enhances the sort of social cohesion that in turn encourages immigrants to engage in national institutions, making further recruitment easier. Drawing forces more proportionately from Canadian society is a nation-building strategy that will enhance Canada's ability to conduct special operations in a global community.

Civil affairs and psychological operations troops, as special units of the Canadian Forces, have a special role to play in Canadian nation-building and overseas operations. Canadian regular units have made a name for themselves through aggressive competence in combat operations and conventional skill at arms. But their reputation goes further. In decades of peacekeeping operations in Cyprus, the Middle East, Asia, the Americas, and the Balkans, tens of thousands of Canadian soldiers, sailors, and airmen and -women have helped to build relationships with communities in conflict. These relationships have helped to reduce the likelihood that Canadian troops will be targetted. Canadian political and military culture makes much of this "nice guy" image, relying as much on communication as on combat skills.[33] Civil-affairs campaigns embody the values and practices of cooperation, relationship-building, and behavioural change that are often associated with successful Canadian missions. While American psychological operations are classed as a form of "offensive fire", Canada established Military Information Support Teams (MIST) in Haiti to perform the psychological-operations function in a transparent and non-offensive way. Civil affairs and psychological operations, as practised by Canada, are more likely to be embraced by Canadians than direct action because they coincide with Canadian values and practices. This includes the values and practices that have proven integral to Canada's longstanding reputation as an immigrant country. These same values should facilitate recruitment of immigrants for this sort of special operation.

Demand has reached unprecedented levels for civil affairs and psychological operations troops. Both capabilities are central to the Brahimi Report on the future of UN peacekeeping.[34] Brahimi identified multi-dimensional cohesion as the core of future UN contributions to peacekeeping. This translates into a focus on local peacekeeping with a view to providing a framework for security and stability. Provincial Reconstruction Teams in Afghanistan exemplify how this might be achieved in practice. As originally fielded by the U.S. in 2003, these teams consisted of 60 to 90 soldiers formed around a 12-man Special Forces "A" team, complemented by civil affairs and psychological operations capabilities. Developing this kind of special operations capability puts Canada in line with UN priorities and at the forefront of international stability missions.

Civil affairs and psychological operations capabilities are an optimal force multiplier for the Canadian Forces. They may thus serve to bridge Canada's continentalist and internationalist imperatives. Since Suez, Canada has engaged in missions that have been difficult for the Americans to take on, due to domestic or international pressures. Canada's peacekeeping in the Congo and peace observation in Kashmir served Cold War objectives. Canada's force in Cyprus helped keep NATO together.[35] More recently, Canada's leadership in Kabul freed up American forces for other missions. The Canadian Navy is one of only two in the world whose ships are fully interoperable with the US Navy, and the U.K. is the only other country whose air force shares the Common Targeting System with Canada and the U.S. Notwithstanding its small size, Canada has a history of making key contributions to American foreign and military policy.

The uncertain future security environments described in Chapter One suggest many opportunities for conflict within states and across international boundaries in a global community. A culturally and linguistically adept military with a substantial diaspora representation is Canada's most promising means of making itself an indispensable partner in any coalition. This will buttress our bilateral relationship with the U.S. and reinforce our capacity to make a unique contribution to multilateral UN efforts. This demands that Canada rethink special operations capabilities.

The best way to turn Canada's demographic advantage into operational capability is to accelerate the development of reserve units with civil affairs and psychological operations capabilities. The Canadian Forces can further enhance the effectiveness of these units by using census data to locate them in areas of high immigrant concentration and by concentrating recruiting efforts on potentially useful immigrant groups. The Governor General's Horseguards in the Greater Toronto Area, Canada's most multi-ethnic reserve unit, is exemplary in this regard. Establishing reserve companies for special operations in Montreal for *la francophonie*, in Toronto for Europe, the Caribbean and Latin America, and in Toronto and Vancouver for Asia-Pacific might be a good start. The units could be seeded with regular and reserve personnel who have already honed their skills in Bosnia, Afghanistan, and elsewhere.

American Special Operations Forces rely heavily on reserves. Of the 46,000 special operations personnel, only 29,000 are on active duty.[36] Sixty percent of America's psychological operations personnel and 97 percent of its civil affairs personnel are in the Army Reserves.[37] And the Army will be adding new civil affairs and psychological operations reserve companies by 2005.[38] Reserves are a cost-effective way to build and maintain special capabilities for use in contingencies. Their appeal results from their deployment on many kinds of operations without large accompanying forces. Because they are not inherently offensive, as direct-action forces are, they can be used in a variety of different circumstances to shape the strategic environment, whether or not large coalition or NATO forces are deployed.

RECOMMENDATIONS AND FURTHER RESEARCH

On the one hand, Canada's military has long been pivotal in its relations with the U.S. On the other hand, that makes its role controversial. Ideally, Canada's comparative advantages should be harnessed in a fiscally responsible and realistic way. I have argued that developing a role for immigrants in special operations is one way forward. Language, culture, phenotype, and local knowledge will be vital in future operations in the global community. Special operations will need to take advantage of networks, local intelligence, human contacts, and social and cultural understanding. Integrating minorities stands to strengthen Canada and its national security and to balance Canada's continental and international imperatives.

Some important recommendations follow from this study of Canada's ethno-demographic edge. Canada should recruit immigrant communities for special operations such as civil affairs and psychological operations. Recruitment should focus on cities such as Toronto, Vancouver, and Montreal. More research is needed on the processes by which immigrants are effectively recruited and integrated in military service, and on the factors that deter or enhance recruitment and international service. This knowledge may facilitate recommendations for change in institutional culture or recruiting practices. Canada's ethno-demographic advantage stands out as the Canadian Forces' ultimate multiplier.

NOTES

1. This research was supported financially by the Counter-Terrorism and Special Operations branch of Canada's Department of National Defence and by the Social Sciences and Humanities Research Council of Canada. The author gratefully acknowledges research assistance provided by Nicolette O'Connor and Natasha Kanerva and is indebted to Randy Richert, Casey Haskins, Terry Loveridge, Joel Sokolsky, and Will Kymlicka for comments and feedback.
2. By peacemaking, the UN and NATO understand diplomatic activity with a very low level of military involvement; by peacekeeping they understand observers and inter-positional forces in a mutually agreed peace; peace enforcement refers to a policy of creating a peace without prior agreement of the parties to the conflict, bringing armed force to bear, if necessary; peacebuilding refers to post-combat operations and is usually associated with the three-block war paradigm where, within a radius of three blocks, a force is providing aid, interacting with local populations, and engaging an armed militia.
3. Leslie Fuller, *US Special Operations Forces in Peacekeeping Operations* (Carlisle, PA: Army War College, 1996), 14-19.
4. Michael Fitzsimmons, "The Importance of Being Special: Planning for the future of US Special Operations Forces," *Defense and Security Analysis* 19, 3 (2003): 208.
5. Not factored into the analysis is these organizations' fundraising efforts pervasive throughout liberal democracies. Furthermore, al-Qaeda is double-counted as Asia and as Middle East.
6. United Nations, *International Migration Report* (New York: Department of Public Information, 2002). Figures are for migrant stock as proportion of population in 2000.
7. Ibid.
8. Andrew Parkin, "How Canada is Changing," in *A Changing People: Being Canadian in a New Century* (Ottawa: Centre for Research and Information on Canada, April, 2003), 5.
9. Timothy J. Hatton and Jeffrey G. Williamson, *The Age of Mass Migration: Causes and Economic Impact* (Oxford: Oxford University Press, 1998).
10. Stephen Castles and Mark J. Miller, *The Age of Migration: International Population Movements in the Modern World*, 2nd ed. (New York: The Guilford Press, 1998 [1993]).
11. Alejandro Portes and Robert L. Bach, *Latin Journal: Cuban and Mexican Immigrants in the United States* (Berkeley: University of California Press, 1985).
12. Statistics Canada, *Census of Population, 2001*; U.S. Census Bureau, 2001.
13. Will Kymlicka, *Finding Our Way* (Don Mills, ON: Oxford University Press, 1998), Chapter 1.

14. Andrew Parkin and Matthew Mendelsohn, *A New Canada: An Identity Shaped by Diversity* (Montreal: Centre for Research and Information on Canada, 2003).
15. Statistics Canada, *Census of Population, 2001*.
16. Statistics Canada's resource tool, E-Stat, was used to track down the data. Through any licensed administrator, such as a registered university or public library, it is possible to identify variables and generate data using the figures documented in Statistics Canada's CANSIM matrices and tables. The data presented for the purposes of this paper are also available in the Statistic Canada's publication, *Profile of Citizenship, Immigration, Birthplace, Generation Status, Ethnic Origin, Visible Minorities and Aboriginal Peoples, for Canada, Provinces, Territories, Census Divisions and Census Subdivisions, 2001 Census, Cat. No. 95F0489XCB01001*. Note that in addition to the category "Total immigrants by selected places of birth", another variable measures "Total recent immigrants by selected places of birth - 20 percent Sample Data". Statistics Canada refers to those persons who immigrated to Canada between 1996 and Census Day, 15 May 2001, as "Recent immigrants".
17. Eighty-five percent of immigrants live in the country's largest 25 urban regions, compared to only 57 percent of Canadian-born citizens. Recent immigrants are most likely to settle in Canada's largest cities. Toronto's immigrant population exceeds 42 percent and Vancouver's 35 percent, followed by Hamilton (24 percent) and Kitchener (22 percent), both within close proximity of Toronto. Nearly three quarters of recent immigrants settled in Toronto, Vancouver, or Montreal, although these cities house only a quarter of the country's population. Recent immigrants are more than twice as likely to live in Toronto than in Vancouver and more than three times more likely to live in Toronto than in Montreal. As a result, Ontario has by far the largest proportion of immigrants (55 percent), followed by British Columbia (18 percent) and Québec (13 percent).
18. Brian Selmeski, "Family and Values in Socializing Ecuador's Conscripts," in *Challenge and Change for the Military: Social and Cultural Change*, eds. David Last, Franklin Pinch, Douglas L. Bland and Alan Okros (Montreal and Kingston: McGill-Queen's University Press, 2004).
19. See Table 1-1, Quality-Quantity Trade-off.
20. Anna Simons, "The Evolution of the SOF Soldier: An Anthropological Perspective," in *Force of Choice: Perspectives on Special Operations*, eds. Bernd Horn, J. Paul de B. Taillon, and David Last (Montreal and Kingston: McGill-Queen's University Press, 2004).
21. Scott Moore describes American Special Forces as potential "global diplomats". See Scott Moore, "Special Operations Forces: Visioning for the Future," in *Force of Choice*, eds. Horn *et al.*
22. In 1941, the US Navy was concerned about sabotage of shipping by the large Italian-American population in New York. It arranged for the release

of imprisoned gangster "Lucky" Luciano to provide guarantees. Later, the embryonic Office of Strategic Services recruited the Mafia to help with the invasion of Sicily. Paul Elliott, *Brotherhoods of Fear: A History of Violent Organizations* (London: Cassell, 1998), 146.

23. Nigel West, *MI6: British Intelligence Operations, 1909-1945* (London: Weidenfeld & Nicolson, 1983); Edward Spiro, *Inside S.O.E.: The story of special operations in Western Europe, 1940-1945* (London: Baker, 1966); David Stafford, *Britain and European Resistance, 1940-1945: A survey of the Special Operations Executive, with documents* (Toronto: University of Toronto Press, 1980).
24. Sheilagh Nataraj Kirby, Margaret C. Harrell, and Jennifer Sloan, "Why Don't Minorities Join Special Operations Forces?" *Armed Forces and Society* 26, 4 (2000): 523.
25. Often closely connected with nativism is a current in American thought insisting that political radicalism has foreign origins. This patterns crops up in the anti-Catholic fears of conspiracy in the 1840s, the anarchist violence of the late-nineteenth century, the post-World War I Red Scare, the fears of fifth columnists during the late-1930s, and in the McCarthy witch-hunts. Radicalism – be it anarchism, bolshevism, fascism, Communism, or a series of others – regardless of its actual origins, was generally ascribed to foreign sources, identified as intrinsically un-American. See Richard Polenberg, *One Nation Divisible: Class, Race, and Ethnicity in the United States since 1938* (New York: Penguin, 1980), 41, 115-119; Robert H. Wiebe, *The Search for Order, 1877-1920* (New York: Hill and Wang, 1967), 209, 288-290; Roger Daniels, *Not Like Us: Immigrants and Minorities in America, 1890-1924* (Chicago: Ivan R. Dee, 1997), 99-100; John Higham, *Strangers in the Land: Patterns of American Nativism, 1860-1925*, rev. ed. (New Brunswick, NJ: Rutgers University Press, 1988). The author gratefully acknowledges Ross Cameron's contribution of this insight.
26. Jeffrey G. Reitz and Raymond Breton, *The Illusion of Difference: Realities of Ethnicity in Canada and the United States* (Toronto: C.D. Howe Institute, 1994); Irene Bloemraad, "Is Multiculturalism Assimilatory? Structure Mobilization and the Political Incorporation of Refugees and Immigrants in the U.S. and Canada," paper presented at the Canadian Institute for Advanced Research, Berkeley, CA, 16-17 January 2004.
27. Simons, "Evolution of the SOF Soldier".
28. Canada, for instance, did not assign Jewish or female soldiers to the United Nations Iran-Iraq Military Observer Group (UNIIMOG, 1988-1991). Similarly, cultural sensitivities altered the selection of units for Suez in 1956.
29. David Last, *From Peacekeeping to Peacebuilding: Theory, Cases, Experiments and Solutions*, Royal Military College of Canada Working Paper, 99/01 (Kingston, ON: RMC, 1999).

30. N. F. Dreisziger, ed., *Ethnic Armies: Polyethnic Armed Forces from the Time of the Hapsburgs to the Age of the Superpowers* (Waterloo, ON: Wilfred Laurier University Press, 1990).
31. This claim has been substantiated empirically for, *inter alia*, Arab-Americans. See Yossi Shain, *Marketing the American Creed: Disporas in the U.S. and their homelands* (Cambridge: Cambridge University Press, 1999).
32. Nataraj Kirby *et al.*, "Why Don't Minorities Join Special Operations Forces?"; Margaret C. Harrell *et al.*, *Barriers to Minority Participation in Special Operations Forces,* RAND MR-1042-SOCCOM (Santa Monica, CA, 1999); Martha Teplitzky, *Minority Representation in the Enlisted Special Forces* (Alexandria, VA: United States Army Research Institute for the Behavioral and Social Sciences, 1992).
33. David Last, *Theory, Doctrine and Practice of Conflict De-Escalation in Peacekeeping Operations* (Cornwallis, NS: Canadian Peacekeeping Press, 1997), 67-89.
34. Lakhdar Brahimi, *Report of the Panel on United Nations Peace Operations* A/55/305 S/2000/809 (New York: United Nations, 2000).
35. Sean Maloney, *Cold War by Other Means: Canada and UN Peacekeeping, 1945-1970* (St. Catharines, ON: Vanwell, 2002).
36. Office of the Assistant Secretary of Defense, "Special Operations and Low-Intensity Conflict and US Special Operations Command," United States Special Operations Forces: Posture Statement (Washington, DC, 2000), 41.
37. Assistant Secretary of Defense, "Special Operations and Low-Intensity Conflict", 52.
38. Marshall Billingslea, Statement Before the Subcommittee on Terrorism, Unconventional Threats and Capabilities, House Armed Services Committee: Concerning Special Operations Forces Acquisition (Washington, DC, 1 April 2003).

APPENDIX
List for the purposes of Part II.1 of the *Criminal Code*

Organization	*Location/Characteristics*
Abu Nidal Organization (ANO)	Middle East – carried out attacks internationally
Abu Sayyaf Group (ASG)	Iran – smallest and most radical Islamic separatist groups fighting to establish an Iranian style Islamic state in Mindanao (Phillippines)
Al Jihad (AJ or Egyptian Islamic Jihad)	Egypt – wants to replace Egyptian government with an Islamic government Involved in the Sadat assassination and US embassy bombings Linked with al-Qaeda and bin Laden
Al-Qaeda	International – central component of a network of Sunni Islamic extremist groups Associated with bin Laden
Al-Aqsa Martyrs Brigade	Israel – armed faction of Islamic Nationalists
Al-Gama'a al-Islamiyya (AGAI or Islamic Group IG)	Egypt – armed religious extremists Objective: overthrow government to establish Islamic rule; focuses on killing Americans Links with bin Laden
Al-Ittihad Al-Islam (AIAI)	Somalia and Ethiopia – internationally established Objective: create a greater Somalia
Ansar al-Islam (AI)	Iraq-Kurdish Sunni organization, Part of the al-Qaeda network
Asbat Al-Ansar (The League of Partisans and many other names)	Lebanon – Sunni extremist organization composed of Palestinians Objective: establishment of Islamic Lebanon
Aum Shinrikyo	Japan – sarin gas in Tokyo subway
Autodefensas Unidas de Colombia (AUD or United Self-Defense Forces of Colombia)	Colombia – right-wing umbrella terrorist organization Closely linked to drug cartels
Babbar Khalsa	India – Sikh Objective: form fundamentalist Sikh state called Khalistan
Babbar Khalsa International (BKI)	India – Sikh Objective: form fundamentalist Sikh state called Khalistan

... *continued*

APPENDIX
(Continued)

Organization	*Location/Characteristics*
Ejercito de Liberacion Nacional (National Liberation Army or ELN)	Colombia – second-largest left-wing after FARC Opposes foreign involvement in Colombia's oil
Euskadi Ta Asakatasuna (ETA)	Basque – called most dangerous terrorist organization in Europe Objective: form a Basque state based on Marxist principles
Fuerzas Armadas Revolucionarias de Colombia (FARC)	Colombia – best-equipped Marxist insurgency Closely linked to drug squads
Groupe Islamique Arme (GIA)	Based in Algeria – anti-secularist and anti-Western Sunni Muslim Affiliated with bin Laden
Hamas	Israel – Sunni Muslim terrorist organizations Objective: kill Jews
Harkat-ul-Mujahedeen (HuM)	Pakistan-based radical Kashmiri Islamist organization Objective: liberate Kashmir from India Calls for a jihad against India and the U.S.A.
Hezbollah	Lebanon – Islamic terrorist Objectives: remove all western influence from Lebanon, liberate Palestinian territory
International Sikh Youth Federation (ISYF)	U.K./India – centres in Canada Objective: establish Khalistan
Islamic Army of Aden	Yemen – radical Islamic organization Objective: overthrow Yemeni government in favour of Islamic government Ties with al-Qaeda
Islamic Movement of Uzbekistan (IMU)	Uzbekistan Objective: overthrow government of Uzbekistan
Jaish-e-Mohammed (JeM)	Pakistan – radical Islamic organization Objective: Liberate Jammu and Kashmir from India and integrate them into Pakistan
Jemaah Islamiyyah (JI)	Southeast Asia – Islamist terrorist Objective: unify Muslims in Thailand, Malaysia, Indonesia, Brunei, Southern Philippines

... continued

APPENDIX
(Continued)

Organization	*Location/Characteristics*
Kurdistan Workers Party (PKK)	Turkey/Iraq – based on Marxist-Leninist ideology Objective: create a Kurdish state in southeast Turkey and northern Iraq
Lashkar-e-Jhangvi	Parkiston – Sunni Islamic organization Objective: create a Sunni Muslim state
Lashkar-e-Tayyiba (LeT)	Pakistan/Kashmir/Jammu – radical Islamist organization
Palestine Liberation Front (PFL)	Europe/Israel/Lebanon – faction of the PLO
Palestinian Islamic Jihad (PIJ)	Israel (West Bank, Gaza, Lebanon and Syria) Objective: Destruction of Israel
Popular Front for the Liberation of Palestine – General Command (PFLP-GC)	Israel – secular Palestinian group guided by Marxist doctrine Objective: Destroy Israel
Popular Front for the Liberation of Palestine (PFLP)	Israel – secular Palestinian group guided by Marxist doctrine
Salafist Group for Call and Combat (GSPC)	Algeria – radical Sunni Muslim group seeking to establish an Islamic government in Algeria Affiliated with or funded by bin Laden
Sendero Luminoso (SL)	Peru – Bombed Canadian Embassy Objective: establish communist peasant revolutionary regime to rid the country of foreign influences
Vanguards of Conquest (VOC)	Egypt – radical armed wing of the AJ Has released assassination lists

Source: National Security Directorate, Ottawa. http://www.PSEPC-SPPCC.gc.ca/national_security/counter-terrorism/Entities_e.asp, December 2004

CHAPTER FIVE

CANADA AND INTERNATIONAL PRIVATE SECURITY COMPANIES

ISSUES AND CHALLENGES FOR SPECIAL OPERATIONS CAPABILITIES

Christopher Spearin

In the early 1990s, as the Canadian government formed JTF 2, international private security companies (PSCs) were also in their nascent stages of development. Although their activities are "mercenary" in the generic sense, the PSC is a post-Cold War phenomenon, intentionally different from those destructive operations by soldiers of fortune that plagued post-colonial Africa from the 1960s onward.[1] But although PSCs strive to differentiate themselves from the pejorative image of the contemporary mercenary, they still pose challenges to the practices of statecraft and the activities of state security agencies. The dual objectives of this chapter are to examine the role played by special operations capabilities in PSCs and to explore their impact on the Canadian Forces (CF) and Canadian foreign policy.

Several questions guide the research: Why are special operations capabilities a part of the PSC business, and what roles of this nature have firms performed in the past? Given the often-publicized manpower limitations of the CF, what are the implications of this private actor in relation to JTF 2? Do PSCs pose a threat to international security, and are they effective in their operations? And finally, recognizing that the PSC is a worldwide phenomenon, what are the current Canadian capacities to manage firms based in Canada?

The chapter concludes that PSCs will influence the longevity, success, and operations of JTF 2 in both positive and negative ways. Likewise, the Canadian government will have to choose the terms on which it recognizes and manages international PSCs. Eliminating PSCs is unlikely because there is a long history of both publicly and privately owned and managed military assets, with first one and then the other in the ascendancy. Neither side has dominated since the advent of the modern state. The PSC is but the latest addition to the "private" side of the ledger. What is more, many prominent international officials, including the current Secretary General of the United Nations, Kofi Annan, see the utility of a private option and wish to keep it on the international stage, albeit under careful management.[2] In this light, the chapter contends that Canada is not yet equipped to deal with the PSC issue. This conclusion has implications for Canada's intent to field a combat-capable, multi-purpose military force that includes special operations capabilities, as well as for its desire to promote stability, good governance, and orderly international relations in its foreign policy.

SPECIAL OPERATIONS CAPABILITIES AND THE PSC

The exact number of PSCs is not known. Observations of general trends indicate that there are perhaps 200-300 firms that, for the most part, are based in the developed world and offer their services to clients operating in the developing world.[3] Canadian firms contribute to these ranks; some examples are Blackbear Consulting, Global Impact, Globe Risk Holdings, and High Energy Access Tools. Firms such as these indicate that their personnel have experience in many of the world's troubled regions: South America, Africa, the Middle East, and the Balkans. But given the commercial dynamics that are evident in any industry, it is difficult to find out precisely how many PSCs there are, Canadian or otherwise, and where they operate. On a regular basis, new firms arrive on the scene, other firms close, firms merge or are bought out, and other firms add and drop services. What is more, the number is even more elusive because PSCs are often part of a larger group of companies, military contractors, that provide logistical and maintenance services to armed forces. The exact number of military contractors, perhaps somewhere in the low thousands, is also unknown.[4]

Anecdotally, the characteristics and capabilities of special operations are prominent in PSCs, including some of the Canadian firms noted above. The dynamics of the industry contribute to this; like special operations units, PSCs generally operate in smaller numbers than conventional forces, in the tens and hundreds rather than in the thousands.

But there are two reasons for the contemporary commercial relevance of special operations capabilities. First, it could be argued that in the absence of any international regulation or standardization for the nascent PSC industry, indications that a firm offers special operations capabilities or employs former special operations personnel serve as a sort of stamp of approval. This advertising tool is a reflection of the high-profile image of special operations in popular culture. The image is reinforced in news reportage, whether it be special operations personnel riding on horseback in Afghanistan with anti-Taliban forces, rescuing Private Jessica Lynch in Iraq, or capturing Saddam Hussein.

Second, state clients often have security sectors of varying quality, or they may lack the full spectrum of capabilities. PSCs help to fill the gaps either by training select state security-sector elements, a task that often falls to special operations personnel, by improving indigenous assets qualitatively and quantitatively by operating alongside, or by conducting independent special operations activities. It is for these reasons that Herbert Howe refers to PSCs as "force multipliers".[5]

Taken together, personnel of this type and firms of this nature have performed a variety of tasks that qualify as special operations in four general categories: small unit operations, training, hostage rescue, and close protection.

Small-Unit Operations

When the government of Sierra Leone hired the South African firm Executive Outcomes (EO) in April-May 1995, the rebels of the Revolutionary United Front (RUF) were just 20 kilometers from the capital, Freetown. Within a year's time, EO personnel, numbering no more than 350, had not only pushed the RUF away from the capital but had also recaptured the country's essential diamond-producing areas and forced the RUF to the negotiating table. EO personnel, drawn mostly from South Africa's defunct Apartheid-era special operations forces, achieved this feat through the use of electronic warfare, coordinated fire support, and air-mobile operations.[6]

It is important to note that in order to achieve this success EO relied upon local forces. EO concentrated its efforts on the Kamajors, an ethnic militia based in the southeast of the country. Formed in 1994 before EO's arrival, two or three thousand Kamajors relied on traditional weapons, hunting skills, and warrior cult beliefs. Under the tutelage of EO, the Kamajors received modern military training and sophisticated weaponry. Their numbers then exploded to at least 20,000, and they provided the guides, the intelligence gatherers, and the supporting fighters for EO.[7] In sum, one EO commander acknowledged the importance of the symbiotic relationship between his firm and the Kamajors: "[T]hey would never have been able to do it without us – the planning and support. On the other hand, we couldn't have done it without them."[8]

Training

Although US Army special operations forces are the lead security-sector units in the State Department-run Africa Contingency Operations Training Assistance (ACOTA), formerly known as the African Crisis Response Initiative

(ACRI), a PSC offers additional flexibility and expertise.[9] U.S.-based Military Professional Resources Incorporated (MPRI) provides much of ACOTA's follow-on programming after special operations forces personnel have left. MPRI's presence is necessary because public special-operations personnel do not have the organizational capability and the numbers of senior staff are not available to conduct ACOTA as currently envisioned. Moreover, the private presence compensates for the rotational requirements of public personnel, which would have otherwise disrupted ACOTA's timetable and instruction.[10] Thus, at any given time, approximately 40 MPRI personnel are present in Africa in support of ACOTA's follow-on modules. MPRI's role in ACOTA ranges from specialized officer training and computer simulations to monitoring, assessing, and advising on training exercises.

Hostage Rescue

In 1996, EO provided five military consultants to train and conduct operations in West Papua alongside Indonesia's Kopassus special operations force. The EO personnel advised on the operational aspects of the May attack against members of the Free Papua Movement who had kidnapped British, Dutch, German, and Indonesian hostages five months earlier in order to attract attention to their calls for independence. It was reported that members of the British and Dutch special operations forces also assisted in the helicopter-borne assault.[11] Although the hostages were not liberated through the attack itself, Indonesian soldiers found them one week later.

Close Protection

In August 2002, the United States government transferred the responsibilities for the close protection of Afghan President Hamid Karzai from US special operations forces to the State Department. Because its Diplomatic Security Service (DSS) special agent force of 1,000 was overstretched, the Department elected to purchase services from the private marketplace to fulfil its responsibilities. The DSS also contended that the private option was the appropriate choice, given current DSS expertise and the challenging conditions in Afghanistan. According to State Department spokesman Richard Boucher, the "Diplomatic Security Service is a civilian law enforcement and security service. It operates in an environment where the rule of law governs; that is not necessarily the situation in Afghanistan".[12] Thus, in November 2002, personnel of DynCorp, a U.S.-based PSC, took over President Karzai's personal security from US Navy Seals. DynCorp will be providing the 40- to 50-man detail, composed of former special operations personnel, until an Afghan close-protection detail is formed and trained.

MANPOWER CHALLENGES POSED BY PSCS

The month after the September 11 terrorist attacks, the Canadian government decided to double the size of JTF 2 to 600 personnel. The decision was taken in the face of evidence uncovered by the Auditor General pointing to reduced rates of recruitment and retention in the CF.[13] The potential impact on JTF 2 is both qualitative and quantitative. Because JTF 2 recruits from serving members of the CF, overall reductions shrink the recruiting pool and number of applicants for JTF 2 positions. JTF 2 historically accepted only about 10 percent of applicants. With the mandate to increase JTF 2 strength, acceptance rates have increased, at the cost of some reduction in the previous standard. No longer must candidates be corporals with at least four years' experience. Only two years of service are now required, regardless of rank. Estimates put JTF 2 strength above 400, but there is some concern that the augmentation came through the dilution of recruitment and training criteria.[14]

Seen in this light, the PSC presence compounds the quantitative and qualitative problems facing JTF 2. The issues are not unique to Canada. EO was accused of poaching South African military expertise.[15] Similarly, Defence Systems Limited (DSC) presented itself as a resource "waiting to hire former military personnel [i.e., British special operations personnel] into legitimate contracts as security consultants, military trainers, or support commercial enterprises with assets in regions of conflicts".[16] Since September 11, the United States has had to issue stop-loss orders preventing the retirement of 25,000 key military personnel, including those in the ranks of the American Special Operations Forces. Opportunities in the private sector increase the lure of early retirement. But one can argue that the pressures are much greater in the Canadian context, given the relatively more severe manpower shortages faced by the CF. Not only have former JTF 2 personnel recently made lateral moves to join the tactical-response teams of public police forces, but they have also started working for American and British PSCs, providing former special operations personnel for clients in Iraq.[17] Undoubtedly, with remuneration rates in Iraq sitting at US$600-1,000 per day for PSC special operations-type personnel, maintaining JTF 2 manpower levels will be a difficult task.[18]

The degree to which these quantitative and qualitative concerns for JTF 2 can be managed is highly circumscribed. Budgetary concerns aside, the CF might be able to develop a special retention program similar to that designed to prevent pilots from being lured to the commercial aviation industry. This would recognize the existence of opportunities in the private sector where JTF 2 members might apply their publicly funded expertise. Nevertheless, increased pay, bonuses, and benefits can go only so far; larger economic and sociological factors still exist. One Canadian assessment contends that the "basic cause of the recruitment and retention crisis is that the increasing need for technically capable and well-educated young men and women to meet the demands of the modern military places the CF in direct competition with major sectors of the economy."[19] Admissions by a body as prominent as the Canadian Senate that the CF is an "Antiques Roadshow" do not push young people to choose the CF over the private sector.[20] But what makes private-sector economic opportunities particularly salient is the decline of nationalism in OECD states. It is no longer the influence that once fuelled the supply of military personnel in the developed world as far back as Napoleonic times.[21] In the Canadian case, surveys starting in the late 1970s show that CF personnel increasingly view their work as an occupation rather than a vocation. These sentiments are relatively stronger in the lower ranks.[22] This trend will not be easy to reverse in the short term. JTF 2 will continue to confront manpower issues, and the government may have to manage and perhaps rely upon PSC options as a consequence.

PSCS AND INTERNATIONAL SECURITY

It follows from the analysis above that PSCs with special operations capabilities may very well present challenges that national forces might have to counter. Furthermore, if a state chooses to rely on a private special-operations force, several issues would affect the utility of the contractual relationship. This chapter focuses on two. First, although PSCs are unlikely to consciously violate human rights or international legal norms, they may contribute to an environment in which such occurrences are more likely. Second, the sustainability of a force motivated by profit rather than patriotism will always be suspect.

Governance and Human Rights Implications

Under current international and commercial conditions, it is highly unlikely that PSC special operations forces will directly oppose a unit like JTF 2 in combat. It is equally unlikely that PSCs will directly instigate human rights abuses in the fulfilment of their contractual obligations. This is because, as stressed by Juan Carlos Zarate, firms "have developed a modus operandi compatible with the needs and strictures of the post-Cold War, state-based international system".[23] PSCs do not want to upset the sensitivities of states, especially powerful developed states. The developed states in which PSCs are based would shut them down if they became a political embarrassment, and a highly public confrontation between a PSC like EO and a national force like JTF 2 would be very bad for business.

PSCs are sensitive to contemporary human rights concerns, and they work hard to distinguish themselves from their unsavoury precursors, the "soldiers of fortune" and "mercenaries" of the 1960s. One EO official noted, "[t]he fastest thing that would get us [EO] out of business is human-rights violations".[24] PSC performance has been relatively good, compared to indigenous forces, state and non-state, in many Third World conflicts. A British parliamentary investigation concluded in 1999 that with respect to EO, "[d]espite much effort by various organisations, allegations of human rights abuses are mostly unproven".[25]

While PSCs may not directly undermine human rights and international norms, they may do so indirectly, potentially requiring a national response from forces like JTF 2. Damian Lilly of International Alert suggests it is an open question as to whether or not PSC activities lead to more effective and professional forces in the client state.[26] In Sierra Leone, for example, the International Crisis Group has documented the decline of operational effectiveness of the Kamajors since the departure of EO.[27] Once the firm left, local operations were no longer as successful and objectives were not achieved, not just for lack of direction by EO but also because of Kamajor practices in its absence. Human Rights Watch has documented harsh Kamajor treatment of RUF prisoners, looting, and rights violations.[28] Even more telling, Sierra Leone's War Crimes Tribunal indicted the Kamajors' leader, Sam Hinga Norman, in March 2003.

In short, the Kamajors are known to have contributed to the general chaos in Sierra Leone, a chaos for which EO was arguably partially responsible.[29] This triggered the arrival of British forces in 2000, including SAS and Parachute Regiment contingents, to execute Operation Palliser, the British mission to assist the beleaguered United Nations peacekeeping force. It also spurred Pretoria to initiate legislation that eventually became the *Regulation of Foreign Military Assistance Act*, to provide better oversight and management of South Africa-based PSCs.

Sierra Leone illustrates that PSCs serve a client that is not necessarily a coherent state with long-term interests. In the process, they might change local power dynamics, absorb national resources, and leave without bequeathing any appropriate structure for governing security organizations. They may thereby cause more disruption than they cure. This also raises the importance of closely monitoring and managing PSC contracts, to ensure that they do not create conditions that demand intervention. This is considered in the Canadian context below.

Force Sustainability

The main legal distinction between public and private military personnel is that the former are subject to an oath of service or to the obligation of unlimited liability. In other words, contracted personnel are not obliged to stay in harm's way. A public employee who fails to execute his or her duties and responsibilities in response to a rise in danger levels is likely to face the military justice system, including a dishonourable discharge from the armed forces. In contrast, if private employees fail in their duties, the company can fire the individuals or the client can fire the company. The qualitative differences between accountability in public and private spheres suggest that there is a greater probability that a PSC client will be left in the lurch when danger levels rise.

Anecdotal evidence suggests that private firms and personnel associated with special operations are not likely to quit a project *en masse* in the face of danger. One can argue that former special operations personnel have a higher tolerance for danger because of their experiences or warrior class attributes. Nevertheless, there have been instances in which intra-firm and client-firm relations have not been good. In Angola between 1993 and 1995, EO had to adjust as several employees elected not to fulfil their contractual obligations to counter UNITA, the main rebel movement in Angola. To its credit, EO continued with its contract, despite the deaths of 20 personnel, and their special operations-style "fix, find, and destroy" activities eventually helped to force UNITA to the bargaining table.[30] This experience, we assume, permitted EO to improve its selection process for the Sierra Leone contract. But other firms have not been able to recover from similar setbacks. Contracted in 1995 by the government of Sierra Leone to train and operate alongside the Sierra Leonean military, the PSC Gurkha Security Guards (GSG) left the country shortly after arrival when an ambush killed several of its employees. Due to the impact this had on GSG's reputation, its business decreased substantially.[31] While this case reveals how the marketplace can punish those firms that fail to fulfil their contractual obligations, it also demonstrates that such a commercial punishment did not deter contract defection in the first instance.

We might argue that PSCs offering special operations capabilities are qualitatively superior to less-specialized security companies. Even if this is true, sub-contracting and out-sourcing could prove to be an Achilles heel. Not all firms possess the full range of operational tools, and like other corporations, PSCs seek ways to reduce costs. Consequently, networks of commercial relationships and contracts might create weak links in the operational chain. A state can field a relatively small force that draws on the full operational capability of a national armed force. The British Operation Palliser in Sierra Leone, for example, fielded only 800 participants but drew on Britain's large armed forces for logistics, communications, intelligence, and support. To achieve the same depth, PSCs must rely on consortiums and inter-firm contracts. The 2003 proposal for a PSC air-mobile strike force to assist the UN Observer Mission in Congo (MONUC) involved five PSCs. TASK International, with the support of MPRI, was to provide combat-capable Gurkhas formerly employed in the British Forces. Logistical support was provided by PAE, and air support and surveillance by ICI and AirScan International.[32]

The concern is that complex contracting arrangements have created operational problems for PSCs in the past. In Liberia in the late 1990s, ICI personnel under State Department contract remained in Monrovia and even helped to defend the American embassy in the midst of heavy fighting. DynCorp, another firm assisting with transportation and logistics, evacuated its personnel and left ICI in the lurch.[33] It is conceivable that while private special-operations personnel may perform admirably in the field, their overall operation may not be a success if other private companies fall short in their contractual support.

CANADIAN REGULATION OF PSCS

If governance and sustainability of PSCs are two of the most significant problems for their employment, are there regulatory solutions? The second issue is unlikely to be solvable, because public and private enterprises are fundamentally different. Only careful contract writing and the discipline of the market will keep problems in check. Regulation, however, might address some of the problems pertaining to quality control and operational impact that are raised by our discussion of governance and human rights.

We can learn from the two states with substantial PSC regulation regimes: the U.S. and the Republic of South Africa. Both the American International Traffic in Arms Regulations (ITAR) and the South African *Regulation of Foreign Military Assistance Act* focus on the contract-approval stage. In the South African case, recommendations about PSC contract approval are made to the Minister of Defence by the National Conventional Arms Control Committee (NCACC). To improve objectivity, the president of the NCACC is a government minister with no direct link to the South African defence industry.

In the American case, the PSC contract can be vetted through a variety of governmental bodies such as the Department of State's Human Rights Office, the department's country and regional desks, American embassies, the Department of Defense, the Department of Energy, and the Treasury Department. If indecision remains, it falls to the Assistant Secretary of State to adjudicate. The Office of Defense Trade Controls (ODTC) in the Department of State is required to notify Congress of any contract with a value of $50 million or more. Congress can deny the approval of an export contract (for goods or services) through a joint resolution.

What is missing from these countries' regulations is oversight of quality and the actual outcomes in the field. These are particularly important for special operations personnel, given their qualitative difference and the disproportionate effect they can have in operations. Under ODTC's management, ITAR requires only that all firms must pay a fee for a licence that is valid for a certain period. No other capability checks are conducted. Similarly, in South Africa, the only initial requirement is that a PSC obtain a licence to offer its services abroad. No specific criteria concerning training or the actual ability to provide the services are considered. As for the early detection and management of negative effects in the field, the American system has no designated formal mechanism or government-wide agency for oversight. Likewise for South Africa, once a South African PSC is operating overseas, there is no standard governmental monitoring presence.

Turning now to Canada, Ottawa might be able to adapt existing Canadian regulation to manage the contract approvals of Canadian PSCs in a manner similar to those employed by Washington and Pretoria. Canada's *Defence Production Act* and the *Export and Import Permits Act* require that International Trade Canada (ITCan) approve individual military- and security-related exports. Input and advice for the vetting procedure can come from within ITCan and can be sought from a variety of Canadian bodies: Foreign Affairs Canada, the Department of National Defence, Industry Canada, the Canada Customs and Revenue Agency, the Atomic Energy Control Board, the Communications Security Establishment, the Canadian Security Intelligence Service, and the Royal Canadian Mounted Police. These numerous actors consider several criteria: whether or not the recipient state poses a threat to Canada, is engaged in or threatened by hostile activity, is under UN sanctions, or has a government accused of human rights violations. While these stipulations are directed only at military goods, they might be modified to cover the export of human services such as PSC expertise.

As for vetting firms for quality control, existing regulations might be adapted to make the Canadian approach superior to those of the United States and the Republic of South Africa. Canada's Controlled Goods Registration Program demands that selected individuals working for an exporting firm must undergo character and security assessments conducted under the auspices of Public Works Canada. In turn, this individual may be held legally responsible for vetting employees who produce or handle military goods. To ensure that the law is respected, the Minister of Public Works is authorized to conduct spot checks and audits. While this process is designed to ensure the trustworthiness of employees working with sensitive goods, it might also be used to ensure that PSC employees have had honourable discharges and possess the necessary special operations expertise. Such an adaptation to existing regulations would ensure that potential clients, both Canadian and international, from the public and private sectors, would worry less about the age-old dictum, *caveat emptor*.

The difficulty for Canada lies in actually monitoring firms in the field, where there is a complete lack of regulation. This is a particularly complicated issue for some special operations, given their secrecy, speed, and sensitivity. For now, therefore, we should concentrate our attention on the long-term developmental activities of PSCs, such as training. The purpose of monitoring would be to ensure that the PSC presence evolves as approved by the regulatory process and does not add to violence or instability. Remaining in a theatre of operations, a PSC may contribute to undermining human rights or good governance, through no fault of its own. For example, legitimate policing techniques might be applied for population control by a coercive regime, or counter-insurgency techniques might be applied against legitimate opposition groups. Contracts might limit the PSC to technical training and to providing constructive advice, which might not be heeded or wanted. Therefore, part of Canada's PSC regulation would have to insist on provisions that allow not only Canadian government oversight of PSCs but also reconsideration of the PSC's contract. This would not resolve all the issues posed by private special-operations personnel, but it would be a useful start for the management of Canadian PSCs.

CONCLUSION

This chapter has identified and examined factors that Canada must consider in its management of both public and private special operations forces. International trends are such that Ottawa will not be able to favour the former or ignore the latter. PSCs will continue to draw personnel away from public forces because their expertise is highly valued by clients. Given the manpower pressures Canada faces and the responsible and positive role it wishes to play on the world stage, Canada would be well served by an expanded regulatory framework along the lines sketched out above. Important regulatory issues for future analysis concern the criteria to ensure quality control, the formal mechanisms through which the Canadian government and PSCs would interact, the fair distribution of regulatory costs, and the provision of appropriate resources for effective regulation. As we direct attention towards these issues, we should keep in mind that the rising importance of special operations expertise in the private sphere is just the latest adjustment to the historic balance between public and private military assets. Governments should recognize this and adapt.

NOTES

1. For an assessment of the differences, see David Isenberg, *Soldiers of Fortune Ltd.: A Profile of Today's Private Sector Corporate Mercenary Firms* (Washington, DC: Center for Defense Information, 1997); David Shearer, *Private Armies and Military Intervention,* Adelphi Paper 316 (London: International Institute for Strategic Studies, 1998).
2. Kofi Annan considered the use of a private rapid-reaction force to handle the problems the United Nations was encountering in its operations in Central Africa in the late 1990s. See United Nations, Office of the Secretary General, "Secretary-General reflects on Intervention," Speech given to the Ditchley Foundation, United Nations Press Release SG/SM/6613/Rev.1 (26 June 1998).
3. Other PSC clients include non-governmental organizations, international organizations, and multinational corporations.
4. For an assessment of the overarching military contactor business, see Peter W. Singer, "Corporate Warriors: The Rise of the Privatized Military Industry and its Ramifications for International Security," *International Security* 26 (Winter 2001/02): 186-220.
5. Herbert M. Howe, "Private Security Forces and African Stability: The case of Executive Outcomes," *Journal of Modern African Studies* 36 (1998): 312, 314.
6. EO personnel were drawn from the 1-5 Reconnaissance Commandos, the 44th Parachute Brigade, the paramilitary unit Koevoet, and the 32nd Buffalo Battalion, the most decorated South African combat unit since the end of the Second World War. Of the pool of 2,000 personnel EO

claimed it could draw upon on a contract basis for its operations, 70-75 per cent were retired black soldiers formerly of the Buffalo Battalion.

7. Some suggest the numbers might have been as high as 37,000 with a further 100,000 potential volunteers waiting in the wings. See Glenn McKenzie, "Unruly Militia Defends Sierra Leone," *Associated Press*, 5 July 2000.
8. Cited in Shearer, *Private Armies and Military Intervention*, 54.
9. Whereas the Clinton Administration created ACRI to train select African militaries to conduct Chapter Six-type operations, the Bush Administration changed the focus, and the name of the program, to cover Chapter Seven-type operations.
10. Initially, the rotational practices made the timing for the follow-on modules highly inflexible, which affected the absorptive capacity of recipient state militaries. Eric G. Berman and Katie E. Sams, *Peacekeeping in Africa: Capabilities and Culpabilities* (Geneva: United Nations Institute for Disarmament Research, 2000), 275.
11. Peter Cronau, "East Timor and West Papua," *Pacific Journalism Review* 6 (January 2000).
12. James Dao, "U.S. Company To Take Over Karzai Safety," *New York Times* (19 September 2002). See also "State Department Regular Briefing," *Federal News Service,* 2 January 2003.
13. Canada, Office of the Auditor General of Canada, *2002 Report of the Auditor General of Canada to the House of Commons* (Ottawa: Minister of Public Works and Government Services Canada, 2002), 3.
14. Given that most aspects of JTF 2 are kept secret, the information noted here was gleaned from Bruce Garvey, "Forces struggling to find 600 soldiers good enough to serve in crack JTF2 unit," *Ottawa Citizen*, 24 October 2003.
15. Jeremy Harding, "The Mercenary Business: 'Executive Outcomes'," *Review of African Political Economy* 24 (March 1997).
16. DSC literature noted in Kevin A. O'Brien, "PMCs, Myths, and Mercenaries: the debate on private military companies," *Royal United Service Institute Journal* (February 2000).
17. Scott Taylor, "Canuck Soldiers Recruited by Police, Security Job Market," *Halifax Chronicle-Herald,* 22 July 2003.
18. Scott Taylor, "Little chance Canadian elite commando unit will expand," *Halifax Chronicle-Herald,* 10 November 2003.
19. Centre for Military and Strategic Studies, "To Secure a Nation: The Case for a New Defence White Paper," Council for Canadian Security in the 21st Century (November 2001), 23.
20. For analysis of the Senate's assertion, see Daniel LeBlanc, "Bring soldiers home, Senate committee proposes," *Globe and Mail*, 13 November 2002.
21. See Christopher Coker, "Outsourcing War," *Cambridge Review of International Affairs* 13 (Autumn/Winter 1999): 95-113.

22. R. B. Byers, *Canadian Security and Defence: the Legacy and the Challenges*, Adelphi Paper 214 (London: International Institute for Strategic Studies, 1986), 52.
23. Juan Carlos Zarate, "The Emergence of a New Dog of War: Private International Security Companies, International Law, and the New World Disorder," *Stanford Journal of International Law* 75 (Spring 1998): 91.
24. Cited in Kevin Whitelaw, "Have Gun, Will Prop Up Regime," *US News & World Report* (January 1997): 48.
25. Citations from the committee's report can be found at www.sandline.com/comment/list/comment11.html.
26. Damian Lilly, *The Privatization of Security and Peacebuilding: A Framework for Action* (London: International Alert, 2000), 25.
27. International Crisis Group, *Sierra Leone: Time For A New Military And Political Strategy,* ICG Africa Report No. 28 (Freetown/London/Brussels: International Crisis Group, 11 April 2001), 8.
28. Letter to Kofi Annan, Secretary General of the United Nations, from Human Rights Watch, 29 November 2000.
29. An example is the disruption of the disarmament processes by the Civil Defence Force (CDF) despite agreements amongst all the parties. Some feared that the CDF was becoming a problem bigger than the RUF. See BBC Focus, "CDF Denies Attacking RUF," 22 July 2001. Regarding CDF lawlessness, see also United Nations, Office for the Coordination of Humanitarian Affairs, Integrated Regional Information Network for West Africa, 16 August 2000.
30. James R. Davis, *Fortune's Warriors: Private Armies and the New World Order* (Vancouver: Douglas & McIntyre Ltd., 2000), 129.
31. See Alex Vines, "Gurkhas and the private security business in Africa," in *Peace, Profit or Plunder? The Privatisation of Security in War-Torn African Societies,* eds. Jakkie Cilliers and Peggy Mason (Pretoria: Institute for Security Studies, 1999), 123-140.
32. "Supporting the MONUC Mandate with Private Services in the Democratic Republic of Congo," IPOA Operational Concept Paper, January 2003.
33. Stephen Fidler and Thomas Catn, "Private Companies on the Frontline," *Financial Times*, 12 August 2003; Barry Yeoman, "Soldiers of Good Fortune," *Independent*, 23 July 2003.

PART II

THE CANADIAN POLICY ENVIRONMENT

CHAPTER SIX

INTERNATIONAL LAW AND SPECIAL OPERATIONS

Susan Breau

The destruction of the World Trade Center in New York on 11 September 2001 moved the issue of international terrorism to the forefront of the international agenda. Two international armed conflicts – in Afghanistan and Iraq – have been partially justified by alleged state sponsorship of terrorism. There was no question of the Taliban regime's support for Osama bin Laden and the al-Qaeda movement. There was some doubt with respect to Iraq's involvement in international terrorism, although Saddam Hussein's regime did provide financial sponsorship for relatives of Palestinian suicide bombers. Since September 11, other terrorist attacks have resulted in civilian casualties. In the midst of all this, Libya recently agreed to pay compensation for its sponsorship of the 747 crash at Lockerbie. Like other governments, Canada has been forced to consider its options for combatting terrorism.

There may be sound operational reasons for using armed force to prevent or terminate a terrorist operation by direct action or by targetting individuals, but any proposed action should comply with the principles of international law. Since World War II, a revolution in international law has created a nascent system of international rule of law. States are bound by international agreements known as treaties and by international customary law; the latter defined as the set of practices accepted by the majority of states to be lawful.[1] All of the operations considered in this chapter trigger both sets of international obligations.

While this chapter offers no definitive answers, it highlights the most controversial areas of international law. It first considers operations conducted outside Canada and then, briefly, internal operations. In each type of operation conducted externally, three important sets of international rules govern.

The first is the *jus ad bellum,* meaning the lawfulness of the use of force in general against another sovereign nation. The second is the *jus in bello*: the conduct of the use of force itself, or what is termed international humanitarian law. Finally, there are those treaties and customary rules that make up international human rights law. The focus of this brief examination is the lawfulness of the initiation of the use of force, with only brief mention of the other two areas although each merits extensive treatment.

INTERNATIONAL OPERATIONS – *JUS AD BELLUM*

Some of the justifications that have been made for expeditionary military action include anticipatory self-defence, rescue of nationals abroad, violations of treaty responsibilities (such as weapons conventions or arms limitations), and reprisals to redress injury. International law limits the use of these justifications in the conduct of special operations and counter-terrorism efforts within the jurisdiction of other states.

Anticipatory Self-Defence

Many operations to combat international terrorism would involve breaching the sovereignty of another territory. Such breaches could involve a force, large or small, entering the sovereign territory of another state to rescue Canadian nationals or to foil an anticipated attack that might threaten Canadian soil or Canadians abroad. The key question of international law is whether an anti-terrorism operation can ever be a lawful use of force against another territory. Article 2(4) of the Charter of the United Nations states:

> All Members shall refrain in their international relations from the threat or use of force against the territorial integrity or political independence of any state, or in any other manner inconsistent with the Purposes of the United Nations.

There are only two exceptions to this prohibition on the use of force, which has the status of a *jus cogens* norm of international law.[2] The first is a collective security action under Chapter VII of the Charter authorized by a Security Council Resolution. The second is an action in self-defence, which encompasses most of the special operations contemplated. Article 51 of the Charter states:

> Nothing in the present Charter shall impair the inherent right of individual or collective self-defence if an armed attack occurs against a Member of the United Nations until the Security Council has taken measures necessary to maintain international peace and security. Measures taken by Members in the exercise of this right of self-defence shall be immediately reported to the Security Council

> under the present Charter to take at any time such action as it deems necessary to maintain or restore international peace and security.

In the *Nicaragua* case, Nicaragua sought restitution for the American mining of its harbors. The International Court of Justice interpreted Article 51 as preserving a "pre-existing right (of self-defence) of a customary nature"[3] and said that the general prohibition on the use of inter-state force was also part of customary international law as well as the law of the Charter.[4]

Can any armed force be used in anticipation of an armed attack and still be considered a lawful action in self-defence? This question is applicable to anti-terrorist operations because one would hope that the purpose of the operation would be to foil an anticipated attack. The academic community and state practice are divided on this point.[5] These two viewpoints have been classified into two schools of interpretation of the Charter, the restrictionist and counter-restrictionist[6] because the language of Article 51 can lead equally to either interpretation. "Inherent" would seem to refer to the pre-existing customary right, while "if an armed attack occurs" would seem to reflect a restriction on the right. The restrictionist scholars would argue that Article 51 is the only contemporary source of the law of self-defence and, as such, prohibits anticipatory self-defence. The counter-restrictionist commentators would argue on two fronts. First, the reading of the whole section includes the previous customary right as set out in the 19th century in the *Caroline* case.[7] Second, the impact of post-1945 developments must be considered in light of the failure of the collective security system, thus requiring greater resort to unilateral and regional action relying on customary international law.[8]

It does appear that the bulk of practice and literature supports a notion of anticipatory self-defence. The debate with respect to anticipatory self-defence began soon after the Charter came into force in 1945, in the context of the development of nuclear weapons. It was clear that the technology of weapons of mass destruction permitted states to launch a first strike, which could cripple the military capacity of the target nation to defend itself. As the eminent jurist Waldock stated in his 1952 Hague lectures:

> [for] if the armed attack becomes manifestly imminent, then it would be a travesty of the purposes of the Charter to compel a defending force to allow its assailant to deliver the first and perhaps fatal blow.[9]

Almost half a century after it was written, the jurist Bowett's treatise on the law of self-defence still resonates. As part of the counter-restrictionist school, Bowett discussed the relationship between Articles 2(4) and 51 of the UN Charter in the following terms:

> action undertaken for the purpose of, and limited to, the defence of a state's political independence, territorial integrity, the lives and property of its nationals (and even to protect its economic independence) cannot by definition involve

> a threat or use of force "against the territorial integrity or political independence" of any other state.[10]

He supported the doctrine of anticipatory self-defence, arguing that self-defence in customary international law had always been anticipatory and that armed force was valid against imminent as well as actual attacks. He cited both the *Caroline* case and the practice of states as evidence to support his conclusion that anticipatory self-defence continued to be legal after the Charter:

> It is not believed, therefore, that Art. 51 restricts the traditional right of self-defence so as to exclude action taken against an imminent danger but before 'an armed attack occurs'...No state can be expected to await an initial attack which, in the present state of armaments, may well destroy the state's capacity for further resistance and so jeopardize its very existence.[11]

In his further analysis of Article 51, Bowett argued that armed attack was not the only form of aggression, but that it would include the right to respond to indirect aggression such as "assistance to revolting minorities, bacteriological or gas warfare, or serious breaches of a Convention on Atomic Weapons."[12] Many years later, in 2002, the legal scholar Frank agreed with this position and argued that Article 51 should not be interpreted to compel a state to await a first, perhaps decisive, military strike.[13]

State practice also seems to support the concept of anticipatory self-defence.[14] However, the United States has attempted to develop the concept even further. In September of 2002, President Bush released *The National Security Strategy of the United States of America,* in which a concept of pre-emptive self-defence was argued in light of a "new deadly challenge" from rogue states and terrorist groups with the greater likelihood of their use of weapons of mass destruction. It was argued that traditional concepts of deterrence would not work and that international law recognized that nations could lawfully take action to defend against an "imminent danger of attack". The concept of imminent threat, it was argued, must be adapted to the potential use of WMD. The critical portion of this doctrine stated:

> The United States has long maintained the option of pre-emptive action to counter a sufficient threat to our national security. The greater the threat, the greater is the risk of inaction – and the more compelling the case for taking anticipatory action to defend ourselves, even if the uncertainty remains as to the time and place of the enemy's attack. To forestall or prevent such hostile acts by our adversaries, the United States will, if necessary, act pre-emptively.[15]

As the debates preceding the war in Iraq revealed, the global community was not in agreement with expanding the concept of anticipatory self-defence.[16] Countries such as France, Russia, and Germany argued that lawful action had to be taken in the face of an imminent threat. This would seem to comply with the criteria established in the *Caroline case*, which consisted of an "instant and overwhelming necessity for self-defence, leaving no choice of means and no moment for deliberation".[17] Therefore, anti-terrorism operations depend on the important concept of imminence. "Instant and overwhelming necessity for self-defence" can be employed in the context of WMD at a much earlier stage, given the possibility that many lives could be lost in the destruction of the weapons themselves. "Leaving no choice of means" would be used in the case of continuing terrorist attacks. "No moment for deliberation" is the critical point in time when the risk has crystallized into a very real threat against a population, but that point does not have to await the launch of the attack. These criteria are starkly illuminated by the controversy surrounding the issue of WMD and Iraq. The global community was divided over the issue of whether Hussein possessed these weapons and whether he could launch a preemptive attack. Termed the affair of the "dodgy dossier" in Britain, this led to the suicide of a noted weapons expert and the discrediting of the claim that the weapons could be launched within 45 minutes.

It is without controversy that any resort to self-defence must comply with the requirements of necessity and proportionality. Although this is not stated specifically in the Charter, it has been accepted in customary international law, as reflected in the *Nicaragua* case and the Advisory Opinion of the *Legality of the Threat or Use of Nuclear Weapons*.[18] Therefore, the use of force must be limited to what is "reasonably necessary and proportionate to the achievement of a legitimate objective".[19]

The factors to be considered with respect to proportionality are the geographical and temporal scope of the conflict, the choice of weapons and targets, and the degree of coercion that can be applied against neutrals.[20] In the context of anticipatory self-defence, the requirement of proportionality requires only that the force used be proportionate to the imminent threat. That could mean the removal of the offensive weapons or units ready to strike.

Necessity requires establishing the need to remove the actual threat existing at the time of the response. It requires an analysis of whether any other measures such as political or economic sanctions would be as effective in removing the threat.[21] Once again, it is in the definition of the term "imminent" that consideration is given for the necessity of an armed attack. If armed aggression is imminent, then quite obviously economic or political sanctions may not be effective.

Another critical threshold question is whether terrorist attacks could be considered an act of war that justifies the use of force in self-defence against a sovereign state. There is no precise definition of an "armed conflict", but there are several indications that terrorist attacks, starting with September11, are viewed as armed attacks. The first is that the United States considered itself to be a victim of an "act of war". The second is that NATO activated Article 5 of the NATO treaty, which meant that the NATO countries, including Canada, deemed an armed attack against the United States had occurred. The third is UN Security Council Resolutions 1368, 1373, 1386 (2001), and 1390

(2002), which condemned the World Trade Center attacks and recognized the inherent right of individual or collective self-defence in accordance with the Charter. Furthermore, other Security Council resolutions have referred to terrorist attacks in general as being a "threat to international peace and security." These include Resolution 731 (1992) with respect to the extradition demands placed on Libya after the airliner crash at Lockerbie and Resolution 1070 (1996) with respect to Sudan and the "suppression of terrorism essential for the maintenance of peace and security". The war with Afghanistan also supports the consideration of major terrorist attacks under the law of armed conflict. Unlike the war with Iraq, this conflict had apparently attracted the support of the majority of states and was initiated in response to Taliban support for the al-Qaeda terrorists.[22] Therefore, it seems that there is a developing rule of customary international law that terrorist attacks are armed attacks and can trigger the right of self-defence.

Rescue of Nationals Abroad

Rescue of nationals abroad is another controversial area in the law on the use of force. Rescue operations trigger the Article 2(4) prohibition on the use of force. Although often discussed under the rubric of humanitarian intervention, rescue of nationals should be viewed as a case of self-defence. Israel's rescue of its nationals at Entebbe in Uganda is one of the best-known international rescue operations.[23] It did not attract condemnation from the UN Security Council; indeed, several states welcomed it. The US attempt to rescue its hostages in Tehran failed and was argued in the International Court of Justice, but there was no definitive ruling.[24] Rescues are not unambiguously legal but are accepted under certain conditions. Case law suggests three conditions for acceptance. First, the country where the nationals are being held is not fulfilling its international obligation to protect citizens of another country. Second, the country whose citizens are being held has made efforts to demand that the state fulfil its responsibility.[25] Third, the citizens must be in immediate peril without a rescue operation.[26] These same criteria can be employed for most of the operations contemplated to combat terrorism.

The Law on State Responsibility and Armed Intervention

In addition to the use of force pursuant to the customary right of self-defence, there is the question of whether or not armed force could be used in the event of serious violations of treaty obligations, such as terrorism or weapons conventions. However, neither the existing treaty framework for terrorist acts nor weapons conventions includes a right of intervention. These international instruments include the Hague Convention for the Suppression of Unlawful Seizure of Aircraft (1970), the Montreal Convention for the Suppression of

Unlawful Acts Against the Safety of Civil Aviation (1971), and the International Convention for the Suppression of Terrorist Bombings (adopted by the General Assembly in 1997). All three include provisions to extradite or try the accused but do not oblige a state to extradite. The last includes measures encouraging assistance and sharing of information, but none entitles a state to act to enforce provisions. The Montreal Convention deals with crimes on board an aircraft rather than attacks like those of September 11.

Can the existing framework handle the magnitude of recent terrorist attacks? The answer depends on whether an attack is interpreted strictly as a "terrorist attack" or as an "armed attack." If it is strictly a terrorist attack, then the Conventions above seem to apply. None of these conventions provides for the use of armed force, but rather they set up a regime of criminal responsibility.[27] Hijacking an airliner is analogous to piracy on the high seas – any state may exercise criminal jurisdiction, applying its law universally.[28] Response to "armed attack" allows more latitude for use of force, but the "war on terrorism" is a highly contested concept and is not accepted by many nations.[29]

Can states act to police proliferation of weapons of mass destruction? The existing treaty network of weapons conventions does not include any right of armed intervention. Table 6-1 lists key international weapons conventions, many of which do not even include sections on compliance. The 1997 Ottawa Convention has extensive provisions on compliance, but it refers any problems to the Secretary-General of the United Nations. There are no provisions for armed force to be used to compel adherence to the treaties.

The fact that these treaties do not contain rights of other nations to intervene to force compliance is hardly surprising. The whole system of international conventions dates from the 1648 Treaty of Westphalia, which established the system of sovereign states. State sovereignty was based on preserving sovereign states from armed intervention, not on allowing such intervention to occur. The United Nations Charter is the only multilateral convention with provisions on collective security that provides for armed intervention, *but only* on the basis of a vote authorizing such actions by the members of the Security Council, including the five permanent members.

Two little-publicized but pivotal developments in international law have been used as an argument to support armed intervention to enforce treaty obligations. The first was the report of the International Commission on Intervention and State Sovereignty, entitled *The Responsibility to Protect.* This argued that the doctrine of state responsibility had expanded to include a duty for other states to intervene in situations of large loss of life, actual or apprehended, that was the product of deliberate state action, state neglect, or inability to act.[30] Although this was framed in the context of humanitarian intervention, the same argument could be made about terrorist attacks with weapons of mass destruction. The second major development bolstering this approach was the adoption in the General Assembly of the Draft Articles on State Responsibility, in the form of a non-binding resolution. Chapter III of these articles, entitled "Serious breaches of obligations under peremptory norms of

TABLE 6-1
Treaties and Weapons Conventions

Convention	*Date of Signing*
Protocol for the Prohibition of the Use in War of Asphyxiating, Poisonous or other Gases, and of Bacteriological Methods of Warfare	17 June 1925
Treaty on the Non-Proliferation of Nuclear Weapons	1 July 1968
Convention on the Prohibition of the Development, Production and Stockpiling of Bacteriological (Biological) and Toxin Weapons and on Their Destruction	10 April 1972
Convention on the Prohibition of Military or any Other Hostile Use of Environmental Modification Techniques	10 December 1976
Convention on Prohibitions or Restrictions on the Use of Certain Conventional Weapons Which May Be Deemed to Be Excessively Injurious or to Have Indiscriminate Effects, 10 October 1980; Amended Protocol II, 3 May 1996, and Additional Protocol (IV) on Blinding Laser Weapons	12 October 1995
Convention on the Prohibition of the Development, Production, Stockpiling and Use of Chemical Weapons and on their Destruction	13 January 1993
Comprehensive Nuclear-Test-Ban Treaty	10 September 1996
Convention on the Prohibition of the Use, Stockpiling, Production and Transfer of Anti-Personnel Mines and on their Destruction (Ottawa Convention)	18 September 1997

general international law", introduced the concept of a second tier of obligations identified as "Aggravated State Responsibility".[31] Article 40 of the Draft Articles states:

1. This chapter applies to the international responsibility which is entailed by a serious breach by a State of an obligation arising under a peremptory norm of general international law.
2. A breach of such an obligation is serious if it involves a gross or systematic failure by the responsible State to fulfill its obligation.

In his recently published textbook on International Law, Antonio Cassese outlined the main factors in aggravated responsibility. The breach is of a community obligation, defined as a fundamental value such as peace, human rights, self-determination, or protection of the environment. Since the community obligation is owed to all other members of the international community, there is a community right belonging to any other state. As a result, this community right can be exercised by any other state, whether or not damaged by the breach. However, this right is exercised on behalf of the international community, not on the part of the Claimant State.[32] Article 40 (2) specifies that the breach must be gross or systematic, which to Cassese must be serious or on a large scale. The examples he gives are aggression, genocide, or grave atrocities against one's own nationals or all persons belonging to an ethnic group.[33]

The consequences of such a breach is outlined in Article 41 of the Draft Articles, which states:

> 1. States shall cooperate to bring to an end through lawful means any serious breach within the meaning of article 40.
> 2. No State shall recognize as lawful a situation created by a serious breach within the meaning of article 40, nor render aid or assistance in maintaining the situation.
> 3. This article is without prejudice to the other consequences referred to in this part and to such further consequences that a breach to which this chapter applies may entail under international law.

The consequences of a serious breach of obligations under peremptory norms represent a departure from the ordinary responsibility of a state. All other states can take action. They may invoke the aggravated responsibility by bringing their claim to the notice of the state, demand cessation of the wrong, claim reparation on behalf of victims, and bring the matter to competent international bodies (such as the UN or regional organization). If that international organization takes no action, then states can take *peaceful* countermeasures on an individual basis. Finally, they may resort to collective self-defence in the case of aggression, provided that the state that is the victim of the aggression makes such a request or gives consent.[34] None of those measures includes unilateral action to prevent or foil a terrorist attack even with weapons of mass destruction.

The Special Rapporteur for the International Law Commission, James Crawford, argues that states are under a positive duty to cooperate in order to bring an end to serious breaches of obligations owed under a peremptory norm of international law. Article 41 does not specify the form this cooperation should take; it could be organized under the auspices of the United Nations, or as "non-institutionalized cooperation".[35] Crawford acknowledged that these provisions might be not part of general international law but a progressive development of the law,[36] and that there may be future development of "a more elaborate regime of consequences entailed by such breaches."[37] In a speech at the Indiana University School of Law, Crawford indicated that movement in international law has been from "sovereignty to obligation" and from "immunity to accountability".[38] However, even strong advocates of international accountability for treaty violations do not support the use of force as a tool for ensuring compliance. A lawyer for the International Commission of the Red Cross argued in 2001 that even grave violations of international humanitarian law could not justify armed intervention.[39]

Our conclusion must be that nothing in the current doctrine of state responsibility accommodates a right of armed intervention to enforce treaty obligations. The deletion of the previous Article 19 of the Draft Articles of State Responsibility on the criminal responsibility of states, and the resistance of some states to aggravated state responsibility, suggests that this is some time off. If the international community cannot agree that states attract criminal responsibility, it is hard to imagine an enforcement component that would allow other states to intervene. As the international community has not accepted the right to intervene, it might be a long time before they accept a duty to do so.

Another threshold for international policing is proof that a sovereign state is in some way responsible for the action of terrorist elements. Even if a country harbours terrorists and refuses to prosecute or extradite them, the countermeasures must be proportionate. Unless the state can be shown to be liable for the attacks, the use of force is not legal. According to the Draft Articles on State Responsibility, "The conduct of a person or group of persons shall be considered an act of a State under international law if the person or group of persons is in fact acting on the instructions of, or under the direction or control of that State in carrying out the conduct." There is precedent in the International Court of Justice in the Iran Hostages Case, in which the Iranian regime was held responsible for failing to protect the United States Embassy from attack or to deal with the militants once it happened. Refusal to prosecute would also signify acquiescence on the part of a government to the acts that have occurred. Thus there would be a sufficient link between the criminal and the state, and this could justify the use of force on grounds of self-defence without a Chapter VII Security Council resolution. This is a critical issue that must be considered in the context of every proposed operation. It would be essential for the Canadian government to determine that the operation in self-defence is against a nation that is shielding the terrorist operations and refusing to take steps to deal with the situation. Even if the military situation seems clear, there must be clear, compelling legal evidence that a nation is not assuming responsibility for its own terrorist problem.

Reprisals

Often confused with self-defence, a reprisal is an action that a state undertakes to redress an injury suffered in peacetime. It is an action that would on its own be a violation of international law but is not regarded as such if it is a response to a prior unlawful act. It may or may not involve the use of force.[40] Bowett's definitive analysis of reprisals begins by stressing their illegality in the modern age: "Few propositions about international law have enjoyed more support than the proposition that, under the Charter of the United Nations, the use of force by way of reprisals is illegal."[41] Bowett considered this illegality to be the logical consequence of Articles 2(3) and 2(4) and the limiting of permissible force by states to self-defence. Moreover, the 1970 General Assembly Declaration on Friendly Relations also considers reprisals to be illegal: "States have the duty to refrain from acts of reprisal involving the use of force."

Bowett deemed it vital to distinguish between self-defence and reprisals – the former being legal and the latter illegal, according to the UN Charter. He stated that reprisals and self-defence are both forms of self-help and that they share three preconditions. The target state must be guilty of a prior international delinquency against the claimant state. An attempt by the claimant state to obtain redress or protection by other means must have been made, and failed, or such an attempt must be inappropriate or impossible in the circumstances. Finally, the claimant's use of force must be limited to the necessities of the case and proportionate to the wrong done by the target state.[42]

The main difference between self-defence and reprisals lies in their purpose. Self-defence has the purpose of protecting the security of a state, while reprisals are punitive: "they seek to impose reparation for the harm done, or to compel a satisfactory settlement of the dispute created by the initial illegal act, or to compel the delinquent state to abide by the law in future." Bowett argued that the apparently obvious distinction between self-defence and reprisals is not straightforward in reality, especially as one moves away from the particular incident and places a single act of violence in context. In the Arab-Israeli conflict, he saw the series of Arab attacks against Israel as justifying an armed response, on the basis of the Israeli argument of accumulation of events and not just an imminent attack. This perspective implies a broader meaning of self-defence that includes anticipatory self-defence. However, Bowett acknowledged that the international community did not accept this argument. Therefore, any action against terrorism risks being labelled a reprisal. The timing of the operation is critical in distinguishing between punishment and prevention.

INTERNATIONAL OPERATIONS – *JUS IN BELLO*

The key question in the conduct of anti-terrorism operations is whether they are part of an ongoing international armed conflict. Canada is bound by he 1949 Geneva Conventions and the 1977 Protocol 1 to the Convention.[43] Protocol 1 applies in the circumstances of an international armed conflict. Therefore, the provisions against civilian casualties and the concept of "military objective" would strictly circumscribe the conduct of anti-terrorist operations. This may be extremely difficult in anti-terrorism operations in which civilians might be used as human shields. Nevertheless, every care must be taken not to target civilian facilities such as schools and hospitals. In case of doubt, the presumption must be that the target is a civilian one.[44]

Many of the limited operations against terrorism may not trigger the obligations of the Geneva Conventions, absent an armed conflict. For any international military intervention, however, it should be argued that an armed conflict exists and that the Geneva Conventions and Protocol I therefore apply. The United States does not accept this restriction, arguing that al-Qaeda operatives are unlawful combattants, not entitled to the protection of the Geneva Conventions. This would seem to be completely in error; the issue is the nature of the conflict, which triggers the obligation. Even if combattant status is dubious, the Conventions provide for a hearing to determine status and, until their status is resolved, individuals are treated as prisoners of war.[45] In other circumstances, the U.S. has indicated that it will comply with the laws of war even if the conflict differs.[46] This should be Canada's position on any military operation, even if it is not accepted that the "war on terror" is an international armed conflict.

International Protection of Human Rights

Canada is bound by a whole set of international human rights treaties but concedes only the jurisdiction of international committees on human rights, whose power is limited to issuing views and making recommendations.[47] Canada has a history of complying with these recommendations[48] but has not agreed to the jurisdiction of the Inter-American Court of Human Rights, which has the power to issue judgments with costs and financial compensation.

The relevant conventions for this study are the International Covenant of Civil and Political Rights and the Convention Against Torture. All persons within Canadian jurisdiction (including those apprehended elsewhere) are entitled to challenge the legality of their detention in court and to be treated with dignity and respect. This is an important consideration in the capture and interrogation of suspects. Is a terrorist suspect captured in another country entitled to undergo an extradition process rather than be spirited away to Canada?[49] It seems that international criminal law overlooks the method of capture. Canada, however, may still be responsible for damages to the country it entered.[50] Furthermore, if a suspect is killed, survivors may bring an action alleging that Canada did not respect the suspect's right to life.

NATO's 1999 air campaign in Yugoslavia offers another relevant case. Family members alleging that the bombing of the Serbian television station in Belgrade was a violation of the civilian's right to life brought the Bankovic case in the European Court of Human Rights.[51] This involved a consideration of both international humanitarian law and international human rights law. The case was dismissed due to lack of jurisdiction because Yugoslavia was not a party to the European Convention on Human Rights, and the important issue of the obligation to respect human rights during armed conflict was not resolved. It is a fair assumption that human rights obligations toward civilians continue even if armed conflict is declared. This is especially relevant if Canada occupies another territory; its human rights obligations would then apply.

OPERATIONS WITHIN CANADA

Even military operations within Canada against suspected terrorists fall under the international legal regime. The traditional doctrine of state responsibility towards foreign nationals applies. They must be treated according to international human rights treaties. According to the International Covenant of Civil and Political Rights, they cannot be tortured, detained without a hearing, or denied right to counsel. The controversy over the US detention centres at Guantanamo Bay illustrates the obligations owed to foreign nationals. It is entirely possible that a nation could bring an action against Canada in the International Court of Justice for damages to its citizens under the traditional remit of state responsibility.

Even armed combat within Canada is subject to international humanitarian law. Protocol II to the Geneva Conventions deals with obligations during an internal armed conflict. The issue will be whether an anti-terrorism operation is a police action or part of a "war against terror". It seems likely that it would be characterized as internal law enforcement, but in that case, the Canadian *Charter of Rights and Freedoms*, which incorporates international human rights obligations, would bind the military personnel.

There is a further question of immigration and asylum law and the obligations imposed by the United Nations Convention on Refugees. Suspected terrorists from other countries are entitled to a judicial process for determination of their status. Anti-terrorism legislation in Canada met with a storm of criticism and is rarely applied.[52] The first annual report concerning investigative hearing and compliance with conditions, delivered by the Department of Justice on 23 December 2002, reported that there were *no cases* for investigative hearing or for failure to comply with conditions.[53] However, there is clearly more scope for police actions within Canada being subject to human rights provisions. UK practice in Northern Ireland and the many cases that resulted in creation of the European Court of Human Rights provide an important backdrop. It is never permissible to arbitrarily kill or to torture detainees.

CONCLUSION

It is clear that special operations such as seizing indicted war criminals or taking unilateral action to destroy weapons facilities are not unambiguously legal. They encompass some of the most controversial legal issues in international law, most particularly the breach of sovereignty of other nation states. Nevertheless, there is no definitive ruling from the Security Council or the International Court of Justice that precludes action in the face of an imminent attack.[54] The absence of a ruling preventing states from interpreting actions by terrorists as an "armed attack" permits states to respond as they would in war. However, it is also clear that no treaties exist that provide a right or duty for a state to intervene in the case of violations of weapons or terrorist conventions. Thus the hope that special operations might contribute to policing international agreements is out of step with current law, although the record of "vigilante" anti-terrorist operations (set out in the Appendix) suggests that the practice will continue.

The work of the International Law Commission on the issue of state responsibility and the report of the International Commission on Intervention and State Sovereignty could constitute the pivotal development in international law. They argue not just a right but a responsibility to intervene when massive loss of life is possible. However, the concept of serious breaches of state responsibility is a new one, and it might be many years before customary law and state practice follow suit.

NOTES

1. The major International Court of Justice cases that define customary international law as a combination of the practice of states and *opinio juris* are the *Asylum* case (Colombia/Peru, 1950), the *Fisheries* case (United Kingdom v. Norway, 1950), the *North Sea Continental Shelf* (Federal Republic of Germany/Denmark; Federal Republic of Germany/Netherlands, 1969), and the *Nicaragua* case (Military and Paramilitary Activities in and against Nicaragua, 1986).
2. For a definitive discussion of the provisions of the Charter on the Use of Force, see Simma, Mosler, Randelzhofer, Tomuschat, Wolfrum, Paulus, Chaitidou, eds., *The Charter of the United Nations: A Commentary* (London: Oxford University Press, 2002).
3. International Court of Justice, *Case Concerning Military and Paramilitary Activities in and against Nicaragua* (Merits), [1986] ICJ Rep. 14, 94; see also *Legality of the Threat or Use of Nuclear Weapons Case* (Advisory Opinion) (1997) 35 *I.L.M.* 809, paragraphs 37-42.
4. Ibid.,102-103.
5. Among the many authors who have discussed this concept are Frank, *Recourse to Force* (2002); Yoram Dinstein, *War, Aggression and Self-Defence Third Edition* (2001); Christine Gray, *International Law and the Use of Force* (2000); Stanimir Alexandrov, *Self-Defense Against the Use of Force in International Law* (1996); Rosalyn Higgins, *Problems and Process* (1994); Anthony Clark Arend and Robert J. Beck, *International Law and the Use of Force* (1993); Sir Robert Jennings and Sir Arthur Watts, eds., *Oppenheims International Law,* 9th edition (1992); William V. O'Brien, *The Conduct of Just and Limited War* (1981); Louis

Henkin, *How States Behave,* 2nd edition (1979); Julius Stone, *Of Law and Nations* (1974); Ian Brownlie, *International Law and the Use of Force by States* (1963); D. W. Bowett, *Self-Defence in International Law* (1958); J. Stone, *Aggression and World Order (*1958); Sir Humphrey Waldock, "The Regulation of the Use of Force by Individual States in International Law," *Recueil des Cours,* Volume 81 (1952); the report from the House of Commons Foreign Affairs Committee, *Foreign Policy Aspects of the War Against Terrorism,* 17 December 2002.

6. These two schools of interpretation also operate with respect to the scope of Article 2(4) of the Charter.
7. *Caroline* Case, *Moore's Digest,* Vol.II, 409. The *Caroline* was a small steamer employed by rebels and Americans supporting them in the Upper Canada Rebellion of 1837. It was destroyed near Niagara Falls. America protested the destruction of property and loss of life, and on investigation, Britain admitted to it and claimed self-defence. Subsequently the Webster-Ashburton exchange of correspondence accepted the action, establishing precedent for self-defence in apprehension of an armed attack.
8. Arend and Beck, *International Law and the Use of Force: Beyond the UN Charter Paradign* (London and New York: Routledge, 1993) 72-73.
9. Ibid., 92 quoting Sir Humphrey Waldock, "The Regulation of the Use of Force, 496-498.
10. Bowett, *Self-Defence in International Law* (Manchester: University of Manchester Press, 1958), 185-186.
11. Ibid., 191-192.
12. Ibid., 192.
13. Frank, *Recourse to Force: State action against threats and armed attack* (Cambridge: Cambridge University Press, 2002), 98.
14. See Appendix for a brief discussion of state practice.
15. President of the United States, *The National Security Strategy of the United States of America,* 20 September 2002.
16. For example, see United Nations Security Council debate no. S/PV.4625 of 16 and 17 October 2002. The debate continued over two full days, and many countries addressed the Security Council. See also S/PV. 4644 of 8 November 2002, S/PV. 4707 of 14 February 2003, S/PV. 4709 of 18 February 2003, S.PV. 4709 (Resumption 1) of 19 February 2003; S/PV. 4721 of 19 March 2003; and after the war began S/PV. 4726 of 26 March 2003 where several countries addressed the Council.
17. *Caroline* Case, *Moore's Digest,* Vol. II, 409.
18. Gray, *International Law and the Use of Force* (Oxford: Oxford University Press, 2001), 106.
19. Christopher Greenwood, "Self-Defence and the Conduct of International Armed Conflict" in *International Law at a Time of Perplexity: Essays in Honour of Shabtai Rosenne*, ed., Yoram Dinstein (Dordrecht: Martinus Nijhoff Publishers, 1989), 273.
20. Ibid., 275.

21. Christopher Greenwood, "International Law and the United States' Air Operation Against Libya," 89 *West Virginia Law Review* 933: 945.
22. This is not a universally held opinion. Judge Guillaume of the International Court of Justice recently argued that the terrorist threat should have been dealt with by means of criminal prosecution. See also M. Schmitt, "Counter-Terrorism and the Use of Force in International Law," *The Marshall Centre Papers*, No. 5, 2003, in which he argues that operations against the Taliban may not have been legally justified, citing the *Nicaragua* case in the ICJ.
23. 4 July 1976.
24. *United States Diplomatic and Consular Staff in Tehran (United States v. Iran)* International Court of Justice Provisional Measures 1979, Judgment 1980.
25. Ibid., in the *Iran Hostages* Case, the Provisional Measures Order of 15 December 1979 demanded that Iran intervene to "secure the immediate release" of all persons of United Sates nationality.
26. Natalino Ronzitti, *Rescuing Nationals Abroad Through Military Coercion and Intervention on Grounds of Humanity* (Dordrecht: Martinus Nijhoff Publishers, 1985); this book is the definitive study of this specialized area of international law.
27. There is continuing work at the United Nations for a comprehensive terrorism convention, but the states cannot agree on the definition of terrorism.
28. *Yunis v. Yunis* (1991) 30 I.L.M. 403.
29. For a discussion of this contested concept, see Christopher Greenwood, "International Law and the 'War on Terrorism'," *International Affairs* 78 (2002): 301-318.
30. International Commission on Intervention and State Sovereignty, *The Responsibility to Protect* (2001), XII.
31. On "Aggravated" State Responsibility, see Cassese, *International Law*, 200-204.Oxford: Oxford University Press, 2001.
32. Ibid., 200-201. Cassese also included obligations to States bound by multilateral treaties, but that topic does not seem to be included in Chapter III.
33. Ibid., 201.
34. Ibid., 203-204.
35. James Crawford, *The International Law Commission's Articles on State Responsibility: Introduction, Text and Commentaries* (2002). See Introduction for a history of the Articles on State Responsibility.
36. Ibid., 249.
37. Ibid., 253.
38. James Crawford, "The Earl A. Snyder Lecture in International Law: Responsibility to the International Community as a Whole," 8 *Indiana Journal of Global Legal Studies,* 303, 307 and 309.

39. A. Ryniker, "The ICRC's position on "humanitarian intervention'," 83 *IRRC* 527 (2001): 527.
40. The definition was developed in the *Naulilaa* case, 1926. *Naulilaa* (1928) 2 R.I.A.A. 1002.
41. D. Bowett, "Reprisals including Recourse to Armed Force," *AJIL 66,* 1 (1972).
42. Ibid.
43. For an excellent discussion on this issue, see A. Roberts, "Counter-terrorism, Armed Force and the Laws of War," *Survival* 44 (2002): 7.
44. The conduct of anti-terrorism operations has received little academic attention. One relevant article is Rona, "Interesting Times for International Humanitarian Law: Challenges from the 'War on Terror'" in 27 *Fletcher Forum on World Affairs"* (2003): 55; for general texts on International Humanitarian Law, see Kalshoven and Zegveld, *Constraints on the Waging of War* (2001) or Leslie Green, *The Contemporary Law of Armed Conflict, Second edition (*2000).
45. Article 5 of the Third Geneva Convention 1949.
46. Roberts, "Counter-terrorism, Armed Force and the Laws of War": 7.
47. The key committee is the Human Rights Committee, which administers the International Covenant on Civil and Political Rights.
48. The Canadian government amended its *Indian Act* to provide status for native women who married non-native men in accordance with a decision of the Human Rights Committee and will not extradite persons to face the death penalty in the United States according to the jurisprudence of the Human Rights Committee and its own Supreme Court.
49. There is a succession of cases, beginning with the Eichmann case, that consider this issue.
50. Israel paid compensation to Argentina for its kidnapping of Eichmann.
51. *Bankovic v. Belgium and Others* (Application No. 52207/99) European Court of Human Rights (Grand Chamber) 19 December 2001.
52. *Anti-terrorism Act,* S.C.2001, C.41and see http://www.parl.gc.ca/common/Committee_SenHome for the evidence from various prominent Canadians.
53. http://canada.justice.gc.ca/en/terrorism/annualreport.html
54. The most recent case, the Case Concerning Oil Platforms (Islamic Republic of Iran v. United States of America) judgement 6 November 2003, did not rule on this issue even though the United States argued imminent further attacks from Iran.

APPENDIX
State Practice in Anti-Terrorism Actions

Date	*Operation and Circumstance*	*Reaction*
1973	Israel raided Entebbe airport to free hostages from a hijacked Israeli aircraft. It argued that it was protecting its nationals abroad because Uganda was not assisting the hijack victims.	International response was mixed; the Security Council debate was inconclusive. Some accused Israel of using excessive force and committing acts of aggression against Uganda; others, including the U.S., recognized Israel's right to protect its nationals abroad.
1985	Israeli planes bombed the headquarters of the PLO near Tunis, Tunisia. The justification was that Tunisia knowingly harboured terrorists who had targetted Israel.	Security Council Resolution 573 condemned Israel's action 14 – 0 (with the U.S. abstaining) saying that the air raid was a threat to peace and security in the Mediterranean region.
1986	US air raid on Libya: result 100 civilians killed – in response to the April 9th bombing of a Berlin nightclub where one US soldier was killed and 50 others wounded. This was justified under Article 51.	A draft Security Council resolution condemning the air raid was vetoed by the U.S. and the U.K., although it had sufficient votes to pass (11 to 4).
1994	U.S. destroyed Iraqi Intelligence Headquarters in Baghdad, causing at least six civilian deaths – in response to unexecuted Iraqi plan to kill President Bush in Kuwait in 1993.	U.S. justified it under Article 51. The U.K., Russia, and France supported this action by the U.S.
1998	US Cruise Missile strikes in Afghanistan and Sudan, in response to the bombing of the US embassies in Kenya and Tanzania, were carried out after repeated efforts to convince the Sudanese government and Taliban regime of Afghanistan to cease cooperation with the Bin Laden organization.	Clinton justified this action as self-defence and retribution for the bombings. It was not condemned in the Security Council.

... continued

APPENDIX
(Continued)

Date	*Operation and Circumstance*	*Reaction*
2001	War on Afghanistan – the primary example of a war in self-defence against an anticipated attack.	Not condemned by the Security Council, which had passed a resolution after September 11 recognizing the right of the U.S. to self-defence. The coalition for this action was much broader than that of the later action in Iraq and seemed to reflect universal agreement.
2003	War in Iraq – part of the justification for this war was anticipation of the use of WMD by Hussein.	The French, German, and Russian opposition seemed to centre on lack of evidence that an attack was imminent.
2003	Israeli attack on terrorist camp in Syria. Israeli armed forces bombed an alleged training camp near Damascus on 5 October 2003. Israeli officials asserted that the attack was in reaction to a suicide bombing that killed 19 people in a restaurant hours earlier and constituted an action in self-defence.	The Israelis alleged that the terrorists involved in the bombing had been trained in the camp in Syria. This argument was based on the traditional Israeli position that an accumulation of smaller terrorist attacks could be regarded as an armed attack. This theory has never found widespread approval by the international community. The Security Council met in an emergency session on the same day; only the United States supported the Israeli action but threatened to veto any resolution condemning the attack.

CHAPTER SEVEN

POLITICAL LEADERSHIP FOR SPECIAL OPERATIONS

Stephanie Mullen

National defence issues have undeniably gained a higher profile in the media since the events of September 11. Unsurprisingly, Canadian political decision-makers and policy-makers have embarked on a period of intensive study of defence issues. Both the Senate and the House of Commons Standing Committees on National Defence Issues have undertaken several major studies, addressing North American defence, coastal surveillance, military expenditures, and military preparedness.[1]

We can assume that the politicians who sit on these committees have the knowledge and experience necessary to engage in a substantive discussion of the new problems of special operations. Personal interviews with 18 Members of Parliament and Senators, conducted between November 2003 and March 2004, addressed five specific aspects of the conduct of special operations. The nature of the respondents' positions within their parties leads us to believe that they should be broadly representative of party views. While the small sample and the volatility of the political climate suggest that we should be cautious about drawing conclusions, these interviews are nevertheless indicative of opinion amongst political leaders, and they represent the first results of their kind.

The interviews followed the general form of the survey approved for use with senior policy-makers and opinion-leaders and were developed in conjunction with COMPAS research. We wanted to know what kinds of operations are acceptable from a political standpoint in the current climate. Who should Canada work with, and whom should we expect to target? What kind of cooperation and sharing of burdens might be appropriate? Finally, we were interested in their views about the role of Parliament in oversight and decision-making concerning special operations.

There appears to be an institutional difference between MPs and senators. Senators seemed more actively engaged and knowledgeable about defence issues. This might be because senators have been exposed to more briefings by DND officials. The short tenure of the opposition critic and committee members in the House of Commons, compared to the more stable membership of Senate Committees, may give senators an advantage. Senators have more time than MPs to devote to research, and members of the Senate Defence Committee have conducted more detailed and issue-specific investigations than their counterparts on the Parliamentary Standing Committee.

Of the 18 respondents, five were from the Liberal Party, four were members of the Conservative Party, one was from the New Democratic Party (NDP), and one was a member of the Bloc Quebecois (BQ).[2] The NDP responses in some cases reflect their policy priority on social justice, which will differentiate them from the other political parties. The BQ represent a desire to have parliamentary oversight of special operations, especially covert actions. These party differences are discussed later in this chapter.

CANADIAN SPECIAL OPERATIONS CAPABILITIES

In the broadest sense, special operations include offensive direct actions to pre-empt attack or destroy weapons facilities, operations to rescue or secure Canadian citizens, managing the consequences of attacks by weapons of mass destruction, and humanitarian actions abroad.[3] How do federal politicians rank these different types of special operation, and how do they compare them to conventional operations by land, sea, and air forces? Most respondents agreed to rate the relative importance (on a 7-point Likert-type scale, where 7 represents very important and 1 the opposite) of different types of special operations, but one leading Liberal member of the Standing Committee on National Defence and two senators did not believe that one type of operation could be given higher priority than another. They argued that all operations listed were equally important and that the Canadian Forces should be prepared to conduct all the operations listed. Respondents who held this view appeared to be well informed about defence policy in general and special operations in particular, and all had served for some time with their respective committees.

Amongst those who did rank the operations, a majority rated operations to help Canadians as the most important. Helping civilians deal with chemical, biological, or radiological attack on a major Canadian city was ranked highest, followed by evacuating Canadian citizens from danger (with or without the consent of the country involved), freeing Canadian hostages (with or without cooperation from a foreign country), and retaking a Canadian commercial ship or aircraft. (See Table 7-1 for rankings by Party.)

TABLE 7-1
Political Attitudes towards Special Operations (Mean Responses)

Type of Special Operation	*Lib*	*Con*	*NDP*	*BQ*	*All*
Help civilians deal with a chemical, biological or radiological attack on a major Canadian city.	7.00	7.00	7.00	7.00	7.00
Free hostages in Canada.	6.25	6.50	7.00	7.00	6.69
Evacuate Canadian citizens from dangerous situations, with the consent of the country involved.	6.75	7.00	7.00	6.00	6.69
Free Canadian hostages in a foreign country, with the cooperation of that country's government.	5.75	7.00	6.00	7.00	6.44
Seize or free a Canadian commercial ship or aircraft taken hostage by criminals or terrorists on the high seas.	6.00	6.75	7.00	6.00	6.44
Provide humanitarian assistance in the case of natural disasters outside North America.	6.75	5.25	6.00	6.00	6.00
Deploy to war-torn regions multidisciplinary teams including medical personnel, aid experts and security advisers.	6.50	5.00	6.00	6.00	5.88
Free Canadian hostages in a war-affected foreign country, without local assistance.	4.50	6.00	6.00	6.00	5.63
Evacuate Canadian citizens from dangerous situations, without the cooperation of the country involved.	6.00	6.50	5.00	4.00	5.38
Work with a multilateral force to destroy a weapons facility in a hostile country.	4.50	6.00	7.00	3.00	5.13
Enhance the security of Canadian civilians working in war-affected or unstable countries by providing security advice, training, or oversight.	6.00	5.50	6.00	3.00	5.13
Work with a multilateral team to disable or destroy large facilities in countries that are a threat to Canada or other democratic countries.	5.00	5.75	6.00	2.00	4.69
Capture and extract an individual at the request of or with the cooperation of a foreign government.	3.50	4.75	5.00	4.00	4.31
Gain covert entry to a computer installation as part of information warfare.	4.25	4.50	5.00	3.00	4.19
Capture and extract vital information from a country hostile to Canada without the knowledge and/or consent of that country.	4.75	4.75	5.00	2.00	4.13
Capture and extract a person without the knowledge/consent of a country hostile to Canada.	2.25	4.25	4.00	4.00	3.63

The Liberal, Conservative, NDP, and BQ respondents agreed on many of the special operations that they believed Canada should be able to undertake, most of which were focused on helping Canadians at home and abroad. For instance, they considered it very important that Canada be able to help civilians deal with a chemical, biological, or radiological attack on a major Canadian city. This was consistently the most important capability for Canada to be able to undertake. Almost all respondents also considered it important that Canada should be able to free hostages anywhere in Canada or abroad.

The responses became more differentiated when the elements of risk and opposition were introduced. When asked how important it was to be able to free Canadian hostages in a war-affected foreign country without local assistance, a majority of Liberal respondents stated that it was not very important, while half of Conservative respondents stated that it was important. One Conservative respondent stated that in its current state the military does not have the capacity to engage in such action. Furthermore, he believed the direction of the military needs to be further defined so that Canada has a domestic reserve force to assist with natural disasters and a force better trained to engage in special operations in Canada and overseas.

Interestingly, all the respondents agreed that it was important for Canada to be capable of evacuating Canadians from dangerous situations, with or without the cooperation or consent of the country involved. They also believed it is very important for Canada to be able to seize or free a Canadian commercial ship or aircraft taken hostage by criminals or terrorists on the high seas.

Political parties were split on matters of Canada's ability to provide humanitarian assistance in the case of natural disasters outside North America. Liberal respondents rated this capability as important, but a majority of Conservative respondents rated it as not important. Liberal respondents also believed that it was important for Canada to be able to enhance the security of Canadian civilians working in war-affected or unstable countries by providing security advice, training, or oversight, while the Conservative respondents did not rate this capability as important. For example, Liberal responses averaged 6.50 on the question of deploying multidisciplinary teams that include medical personal, aid experts, and security specialists to war-torn regions.

Most Important Special Operations

When asked to choose one type of special operation as the most important capability for Canada to develop, some parliamentarians had difficulty complying because they believed that several of the types listed are important, if not all. For those who did choose one type above all the others, a majority of respondents stated that Canada has to be able to help civilians deal with a chemical, biological, or radiological attack on a major Canadian city. This appears to be an overall concern shared by both federal politicians and Canadians in general.[4] The ability to evacuate Canadian citizens from dangerous situations with the consent of the country involved was also mentioned in unprompted responses. These responses demonstrate a commitment to domestic security but also a focus on rendering assistance to Canadian citizens in distress. It was clear that participating politicians believed our special operations capability should focus on helping Canadian citizens directly at home and abroad.

Politicians were asked whether and to what extent Canada might suffer if it were unable to conduct the special operations that they deemed most important. In their responses, they reflected on the close geographic and diplomatic ties that Canada has with the U.S., and concerns over Canada's reputation on the international stage with the U.S. and U.K. Most politicians believe that Canada would suffer a great deal if it were not able to conduct these operations successfully. When asked to provide greater detail on how Canada would suffer if it could not conduct those operations identified as the most important, the overwhelming response from both Conservative and Liberal respondents was that Canada would lose credibility in the international arena. Politicians further expressed the views that innocent Canadians would suffer if such action could not be taken and that the public could lose confidence in the federal government. A majority of respondents believed that Canadians would have to rely increasingly on the U.S. or other countries for defence and security. This was a particular concern on the part of members of the Senate, who believed that Canada should be able to conduct special operations independently of the U.S. or other nations or organizations.

The few parliamentarians who stated that Canada would not suffer at all believed that other nations such as the U.S. would come to our aid. In fact, the opinions expressed in this interview question were strongly associated with the answers later in this chapter about whether it is important for Canada to be able to act unilaterally.

Least Important Special Operations

Most politicians were in agreement on which operations were less important. They agreed that the ability to capture and extract a person at the request of, or with the cooperation of, a foreign government was not important. One exception arose on the question of whether Canada should have the capability to gain covert entry to a computer installation as part of information warfare. Half of the Conservative and BQ respondents believed it was important, whereas a majority of Liberals and NDP respondents thought it was not important. Likewise, all four political parties regarded the capture and extraction of a person or vital information without the knowledge or consent of a country hostile to Canada as less important. This may reflect the reality that such operations would face serious obstacles under international law.[5]

Some of these operations were rated as having low importance because respondents believed Canada does not spend enough on defence to be capable of carrying out special missions. Another reason may have been their limited knowledge of special operation. Not all MPs seemed to be aware of the importance of particular operations in a conflict. Senators on the National Defence Committee who had been briefed on Canadian special operations capabilities clearly had more detailed knowledge than MPs.

Special Operations and Other Military Priorities

Overall, the majority of political respondents rated a few conventional operations higher than special operations. A majority of respondents from both major parties rated typical missions of the Canadian army or land forces as more important. However, a majority of the Liberal respondents also rated typical missions of the Canadian air force as more important, while the majority of Conservative Party representatives regarded typical missions of the Canadian army, navy, and air force as more important than special operations. Politicians believed that most of these operations were only slightly more important than special operations. The BQ and some other parliamentarians wanted the federal government to put forward a new white paper on defence, citing a need to debate mission priorities and to determine the importance of special operations compared to other military priorities.

Interestingly, one response that was rated by a majority of Liberal respondents as unimportant was investment in new technologies. In contrast, Conservative respondents scored this as important. This might reflect a desire to direct funding to build up Canada's forces and capabilities before taking on new commitments.

PARTNERSHIPS FOR SPECIAL OPERATIONS

Both Liberal and Conservative respondents felt that it was important for Canada to conduct special operations. Interestingly, the Liberal responses were more diverse, while Conservative responses were consistently in favour of special operations. However, when asked how important it was for Canada to be able to conduct such operations unilaterally, responses reflected a diversity of opinion within the parties. A majority from the Liberal and Conservative Parties believed that it was important for Canada to be able to act unilaterally in conducting special operations. This belief has special implications, not only for doctrine but also for the direction of military spending and policy.

Clearly the responses from this section of the survey suggest that political leaders believe it is important to conduct special operations that protect Canadian citizens and that we must be able to do this unilaterally. Some parliamentarians went so far as to connect the ability to conduct such operations unilaterally with Canada's national sovereignty and with the safety and well-being of our nation.

For larger or more ambitious special operations, each party believed it was a very good idea to commit Canadian resources only after a full public debate and with parliamentary support. While several respondents stated that parliamentary debate is necessary in our democratic society, most accepted that security concerns would not allow it in every instance.

Liberal respondents were evenly split on the importance of unilateral operations on Canadian soil without public disclosure or parliamentary debate. In contrast, a majority of Conservatives believed it was a very good idea. Liberal and NDP responses to unilateral operations overseas without public disclosure or parliamentary debate were more negative than positive, but again, a majority of Conservatives viewed these as very important.

Multilateral Teams

As indicated in Table 7-2, there also appeared to be mixed opinions regarding Canada's participation in multilateral actions. The Conservative members tended to view multilateral action more favourably than the Liberals did. When a choice between unilateral and multilateral operations was presented, Tory support strengthened. Specifically, the Conservatives and the BQ mainly preferred multilateral operations, while the Liberals preferred unilateral action with full parliamentary debate and support. The BQ did express a desire for flexibility, on a case-by-case basis, as to partners for multilateral actions, but their overriding concern is to have Parliamentary control over special operations – especially covert special operations.

One possible explanation for these results is that parliamentarians prefer unilateral action to assist Canadians over assertive multilateral action in foreign countries. This choice was most obvious when they were presented with a list of operations in which most appear to be unilateral actions, as was the case in the first section of this chapter. However, when they were presented with a list of partners, it was assumed that the question related to a foreign action only – in which case, parliamentarians would prefer to engage in joint operations. One senator, who believed Canada should have a domestic force to deal primarily with natural disasters and a specialized force to handle difficult operations in partnership with other nations and organizations, presented this scenario.

Partners – Legitimation, Material Support, and Interoperability

On the questions relating to potential partnerships for Canada, a Liberal respondent stated that Canada should be able to choose its allies on a case-by-case basis. This clearly emphasizes the belief of politicians that Canada should have the flexibility to choose its partners in different operations. It also implies significant autonomy in the conduct of operations.

TABLE 7-2
The Nature of Potential Partnerships

Potential Partners for Special Operations	*Lib*	*Con*	*NDP*	*BQ*
Authorized by a resolution of the UN Security Council	6.25	5.50	6.00	7.00
Under NATO	6.25	6.33	6.00	5.00
Sponsored by regional organizations (OSCE, OAS)	5.25	4.00	5.00	n/a
Authorized as policing under rules	4.75	3.33	5.00	n/a
Authorized by the International Criminal Court	5.25	3.00	6.00	n/a
Requested by or undertaken by commercial or non-governmental organizations	3.00	4.00	5.00	n/a
In a multilateral operation with full public debate and Parliamentary backing	6.75	6.67	6.00	7.00
In a multilateral operation without public disclosure or parliamentary debate due to the need for secrecy in order to ensure the success of a special operation	5.25	6.67	5.00	1.00
In a multilateral operation without public disclosure or parliamentary debate because of the need for secrecy in order for the special operation to be successful but with secret consultation with the Leader of the Official Opposition in Parliament	6.00	6.67	3.00	3.00
That are unilateral and with full public debate and parliamentary support	7.00	6.33	6.00	7.00
That are unilateral on Canadian soil and without public disclosure or parliamentary debate	5.50	6.00	6.00	1.00
That are unilateral and abroad and without public disclosure or parliamentary debate	3.50	5.00	3.00	1.00

A Conservative respondent stated that Canada should commit Canadian assets whenever an international natural disaster occurs. The rationale was that creating an environment of stability out of confusion would also help establish political and social stability. Another Conservative respondent believed that Canada should commit Canadian resources that involve "Strategic Intelligence Gathering."

When asked about committing Canadian resources to operations relying for their success on command, intelligence, or logistic support from different countries or organizations, a majority of Liberal and Conservative respondents stated that NATO and ABCA (America-Britain-Canada-Australia) partnerships were preferred in multilateral operations. Liberal respondents were evenly split on US operations and British operations. Liberals viewed special operations led by the UN as a bad idea. The NDP, in contrast, favoured the UN over other partners.

Ancillary functions related to special operations were mentioned in several of the interviews. A Conservative respondent stated that Canada should commit more medical assistance, food, and clothing to operations. The NDP believed that Canada should provide material support to NGOs working in war-torn areas. Politicians also sought to have more RCMP and other police officers committed to train foreign police. The interviewees also indicated that the Canadian coast guard needs more powers in order to protect our maritime approaches.

When discussing interoperability of equipment and training, a majority of parliamentarians believed that it was very important to have compatibility with NATO forces, ABCA, the U.S., and Britain. A majority of parliamentarians also indicated that compatibility with United Nations forces is not as important, although the NDP rated this organization the highest, along with NATO.

TARGETS OF CANADIAN SPECIAL OPERATIONS

Although most politicians believed scenarios involving direct action should be considered on a case-by-case basis, a majority considered it very important to be able to take direct action against groups or individuals within Canada when necessary. This is most likely related to Canadians' fears that a terrorist attack on Canadian soil is very likely.[6]

A difference of opinion based on Party affiliation was evident for some scenarios. First, a majority of Liberals believed that it is not important to take direct action against non-state actors, the opposite view of a majority of Conservative and NDP parliamentarians. Second, Liberal and NDP parliamentarians also saw direct action against commercial companies as important, but not covert actions. A majority of Liberal and NDP respondents believed that direct action against countries other than the U.S. is very important; however, Conservatives were evenly split between those who believed it is not important and those who believed it is. Furthermore, Conservatives believed that countries other than the U.S. are also very important potential targets for *covert* action. The BQ believed that none of these scenarios are important because Canada should focus on peacekeeping and humanitarian assistance. This opinion probably relates directly to their discomfort over the secret nature of special operations and perceived lack of parliamentary control or oversight.

The Media's Role in Special Operations

A majority of Liberals believed that it is important for the media to cover issues of national security, terrorism, and typical missions of the army, navy, and air force. However, they were evenly split on the importance of media coverage of peacetime preparations for special operations. The Conservatives believed the opposite: that every item, including peacetime special operations, is an important subject for coverage, unless it undermined national security. The BQ believed in media coverage of special operations except those related to terrorism. It is interesting that only the senators saw a connection between national security concerns and peacetime preparations for special operations, yet these go hand in hand. Liberals thought that media coverage of security operations is more important than coverage of preparations for future engagements, while Conservatives believed the opposite and the NDP rated each as equally important.

PARLIAMENT'S ROLE IN SPECIAL OPERATIONS

Politicians generally agreed that it is important for parliamentarians to be apprised of special operations to some degree, as indicated in Table 7-3. A majority of Liberal respondents believed that it is important for parliamentarians to be briefed on issues of national security, terrorism, and typical missions of the army, navy, and air force.

TABLE 7-3
Parliamentary Oversight

Operations on Which Parliamentarians Should Be Briefed	*Lib*	*Con*	*NDP*	*BQ*
Peacetime preparations of special operations	5.50	5.67	6.00	7.00
Issues of national security	5.75	5.33	6.00	7.00
Terrorism	5.75	5.67	4.00	7.00
Typical missions of the army, navy, and airforce	5.75	6.33	6.00	7.00

Respondents also believed it is moderately important that Parliament be briefed on matters related to peacetime preparations for special operations. Conservative politicians believed that it is not as important to be briefed on issues of national security, but a majority rated the remaining responses as important for parliamentarians to be briefed on. Interestingly, the NDP rated three of the four scenarios as important for parliamentarians to be apprised of, but were comparatively more ready to be kept in the dark about terrorism. The BQ, on the other hand, rated all four areas as very important. In fact, the BQ does not accept the veil of secrecy surrounding JTF 2 operations, although the capability they represent might gain BQ approval if DND officials were more open with parliamentarians, the defence committee, or each party's defence critic at the very least. The BQ believed very strongly that special operations of all types, including those touching on the most sensitive matters of national security, must be open to parliamentary scrutiny, and not just government oversight.

The secrecy surrounding special operations makes it difficult to discuss. Some of the respondents knew few operational details about capabilities or requirements. Until the House of Commons Defence Committee is properly briefed, it will be difficult for parliamentarians to make an informed judgement about the appropriate level for their involvement. Several politicians suggested that it might be appropriate to have different levels of briefing about special operations, including both government and opposition members. For example, Parliament as a whole might be briefed before a debate and a vote. Members of the Defence Committee might be briefed in camera in preparation for key decisions. Certain key figures (such as the leaders of opposition parties) might be briefed at the highest level, to ensure a policy consensus on sensitive operations affecting national security. A Conservative respondent reiterated the concern that the Leader of the Official Opposition must be brought into the government's confidence when matters are too sensitive to be brought to Parliament:

> There are methods by which a government can brief an opposition on serious national security matters. During the Gulf War the PM made Party leaders Privy Council Members so that they could be briefed on the conduct of the war. During Kosovo Clark received a Privy Councillor's briefing that he could then share. Additionally, things can be done quietly. Prior to the bombing campaign in Kosovo, Defence Critics were informed that a NATO attack was imminent.

When politicians were asked about the source of funding for special operations, a majority from all the parties named the DND budget (see Table 7-4). One Senator stated that the federal government should have the courage to publicly increase the funds going to the DND budget, instead of trying to hide the true cost of the military by taking money from other departmental budgets. Interestingly, only a few parliamentarians stated that funds should be apportioned from other appropriate departments. A small group believed funding should come directly from central funds.

TABLE 7-4
Sources of Funding for Special Operations

Funding Source	*Number Responding in Each Group*			
	Lib	*Con*	*NDP*	*BQ*
DND's Budget	4	3	1	1
Central Funds	3	3	0	0
Apportioned from other appropriate departments	2	1	0	0

A majority of politicians (with the exception of the NDP and BQ) believed that employment equity and human rights need to be adjusted or waived for individuals, units, or formations due to the nature of special operations. However, there was a divergence of views on whether special operations should be excluded from the *Access to Information Act*. Liberal politicians split evenly on a yes/no dimension, whereas the Conservatives had some "no" responses, but a majority still believed that access to information should be waived or adjusted for sensitive special operations. The NDP and BQ respondents believed there should be no adjustments, especially when it came to human rights. A Conservative put the opposite view: "Basic rights should never supersede the security and preservation of national interests. The Third World War in which we are now engaged (terrorism) will test our Charter. Freedoms often are limited and sometimes curtailed in defence and national interests."

The NDP respondent argued that the government needs to think beyond officers and remember soldiers and their families as well, stating that "we must ensure that we give the troops and their families all the support that we can offer."

SUMMING UP

This chapter has examined the attitudes of federal political leaders with some knowledge of defence issues towards several broad subject areas related to special operations. Responses about types of special operations, preferences about authorization, anticipated allies, and likely targets indicate broad areas of agreement among federal politicians from the major political parties. They agree that special operations that manage consequences and help to rescue Canadians are the most important and direct action and covert missions are the least important. A common thread throughout the responses was the desire to give the military adequate funding to permit more unilateral actions, should these be necessary. Although multilateral operations are important, the desire to be able to act independently was articulated across the political spectrum.

Parliamentarians have great respect for the military and believe that it should be capable of carrying out a multitude of diverse special operations. Providing assistance to Canadians within our country and throughout the world were top priorities for this group. Nevertheless, there was recognition of the fact that offensive actions are sometimes necessary to secure the safety and wellbeing of Canadians. Although most parliamentarians were willing to permit the military to conduct some special operations without their knowledge, they insisted on being kept informed of major actions, such as Canada's participation in direct action and acts of war. In such cases, the opinion was that the leaders of the opposition parties should be briefed at a minimum; however, full parliamentary debate and public support were preferred.

This sample of only 18 politicians from the 128th session of Parliament cannot reflect the full diversity of opinion likely to be found in any assembly of elected politicians and appointed senators. Nevertheless, the qualitative aspect of extended structured interviews provides a unique insight into the thinking of Canada's political leadership about counter-terrorism, consequence management, and special operations in the age of the global war on terror.

NOTES

1. Senator Colin Kenny, *et al., Canada's Coastlines: The Longest Under-Defended Borders in the World,* The Standing Senate Committee on National Security and Defence (Ottawa: Government of Canada, October 2003). Senator Colin Kenny, *et al., The Myth of Security at Canada's Airports,* The Standing Senate Committee on National Security and Defence (Ottawa: Government of Canada, January 2003). Senator Colin Kenny, *et al. For an Extra $130 Bucks....Update On Canada's Military Financial Crisis: A View From The Bottom Up,* The Standing Senate Committee on National Security and Defence (Ottawa: Government of Canada, November 2002). *Canadian Security And Military Preparedness,* The Standing Senate Committee on National Security and Defence (Ottawa: Government of Canada, February 2002). *Defence Of North America: A Canadian Responsibility,* The Standing Senate Committee on National Security and Defence (Ottawa: Government of Canada, September 2002).
2. Conservative respondents included both Progressive Conservative and Canadian Alliance Members of Parliament and the Senate. One Progressive Conservative Senator did not join the new Conservative party and, at the time of publication, is sitting as a Conservative in the Senate. The NDP's defence critic indicated that his Party did not have an official policy towards special operations, so he could not participate in the study. Nevertheless, other NDP MPs were contacted in order to gauge whether there was homogeneity or a diversity of views towards special operations within the NDP caucus.
3. The doctrinal definition of special operations and the types of operations discussed are listed in the preface.
4. Associated Press/Ipsos Poll: "Many In Neighboring Countries, Europe Believe Iraq War Increased Terrorist Threat," 5 March 2004.
5. See Chapter Six of this volume.
6. Associated Press/Ipsos Poll, "Iraq War Increased Terrorist Threat."

CHAPTER EIGHT

ELITE OPINION ABOUT SPECIAL OPERATIONS

David Last and Hugh Thorburn[1]

The absence of Canadian doctrine on special operations reflects some ambivalence about the use of Canadian forces in operations like the current "war on terror". Canadian policy has been to support a rules-based international order, but Canada also has many interests that are closely aligned with those of the United States, and the Canadian Forces have a history of working closely with first British, then American forces. What do informed policy-makers and opinion-leaders think about the limits and utility of special operations?

An elite survey was conducted to explore the limits of acceptable operations for Canadian forces, as seen by senior policy-makers and opinion-leaders. The rationale of the study is that military planners and the public alike should think about the limits of acceptable operations. Without discussing specific circumstances, the views of policy-makers and opinion-leaders provide the best starting point to describe the broader current Canadian views on these matters.

CONCEPTS AND METHODS

The term "special operations" can have a variety of meanings for different audiences. There is not yet an official Canadian definition, but widely circulated NATO and American definitions include at least six elements that are important to an exploration of Canadian views. Special operations are conducted by forces that are specially trained, organized, and equipped. These forces work in hostile, denied, or politically sensitive areas (including Canadian territory). The operations can be conducted in any phase of peace, conflict, or war. Because they are strategically and politically significant, they cannot be governed by strictly military decision criteria. Finally, they differ from conventional operations in risk, techniques, independence, and need for intelligence and local support.[2]

Elite surveys work on the assumption that certain sections of the population have a disproportionate knowledge of, or influence on, the matters under investigation. In the case of policy-making, senior bureaucrats and the owners, editors, and lead writers of national media were identified as two groups that play an important role in national policy with respect to special operations and are likely to influence the type of operations that Canada undertakes or prepares for. Using government telephone directories, researchers identified about 650 key appointments in more than 50 government departments and agencies. Many of these have direct connections to security (DND, Foreign Affairs Canada, RCMP, Solicitor General, etc.) while others have more peripheral interests that are nevertheless significant within the new threat environment (e.g., Transportation, Health Canada, Pilotage Authorities, Race Relations Commission). From this pool of policy-makers, researchers from COMPAS conducted 123 computer-aided telephone interviews with policy-makers. They conducted a further 55 interviews with an additional pool of national media opinion-leaders. The interviews were conducted between 24 November and 19 December 2003. Since this period coincided with the transition between the Liberal governments of Jean Chrétien and Paul Martin, the responses probably reflect something of the sensibilities of the new government but are dominated by the sensibilities of the established Chrétien administration. Few of the respondents were political appointees, and we would expect the results to be substantively the same if we repeated the survey today. The changing decision-making process is addressed in a later chapter.

In surveys of the general population, a sample of 178 would be deemed to have a margin of error of 7.4 per cent, 19 times out of 20. In practice, the population of interest is considerably smaller, and the sample of 178 might be considered accurate to within 6.2 per cent 19 times out of 20 for the population of 600 policy-makers and opinion-leaders. In the following report, relationships are statistically significant unless otherwise indicated.

IMPORTANCE OF SPECIAL OPERATIONS

The study's most significant finding is that both policy-makers and opinion-leaders ascribe exceptionally high importance to special operations, compared to other military capabilities. This requires explanation. As reported in the previous chapter, parallel interviews with a small number of political leaders revealed that most parliamentarians surveyed consider special operations capabilities to be less important than conventional army, navy, and air force capabilities. The larger sample of policy-makers and the detailed responses permit us to model the key factors that are statistically associated with a belief in the importance of special operations.[3] The desire to help civilians faced with chemical, biological, and radiological (CBR) threats is the single most powerful driver and was a consensus among respondents. Other drivers were the need to evacuate Canadians, seize ships or aircraft, free hostages, conduct direct action, and provide humanitarian assistance.

Since respondents were not assumed to know much about special operations, they were provided with a list of the types of operations that might be encompassed in a broad understanding of the term, including response to asymmetrical threats such as terrorism, weapons of mass destruction, and information attack. The list of operations appears below in Table 8-1. The shorthand, "post-hoc" labels associated with each example (shown in square brackets) were not provided to respondents. The right-hand column reflects the mean value ascribed to each by respondents, using a 7-point scale in which 7 represented "very important" and 1 the reverse. The first column reflects the mean for all respondents, the second for policy-makers, and the third for media opinion-leaders.

TABLE 8-1
Examples of "Special Operations" and Mean Importance Ascribed

#	*Post-hoc Label*	*Description from Survey*	*All*	*Policy-makers*	*Media*
1.	CBR response	Help civilians deal with a chemical, biological, or radiological attack on a major Canadian city	6.5	6.5	6.6
2.	NEO[4] with consent	Evacuate Canadian citizens from dangerous situations, with the consent of the country involved	6.4	6.4	6.3
3.	Domestic hostage	Free hostages anywhere in Canada, for example by storming a building where they may be held	6.3	6.3	6.1
4.	NEO without help	Evacuate Canadian citizens from dangerous situations, without the effective cooperation of the country involved	6.1	6.2	6.0
5.	Repossession operations	Seize or free a Canadian commercial ship or aircraft taken hostage by criminals or terrorists on the high seas	6.0	6.0	6.0
6.	Foreign hostage	Free Canadian hostages in a foreign country, with the cooperation of that country's government	5.9	5.9	6.0

... *continued*

TABLE 8-1
(Continued)

#	*Post-hoc Label*	*Description from Survey*	*All*	*Policy-makers*	*Media*
7.	PRTs[5]	Deploy to war-torn regions multi-disciplinary teams including medical people, aid experts, and security specialists	5.8	5.9	5.6
8.	Security assistance	Enhance the security of Canadian civilians working in war-affected or unstable countries by providing security advice, training, or oversight	5.6	5.6	5.5
9.	Foreign hostage without help	Free Canadian hostages in a war-affected foreign country, without local assistance	5.6	5.6	5.5
10.	DART	Provide humanitarian assistance in the case of natural disasters outside North America	5.3	5.3	5.1
11.	Direct action	Work with a multilateral force to destroy a weapons facility in a hostile country	5.0	5.0	5.0
12.	Large direct action	Work with a multilateral team to disable or destroy large facilities such as a military headquarters in countries that are a threat to Canada or other democratic countries	4.9	4.8	5.1
13.	Covert entry	Gain covert entry to a computer installation as part of information warfare	4.5	4.5	4.5
14.	Covert info operations	Capture and extract vital information without the knowledge or consent of a country hostile to Canada	4.3	4.2	4.3
15.	International arrest	Capture and extract an individual such as an indicted war criminal from a hostile region at the request or with the cooperation of the country's own government	4.3	4.2	4.3
16.	International abduction	Capture and extract a person without the knowledge or consent of a country hostile to Canada	3.3	3.2	3.7

Each of the 16 examples of special operations in Table 8-1 is derived from contemporary cases and recent work by Canadian force-development staff. Taken together, they are intended to explore the range of capabilities that might conceivably be included in the evolution of special operations forces to support the national interest or deal with asymmetrical threats. The first task, for example, reflects the mandate of the national nuclear, biological, chemical, and radiological response team (NBCRT). The second and fourth reflect noncombattant evacuation operations (NEO), which might involve conventional or special forces or both. Examples 3, 5, 6, and 9 fall within the current mandate of JTF 2, Canada's national hostage-rescue unit. JTF 2 operates under the authority of the Solicitor General in Canada and under the direction of the Chief of Defence Staff outside Canada. Examples 7 and 10 reflect the sort of work sometimes done by American Special Forces, currently within the mandate of Canada's Disaster Assistance Response Team (DART). Examples 7 and 8 reflect both civil-military cooperation or civil-affairs skills and the foreign military training teams deployed by US Special Forces to enhance security in a failed state or a state under attack by insurgents.[6] Examples 11 and 12 might require larger forces with more firepower and mobility, suggesting light infantry battalions or forces like US Ranger battalions. These larger forces might also be involved in supporting small teams needed for examples 13 to 16. Capabilities for tasks 13 and 14 are nascent in bodies such as network vulnerability assessment teams and computer incident response teams, which have been formed at various points in response to specific threats.

It can be assumed that military respondents were familiar at least with the concepts involved in doctrinal special operations, if not with the specific examples and force-development questions that have been discussed in relation to each.[7] Military respondents, however, made up only a small proportion of the total sample – fewer than 30 of 179. The way in which these tasks clustered according to the survey responses is therefore instructive. It gives us insights into the way in which the policy environment views special operations, independent of the way in which DND or other departments are organized to carry them out. This could be important for developing policies about new capabilities.

Factor analysis was used to group the responses to the 16 tasks listed above. Three clusters of operations emerged, illustrated in Table 8-2. Of the three categories listed, offensive action is perceived to be significantly less important than the other two.[8] Averaging the factor scores for each group, on the same 7-point scale, the mean for offensive action was 4.6, while for the other two it was 5.9.

The single most important type of special operation is helping civilians deal with a CBR attack on a major Canadian city. More than three quarters (77 per cent) of respondents assigned the highest possible importance score (7 on a 7-point scale) to this type of operation (mean 6.5). "CBR response" significantly outscores all other types of special operations. Only "NEO with consent" comes close, with 63 per cent assigning a score of 7, for a mean of 6.4.

TABLE 8-2
Types of Special Operations

Offensive Action (importance = 4.6 of 7)	*Helping Canadians Abroad (importance = 5.9 of 7)*	*Humanitarian Aid (importance = 5.9 of 7)*
14. Covert Info ops	4. NEO without help	10. DART
11. Direct action	9. Foreign hostage no help	1. CBR response
12. Large direct action	6. Foreign hostage	7. PRTs
13. Covert entry	2. NEO with consent	
16. International abduction	5. Repossession ops	
15. International arrest	8. Security assistance	
3. Domestic hostage		
5. Repossession ops		

As we move down Table 8-1 from most to least important, there is little difference between policy-makers and opinion-leaders in their perceptions of the importance of different types of operation. Overall, opinion-leaders are less enthusiastic about the importance of special operations than policy-makers. But they seem slightly more enthusiastic about CBR response, large direct actions, and international abductions. The latter two present significant legal challenges, which were not discussed with the respondents but are considered in some depth in Chapter Six.

Both policy-makers and opinion-leaders who identify CBR response as the most important feel very strongly about this. Two thirds (69 per cent) say that Canada would suffer a great deal (7 on the 7-point scale) if it were unable to carry out this type of special operation.[9] Among those identifying CBR response as the top priority, 93 per cent feel that the biggest consequence would be that innocent Canadians would suffer.[10] Other consequences identified include loss of confidence in the national government (89 per cent), loss of credibility in the international arena (64 per cent), and loss of credibility as an ally (60 per cent).

Exploratory causal modelling through regression analysis demonstrates the importance that respondents attach to helping Canadians in danger. Overall, the degree to which respondents think Canada would suffer if the top-rated special operation could not be carried out is driven by the importance of helping civilians deal with attacks and of evacuating Canadian citizens from dangerous situations. Thus, the two drivers or dominant factors are reactive rather than preventive or proactive. Respondents are more concerned about responding to evident problems than preventing problems from arising.

Although suffering of innocent Canadians is the focus for the group that placed CBR response as its highest priority, loss of confidence in the national government is the most prominent concern for the group as a whole, both policy-makers and opinion-leaders. This suggests that the central concern of caring for Canadian citizens is tempered by a healthy sense of the importance of government credibility. This insight has implications for selling special operations as part of a strategy of preventive security.

Although offensive action appears relatively less important than aid and humanitarian operations (as indicated in Table 8-2), the perceived importance of offensive action is statistically associated with strong support for special operations in general. This is not limited to core security agencies like DND and RCMP but seems to be spread across government agencies. Some of those who believe special operations capabilities are important see their offensive edge as part of their contribution. This means that DND has potential allies in other government agencies to support the development of special operations. To build these alliances, DND might strive to educate the public and other government departments on the need for offensive action as part of a preventive strategy. Alternatively, DND might avoid discussing offensive action, focusing instead on helping and humanitarian operations, which have the greatest intrinsic support in policy circles.

The more awareness there is of terrorism, the greater the acceptance of offensive operations, and the greater the support for special operations in general. Education about the risk of terrorism is therefore a logical component of a strategy to push proactive special operations. The importance of special operations is also reflected in respondents' views about media coverage. Most (77 per cent) considered it important or very important for the media to cover terrorism, and 70 per cent considered it almost as important to cover issues of national security. Enthusiasm for coverage of typical army, navy, or air force missions is considerably lower. This finding is related to a preventive education strategy. Perception of the overall importance of special operations varies directly with perceived importance of media coverage of terrorism. Incidentally, this relationship explains the aggressive "marketing" of America's Homeland Security threat assessments, as part of the national strategy of preemptive engagement. Clearly we should think carefully about such a strategy for Canada.

Respondents were asked to compare special operations to typical missions of the army, navy, or airforce, as well as to new investments in space-based technology and national missile defence.[11] The wording of thes questions was chosen to ensure a positive image for each of the conventiona missions, by linking them to recent events. For example, "Typical missions c the Canadian navy or maritime force including surveillance and interdicti of shipping to support sanctions, as in the Adriatic or the Gulf, or particip tion in US aircraft carrier task groups, as in support during the war Afghanistan." We were surprised that special operations were considered by spondents in general to be more important than these typical missions or t new investments in space-based technology and national missile defence. mean scores were consistently over 4.0 (neutral), with the highest means ev in comparisons with traditional army or land force missions and closest to n comparisons with space-based technology and national missile defence. Over-ı, this suggests greater readiness to consider new missions and probably corresponds to a general sense that our security environment is changing.

PARTNERSHIPS FOR SPECIAL OPERATIONS

Respondents place a very high value on being able to conduct special operations, with 65 per cent scoring 6 or 7 on the 7-point scale. However, there is less emphasis on being able to conduct these operations unilaterally. Only 30 per cent felt that the capacity to carry out special operations unilaterally was important or very important. This implies a broad assumption that Canada will conduct these operations in collaboration with other states more often than unilaterally. Male respondents are more likely to accept unilateral operations (4.6 compared to 3.7 factor mean for females). As women continue to make advances in the upper levels of the civil service, we would expect greater reluctance to engage in unilateral expeditionary operations.

Table 8-3 summarizes the degree of support for operations authorized under various auspices. The strongest support is for high-profile, publicly approved operations. Asked how good an idea it is to commit Canadian resources to multilateral operations with full public debate and parliamentary backing, the mean response is 6.0 (6.2 for policy-makers and 5.6 for opinion-'eaders). Operations under NATO and UN Security Council authorization are qually attractive at a slightly lower level (5.6). Unilateral operations with 'l public debate and parliamentary backing, and secret multilateral opera-ıs with bipartisan support are equal at 5.3.

Operations that might be authorized under less open or less familiar cir-tances are much less likely to be seen as a good idea. Here the onnaire departed from strictly factual scenarios and included several re intended to test the tolerance for innovation. Scenarios 7, 9 and 10 8-3 suggest a framework of international law in which states are asked e international agreements, to arrest indicted war criminals, or to regional order. The hesitation to endorse such operations may re-iarity with international law, which does not yet support such or it may reflect general reservations about the encroachment on reignty that such operations imply.[12] The final scenario suggests f state resources at the behest of corporate interests, which was ıed not to be a good idea.

ers in Table 8-3 obscure some of the details that emerge from estions. In general, respondents feel that it is a better idea to to operations relying on NATO or ABCA than on single ey are also more confident of support from the U.S. or the om the UN. This result would have been predictable if

TABLE 8-3
Support for Special Operations under Various Auspices

	How good an idea is it to commit Canadian resources to operations…	*All*	*Pol*	*Med*
1	In a multilateral operation with full public debate and Parliamentary backing	6.0	6.2	5.6
2	Under NATO	5.6	5.5	5.8
3	Authorized by a resolution of the United Nations Security Council	5.6	5.8	5.4
4	In a multilateral operation without public disclosure or parliamentary debate because of the need for secrecy in order for the special operation to be successful but with secret consultation with the Leader of the Official Opposition in Parliament	5.3	5.4	5.1
5	That are unilateral and with full public debate and parliamentary backing	5.3	5.3	5.2
6	In a multilateral operation without public disclosure or parliamentary debate because of the need for secrecy in order for the special operation to be successful	5.1	5.2	5.0
7	Authorised by the International Criminal Court	4.8	4.9	4.6
8	That are unilateral on Canadian soil and without public disclosure or parliamentary debate	4.6	4.5	4.8
9	Authorised as policing under rules, for example, of the International Atomic Energy Agency	4.4	4.4	4.6
10	Sponsored by international organizations (e.g., Organization for Security and Co-operation in Europe OSCE, or the Organization of American States, OAS)	4.4	4.4	4.3
11	That are unilateral and abroad and without public disclosure or parliamentary debate	3.5	3.4	3.7
12	Requested by or undertaken by commercial or non-governmental organisations, such as SNC Lavalin asking for military assistance to free non-Canadian civilian employees detained by a hostile group	2.8	2.6	3.0

obtained from a purely military group, particularly one familiar with the ABCA heritage. That it is obtained from a mixed group of predominantly civilian respondents suggests that our cultural preference for cooperation with the U.S., Britain, and Australia (ABCA) is still pervasive. We might surmise that this is a result of collective memory and historical experience.

This preference is clear in the choice of potential partners for special operations. Respondents were asked how important it is that Canada be compatible with various potential partners. The U.S. rates highest, with a factor mean of 6.2 and 82 per cent of respondents scoring it 6 or 7. The ABCA group scores a mean of 6.0, with 75 per cent scoring 6 or 7. The U.K. alone scores 5.8. Although the UN scores significantly lower as a potential partner, two observations are important. First, it scores significantly higher among female than among male respondents (5.7 compared to 4.4). Second, it scores significantly higher for those who place a high value on humanitarian operations.

A final observation on partners for special operations is that these responses provide more evidence of ambivalence about unilateral operations. It is a bad idea to commit resources to unilateral overseas operations without public disclosure or parliamentary debate, and it is a bad idea to commit any resources on the request of commercial or non-governmental organizations.[14] The distinction between "kinetic" and "non-kinetic" special operations is useful. Kinetic operations, involving speed and violence, should be undertaken with our traditional wartime allies, not by ourselves. Non-kinetic operations, involving patience and cooperation, should be multilateral, using international organizations and the UN. Men may tend to focus on the former, and women on the latter. Both the gender difference and the greater support for helping and humanitarian missions in general are significant factors in any attempt to educate decision-makers.

TARGETS FOR SPECIAL OPERATIONS

Questions about the legitimate uses of direct or covert action resulted in three groups of potential targets. Respondents were asked how important it was for Canada to have the capacity to take direct or covert action against targets in Canada, in the U.S., and globally. The questions further distinguished between state and non-state actors and treated commercial companies as a particular case. Direct action was defined in the question as destroying property and seizing or killing individuals. Covert action was defined as surreptitious entry and information retrieval. Although violence against property or individuals was not specified in the question on covert action, there was no significant difference between ratings for direct action and those for covert action, nor do they appear in different groups under causal modelling. This suggests that respondents do not distinguish between these two types of operation. One possible explanation is the assumption that everything will eventually be known – nothing is covert forever – and policy-makers should therefore assume that the consequences would be comparable for direct action and covert action. Another possibility is the assumption that discretion and a low profile would be necessary for a comparatively weak actor to conduct a direct operation, while any covert action is somehow sneaky and offensive.

Table 8-4 illustrates the three target categories for which mean importance scores were calculated. Within each category, the mean importance scores were virtually identical for direct and covert action. Domestic targets presented the only significant difference, with an importance score of 5.4 for direct action and only 5.0 for covert action.

TABLE 8-4
Clusters of Potential Targets for Special Operations

Domestic Targets (factor mean = 5.2)	*Global Targets (factor mean = 4.8)*	*US and Industry Targets (factor mean = 3.3)*
Groups or individuals within Canada (direct)	Non-state actors (covert)	The U.S. (direct)[15]
Groups or individuals within Canada (covert)	Other countries (direct)	Commercial companies (covert)
	Non-state actors (direct)	Commercial companies (direct)
	Other countries (covert)	

There was general agreement about the relative importance of these three types of targets, with domestic targets being most important and targets in the U.S. and industry targets being the least important. In fact, the factor mean of 3.3 suggests that on the whole the group feels it is a bad idea to attack US or industry targets (mean is less than 3.5). Again, gender plays a role, with female respondents being more likely to see some importance in a capacity to take action against both American and commercial targets. The salience of domestic targets is understandable, given the focus on protecting Canadians from terrorist attack. But this also suggests a task for public education. If the targets are more threatening once they are in Canada, would it be useful to advocate attacking threats *outside* Canada as a preventive measure? We will return to the problem of prevention and its implications for public education.

LEGISLATION AND FUNDING

The new security environment has raised questions about the legislative framework for special operations. Should legislation with respect to employment equity, access to information, or human rights be waived or adjusted for individuals, units, or formations, due to the nature of special operations? There is acceptance of the need for secrecy but surprisingly little flexibility on human rights and employment equity. A majority, 65 per cent, agreed that access to information legislation should be waived (21 per cent) or adjusted (45 per cent) for sensitive special operations. Comparing groups of respondents, opinion-leaders were more inclined to waive the legislation (29 versus 17 per cent), while policy-makers were more inclined to adjust it (48 to 38 per cent).

The majority of respondents (54 per cent) would agree to adjusting (29 per cent) or waiving (25 per cent) employment-equity provisions for special operations. Policy-makers are more favourably disposed to the status quo than are opinion-leaders (43 to 31 per cent for no change). On the other hand, most respondents say that there should be no change to legislation on human rights (62 per cent).

Respondents were asked where special operations funds should come from, and they were given the option to choose one or more sources.[16] The majority (84 per cent) agreed that the DND budget should fund special operations. However, two thirds (65 per cent) also identified central funds and almost half (47 per cent) also argued for an apportionment among appropriate departments. Thus, although special operations is generally seen as a military problem, to be funded from DND's budget, there may be growing awareness that it is of national significance and requires interdepartmental effort. Mullen's findings amongst political leaders also highlighted a desire to see adequate funding for special operations through DND's budget. Both the political leadership and the policy-maker/opinion-leader surveys may reflect a new desire to see necessary expenditures clearly allocated to security.

PREVENTION AND EDUCATION

Elite response to the importance of special operations raises an interesting question about prevention, which may be the central policy issue. We want to be able to help if a city is attacked with CBR weapons, but we are hesitant to engage in direct action overseas. We want to be able to rescue Canadians from nasty places, but we are reluctant to engage in policing the international order. We are more concerned with addressing threats inside our borders than outside them. It is not surprising that policy-makers and opinion-leaders focus on helping Canadians and on humanitarian operations. They seem to be influenced by a strong ethic to serve and protect Canadian citizens. Obviously, it would be preferable for Canadian cities not to be attacked by CBR agents and for Canadians not to need rescuing abroad. Some of the missions identified as *less* important may be considerations in preventive strategies. That they are nevertheless seen as less important is not surprising but does require some exploration.

The policy dilemma of prevention is well understood. Resources devoted to successful prevention may be difficult to justify. It may be hard to demonstrate the efficacy of preventive strategies, or the direct connection between preventive action and avoidance of negative consequences. Some preventive strategies may be associated with increased risk. For example, direct action to destroy a chemical factory overseas may increase motivation to target the countries conducting the raid.[17]

To see the policy connection with different types of special operations, it may be useful to differentiate types of preventive action.[18] Primordial prevention inhibits the emergence of threats by addressing environmental, economic, social, and behavioural conditions known to be associated with them.[19] This suggests the type of "roots and causes" development policies advocated in the wake of September 11, although there is often dispute about the direct connection between social and economic factors and the emergence of physical threats like terrorism, just as there is in discussions of some patterns of disease. Peacebuilding and development assistance are associated with this policy (tasks 7 and 8 in Table 8-1).

Primary prevention protects against threats by communal efforts and is associated with public health. The security analogue is to control coercive forces, manage weapons, and limit technology transfers. Security-sector reform, small-arms control, the missile technology-control regime, technology tracking, and enforcing international law and regulatory regimes would support primary prevention of violent threats in general, and weapons of mass destruction in particular. Tasks 8 and 13 to 16 in Table 8-1 suit this objective.

Secondary prevention in medical terms implies early detection and prompt intervention to control disease and minimize disability, through screening and preventive medicine. The security analogue involves identifying emergent threats and taking direct action to prevent the use of offensive capabilities. Direct action to destroy facilities or seize individuals might support secondary prevention of terrorism or non-state violence.

Tertiary prevention in medical terms implies softening the impact of long-term disease and disability by eliminating or reducing impairment and disability and by rehabilitating victims. The security analogue is consequence management, which includes hostage rescue, evacuations, repossession operations, and clean-up after major attacks (Tasks 1 to 6, 9, and 10 in Table 8-1).

Surveys of attitudes to health and medicine typically demonstrate that people value tertiary prevention but have limited appreciation for primary prevention. While we recognize that it is important to treat people once they have diseases, and we are prepared to expend considerable resources on doing so, it is more difficult to find support for primordial and primary prevention.

Five steps are necessary for prevention. There must be recognition of the problem, understanding of the cause, and capability to respond. Social values must support collective action, and there must be political will to follow through and take sustained action that may be expensive and take a long time to show results (although decision-makers may be held to account only at short intervals).[20] In many instances, we have insufficient knowledge of causes to make a compelling case for primordial and primary prevention.

The revolution in hygiene and sanitation in the nineteenth century demonstrated the power of prevention when we get the causes right and mobilize social values behind change. Legislation and changing attitudes to smoking and impaired driving have directly affected death rates. For similar changes to occur in the international system, the five stages necessary for prevention must be present. Our cautious elites are right to be sceptical about the preventive value of direct action to prevent terrorism and war. Those who are responsible for special operations must learn more about the causes of threats, the effects of special operations, and the means available to educate both elites and society.

NOTES

1. Thanks to Conrad Winn, Robert Laufer, and Tamara Gottlieb for their work on the survey and statistical analysis of the results. Space does not permit the full report to be presented here. This chapter provides highlights relevant to the policy questions raised by this book. Any errors in interpretation are the responsibility of the authors.
2. This is drawn from the US definition of special operations, which was included in the letter of introduction to respondents.
3. Multiple regression analysis identified key factors that were statistically related to belief in the importance of special operations and are therefore considered to be "drivers" of strong support for these capabilities.
4. Non-combattant Evacuation Operation.
5. For Provincial Reconstruction Teams (PRTs) under discussion for the expansion of the secure zone in Afghanistan, see Chapter Twelve of this volume.
6. Susan L. Marquis, *Unconventional Warfare: Rebuilding US Special Operations Forces* (Washington, DC: Brookings, 1997), 184.
7. One study that helped define the potential range of special operations tasks was directed by Brigadier General V. Kennedy, Director General of the Land Staff, "Staff Planning Directive: Special Operations Capability Working Group," 3185-1 (DLSC 3), November 2001.
8. "A mean score was computed for each factor by calculating the average of respondent scores for all the variables contained within a given factor. Under this procedure, each factor mean is on the same 7-point scale as the individual questions."
9. Question 4: "To what extent do you think Canada would suffer if it were not able to help civilians deal with a chemical, biological, or radiological attack on a major Canadian city? Please use a - point scale where 7 means suffer a great deal and 1, the opposite."
10. Question 5: "In which of the following ways would Canada suffer or be at a disadvantage?"
11. "Question 6B: "Now using a 7-point scale where 7 means that *special operations in general* are much more important and 1 the opposite, how would you rate the importance of special operations relative to (rotated)

Investment in new technology such as space-based surveillance and communications, or a National Missile Defence; Typical missions of the Canadian army or land force today including battle group contributions to peacekeeping or mid-intensity combat like the recent war in Iraq; Typical missions of the Canadian air force today including combat air patrol as in the 1991 Gulf War, or strategic bombing as in the 1999 NATO bombing campaign in Kosovo; Typical missions of the Canadian navy or maritime force today including surveillance and interdiction of shipping to support sanctions, as in the Adriatic or the Gulf, or participation in US aircraft carrier task groups as in support during the war in Afghanistan.

12. See Chapter Six of this volume.
13. ABCA, for America, Britain, Canada, Australia (and New Zealand), is the wartime alliance set up in 1940 to enhance technical and doctrinal cooperation and is one of the longest-standing and most successful means of sharing military expertise. Even without knowledge of the organization, there was a strongly positive response to cooperation with traditional allies, the U.S., the U.K., Australia, and New Zealand. That New Zealand elicits this response suggests the importance of Huntington's notion of "kin countries" in establishing special operations partnerships.
14. Commercial and non-governmental organizations were grouped because, although the former is likely to be viewed as self-interested and the latter as altruistic, both have interests distinct from the state.
15. The question was, "Is it important for Canada to have the capacity to take direct action against targets in the U.S. which threaten Canada?"
16. The question was, "Which of the following sources should provide funding for special operations?"
17. This is one of Ted Galen Carpenter's arguments against foreign entanglement in general. See, for example, Ted Galen Carpenter, "Foreign Policy Masochism: The Campaign For U.S. Intervention In Yugoslavia," Foreign Policy Briefing No. 19 (Washington, DC: The Cato Institute, 1 July 1992).
18. John M. Last, ed., *A Dictionary of Epidemiology,* fourth edition (London: Oxford University Press, 2001), 141-2.
19. Ibid.
20. John M. Last, *Public Health and Human Ecology* (Toronto: McGraw-Hill, 1997), 367.

CHAPTER NINE

NATIONAL SECURITY DECISION-MAKING

David Last and Glen Milne[1]

Special operations are undertaken for strategic purposes to deal with crises or strategic threats. A state without a decision-making process to identify and manage such threats is not positioned to use special operations effectively. As we develop thinking in Canada about the capabilities we would like to have and the ways in which we would like to use them, we have to consider how we actually make national security decisions. Possible scenarios that might require such capabilities range through various forms of physical or economic attack on Canadians. Missing or misdirected aircraft could presage a repeat of the attacks on September 11. Canadians taken hostage abroad while on national service could affect foreign and defence policy. Events on Canada's vulnerable high-density border crossings with the U.S. could have sudden and direct repercussions affecting millions of Canadians. A gradual increase in targetted computer attacks on Canada's financial infrastructure could have dire economic consequences. Even afflictions like mad cow disease (bovine spongiform encephalopathy, BSE) or severe acute respiratory syndrome (SARS) might derive from hostile actions that require more than a purely defensive response.

This chapter describes the policy environment within which national security decisions are made, then considers the pattern of decision-making for optional foreign ventures, evolving threats, and immediate crises. It concludes with recommendations about how to ensure that a national plan for special operations might accord with characteristic Canadian approaches to making decisions on national security.[2]

Asymmetric threats include, but are not limited to, terrorism, weapons of mass destruction, information warfare, and direct attacks on unprotected Canadians or Canadian interests.[3] The responses on which we are focused involve "special operations". These include the unconventional employment of conventional forces (e.g., direct action by specially prepared infantry units to destroy a weapons facility) employment of specially selected and trained forces such as JTF 2, network vulnerability assessment teams (NVAT), or interdepartmental task forces, and any novel combination of forces and capabilities to meet new threats. Even the employment of conventional capabilities can be encompassed in the phrase "special operations" when a national command authority directs their use for strategic purposes. The National Counter Terrorism Plan (NCTP), an interdepartmental plan for response to terrorist incidents, is an example of the sort of document that might result from a review of decision-making for special operations.

THE POLICY MARKETPLACE

Responsibilities for national security decision-making in Canada are not precisely defined. The recent Senate Committee Report on Issues of Maritime Security, for example, pointed to the confusing variety of potential decision-making processes as a deficiency for both accountability and efficacy.[4] But this is a longstanding feature of Canada's political environment for decision-making in general. Albert Legault's report to the Prime Minister in 1997 rejected the bureaucratization of security outside political control.[5] Jane Boulden's work at Queen's University reinforced this, suggesting dubious benefits for expanded costs.[6] Even military officers examining the problem have argued against a national security council, which would violate Canadian principles of parliamentary democracy and accountability.[7]

Security studies sometimes overlook the reality that Canada's survival still depends on an accommodation of English and French Canadian realities and increasingly diverse regional interests. The parliamentary system, Cabinet structure, patronage, bilingual bureaucracy, and other aspects of the "policy marketplace" help to maintain the balance, and are at the heart of national security, whether or not they are articulated in policy. The events of September 11 did not change Canadian politics but did generate some thought about continuous attention to security problems. The attacks were cited in calls for a national command council,[8] and Canada's response to changes in the U.S. directly affected the the Privy Council Office (PCO). To understand these changes, we need to describe the federal policy-making environment.

The policy marketplace has concentric rings of decision-making that surround the final authority – that is, the Prime Minister and Cabinet. Decision-making power and influence increase as we move towards the centre, but important powers and responsiblities are vested in the outer rings, beginning with the central agencies and extending to departments, oversight bodies such as the Privacy and Information Commissioners, and then to the public, the media, and interest groups, which press the system from the outer ring. The whole network of activity illustrated in Figure 9-1 constitutes the policy marketplace.[9]

FIGURE 9-1
The Policy Marketplace

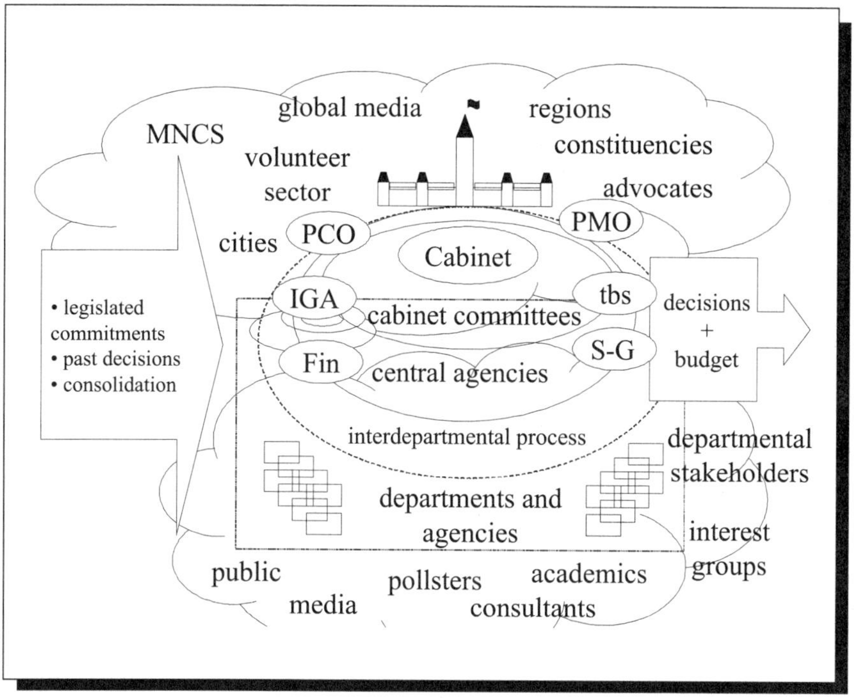

Source: Glen Milne, *Making Policy* (2004).

The theory of parliamentary democracy is that Cabinet as a whole exercises control over decision-making, but the fact is that prolonged prime ministerial mandates, combined with the powers of appointment, have tended to concentrate power in the hands of the Prime Minister. He appoints Cabinet ministers and senior civil servants, sets the agenda for Cabinet, structures its committees, summarizes its conclusions, and divides administrative responsibilities. From Borden (1918) to Trudeau (1965), Cabinet averaged 19 ministers but then increased steadily to a total of 40 under Mulroney. As both Cabinet and its responsibilities grew, Trudeau introduced the Priorities and Planning Committee of senior ministers to direct the work of other Cabinet Committees and ministers. This was accompanied by the growth of the Prime Minister's Office (PMO), which increased the Prime Minister's access to information and his capacity to channel it to manage his Cabinet colleagues.[10] The growing importance of intergovernmental decision-making, special expertise, international arrangements, and knowledge management under the constraint of time all reinforce the central role of the Prime Minister.[11]

Moving outwards to the government departments, we can use a number of different lists to identify the departments that have an interest in national security. The shortest list would include those involved in decisions about a foreign military venture, such as the decisions concerning Iraq and Afghanistan in 2003. This was limited to Foreign Affairs, Defence, Solicitor General, and Finance. The Interdepartmental Policy Advisory Group (IPAG) to address domestic terrorism includes all these except Finance and adds Justice and Transport. Senator Kenny's report includes all these and adds Health and Immigration.[12] The National Operations Centre (NOC) is the venue where the representatives of the key departments would come together to support national decision-making. Departments that might find a seat at the table there would depend on the nature of the crisis. Federal Emergency leglislation lists 16 departments with specific responsibilities, including all those mentioned above plus Industry Canada, the Food Inspection Agency, Agriculture and Agrifood, Natural Resources, the Nuclear Safety Commission, and so on. The loose connections between these departments, the proliferation of "operations centres", and the problem of interdepartmental coordination were never satisfactorily resolved by the Chrétien government.[13] Nevertheless, Table 9-1 gives a sense of the size of the new national security community and the kinds of expertise involved in addressing asymmetric threats.

TABLE 9-1
Departments Involved in Security

Department	*PCO Iraq Group*	*IPAG (NCTP)*	*Kenny List*	*NOC in Ottawa*	*Federal Emergency Legislation*
Foreign Affairs	•	•	•	•	•
Defence	•	•	•	•	•
Solicitor General	•	•	•	•	•
Health			•	•	•
Transport		•		•	•
Finance	•		•		•
Justice		•	•		•
Immigration			•		•
OCIPEP				•	•
Environment					•
Fisheries & Oceans					•
Nuclear Safety Commission					•
Natural Resources					•
Agriculture and Agrifood					•
Food Inspection Agency					•
Industry Canada					•

Prime Minister Chrétien concentrated decision-making power in the hands of the executive and his key advisors in the PMO. In 1993, Chrétien reduced Cabinet to 23 Ministers and limited it to four committees: Economic Development, Social Development, Treasury Board, and Regulations. With work divided largely between the first two committees, ministers relied heavily on the PMO and PCO for continuity and coordination. By 1999, decisions about security were not being made in Cabinet, but by Chrétien and close advisors like Jean Carle and Jean Pelletier.[14] The milestones for the Chrétien governments' decision-making on national security issues might be summarized as "passenger" status on the UN operations in the Balkans, Horn of Africa, and Rwanda, followed by Operation Assurance in 1996 – the abortive attempt to lead an international humanitarian operation to the Congo. Kosovo operations from 1997 to 1999, including the Kosovo Verification Mission and the NATO bombing campaign, were followed by the use of Cold War machinery plus improvization to respond to the September 11 events. Finally the government decided to abandon the American-led Operation Enduring Freedom (OEF) in Afghanistan in favour of the UN-approved and NATO-led International Security Assistance Force (ISAF) in Kabul, and to commit to Afghanistan rather than Iraq in 2002-2003.[15]

Some have ascribed these milestones to the iron grip of the Prime Minister.[16] Both historian Michael Hennessy's work and the Auditor General's review of Operation Assurance suggest that official structures were bypassed in the effort to respond to the PMO.[17] But the "marketplace" within which security decisions were made can be described in some detail. The response to the 2003 Iraq war was a prelude to a new and more structured approach to security decision-making. The need for daily advice on the progress of the war in Iraq from March to September 2003 resulted in a *de facto* Committee of Affected Deputy Ministers, which seems to have functioned much as a National Security Council might but without the permanence or bureaucratic interests that might be vested in a powerful permanent body. We describe it here as the final evolution of security structures under Chrétien, and the starting point for the Martin government.

The Secretary of the Foreign and Defence Committee of the PCO, a career foreign-service officer, chaired the Committee of Affected Deputy Ministers. It met daily, or as required by circumstances, supported by analysts provided by Defence and Foreign Affairs. Deputy Ministers from affected departments participated – typically Foreign Affairs, Defence, Solicitor General, and Finance. Canada's senior civil servant, the Clerk of the Privy Council, served to link the committee directly to Prime Minister Chrétien, while the Deputy Clerk of the Privy Council typically worked with the Deputy Prime Minister, John Manley, who was assigned responsibility for homeland security issues. There were thus two direct links with the United States on security issues. The Chair of the Foreign and Defence Committee of the PCO dealt directly with the US National Security Advisor, Condoleeza Rice, and the Deputy Prime Minister dealt directly with the Secretary for Homeland Security, Tom Ridge. These links reinforced the parallel Canadian system, but

FIGURE 9-2
PCO/PMO Decision Support

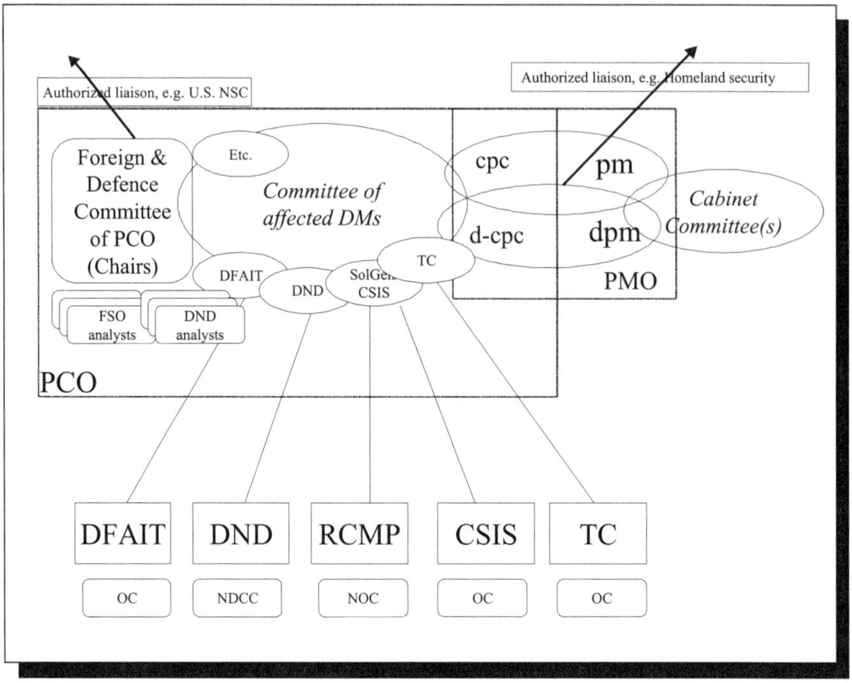

without involving Cabinet as a body. Under Chrétien, Cabinet was involved only to the extent that the Prime Minister or Deputy Prime Minister chose to involve individual ministers. The Committee of Affected Deputy Ministers provided a continuous review of security issues and advised the Prime Minister and Deputy Prime Minister as executives, rather than advising Cabinet as a body.

But while this worked well for policy questions like involvement in Afghanistan and the Iraq war, it was narrowly focused on traditional foreign and defence issues and did not help with a series of human and economic disasters that hit Canada in 2003. SARS, BSE, power failure, hurricane, and forest fires evoked little evidence of coherent federal response or national leadership. In November 2003, as the Martin team was preparing the transition, these crises figured prominently in thinking about how best to structure the cabinet and its supporting central agencies and government departments.

Prime Minister Paul Martin took a more structured approach to decision-making. His leadership manifesto emphasized the need to mobilize the national will to achieve public purposes.[18] Ensuring Canada's place in the world was one of four goals Martin set. A national security policy would be central to this:

> Canada must be prepared to act in our national self-interest and advance [with the U.S.] the mutual objective of a safe and secure North America...A new national security policy would direct and co-ordinate military and non-military efforts. It would include internal security, intelligence, policing, the coast guard, customs and emergency preparedness, all focused on protecting our country against terrorist threats that emanate from beyond our shores, or within our borders...[19]

The new cabinet structure announced 12 December 2004 resurrected the Priorities and Planning Committee introduced by Trudeau to guide the executive agenda. It was a large body – 16 ministers constitute almost half the cabinet. The Operations Committee, responsible for day-to-day management, was more manageable with just six members. Chaired by the Deputy Prime Minister and including the ministers of Transport, Finance, Health, Treasury Board, and Public Works, this was the inner circle that might be expected to formulate federal response to the crises that had afflicted Canada in 2003. The leadership for coordinating that response, however, would have come from the Cabinet Committee on Security, Public Health, and Emergency Preparedness (SPHEP), which "Manages national security and intelligence issues and activities, and ensures co-ordination of the federal response to all emergencies, including natural disasters, public health, and security."[20]

Nine of the eleven ministers in SPHEP had security-related portfolios: Foreign Affairs, Coast Guard, Transport, Defence, Justice, Immigration, Civil Preparedness, and Public Health. Note, however, that security is defined in broad terms to include both the sort of threats without aggressors that ravaged the Canadian economy in 2003 and "asymmetric threats" such as illegal immigration, weapons of mass destruction, terrorism, and cyber attacks.[21] Reorganizing government departments to respond to this new, more eclectic vision of security created tensions at the deputy minister level. Creating a new department for Public Safety and Emergency Preparedness, built around the Solicitor General's Department but incorporating the Office of Critical Infrastructure Protection and Emergency Preparedness (OCIPEP), was one of Martin's first challenges to the bureaucrats.[22]

Judging from the proportion of security-related portfolios within each of Martin's Cabinet committees, SPHEP might be the most closely related to security decisions, both at home and abroad.[23] It is followed by the Committee on Canada-U.S. Affairs, with the mandate to ensure an integrated, government-wide approach to Canada-U.S. relations. This included Ministers for Transport, Defence, Justice, and Immigration.[24]

Paul Martin's 12 December release described new structures in the PMO and PCO that would certainly have affected decision-making on security issues. The Cabinet Committee for Canada-U.S. affairs would be supported by a new Canada-U.S. secretariat in the PCO, and a new Aboriginal Affairs Secretariat would support the Cabinet Committee on Aboriginal Affairs, which the PM intended to chair himself. The appointment of National Security Advisor Rob Wright, formerly a key player on the Foreign and Defence Secretariat of the PCO, began to consolidate a holistic view of national security, which was signalled with the 2002 budget allocation of security funds to CSIS, RCMP, and Transport, rather than to Defence. The April 2004 National Security Policy articulated a focus on human security and homeland security, with international security added as an afterthought.[25] Taken together, the changes undertaken by the Martin team shift the decision-making focus from expeditionary military forces supporting collective security through the UN and NATO to multi-agency homeland security efforts, in line with American fears.

INTELLIGENCE SUPPORT FOR DECISION-MAKING

As we bridge the interdepartmental space surrounding central agencies and approach departmental stovepipes for managing information and supporting decision-making on national security issues, we encounter a variety of structures and processes that are tailored to specific tasks. Security and intelligence committees form a well-articulated network that cascades downwards from Cabinet to the director level within departments. Intelligence architecture is a sensitive subject, and the following description is illustrative only.

At least ten separate committees address various aspects of security and intelligence at four distinct levels, as shown in Table 9-2. At the ministerial level, the Ministers' Meeting on Security and Intelligence (MMSI) is chaired by the Prime Minister, and the Ad Hoc Committee on Public Security and Anti-Terrorism (PSAT) is chaired by the Deputy Prime Minister. Support for both is provided by the Intelligence Advisory Secretariat of the PCO, with the Clerk of the Privy Council supporting the MMSI and the Associate Clerk supporting the PSAT. By default, new matters are addressed by the MMSI, while the PSAT deals with established areas in Canadian-American security relations. The labels "primary", "senior", "secondary", and "junior" as used in the table are descriptive, rather than official.

Mirror committees at the levels of Deputy Minister (DM) and Assistant Deputy Minister (ADM) support and feed these ministerial committees. The Interdepartmental Committee on Security and Intelligence (ICSI), includes Deputy Minister-level representatives of Foreign Affairs, Defence, Public Safety, the Communications Security Establishment, CSIS, the RCMP, and Justice and is chaired by the Security and Intelligence (S&I) Coordinator of the Privy Council Office. It is also important that the specific appointees attending any given meeting are not predictable to an outsider. The third body at DM level is the DM Mirror Committee to the PSAT, which is also chaired by the Security and Intelligence Coordinator, providing built-in coordination among the three committees at DM level.

The pattern of secretarial co-ordination is continued to the ADM- and Director-level committees. The Assistant Secretary, Security and Intelligence, who attends DM-level committee meetings, chairs the Intelligence Policy Group (IPG) at the ADM level. The Public Safety Committee is chaired by the Senior Assistant Deputy Solicitor General, who in practice may attend the DM Mirror PSAT. The Director General National Security of the Solicitor General's Department chairs the Interdepartmental Policy Advisory Group (IPAG), which is empowered under the National Counter-Terrorism Plan. At the Director level, the Section 16 Committee (S16) is chaired by the Assistant Secretary, Security and Intelligence, and the Intelligence Assessment Committee is chaired by the Assistant Secretary of the Intelligence Advisory Secretariat.

TABLE 9-2
Intelligence and Security Committees

<table>
<tr><th>Level</th><th colspan="2">Primary (Senior)</th><th colspan="2">Secondary (Junior)</th></tr>
<tr><td>Ministerial</td><td colspan="2">MMSI
(Chair: Prime Minister)</td><td colspan="2">PSAT
(Chair: Deputy Prime Minister)</td></tr>
<tr><td>DM</td><td>ICSI
(Chair: Clerk)</td><td>Ex-ICSI
(Chair: S&I Coord)</td><td colspan="2">DM Mirror PSAT
(Chair: S&I Coord)</td></tr>
<tr><td>ADM</td><td colspan="2">IPG
(Chair: Asst Sec S&I)</td><td>PSC
(Chair: Sr ADSG, SolGen)</td><td>IPAG
(Chair: DG National Security, SolGen)</td></tr>
<tr><td>Director</td><td colspan="2">S16
(Chair: Asst Sec S&I)</td><td colspan="2">IAC
(Asst Sec IAS)</td></tr>
</table>

While it might appear that chairs, membership, and secretarial responsibilities leave some room for disconnects between the two columns illustrated in Table 9-2, the reality is that this is a very small community, and individual members may attend meetings from time to time in different committees. Nor is the committee structure a clear guide to decision-making. The mandate of each committee is sufficiently vague to permit considerable latitude, and specific decisions may be made "off-line" and brought before committees for information or action. This reflects both the culture of the intelligence community and the decision-marketplace of the senior levels of the Ottawa bureaucracy. For these reasons, without knowledge of personalities, knowledge of structures and committee names is almost meaningless. By virtue of their work with Cabinet, these structures are also well-protected from access-to-information requests, which allows their members considerable latitude.

DECISION-MAKING FOR OPTIONAL FOREIGN VENTURES

There are several scenarios in which a conscious decision to deploy national assets could lead to the use of lethal force. Rescuing Canadian citizens, seizing persons indicted for war crimes, covert inspection of alleged weapons facilities, or destruction of non-state weapons or research facilities are examples of optional foreign ventures. The scenario might evolve over days, weeks, or months and would be accompanied by contingency planning that may involve multiple departments and agencies.

Any decision would be made by the Prime Minister, with supporting contributions from the decision-making "marketplace" illustrated in Figures 9-1 and 9-2. There are several examples over the last decade of JSAT planning groups that have involved more than one department. Planning evacuation of Canadian citizens from a war-affected country has been led on at least one occasion by DFAIT, with planning involvement by the RCMP, and CF (JTF 2). In this case, the plan was taken to PCO with DM approval by a senior Foreign Officer responsible for consular affairs, and further planning guidance was provided by the Foreign and Defence Committee of the PCO. The Chair of the Foreign and Defence Committee of the PCO did not seek political approval of the plan, on the assumption that there would be sufficient warning to obtain approval if the plan needed to be executed and that no approval in advance of the circumstances calling for evacuation would be forthcoming in any case. (This assessment was realistic in the Chrétien era but does raise the risk of surprises for the staff at the point of execution.) Of particular concern to planners was the potential for restrictive rules of engagement that might increase the risk to a rescuing force.

Peace-support operations, or operations mandated by an international organization, constitute a discretionary use of Canadian defence assets usually accompanied by diplomatic (DFAIT) and often development (CIDA) efforts. The structures and processes involved are therefore instructive as to the ways in which discretionary deployment of special operations resources might be handled for a variety of other purposes. Key institutions are the Prime Minister and Cabinet, Parliament and its defence-related committees (the Standing Committee on National Defence and Veterans' Affairs, SCONDVA, and the Senate Committee on National Defence and Security Affairs, SCONDSA), the PCO, and the Departments of Foreign Affairs and National Defence. International organizations (e.g., UN, NATO, OSCE), other government departments and agencies (e.g., CSIS, RCMP, CIC) and even non-governmental or commercial organizations with local knowledge might provide useful input to the decision-making process.[26]

Requests may be initiated by organizations to which Canada belongs, or bilaterally by allies. They may specify certain types of assistance. Requests for Canada to participate in sanctions or embargoes under the UN system are assessed by DFAIT. Requests for humanitarian aid are managed by CIDA. Requests for police personnel or training are evaluated by the RCMP, and DND would advise on requests for military personnel or equipment. Requests can come in a variety of forms and through many different channels, some less formal than others. For example, the request for Canadian involvement in the Congo in 1996 involved an attaché at an embassy in Ottawa.

The actual decision-making process is collegial and personal, frequently involving senior or mid-ranking officials of different departments who know each other personally and have responded to similar situations in the recent past. The Peacekeeping Section of the Regional Security and Peacekeeping Division in Foreign Affairs meets with the DND's Director of Peacekeeping Policy at least two or three times a week. A typical focus for these meetings is capabilities: What capabilities are available? What might be appropriate in responding to a particular request? What might Canada offer, and how might that affect other commitments?

One sequence of decision-making events, which could take as long as several weeks or only a few hours, might entail an external request, internal assessment (with or without strategic reconnaissance), Cabinet decision (with or without formal consultation with Parliament), and directed action. This is illustrated below, and described in the following paragraph.

FIGURE 9-3
Launching an Operation

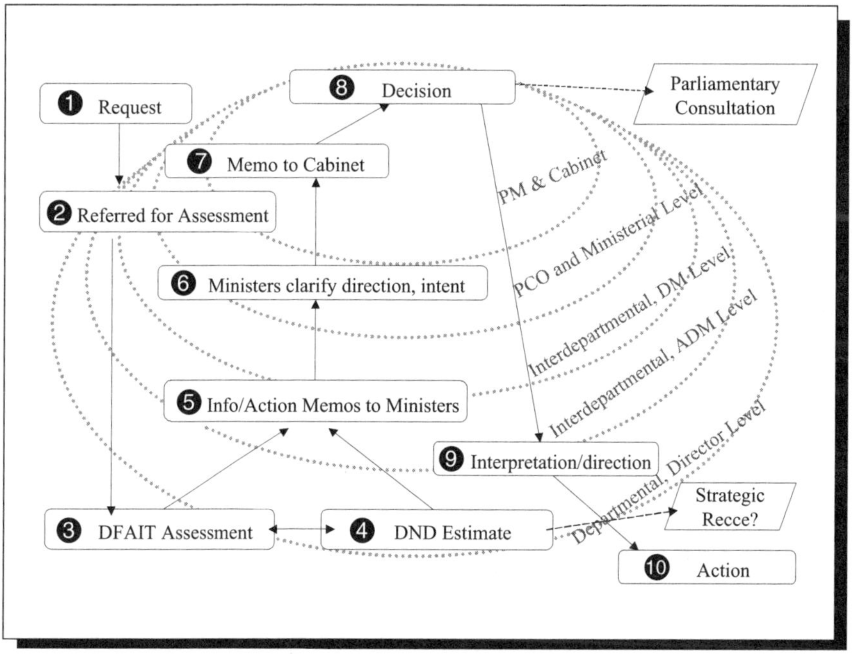

Canada's ambassador at the United Nations might have a conversation with the Prime Minister, indicating a new request for Canadian assistance. Through the PCO, the DM at Foreign Affairs and a senior officer of the CF might be consulted on what the Canadian role might be. This initial conversation might constitute the DFAIT assessment, provided to DND along with the details of the request in order to generate an appreciation of the situation and a tentative plan. A strategic reconnaissance might be launched (led by DND but possibly including other interested agencies, depending on the potential contribution). Working at staff level (that is, below Director level), staff of DND and DFAIT would simultaneously prepare information memoranda for their respective ministers, consulting with PCO and other agencies as required while doing so. These information memoranda would probably be followed by action memoranda, recommending courses of action for each Minister. After the Ministers have agreed, a Memorandum to Cabinet (MC) would be prepared, embodying the Chief of Defence Staff's advice and incorporating political considerations. This may become the basis for parliamentary consultations, which might involve statements and questions in the House, *in camera* committee meetings, or private consultations with individual Members. Time permitting, "sounding out" of MPs and their staff is a common method of consultation that is informal, non-committal, and helpful in building political consensus. This process may appear exclusive, but it is seldom haphazard. One participant explained: "The system is inherently informal and relies as much on relationships as anything else."[27]

DECISION-MAKING FOR EVOLVING THREATS

Some threats might evolve over a period of weeks or months while it becomes evident that a national response is obligatory. For example, we discussed with some officials the possibility that a number of departments or agencies might become aware of systematic attacks on information technology, whose cumulative effect was beginning to damage government operations and perhaps the national economy. OCIPEP, the National Research Council, Industry Canada (Telecommunications), the Bank of Canada, and other agencies might have contributed to this gradual awareness. Individual Deputy Ministers might bring the matter to weekly meetings with the Clerk of the Privy Council. The Clerk might designate a lead DM or involve a group of affected DMs in preparing reports and assessments. A DM might have been designated to brief Cabinet or its Planning and Priorities Committee.

Questions from the DMs to their departments would be both generic and unique to departmental mandates, and they would filter rapidly downwards through the department. During this process, some Directors General would be identified as being closer to the problem than others and thus as having greater understanding and capacity to respond. A Task Force or Interdepartmental Committee might put a limited number of people onto the problem full-time. People might be seconded from departments and agencies, or new people engaged, according to the expertise demanded. Cabinet might task Treasury Board to find emergency funds, or the Finance Department might divide the bill among departmental budgets. Alternatively, Cabinet might allocate funds from a reserve.

If the national response were strictly domestic, reactive, and defensive, then the multiple decision-points illustrated in the following section in Figure 9-4 might be involved. If it emerged that national expeditionary action were warranted, a department (probably National Defence) would be tasked to prepare options. The planning process described above and the steps illustrated in Figure 9-3 for launching an operation might be expected to be in evidence, but there would be no guarantee that Cabinet would adopt any of the courses of action prepared.

DECISION-MAKING FOR IMMEDIATE CRISES

Over the last decade, a decision about an immediate crisis might have evolved over a period of hours to days and would probably have involved one core group of advisors close to the top and centre of the decision-making structure in Ottawa. The exact appointments could only be guessed in advance, but insiders would have a good idea about the individuals most likely to be involved.

Low-level security, such as a coast guard vessel, municipal police force, or airport security might have provided the first warning of an imminent threat or ongoing incident. The evident gravity of the situation might have caused rapid referral of the incident to the PCO. Potential loss of life, international visibility, and national repercussions are some of the factors that might have accelerated consideration by the PCO. Natural friction in the passage of information about an incident has typically included immediate response at lower levels and unwillingness to accept responsibility for a crisis at higher levels. National media images may have filled in for passage of information through ponderous official channels, cutting directly to the top.

Once alerted, the PCO might be expected to consider options with the involvement of hastily assembled Deputy Ministers. The Clerk, Deputy Clerk, or a senior Parliamentary Secretary might have assumed a coordinating role.[28] Foreign Affairs would be involved in opening lines of communication to countries or organizations in a position to provide information or support. The Clerk of the Privy Council would probably have taken a brief for decision to the Prime Minister, who would have made a decision, either alone or with the aid of a hastily assembled Cabinet committee. The Deputy Clerk of the Privy Council, working with the Deputy Prime Minister, might have been involved in subsequent management of the situation and follow-up. Damage control, follow-up, and remedial action might have been delegated to a committee of affected Deputies, which would prepare decision briefs for Cabinet.

While any international deployment requires a decision at the top and centre of the policy process, response to emergencies is designed to emanate from the lowest level possible, including "first responders" (fire, police, ambulance, and other emergency measures) at municipal level. Given the disruption to national communications that might be expected to follow a serious national emergency, this makes sense. However, it is generally accepted that plans should be based on existing organizations and procedures rather than new procedures cobbled together in a crisis. In practice this has meant that there is no coherent national strategy for disaster response and very little capacity exists to coordinate local responses at a national level.

Responsibilities for disaster preparedness have hitherto been dispersed among all those ministers whose own portfolios include responsibility for preparedness. National emergency arrangements include the National Support Plan, the National Earthquake Support Plan, the National Counter-Terrorism Plan, the Federal Nuclear Emergency Plan, and the emergency plans for each federal government department. Bilateral plans with the U.S. date back to the "Agreement on Co-Operation in Comprehensive Civil Emergency Planning and Management", signed in April 1986. Since September 11, it has been extended from cooperation with the US Federal Emergency Management Authority (FEMA) to include the Department of Homeland Security and the Bi-National Planning Group.[29]

Of particular interest in this context are OCIPEP's Counter-Terrorism Consequence Management Arrangements (CTCMA). The province in which a terrorist event occurs has primary responsibility for managing its consequences. The provincial government assumes a lead role and in turn looks to the federal government for assistance; the Consequence Management Arrangements would be invoked only if local resources are overwhelmed. There are two exceptions: Health Canada takes the lead for management of pandemic or emerging contagious diseases and for response to the release of ionizing radiation, and OCIPEP would establish the National Support Centre (NSC) and provide support for five groups of experts, shown in descending order in Table 9-3.

Since consequence management is bottom-up and largely reactive, we could expect most decisions to rise no higher than the first of these groups, which is designated a national decision-making body.[30] At least sixteen different government departments might provide expertise under emergency legislation. The range of other places in which decisions might be made is a tribute to flexible response. Figure 9-4 illustrates a simplified response to an event requiring consequence management. It is easy to envision multiple decision-centres, with an incomplete network of liaison and communications.

An event would involve first responders (fire, police, ambulance, and hospitals) from the local community. Canadian Forces units might be assigned from the Land Force Area Headquarters responsible for the area under attack. Information would be expected to flow from the site of the event to the National Defence Command Centre and to the Canadian Forces Liaison Officer at the NSC. Local mayors and officials and local Emergency Measures officials would also be taking decisions and providing information through provincial Emergency Measures liaison to the NSC. Above the Executive

TABLE 9-3
Consequence Management Support

Executive Group (EG)	Senior representatives from institutions having relevant expertise; provides policy review, guidance, strategic assessment, decision-making related to the national effort
Coordination and Operations Group (COG)	Under the direction of the EG, includes officials involved in the response; coordinates national response to requests for assistance; advises the EG
Public Affairs Group (PAG)	Public information representatives from organizations involved; serves as the central federal public information coordination point for distribution to media and public
Technical Advisory Group (TAG)	Scientific and technical advice, guidance and information for the NSC
Government Emergency Operations Coordination Centre (GEOCC)	Located at OCIPEP headquarters; the main source of communications and technical support to the NSC

FIGURE 9-4
Response Structure for Consequence Management

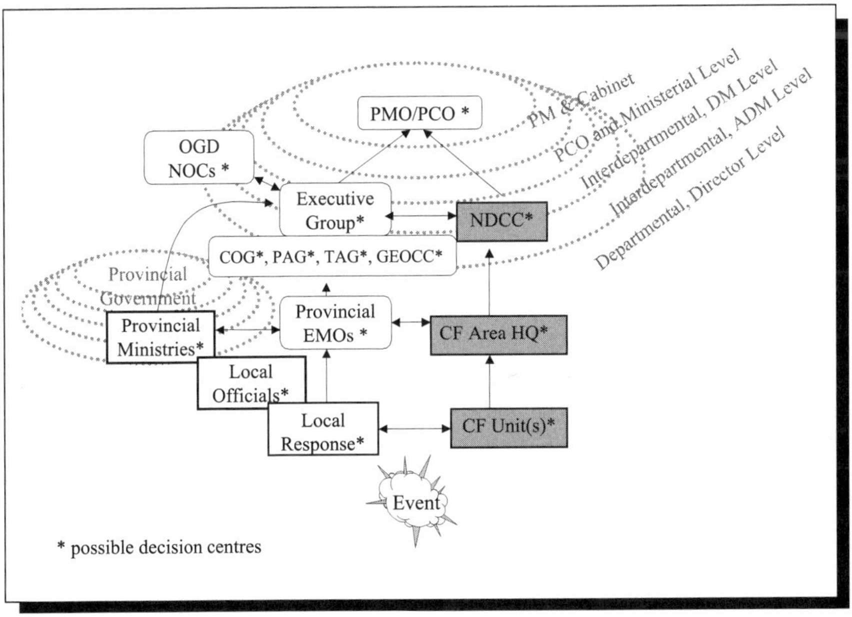

Source: Adapted from OCIPEP Briefing, 18 September 2003.

Group, it is easy to imagine a Committee of Affected Deputies advising Cabinet (as in Figure 9-2), but it is likely that they would be no better informed than the senior officials in the Executive Group – perhaps less so. However, given a choice of locations, Deputy Ministers are likely to choose the PCO venue over the OCIPEP venue, on the basis that it is likely to be closer to the political decision-makers.

DEVELOPING DECISION-MAKING FOR SPECIAL OPERATIONS

The decision-making environment described above is both stable and transient. The broad outline of concentric rings of power, cascading committees, and departmental expertise surrounding the ultimate authority of Prime Minister and Cabinet has been remarkably stable. The processes for launching overseas operations and responding to domestic crises have been stable and serviceable over the life of several governments, although they clearly have *ad hoc* elements and do not always follow the desired sequence. On the other hand, the make-up of individual committees, the personalities involved in key decisions, and the allocation of responsibility for specific portfolios are transient and can change as rapidly within an administration as with an election. This brings us to some important deductions for the broader special-operations community.

The first deduction is that the special-operations community must be bigger and perhaps more amorphous than it has been in the past. A national counter-terrorist unit like JTF 2 is not in a position to fulfil all the expectations of political leaders for non-conventional capabilities to address national security threats. Staff officers involved in planning special operations will need to be acquainted with the departments listed in Table 9-1, the expertise available, and the circumstances that might result in deployment of special capabilities. Scenario-based planning with other government departments can be a basis for developing mutual understanding and for making political leaders aware of the capabilities that might be useful in foreseeable or imaginable circumstances.

The second deduction is that special operations will be marginalized and ineffective if its staff are confined within a single department. It is in central agencies like the PCO and PMO that security information is managed and national security decisions made. If special operations are to be used as a strategic tool, they must be connected to this level of decision-making. If this cannot be done formally, it might be done with informal connections. In building networks and connections to support special operations, the intelligence community is important, particularly wherever it intersects with multiple departments and agencies, as in the committee structure. Participating in intelligence committees might be a vital interest for senior leaders and staff engaged in special operations.

The third deduction is that the special-operations community needs insider intelligence about who the players are and how the national security game is being played. The decision-making environmet is fluid, and detailed knowledge of both structures and personalities is necessary for anyone who expects to shape that environment or to be ready for the demands of one that is changing. This kind of knowledge is not gained easily or quickly. It must be cultivated gradually, with confidence reinforced over time.

Canada's capacity to understand threats and security accurately, and to take timely decisions in the national interest, may be our most important strategic asset. Since Trudeau's government, a succession of Prime Ministers from Québec have honed bureaucratic and political responses to the central problem of keeping the country together. But America's reaction to September 11 has highlighted new risks – Canada-U.S. relations, internal security, and the global war on terror. Our most important strategic asset might be renewed by the efforts to articulate a National Security Policy and restructure decision-making, but it will take more than decisions to achieve security. Canada will need both special and conventional capabilities that are responsive to decision-makers.

NOTES

1. The authors are grateful for the assistance of numerous collaborators who gave generously of their time and knowledge. Any misinterpretation is ours alone.
2. This is an abbreviated version of a more detailed discussion paper submitted to the Asymmetrical Threat Working Group of the Department of National Defence, March 2004.
3. "...asymmetric threat is a term used to describe attempts to circumvent or undermine an opponent's strengths while exploiting his weaknesses, using methods that differ significantly from the opponent's usual mode of operations..." This definition, taken from US DoD Joint Staff, was endorsed by Canada's Armed Forces Council (AFC) 18 April 2000.
4. Senator Colin Kenny, *et al., Canada's Coastlines: The Longest Under-Defended Borders in the World,* Standing Senate Committee on National Security and Defence (Ottawa: Government of Canada, October 2003), 2.
5. Albert Legault, "Bringing the Canadian Armed Forces into the Twenty-First Century," paper submitted to the Prime Minister, March 1997.
6. Jane Boulden, *A National Security Council for Canada?*, Claxton Papers No. 2, (Kingston: Queen's University School of Policy Studies, 2000).
7. Colonel R. M. Williams, "A Measure of Realism: Why Canada does not need a National Security Council," Canadian Forces College, National Securities Studies Course 3, April 2001.
8. Colonel C. S. Sullivan, "Responding To Crises: A National Command Council for Canada's Political Leadership," Canadian Forces College, National Security Studies Course 5, 2003.

9. Glen Milne, *Making Policy: A Guide to the Federal Government's Policy Processes,* May 2004 Edition (Ottawa: Glen Milne, 2004). Available from ggdm@istar.ca
10. George Perlin, *Canadian Politics, Volume 2: Canadian Democracy in Critical Perspective* (Toronto: Interactive Productions, 2001), Chapter 1, 13, note on Cabinet committees.
11. Ibid., 18, note on concentration of power.
12. Kenny, *Canada's Coastlines.*
13. Ibid., 117
14. Donald J. Savoie, *Governing from the Centre: The Concentration of Power in Canadian Politics* (Toronto: University of Toronto Press, 1999), 260, and 362 on Cabinet in general. Our interviews in PCO and PMO in November 2003 support Savoie's conclusion with respect to security decisions.
15. The period 1989 to 2003 is characterized as one of "stability operations" by Douglas L. Bland and Sean M. Maloney, *Campaigns for International Security: Canada's Defence Policy at the Turn of the Century* (Montreal and Kingston: McGill-Queen's University Press, 2004), 3-5.
16. Bruce Wallace, "For the Love of Power: Is Jean Chrétien a closet autocrat?" in *Canadian Politics*, fifth edition, eds. Gregory S. Mahler and Roman R. March (Guildford, CT: Dushkin/McGraw-Hill, 2000), 47-51.
17. Michael A. Hennessy, "Planning a Multi-national Force for Rwanda-Zaire," *Canadian Military Journal*, Spring 2001, 11-20. Comments by those involved in the Auditor General's review of operations, made at the Peacekeeping Intelligence Conference, Ottawa, 5 December 2003, substantiate the criticism.
18. Paul Martin, *Making History – the Politics of Achievement,* Ottawa, 15 November 2003.
19. Martin, *Making History,* 9
20. Office of the Prime Minister, *Release: Prime Minister Martin Announces New Government Will Be Guided by a New Approach,* Ottawa, 12 December 2003.
21. Government of Canada, *Securing an Open Society: Canada's National Security Policy* (Ottawa: Privy Council Office, April 2004).
22. Interviews, Ottawa, 29 January 2004.
23. This criterion has limitations. According to interviews with staff at PCO and Parliament, regional representation and personality, among many other factors, are at least as important as portfolio in selecting members of Cabinet committees. Interviews, Ottawa, January 2004.
24. It is too early to define the work of these committees; however, trade will probably dominate the agenda for the Canada-U.S. Committee, with security relations, ballistic missile defence, and Canada's support to the War on Terror also getting some attention from it. Cabinet Committees on Global Affairs and Domestic Affairs might also evolve to address security issues.

25. Interviews, Ottawa, March 2004.
26. This section draws on interviews with staff at Foreign Affairs Canada and briefing notes provided by Foreign Affairs Canada.
27. Interview conducted by Glen Milne, Foreign Affairs Canada, 15 December 2003.
28. Parliamentary Secretaries are elected Members of Parliament (there are 28 in the current 38th Parliament). It is Martin's stated intent to use Parliamentary Secretaries to involve MPs more in Cabinet proceedings.
29. Dave Noble, OCIPEP Liaison to DND/CF, "Emergency Management in Canada," Joint Staff Orientation Briefing, 18 September 2003.
30. Emergency Preparedness Canada, *Counter-Terrorism Consequence Management Arrangements*, Ottawa, 18 September 1998, and cover document dated September 2002.

PART III

CONTEMPORARY SPECIAL OPERATIONS

CHAPTER TEN

SPECIAL OPERATIONS FORCES IN KOSOVO AND AFGHANISTAN

Sean M. Maloney

Canada will continue to use forces capable of special operations in its pursuit of national objectives around the world. Any analysis of future tasks, force structure, and doctrine should be firmly based not only on the historical development of special operations roles and missions as they pertain to Canada but also on an analysis of the most recent large-scale coalition operations that will ultimately form the basis of future operations in which Canada may be involved. There has been a lot of media commentary about the American-led "Operation Enduring Freedom" in Afghanistan from 2001 to 2003: some even have dubbed it the first special operations war. There has, however, been little discussion of the employment of special operations forces in and around Kosovo between 1998 and 2001. Both operations offer a plethora of examples and lessons, which apply to the future employment and structure of Canadian special operations.

How, then, were special operations forces employed by the Western coalitions that fought in Kosovo and Afghanistan? Military operations in both theatres can be broadly divided into three phases. Phase I is a pre-war manoeuvring phase in which general hostilities have not yet broken out and conventional forces have not been employed in combat. Phase II is a combat phase in which conventional and unconventional forces are openly employed against enemy conventional and unconventional forces. Phase III is a stabilization phase: conventional combat operations have been completed, and the coalition forces are employed to stabilize the occupied area. Drawing on open sources, interviews, and field research in each theatre, this chapter draws lessons from each of these three phases, avoiding any classified details about roles, sizes, training, and equipment of special units.

We can assume that Canadian forces capable of special operations will work closely with American and other NATO special operations forces on future operations. NATO nations tend to use American terminology when referring to various types of special operations. In the absence of approved Canadian terms, this chapter does likewise. American Special Operations Forces (SOF) include units for Civil Affairs (CA) and Psychological Operations (PSYOPS) as well as units designed for direct-action combat missions. The Canadian Forces does not, at this time, group personnel trained in Civil-Military Cooperation (CIMIC) activities or those personnel trained in PSYOPS into CIMIC or PSYOP units, nor does it categorize CIMIC and PSYOP as special operations. Specialized information operations conducted by units like the Canadian Forces Information Operations Group (CFIOG) also differ from "special operations" and will not be considered in this chapter. Consequently, the following terms are used to describe the six principal SOF missions according to American doctrine:[1]

Foreign Internal Defence (FID): Assisting host-nation military capabilities to forestall or defeat insurgent activity.

Direct Action (DA): Short-duration strikes and other small-scale actions to seize, destroy, capture, recover, or inflict damage on designated personnel or material.

Counter-terrorism (CT): Anti-terrorism (defensive measures taken to reduce vulnerability to terrorist acts) and counter-terrorism (offensive measures taken to prevent, deter, and respond to terrorism throughout the entire threat spectrum, sometimes conducted by Special Mission Units to resolve or preempt terrorist incidents abroad.

Special Reconnaissance (SR): Clandestine operations in hostile territory to gain information on capabilities, intentions, and activities of an actual or potential enemy. The NATO term is "Strategic Reconnaissance."

Unconventional Warfare (UW): Support to military and paramilitary operations, normally of long duration, predominantly conducted by indigenous or surrogate forces. This includes guerilla warfare and other low-visibility operations.

Counter-proliferation of weapons of mass destruction (CPWMD): Actions taken to seize, destroy, capture, or recover weapons of mass destruction.

In addition to the six principal SOF missions above, the following five missions are described by American doctrine as collateral SOF missions.

Combat Search and Rescue (CSAR): Operations conducted by rescue forces to effect the recovery of distressed personnel during wartime or contingency operations.

Coalition Support: Actions to improve the ability of coalition partners to coordinate and synchronize combat activity through training on tactics and techniques and by providing communications.

Counterdrug Activities: Active measures taken to detect, monitor, and counter the production, trafficking, and use of illegal drugs.

Security Assistance: The provision of military training, defence equipment, and defence-related services in furtherance of national policies and objectives.

Special Activities: Actions conducted abroad in support of national foreign policy objectives that are planned and executed so that the role of the US Government is not apparent or acknowledged publicly. Such actions require presidential finding and congressional oversight.

American planners refer to Tier I, II, and III Special Operations Forces. These are gradations of capability and readiness and are sometimes used to compare foreign contributions to equivalent US forces. Tier I represents short-notice availability and the pinnacle of specialized capability. Tier II forces have a habitual training relationship with Tier I forces, and Tier III consists of larger units that are closer to conventional forces in their capabilities. The most difficult and dangerous missions are reserved for Tier I and II forces. Hostage rescue or seizure of an important individual (such as arrests of indicted war criminals in Bosnia) would be a Tier I mission, and special reconnaissance would typically be a Tier I or Tier II mission, depending on the circumstances.

KOSOVO 1998-2001

Tensions between the rising Albanian and declining Serbian populations of the province of Kosovo led Slobodan Milosevic to revoke Kosovar Autonomy in 1989. The rising violence had become a regional problem for the Balkans by the mid-1990s. The antagonists struggled over political power and ethnic self-determination in the face of violence generated during the breakaway of several former Yugoslav provinces from 1991 to 1995. Milosevic's regime in Belgrade used ethnic identity to focus and mobilize discontent during a period when UN-mandated sanctions disrupted the economic foundations that supported the regime. Non-violent resistance by Kosovar Albanian nationalists under Rugova collapsed when Serb security forces acted disproportionately in several incidents. A series of loosely organized armed nationalist groups emerged. Generally called the UCK or the Kosovo Liberation Army, many of them were based on family and clan structures. Between 1996 and 1998, the level of violence escalated, prompting the Milosevic regime to employ increasingly disproportionate force.

Ethnic cleansing began in 1998. In addition to the obvious humanitarian disaster in the offing, the situation threatened to destabilize the region and plunge Bosnia, Macedonia, Albania, and even Greece into ethnic conflict, producing a refugee crisis that would affect Italy and Western Europe. NATO members dithered throughout 1998, hoping that diplomatic efforts would calm the situation in Kosovo. Military options to evict Belgrade's forces from Kosovo were examined. The decision to go to war over Kosovo was in the balance in late 1998. Under pressure, Belgrade consented to the multinational OSCE-sponsored Kosovo Verification Mission (KVM) to monitor (within limits) a ceasefire. At the same time, efforts were made to reinforce stability in neighbouring countries and to establish potential bases for operations against the Milosevic regime.[2]

Phase I: Pre-War Manoeuvring

Activity by special operations forces in Phase I was diverse, owing to the convoluted way in which the Kosovo crisis evolved into war. The NATO leadership was actively discussing options for intervention in a vacuum, with little detailed information coming out of Kosovo. The diplomatic agreement between US negotiator Richard Holbrooke and the Milosevic regime created a small Kosovo Diplomatic Observer Mission, but it was unable to cover the province effectively. In time, the OSCE sponsored a larger mission called the Kosovo Verification Mission. The KVM's job was to verify withdrawals of both UCK and Yugoslav security force to cantonments and to investigate and report on any incidents. The American component of the KVM was contracted out to DynCorp, a private military corporation composed of former American military personnel. The Canadian, British, French, and Russian contingents were regular military personnel. The head of the KVM, American Ambassador William Walker, was protected with a bodyguard detachment provided by the Polish special operations unit, *Grupa Reagowania Operacyjno Mobilnego* (GROM).[3] The mission was assisted by Unmanned Aerial Vehicles (UAVs) provided by Germany, the United Kingdom, and the United States. A Kosovo Verification Coordination Centre was set up in Macedonia to fuse information coming in from the KVM and national sources.

A French-led multinational Extraction Force was established in Macedonia. Referred to as "the Dentists," the Extraction Force consisted of an airmobile light-infantry brigade with a capability for hostage rescue in a non-permissive environment if the verifiers had to be removed. It is generally assumed that the special operations capability in the Extraction Force was French and drawn from the *Commandement des Opérations Spéciales* (COS), probably a detachment from the 1st RPIMa (Régiment de Parachutistes d'Infanterie de Marine) and the CPA.[4]

The establishment of these mechanisms and organizations illuminated an important problem for those seeking to distinguish between strategic intelligence-gathering and the use of special operations forces: all of these structures were gathering information on the ceasefire and humanitarian situation in Kosovo, and that information could also be used for targetting purposes by NATO military forces. It was seamless and impossible to separate. This led to charges by the Milosevic regime and its supporters that the KVM was a NATO intelligence-gathering exercise under the cover of the OSCE. The same charge had been levelled at a similar OSCE-mandated European Community Monitor Mission in the early 1990s.[5] The presumption that the DynCorp KVM verifiers included embedded US Special Forces and CIA personnel was prevalent in these charges.[6] There is probably some truth to the charge that contract personnel who were former Special Forces or CIA in the KVM were providing strategic targetting data and liaising with UCK elements. However, there is no proof. The KVM situation is an example of the extent of uncertainty, ambiguity, and opaqueness common to special operations in the 1990s and today. The lesson is, you won't know for sure.

Groups like the British Special Intelligence Service's "The Increment" serve to add another layer of opacity. The Increment is a small group of seconded or former SAS and SBS personnel that conduct special operations directly for the SIS; in other words, the British version of "Special Activities." The French have a similar organization, as do the Americans. A disaffected SIS officer claimed that "The Increment" was scheduled to assassinate Slobodan Milosevic in an ambush in the same way SOE operatives assassinated Reinhardt Heydrich during the Second World War.[7]

Another example of ambiguity is Military Professional Resources Incorporated, another American-based PMC that consists of former military personnel, including special forces personnel.[8] The organization provided military training for the Croatian Army (HV) before 1995. Some Kosovar Albanian members of the HV who were trained by MPRI returned to Kosovo. One of them even led the UCK. In this case, there have been spurious charges that the CIA "controlled" the UCK through MPRI and its contract special-forces personnel. Again, there is no proof and in any case, the UCK was not as well-organized or centrally controlled as is commonly believed. Some small PMCs claim to have been involved in advisory activities in Macedonia.[9] One reliable media report indicated that MPRI trained UCK personnel in 1998-99, assisted by former SAS personnel from two British PMCs, and either the GSG 9 or Kommando Spezialkräfte (KSK) special operations forces from Germany. The training apparently took place in Italy, Turkey, and Germany.[10] It is unclear as to how much of this overlap was arm's-length covert activity designed to improve the UCK to affect some balance of power vis-à-vis Belgrade, how much was outright disinformation, and how much was instigated by the UCK elements themselves with support from their financially generous diaspora and various criminal enterprises.

Whatever the truth about western support for UCK training in 1998-1999, special operations forces from several NATO-member countries were in contact with UCK units in Kosovo just prior to the start of the air campaign, Operation Allied Force. NATO special operations forces, including Norway's Parachute Ranger Commandos (Fallskjermjegerkommandoe) and the Marine Hunters (Marine Jagerne), also conducted training for individual UCK soldiers and UCK sub-units in Albania during this time. This training apparently involved conduct of ambushes and small-unit tactics. Reliable media reports announced that the Norwegian units and the US Special Forces were the first confirmed in-theatre special operations forces to conduct this training.[11] Other reports suggest that certain UCK personnel at this time were trained to use laser designator devices to support the upcoming air campaign, but it seems doubtful that NATO member countries would have released such valuable pieces of equipment to the UCK without supervision.

NATO special operations forces, including French and American organizations, were deployed into hides just inside Serbian territory to provide early warning in case the Yugoslav forces (VJ) attempted a raid from the Presevo Valley into Macedonia to disrupt NATO ground forces and their logistics bases as they were preparing to enter Kosovo to eject Serbian forces.[12]

The distinction between special operations in the narrower NATO sense (mainly direct action) and more inclusive American concepts of special operations employment blurred in the run-up to the air campaign. Psychological operations and special operations overlapped. An AFSOC AC-130 gunship conducted aerial night observation of the Kosovar Albanian refugee flow into Macedonia. On successive nights, Serbian auxiliary policemen controlling the flow would pull out young girls and rape them in the bushes. It was evident from the tapes that specific individuals could be identified conducting the crimes. The AC-130 crew was authorized to surgically kill those who participated with a single 40mm round from the gunship's Bofors cannon. The objective was to leave other Serbian personnel alive so they could pass on what happened and spread alarm.[13]

Phase II: Combat

Missions by special operations forces during the NATO air campaign, Operation Allied Force, included the deployment of substantial Combat Search and Rescue (CSAR) resources. Most of these were drawn from the US Air Force's AFSOC units. Traditionally, CSAR was not a special operations mission. With the emergence of omnipresent media coverage, however, the exploitation of captured air crew for psychological purposes achieved new significance during the Vietnam War. This lesson was re-learned during the 1990-91 Gulf War when the Hussein regime paraded American and British air crews on television, and in Somalia when Michael J. Durant of the 160th Special Operations Aviation Regiment (the "Nightstalkers") was captured and exploited to great effect by the Aideed faction in 1993. Seizure, and even the posthumous mutilation of allied aircrew in a public forum, therefore, was a potentially strategic event in the information war. CSAR was designed to deny the enemy that opportunity. During Operation Allied Force, two major CSAR operations took place inside Serbia. On 26 March 1999, an F-117 Nighthawk crashed, and on 2 May an F-16 went down due to engine failure. Both pilots were extracted by the 352nd Special Operations Group operating MH-53 Pave Low and MH-60 Pave Hawk helicopters refuelled by MC-130P Combat Talon tankers. The helicopters carried AFSOC Special Tactics Teams and Pararescue commandos.[14]

Political restrictions placed on the air campaign, coupled with excellent camouflage and deception (*maskrovia*) practised by Serbian forces, seriously reduced the effectiveness of NATO bombing in the early days of operations over Kosovo. Consequently, the decision was taken to stimulate the UCK into conducting raids to threaten Serb forces and thus get them to move, in order to improve the probability of detection. The media referred to this as Operation Picnic, although its actual code-name remains obscure. Special operations forces were used to support this in a number of ways. First, the rudimentary training provided to the UCK factions was put to good use, sometimes with a single SAS soldier sent along to "observe."[15] Second, American Special Forces personnel (reported by the Serbs to be from the 1st Battalion, 1st Special Forces Group) using laser designator equipment assisted the Allied Force effort directly, sometimes accompanied by UCK personnel and allegedly sometimes operating while wearing Serbian special forces uniforms.[16]

The matter of laser designation requires clarification. The primary form of intelligence on VJ dispositions came from UAVs, not ground spotters. A substantial amount of disinformation was deployed in the media about NATO-member special operations forces and laser designators during the campaign.[17] Even Belgrade fell into the trap when it announced that it had killed "mercenaries from the French Foreign Legion, mujaheddin, and members of the British SAS."[18] Indeed, there were mistaken reports that Canada's JTF 2 was engaged in target-acquisition activity.[19] When similar tactics were employed in Afghanistan in 2001, the US Air Force Chief of Staff noted in an interview that it was "a feature I wish I had in Kosovo."[20] The French armed forces chief of staff, General Jean-Pierre Kelche, put it best during the Kosovo campaign when he was wryly quoted: "Everything is possible with special forces."[21] There is no doubt, however, that what an American military journal referred to as "the indirect penetration of a denied area [will] seriously effect the enemy's ability to conduct the type of deception and denial operations employed [in Kosovo]."[22]

Phase III: Stabilization

The shift from combat to stabilization in the Kosovo crisis was not clear-cut. A NATO land force was building up in Macedonia and Albania to apply pressure while negotiations were being conducted and then to force out Serbian forces if necessary. While the Kosovo Force (KFOR) was building up, specialist personnel were brought in from several NATO force contributors to handle anti-terrorism and counter-terrorism tasks. Belgrade had deployed a limited number of its special operations forces into Macedonia to stimulate antagonisms internally and to target NATO forces with sophisticated propaganda. Several attacks, mostly minor in nature, were conducted against KFOR. The absence of more serious attacks is attributable to Macedonian security forces who received additional training and equipment from NATO-member special operations forces.[23]

Once the agreement was signed to permit the deployment of KFOR into Kosovo while the Serbian forces conducted a phased withdrawal, a plan was implemented to insert SAS personnel by air into Pristina. The exact purpose of the mission is unclear. It may have been to pre-empt a Russian move on Pristina Airport. The C-130 aircraft with the team on board crashed in Albania, and the mission was aborted.[24]

Once KFOR entered Kosovo, it was critical that the power vacuum left by the Serbian forces be filled before the UCK could consolidate, take control, and then conduct revenge attacks against the Serbian minority in Kosovo. Without this, hostilities would be quickly renewed. SAS personnel who worked with the UCK elements now worked in a liaison capacity to ensure that there were no "blue on blue" incidents between the UCK and NATO forces. Another purpose was to keep track of the UCK until it was disbanded, gathering information on it so that if the fighters got out of hand, KFOR could deal with it.[25]

The foreigners who had come to Kosovo to fight alongside the UCK factions were a particular problem for KFOR. The affiliation of these individuals ranged from al-Qaeda and Hizbollah to European Neo-Nazi extremists.[26] The assumption was that radical Islamist individuals or groups would turn on and attack the American component of KFOR. Consequently, a contingent of US Navy SEALS, most likely the Tier I JSOC unit (formerly called SEAL Team 6), was brought in, along with specialized helicopter support from 160th SOAR. There were no radical Islamist attacks on US forces.

At this time, the main problem was not the radical Islamists. It was the more radical UCK personnel and some Neo-Nazi groups supporting them who did not want to stop fighting. Their energy flowed in several directions. Some left Kosovo and entered the Presevo Valley in Serbia and continued the fight outside of NATO's jurisdiction. Others drifted home. Others contemplated guerilla war against KFOR and attacks against Serbian civilians in Kosovo.

KFOR contingents brought in special operations forces, as they had in Macedonia, to conduct anti-terrorist and counter-terrorist operations. Portugal deployed a 13-man unit with the Italian-led Multi-National Brigade (West), while the Swedish contingent brought in the Fallskarmsjagerkola (FJS) and SSG "Special Protection Forces". The FJS came to Kosovo in September 1999 to handle intelligence-gathering, control of human intelligence (HUMINT), and special reconnaissance tasks.[27] At the same time, the United Nations Mission in Kosovo (UNMIK) multinational police force was accompanied by members of Germany's GSG 9 to conduct training for the Kosovo Police Service and to provide a hostage-rescue capability for UNMIK police if they were seized. On at least one occasion, special operations forces contributed to UNMIK were employed to extract a Swedish officer from a barricade situation.[28]

A former UCK element did ultimately succeed in blowing up a KFOR-escorted bus, killing ten people and wounding forty-one in the process. An SAS unit was deployed to Kosovo and, working with KFOR intelligence and UNMIK police organizations, conducted a successful direct-action operation, which eliminated this UCK element.[29]

AFGHANISTAN 2001-2003

In 1996, al-Qaeda, a radical Islamist group led by Osama Bin Laden with characteristics of both a corporation and a cult, declared war on what it labelled Arab apostate regimes and their Western supporters. The al-Qaeda network included construction companies, non-governmental relief organizations, a light-infantry brigade sub-contracted to the Taliban regime in Afghanistan, numerous supporting financial organizations, and what amounted to a multinational "foreign legion" of radical Islamist terrorists. al-Qaeda conducted or planned operations that included terrorist attacks against American embassies, aircraft, and ships. In 2001, it ultimately succeeded in destroying the World Trade Center in New York and causing significant damage to the Pentagon in Washington. The heroic efforts of the passengers of another hijacked aircraft prevented a fourth attack.

The al-Qaeda organization operates like a parasite within established nation-states. This limits the application of conventional military force; for example, al-Qaeda used the Sudan and Taliban-controlled Afghanistan as host states: terrorist-training sites, communications systems, command elements, and financial mechanisms were all operated by al-Qaeda with the consent of the host regime. The Sudanese government realized in time (fortunately) that al-Qaeda was manipulating its security and diplomatic services. In the case of the Taliban, the close personal contacts established during the anti-Communist Jihad between al-Qaeda and Taliban leaders made it difficult to tell where al-Qaeda left off and the Taliban started. The bulk of al-Qaeda infrastructure was moved from the Sudan to Afghanistan. In Afghanistan, al-Qaeda pursued the acquisition of both ready-made weapons of mass destruction and the technology required to produce more. Both the Taliban and the Sudanese governments served as shields to deflect allied efforts to gather information about and launch attacks on al-Qaeda. To get at al-Qaeda, and to prevent it from attacking North American targets with weapons of mass destruction, the shield had to be pierced.[30]

Phase I: Pre-War Manoeuvring

Anti-al-Qaeda operations involving American special operations forces were under way long before the September 11 attacks. After the embassy bombings in Kenya and Tanzania in 1998, the Clinton administration stationed a

Tomahawk-equipped attack submarine off the Pakistani coast. If intelligence assets could locate Osama Bin Laden and the green light were given, the submarine was permitted to fire. Experiments with prototype Predator UAVs to locate high-value al-Qaeda targets were successful, but the problem with initiating an attack was both political and legal. Another option was for the United States to train a select group of six Pakistani Special Service Group operators to enter Afghanistan and either apprehend or kill the al-Qaeda leadership. This operation was scuttled when a coup in Pakistan altered the political landscape. Mass insertion of American special operations forces was vetoed by the JCS and was unpalatable to the Clinton administration. Liaison between a CIA/NSA team and the anti-Taliban Northern Alliance was achieved: Ahmad Shah Massoud attempted to kill Bin Laden on three occasions, but the Clinton administration feared that such a move was illegal and called off the CIA and NSA support.[31]

Between September 11 and the start of the air campaign in Afghanistan on 7 October 2001, a number of overlapping special operations were conducted in and around Afghanistan. The CIA used its special operations capacity: resembling a larger version of the British "Increment", members of the Special Activities Division, which consisted of former American special operations personnel formed into a Special Operations Group (SOG), were inserted to work with the Northern Alliance. This SOG used its own deniable air assets, usually Russian Mi-17 helicopters. It also operated Gnat and Predator UAVs. The SOG, sometimes called the Northern Alliance Liaison Team (NALT) and sometimes by the code-name "Jawbreaker" in media reports, prepared the way for a larger US Special Forces presence and initiated human intelligence links with the Northern Alliance.[32]

Once the NALT had established good relations with the Northern Alliance, the JSOC intelligence-gathering unit, called "Grey Fox" by the media, was brought in. This unit was the descendent of the *ad hoc* arrangements established in the run-up to the 1979 hostage-rescue attempt in Iran. Its job was to gather intelligence on high-value leadership targets.[33] A plethora of intelligence-gathering platforms orbiting Afghanistan and adjacent countries provided inputs: EP-3 Aries III, RC-135 RIVET JOINT, CIA Predators and Gnats, satellites, and U-2s were employed. Since little was known about Taliban forces, specific information had to be gathered on their communications, equipment, order of battle, and command structure before any offensive operations could be launched. British intelligence-gathering operations, assumed by the media to be SAS but which may in fact have been The Increment, were also conducted in Kabul.[34]

Phase II: Combat

AFSOC CSAR units were deployed prior to the initiation of air operations on 6-7 October 2001: one (based on the 16th Special Operations Wing) to Uzbekistan, and another to Pakistan. They were deployed for the same reasons that CSAR had been deployed over the Balkans; that is, to prevent the strategic exploitation of American personnel in danger of capture by enemy forces. At the same time, these units worked with deployed intelligence-gathering assets and other SOCOM aviation elements assigned to JSOC units that were prepared to lift high-value targets if the opportunity arose. At the same time, the NALT laid the groundwork for the insertion of Task Force Dagger and Task Force K-Bar. TF Dagger was a Joint Special Operations Task Force (JSOTF) for northern Afghanistan based in Uzbekistan, while TF K-Bar was designated the southern JSOTF and based in Pakistan. Each JSOTF handed CSAR and Tier II special operations in their geographical areas of responsibility.[35]

TF Dagger, which included the 16th Special Operation Wing and the 5th Special Forces Group, deployed combined teams to support Northern Alliance forces fighting against Taliban and al-Qaeda forces. TF Dagger deployed several Operational Detachment Alphas (ODAs), each of which had members of the US Air Force's Special Tactics Teams and Pararescue personnel attached. The US Army personnel handled unconventional warfare tasks, while the US Air Force personnel called in air support to assist the Northern Alliance forces.[36]

Another organization, Task Force 11, included all of the JSOC Tier I units conducting direct-action, counter-terrorism, and counter-proliferation missions. These organizations and their air support operated mostly from Pakistan and were embedded into Task Force K-Bar for concealment purposes. A new term also emerged at this time: Sensitive Site Exploitation or SSE. Any camp or building that might provide intelligence or evidence of weapons of mass destruction might be designated a sensitive site. Exploiting it might mean capturing personnel or finding material evidence. An SSE mission might involve a Tier I unit plus additional specialist personnel skilled in forensics, computer seizure, or WMD seizure. In general, TF 11 pursued high-value targets (personalities) and conducted SSEs.[37]

The air campaign component of Operation Enduring Freedom softened the opposition forces to the extent that coalition forces could establish forward operating bases inside Afghanistan proper. One of these operations involved the use of a Ranger battalion and an AFSOC Special Tactics Team to seize an airfield designated "Rhino", near Kandahar. Forward Operating Base Rhino became the secure location from which TF 11 units conducted their operations.[38]

ODAs were also brought under TF K-Bar into southern Afghanistan, where they conducted missions similar to those undertaken by TF Dagger in the north. More and more coalition special operations forces were employed as the mission progressed, including the British SAS and SBS. The latter secured Bagram air base in November 2001 in the face of some friendly fire, while a French special operations team secured an airfield near Mazar-e-Sharif. New Zealand SAS personnel were employed to enter Taliban-controlled territories covertly and to control air strikes directed against enemy facilities and units. Special reconnaissance was the order of the day in all areas prior to the insertion of larger light-infantry units by helicopter. At least three SEAL teams were employed in this way. In the main, NATO countries possessing Tier II capabilities were employed in the special reconnaissance role throughout the combat phase, while certain countries with a Tier I capability worked with JSOC units.[39]

Phase III: Stabilization

Taliban and al-Qaeda remnants retreated to southeastern Afghanistan, particularly the mountainous regions adjacent to the Pakistani border. The International Security Assistance Force entered Kabul, while OEF forces consolidated with local Afghan Militia Forces (AMF).[40]

In Kabul, both OEF and ISAF special operations forces were active, and the variety of combinations is instructive. US Special Forces – in this case, reserve special forces units – assisted in training the new Afghan National Army. OEFs Tier I and CIA SOG capabilities were employed in Kabul to track down and apprehend high-value targets. ISAF, on the other hand, was subject to low-level attacks by some factions. ISAF special operations personnel were employed in special reconnaissance tasks designed to reduce rocket attacks on ISAF facilities. Police training, conducted under bilateral arrangements similar to that in Kosovo, included training by German GSG 9 personnel. OEF coalition special operations forces of one particular nationality had a dual role. They had Tier I direct-action tasks to secure national objectives in Kabul (the embassy and national NGO personnel) in the event of seizure. They also had Tier II special reconnaissance tasks under OEF. The Russians were suspected of deploying special operations forces under the guise of "security personnel" for a Russian field hospital. ISAF originally had the close protection function for the President and staff, but this was taken over by DynCorp under a contract with the US State Department.

In the OEF operating areas, US Special Forces ODAs were the main link between OEF and AMF units, operating to support the coalition. There was overlap with the unconventional warfare role, however, as US Special Forces were the focal point for joint AMF-ANA-OEF operations conducted to eliminate Taliban remnants. Coalition special operations forces continued to carry out special reconnaissance tasks in support of light-infantry insertions. Tier I units and their air support were on standby to respond to any potential high-value-target direct-action mission and to conduct SSEs when the need was identified. In the main, the US Special Forces operating with the AMF and CIA SOG enabled intelligence collection that would generate a Tier I mission. Civil Affairs and PSYOPS units, working alongside Special Forces, contributed to this effort while at the same time stabilizing the region and facilitating humanitarian aid and nation-building assistance.

The Provincial Reconstruction Team (PRT) concept emerged from this activity. When special operations forces were deployed to work with the AMF, they established a series of "safe houses" in key areas. Follow-on CA and

PSYOPS teams and improved AMF links made these "safe houses" a clearing house for information on all sorts of areas: economic, infrastructure, enemy forces, and so on. In time, these areas became the prototypes for the PRTs, whereby NGOs could coordinate with OEF and the AMF.[41]

CONCLUSIONS

We can draw important conclusions about the conduct of special operations in contemporary warfare. These conclusions are as valid for the smaller states contributing to operations like those in Kosovo and Afghanistan as they are for the U.S. taking the operational lead.

The use of special operations forces is continuous from before the armed conflict starts, through the combat phase, and into lengthy post-conflict stabilization operations. If the old model of a clear separation between diplomatic communication, war-fighting, and post-conflict peace was ever accurate, it is not so now.

Strategic intelligence- and information-gathering operations cannot be compartmentalized into the three phases, or even confined to the territory involved in the conflict. Intelligence-gathering is global and continuous, with a focus on the region in conflict, not just the affected country.

Canada has a Tier I capability in JTF 2. However this capability evolves, it will need effective intelligence to conduct useful operations with American-led coalitions. We should consider the sort of structure that might be able to provide field intelligence for Canadian special operations. For example, would the mandate of CSIS to conduct overseas investigations in support of Canadian security extend to supporting the security of deployed Canadian forces? Or would this undermine CSIS's primary function in securing Canadians at home? This question highlights the significant overlap between civilian agencies and military special-operations forces when they conduct strategic operations. Because forces like JTF 2 are a strategic asset, they will inevitably be involved with other national assets that can contribute to Canadian security objectives.

As Canada becomes more involved in operations like those in Kosovo and Afghanistan, we will need to articulate policies about the conduct of "covert operations" by civilian agencies in collaboration with military special forces, and "special operations" conducted by military organizations, sometimes with civilian assistance. Without the luxury of large organizations and redundant capabilities, smaller players like Canada may need a more flexible legal framework, so that the same individual can play on a CSIS team today, a CIA team tomorrow, and a JTF 2 team the next day.

The special operations described above include civil affairs, psychological operations, training missions, and counter-terrorism. What do special operations mean to Canada? If we establish separate organizations for special operations, should they include CIMIC, PSYOPS, and FID, or can these functions be left to conventional forces? On the other side of special operations is the murky territory of Special Activities – assassinations, sabotage, and dirty tricks. Even if Canada does not engage in Special Activities, Canadian organizations may be employed alongside allied organizations that do. Should they turn a blind eye? Should they disengage quickly? How pure can we be in today's wars? Evolving Canadian doctrine for special operations has to address these difficult questions with the knowledge of what really happens in modern wars.

NOTES

1. These definitions are compiled from the following sources: SOCOM Briefing, "Joint and SOF Doctrine 101"; Edward F. Bruner, Christopher Bolkcom, and Ronald O'Rourke, *Special Operations Forces in Operation Enduring Freedom: Background and Issues for Congress*, CRS Report for Congress, 15 October 2001; AUSA Background Brief, "Special Operations Forces: An Overview," Institute for Land Warfare, March 1999; Department of Defense, *United States Special Operations Forces Posture Statement 2000* (Washington, DC: Department of Defense, 2000), Appendix A.
2. Sean M. Maloney, *Operation KINETIC: The Canadians in Kosovo 1999-2000* (forthcoming: 2006).
3. Edmund Walendowski, "Grupa Reagowania Operacyjno Mobilnego (GROM) Unit Profile" http://www.specialoperations.com
4. Maloney, *Operation KINETIC*; Peter Humi, "French History of Fighting Terror," 19 September 2001, www.cnn.com
5. Sean M. Maloney, "Operation BOLSTER: The First Two Years of the ECMM", *International Peacekeeping,* Vol. 4, No. 1 (Spring 1997).
6. The charges that were made against the KVM come from the usual assortment of left-wing conspiracy theorists, some of who were manipulated by Belgrade. See, for example, Jared Israel, "Humanitarian Spies" and "The Cat is Out of the Bag" at http://aaart.tripod.com/spies.htm and, of course, our old Cold War friends at *Pravda*: "Who is the So-called Kosovo Liberation Army? German Document Reveals Secret CIA Role," 21 March 2001. For a corrective, see Peter Wuttke, "Racak-Mutation of a Massacre: Leftist Conspiracy Theories and Serbian Propaganda" at http://www.glypx.com/BalkanWitness/wuttke.htm. This article was originally published in the German magazine *analyse und kritik.* See http://home.nikocity.de/schmengler/balkan/ak432.htm, English translation (March 2002) by Mitchell Cohen in Berlin published here with the author's cooperation. The role of DynCorp and the KVM is expertly explored in P. W. Singer, *Corporate Warriors: The Rise of the Privatized Military Industry* (Ithaca: Cornell University Press, 2003).
7. See Richard Tomlinson, *The Big Reach: From Top Secret to Maximum Security* (Edinburgh: Cutting Edge Press, 2001), 73-78; Ken Connors alludes to "The Increment" in *Ghost Force: The Secret History of the SAS*

(London: Weidenfield and Nicholson, 1998), Chapter 16. Note that a unit similar to "The Increment" was portrayed in a short-lived late-1970s British television drama called "The Sandbaggers." The scriptwriter had served with various arms of the British intelligence community and mysteriously disappeared during the first season of the show.

8. Again, I defer to Singer's *Corporate Warriors* for information on MPRI.
9. See "STTU Military Advisory" on the web site of Specialized Tactical Training Unit (STTU), which describes itself as "a contract Training & Studies group dedicated to the training of law enforcement and military special operations teams required to operate in high-risk environments." http://www.sttu.com
10. Christian Jennings, "Private US Firm Training Both Sides in the Balkans," *The Scotsman,* 2 March 2001.
11. Greg Seigle, "Special Forces Involvement Confirmed," *Jane's Defence Weekly,* 20 April 1999.
12. Ibid.; Richard Norton-Taylor, "Clouds defeat air war hopes," *The Guardian,* 31 March 1999.
13. This anecdote was passed from American personnel who were in a position to describe the events in extreme detail, and it has been incorporated into Maloney, *Operation KINETIC.*
14. Michael J. Durant and Steven Hartov, *In the Company of Heroes* (New York: GP Putnam's and Sons, 2003); Mike McKinney, *Chariots of the Damned: Helicopter Special Operations from Vietnam to Kosovo* (London: Harper Collins, 2001), Chapter 10.
15. Maloney, *Operation KINETIC.*
16. Hugh Barnes, "KLA Helps NATO," *The Independent,* 16 May 1999; Balkan Repository Project, "NATO Aggression Against Yugoslavia: Reports on NATO Losses." http://www.balkan-archive.org.yu/kosovo_crisis/nato/
17. Examples include pieces like "Britain denies SAS man is missing," *The Irish Examiner,* 6 May 1999.
18. Balkan Repository Project, "NATO Aggression Against Yugoslavia: Reports on NATO Losses." http://www.balkan-archive.org.yu/kosovo_crisis/nato/
19. An example is Jean-Pierre Husson's otherwise excellent *Encyclopédie des Forces Spéciales du Mond, Tome 1* (Paris: Histoire et Collections, 2000), 98.
20. Robert Wall, "Targeting, Weapon Supply, Encumber Air Campaign," *Aviation Week*, 22 October 2001.
21. Norton-Taylor, "Clouds defeat air war hopes".
22. Michael R. Kershner, "Army Special Forces' Training Focuses on Unconventional Warfare," *Army Magazine*, July 2001, 1-5.
23. Maloney, *Operation KINETIC.*
24. Mike Ryan, *Secret Operations of the SAS* (St. Paul, MN: MBI Publishing, 2003), 168-170.
25. Maloney, *Operation KINETIC.*
26. Ibid.

27. Magnus Norell and Karin Stroeberg, "Special Forces in International Operations: Challenges for the Future," Swedish Defence Research Agency, FOI Memo 1178/S, December 2001. http://www.client.foi.se/
28. This information was collected on a 2001 research trip to Kosovo. For the operation involving the Swede, see "UNMIK Police Update: 18 December 2000."
29. The author was present in Kosovo when this operation was under way.
30. Sean M. Maloney, *Enduring the Freedom: A Rogue Historian Visits Afghanistan* (Fairfax, VA: Potomac Books, 2005).
31. These operations are described in Daniel Benjamin and Steven Simon, *The Age of Sacred Terror* (New York: Random House, 2002); Richard Miniter, *Losing Bin Laden: How Bill Clinton's Failures Unleashed Global Terror* (Washington, DC: Regenery Books, 2003); and Ronald Kessler, *The CIA at War: Inside the Secret Campaign Against Terror* (New York: St Martin's Press, 2003).
32. Bob Woodward, *Bush At War* (New York: Simon and Shuster, 2002); James F. Dunnigan, *The Perfect Soldier: Special Operations, Commandos, and the Future of US Warfare* (New York: Citadel Press, 2003).
33. See Association of Former Intelligence Officers, "Weekly Intelligence Notes #43-02, 11 November 2002, "Defense Covert Ops Role"; David Ignatius, "Get Ready for the American Ninjas," *The Washington Post*, 25 February 2003; William M. Arkin, "The Secret War," *Los Angeles Times,* 27 October 2002.
34. Dunnigan mentions the SAS in Kabul in *The Perfect Soldier* on page 213. Mark Nichol, who had access to some SAS Afghan operations, suggests that the SAS was deployed much later. See Mark Nichol, *Ultimate Risk: SAS Contact Al Qaeda* (London: Macmillan Publishing, 2003).
35. Denis P. Doty, "Command and Control of Special Operations Forces for 21st Century Contingency Operations," a paper submitted to the faculty of the Naval War College in partial satisfaction of the requirements of the Department of Joint Military Operations, 3 February 2003.
36. These activities are detailed in Robin Moore, *The Hunt for Bin Laden: Task Force Dagger* (New York: Random House, 2003) and Michael Hirsh, *None Braver: US Air Force Pararescuemen in the War on Terrorism* (New York: New American Library, 2003).
37. Doty, "Command and Control of Special Operations Forces".
38. Maloney, *Enduring the Freedom.*
39. Ibid.
40. This entire stabilization section is based on data contained in Maloney, *Enduring the Freedom.*
41. Making the transition from PRTs to support the hunt for al-Qaeda to PRTs to support reconstruction is the subject of Chapter Twelve of this volume.

CHAPTER ELEVEN

INFORMATION OPERATIONS IN SUPPORT OF SPECIAL OPERATIONS

Sylvain P. Leblanc and G. Scott Knight[1]

The wars in Afghanistan and Iraq in 2001 and 2003 have demonstrated the speed and sophistication of modern conflict and the essential role played by information. Military forces have departed from the linear sequences that characterized the 1991 Gulf War and the Kosovo air campaign of 1999. The new "rapid decisive operations" (RDO) achieve victory by attacking the enemy's coherence and ability to fight.[2] Effects-based operations (EBO) aim at delivering specific impacts on an adversary's key nodes and vulnerabilities.[3] We expect these two types of operations to become the norm for conflicts waged by 21st-century Western forces.[4] Although many of the missions associated with RDO and EBO have historically been conducted by special forces, this is no longer the case, with conventional forces adopting new techniques and commanders demanding more speed and flexibility from them.

Special operations and information operations are both important aspects of modern military practice in peace and war. To accommodate new forms of operations, force developers in the West are aiming to make conventional forces more like their special operations counterparts: "...lighter, faster, more precise, coherently joint, and politically astute."[5] The success of any "special" force in a future joint task force will depend on its ability to integrate with transforming conventional forces while preserving its unique and critical capabilities as a special force.

Special operations forces are well equipped and make extensive use of specialized weapons technology. We believe, however, that more attention should be paid to the support that information operations (IO) can provide. This chapter examines the contributions that IO can make in the typical phases of missions conducted by special operations forces, and to combat power in general. Conversely, many of the missions typically associated with special operations forces can be conducted in support of IO to accomplish strategic aims; for example, we can imagine infiltration of enemy territory to destroy a communication link, to implant a listening device, or to tamper with computer equipment.

INFORMATION OPERATIONS

Information Operations are defined as "actions taken in support of political and military objectives which influence decision makers by affecting others' information while exploiting, or fully utilizing, and protecting one's own information."[6] This definition is very broad, and an argument can be made that virtually all operations are information operations because every operation gathers information about military adversaries, civilian populations, and other parties. Discussion of IO in this chapter is restricted to those operations that are conducted with the explicit purpose of affecting others' information while exploiting and protecting one's own.

Forces capable of special operations, like Canada's JTF 2, are highly trained and operate in an environment that requires a high level of operational security. One of the tenets of information operations is the protection of information. The information derived from such operations, and the IO assets and operations themselves, are often very sensitive and are protected in a "close-hold" security environment. This is well recognized in Canada, where a special category of IO, termed *Special Information Operations*, has a more stringent process for review and approval because these operations are of a sensitive nature, have significant potential impact, have special security requirements, and may pose risks to national security.[7] Therefore, operations involving sensitive IO assets are not possible within the context of the larger joint force, but are the purview of special operations forces.

In American doctrine, IO encompasses a wide range of disciplines, as shown in Figure 11-1. Just as some countries do not include civil affairs and psychological operations in their consideration of special operations, so it is common outside American doctrine to treat public affairs and civil affairs as separate disciplines, although they contribute to the conduct of information operations. This chapter focuses on the contributions that signals and electronic capabilities can make to special operations, particularly offensive and defensive IO. The arguments, however, can be applied equally to other disciplines, such as civil affairs, public affairs, and psychological operations.

FIGURE 11-1
Information Operations Disciplines[8]

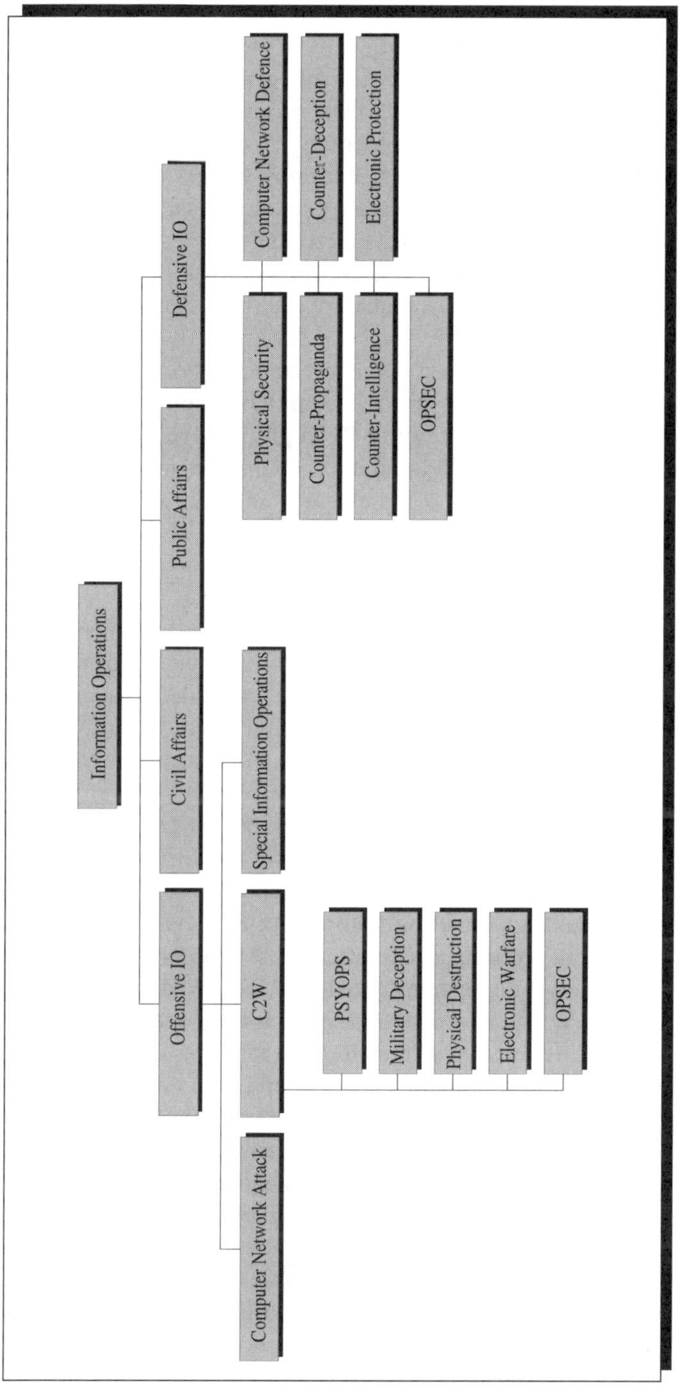

Offensive IO include those actions taken to influence enemy decision-makers.[9] The aim of operations is to prevent the adversary's decision-making process from achieving its desired results. Conversely, defensive IO are the actions taken to protect one's own information so that friendly decision-makers can have timely access to necessary, relevant, and accurate information.[10] This will include actions taken to minimize the effect of the adversary's offensive IO on friendly decision-making processes. To achieve this, defensive IO have three distinctive elements: protection, defensive counter-IO, and offensive counter-IO. Protection aims at protecting the most important elements of friendly information from enemy efforts to disrupt them. Defensive counter-IO responds to enemy attacks and aims to restore friendly information that may have been affected by enemy actions. For example, we might minimize enemy effect on our strategic communications by using redundant Internet channels. Offensive counter-IO might involve identifying enemy communications experts and hiring them (or killing them).

While Figure 11-1 represents a generally accepted classification of IO, a few aspects transcend this taxonomy because they are applicable to all IO. Both Signals Intelligence (SIGINT) and Computer Network Operations have important applications for special operations.

NATO defines Signals Intelligence as the intelligence that is derived from electromagnetic communications and communications systems, as well as electronic non-communications systems, by other than intended recipients or users.[11] Signals intelligence may be able to acquire information by such means as eavesdropping on communications that pass freely through the radio frequency spectrum or targetting specific points of interest in communications and computer networks. Information can be gathered by examining and extracting information-content from the text of an intercepted message, or by examining the characteristics of the communication medium. For example, in radio-frequency direction finding, even though it may not be possible to understand the meaning of an encrypted radio communication, the location of the sender might be determined from observed radio-transmitter activity.

Since the capabilities of signal intelligence systems are classified, only concepts are discussed here. Some capabilities may already exist, while others have useful operational potential and so may be worthy of development. Virtually any communications media in use by an enemy can theoretically be exploited. These might include military radio nets, copper and optical-fibre cable networks, microwave communications trunks, and commercial telephone and cell-phone networks. Depending on the theatre of operations and the nature of the enemy force, the target communications systems might be either localized within a well-defined theatre of operations or truly global in nature.[12]

Computer networks are present in every aspect of modern life, including military operations, and they play an especially important role in IO. The term "Computer Network Operations" (CNO) is used to represent all aspects of computer-related operations, but they have three distinct components: defence, attack, and exploitation.[13]

Computer network defence (CND) comprises all aspects of the protection of computer networks, including the actions described above to protect information systems. CND must defend against any type of attack. It also involves monitoring computer use, analyzing operating characteristics in order to detect and respond to unauthorized use, and monitoring other information technology resources; for example, an enemy might use a hand-held computer to transmit a virus to a computer network by synchronizing a calendar entry through an infrared port. CND is so important that it is considered a core IO capability and is actively practised by the Canadian Forces.[14]

Computer network attacks (CNA) are an aspect of computer network operations that are directed at the enemy. They aim to disrupt, deny, degrade, or destroy information resident in information systems, or the information systems themselves. CNA can involve everything from viruses to power surges and cutting cables. Computer network exploitation (CNE) is aimed at gathering data about the enemy through analysis of their information systems or computer networks. Analysis can be accomplished through a combination of intelligence collection or operations aimed at information-gathering. This kind of exploitation may be particularly well-suited to support special operations through provision of background information for a mission. Similarly, special operations may be used to infiltrate protected areas, plant devices, or otherwise support CNE.

HOW IO CAPABILITIES SUPPORT SPECIAL OPERATIONS

IO capabilities and activities can support special operations in a variety of ways. The most obvious and traditional support is in the form of intelligence products derived from IO, which can be used to provide an understanding of the enemy's capability, order of battle, and disposition. A special operations force requires this information both at a strategic level and within a specific tactical context.

The special operations force itself depends upon the integral communication and information assets it employs and upon the assets of the units that directly support the mission. These assets – communications systems, computer networks, and sensors – are vital and must be defended against attack and exploitation by the enemy. Specialized IO protection techniques and defensive counter-IO are therefore important elements of the mission.

IO capabilities can be used to shape the battlefield in order to permit a mission to be conducted under favourable circumstances. An IO might be used to modify the behaviour of the enemy to create an opening for a special operation, perhaps by creating a virtual diversion, disrupting systems to occupy enemy command and control. Alternatively, degrading command and control systems of the enemy might delay or nullify a response to our actions. Another approach might be to disrupt or compromise a communications channel, in order to shift enemy communications to a channel that can be more easily exploited to glean information relevant to our mission. Information might be manipulated to force the enemy to react, revealing defensive capabilities and tactics in use. Finally, the enemy might be induced to deploy from garrison to field positions at a time that provides an opportunity for special forces to exploit a vulnerable position.

IO capabilities can be used in targetting. Information can be collected to help us understand the vulnerabilities of a possible target. What frequencies is the enemy using? Where are the most active nodes? It can also provide real-time target information. Telephoning a key leader on his cell phone, then using a frequency-riding missile to target the cell phone is an example of smart targetting. It is also something not yet within the scope of conventional forces and standard equipment. Using IO to support a mission may require specialized equipment and highly trained personnel who may have to be attached to, or become integral to, a special organization, which might train for weeks or months for a particular mission.

We now consider IO capabilities in the context of special operations. The list of primary and collateral special operations provided by Maloney in Chapter Ten is a good starting point. Information Warfare (IW) or Command and Control Warfare (C2W) are included, but not civil affairs or psychological operations. IW/C2W is an emerging special operations forces mission that involves the exploitation, dominance, or destruction of an enemy's information systems while maintaining the integrity of our own against attack.

Direct action comes readily to mind when we consider special operations. The mass media images of black-clad super-warriors carrying an impressive array of weaponry on secretive missions "behind enemy lines" are firmly fixed in the public imagination. However, other primary missions such as special reconnaissance, unconventional warfare, combatting terrorism, and counter-proliferation are also important special operations. The remainder of this chapter shows how IO can contribute to the success of these missions.

EXAMPLES – FROM SELECTING OBJECTIVES TO ASSESSING RESULTS

Our examination of the aspects of special operations that would be well served by improved IO support is based on a typical targetting process consisting of five phases: Objective Selection, Target Development, Execution Planning, Mission Execution, and Mission Assessment. [15] For each of these phases, we suggest potential contributions at the strategic and tactical levels, offering scenarios that illustrate some of the ways IO can contribute to the effectiveness of special operations. Examples at the tactical level address the deployment of the special operations units or task forces, while those at the strategic level examine the contributions that IO can make to higher commands and national objectives.

Objective Selection

As the basis of the targetting process, the first task is to select the objective that is to be accomplished. Objectives are selected at the highest possible level of the organization because they must support the commander's aim.

CNE to gain information in counter-proliferation operations provides an example of IO support at the strategic level. The commander must have accurate information and timely warning of threats, including nearly real-time knowledge of the movement of WMD that are to be intercepted or attacked. Relevant indicators may come from a variety of sources; for example, analysis of logistic information may reveal patterns of parts delivery or other activity that indicates WMD assembly or support.

Computer network exploitation can also help with selecting objectives. Although WMD disposition would be a closely guarded secret, information about status might be derived from enemy computer networks. CNE can permit the analysis of these networks and provide commanders with intelligence for timely decisions. CNE can assist in inferring changes in the status and location of WMD. Special forces might then attack completed weapons directly or interdict logistics support for WMD construction efforts.

An example of tactical IO support for selection of objectives in special operations can be found in unconventional warfare. SIGINT can be used to identify additional targets on the way to a main objective. In unconventional warfare, planning resources will be limited because small special forces work closely with indigenous forces, often isolated from support for prolonged periods. Direct support from SIGINT can intercept radio or telephone signals, to help a local commander select the objectives that will have the greatest impact. It may not be possible to determine in advance what kind of SIGINT will be most helpful, so the ability to generate new SIGINT tasks in support of their mission as it evolves would be a significant asset.

A special operations force involved in unconventional warfare may have to maintain a covert presence in its area of operation for some time. Intermediary targets are selected to accomplish the main objective, and other enemy elements are identified and tracked to help the special operations forces remain undetected. The force must be able to gather information about its tactical environment throughout the mission, a role in which SIGINT can be very effective. Monitoring enemy tactical communications can help special operations forces determine if enemy elements threaten to discover them and can give warning of new threats. Even if it is not possible to read message communications, direction-finding can help track the movement of enemy elements through their electro-magnetic emissions.

Target Development

Once the objective has been set, the means to accomplish the commander's aim are refined by the selection of potential targets. Adversary systems and installations are assessed to analyze their vulnerability to attack and to determine their importance to the enemy. This analysis helps to determine which targets should be attacked and the extent of desired damage to the targets. The latter is used to evaluate the success of the mission.

A strategic application of IO to target development might involve using computer network defence to learn about enemy information systems. We know that a variety of attacks are possible on military networks and that these attacks have been taking place for years.[16] CND is what we do to protect our information systems from these attacks. As we conduct the defence, we learn about the techniques and tools used by adversaries in their attempts to disrupt or destroy friendly technology. Over time, information gathered through CND reveals trends in the technology and assets used by adversaries. These assets are potential objectives for friendly offensive IO. We can learn about the importance of particular assets through probing CNA, or we might launch a special IO mission. For example, CND may detect a covert enemy facility compromising friendly command and control networks. It may provide enough information to permit the facility to be identified and targetted. A raid may be mounted to disable the facility and capture the enemy operators. Capture denies the use of a valuable asset, and questioning the captives may disclose the extent of the compromise.

A tactical application of target development might involve SIGINT to support law enforcement during collateral activities. Special operations units may be involved in counter-drug operations or border protection. Organized criminal elements operating outside Canada or along our borders use a wide variety of technologies to communicate, including radio, telephone, and cell phone. SIGINT helps to identify key players and critical installations, both of which can become targets for forces involved in collateral activities.

Execution Planning

Once targets have been selected for attack and the desired effect on these targets has been determined, units and task forces can be assigned the mission of engaging these targets and must then plan for execution. Both special and conventional forces will be employed, and they will make extensive use of information.

Defensive IO to ensure the secrecy of the mission is an example of important strategic support. All forces must be able to rely on operational security to ensure that their plans and information about friendly forces are not disclosed to the enemy. Special operations units and forces have an even greater need for operational security because they are often called upon to work in hostile or denied territory or in politically sensitive environments. This is particularly true for special reconnaissance, unconventional warfare, and collateral activities, but it is also increasingly important as we begin to work in more diverse teams. Sharing information across organizational boundaries – between military and police, for example – creates new opportunities for exploitation and thus increases the importance of defensive IO.

The Protect function (part of defensive IO) is exercised to protect the special operations forces from the enemy's attempt to disrupt or exploit friendly information. It can provide the friendly special operations commander with assurance that information resources can be relied upon in planning the mission and that the enemy is not using IO techniques to compromise the systems in use by friendly forces and supporting units. The commander may also be assisted by offensive IO. It may be possible to deceive the enemy into drawing erroneous conclusions about the mission's true objectives.[17] Information gathered and analyzed during computer network operations may also make it possible to physically destroy enemy assets that might interfere with the mission.

IO can help plan the execution of a mission. A tactical application in support might involve fixing the location of targets through the Internet during special reconnaissance. A special force equipped with IO assets may be able to locate the source of specific communications. This capacity would allow the special operations unit to fix the location of its targets and to plan special reconnaissance operations, such as the emplacement of sensors. With the right IO assets, it may be possible to identify and fix the location of a target that is using almost any communications system. It is clearly possible to do this for targets in a mobile conventional military environment, using military radio networks. It is also theoretically possible in the case of unconventional enemy forces using commercial telephone, fax, cell-phone, and satellite-phone services. It may be possible to fix the location of targets using computer networks through the World Wide Web and Internet to communicate. The extent of IO capabilities in this area is classified, and the existence of any particular capability is hypothetical, but the potential for such a capability has important implications for developing special operations concepts and doctrine and will influence the ability of IO to support special operations.

Another tactical application of IO to support planning a mission might involve computer network attack to force the enemy onto more exploitable communications channels by denying or compromising the preferred means. CNA can be used to help gather information about the target of a special operations mission. For example, imagine collateral operations targetting organized crime. CNA against the computer network might force the organization to communicate by telephone, making tapped telephone lines much more productive and thus increasing the amount of information available to friendly forces.

Mission Execution

During the execution of the mission, special operations forces will be able to make use of information operation assets in a variety of ways. Deception (an

Offensive IO) could be used to increase forces' ability to go undetected. A superior commander may decide to mount a conventional Direct Action to divert the enemy's attention away from the special operation.

As a mission is being executed, it may be necessary to verify the location of the target. SIGINT can provide immediate assistance; by tracking the electronic signature of a target, it can improve the force's ability to confirm the target location.

Mission Assessment

Once any operation has been conducted, its effectiveness must be assessed. In some cases, this can come only from the force conducting the operation. For example, a direct-action mission requiring the capture of an enemy combattant is assessed by the return of the force with the captive. Other missions will have less well-defined indicators of success, and IO can be an important asset in making an assessment. SIGINT elements can track a particular electronic signature, for example: while the absence of a signature is not proof that the target has been destroyed, its presence can be an indicator that the target is still operating.

Computer network exploitation and SIGINT can also make a strategic contribution. After a mission has been executed, SIGINT analysis of intercepted enemy communications may reveal whether the mission had the desired effect on enemy operations. CNE can serve the same purpose by assessing the impact of an attack on a computer network.

THE COMBAT POWER OF INFORMATION OPERATION

The majority of this chapter has been devoted to the contributions that IO can make in support of special operations. However, now that IO is an integral part of a modern force's combat power,[18] there are two additional aspects of the relationship between special operations and IO that must be considered. First, special operations forces can take a very active role in supporting IO; second, IO assets can be used to carry out special operations.

The use of special operations forces in support of IO is so important that IW/C2W is recognized as a primary mission for special operations forces. They can be used to emplace or recover listening devices or sensors in computer networks or other communications systems. They can be used to capture enemy information systems for analysis, and they can physically destroy enemy IO assets.

The disruptive power of IO has long been recognized; electronic warfare assets have supported military operations since the Second World War, for example, by jamming enemy communications or radar facilities in support of an attack. Modern information systems, however, are reaching the point where they can be used to conduct operations, not simply support them. CNA can be used to conduct information warfare. If the objective of an attack is to destroy information in an enemy database or on a particular server, the friendly IO force will need information about the computer network where this server resides and about the CND techniques being employed by the enemy. It may be possible to get this information electronically (for example, by gaining clandestine access through the Internet) or special operations forces may be tasked to collect it. Armed with knowledge about servers, networks, and security measures, the IO force may be able to execute the attack through a computer network attack or other offensive IO technique. By fully exploiting the enemy computer network, CNE can help to identify critical intermediary targets on the network that will enable the friendly force to reach the server or to remove evidence of its attack.

CONCLUSION

Many advocates of special operations argue that they provide a cost-effective solution to difficult operational problems. Special operations are an important aspect of modern conflict, and their significance will probably grow with the increasingly asymmetric nature of warfare. Information operations provide vital tools to support special operations across the entire spectrum of their activities, from selecting objectives at the highest level to assessing the impact of a mission at the lowest level. It is hard to imagine complex modern special operations being conducted, whether by military forces alone or by multi-agency teams, without competent information support. Developing skilled information operators and keeping abreast of technological change will be a challenge for special operations, one that will only be made more daunting by the need to work across national and organizational boundaries.

Given the current efforts to achieve information supremacy, we should expect that the relationship between special operations and information operations to become even stronger in the future. Information operations contribute to combat power in their own right. They will play an increasingly important role in future military operations, and as this happens other forces will surely become more closely involved with, and more dependent upon, effective information operations.

NOTES

1. The opinions and ideas expressed in this paper are those of the authors alone. They do not necessarily reflect current Department of National Defence or Canadian Forces policy or doctrine.
2. A good description of Rapid Decisive Operations can be found in the following unattributed article, *Decisive Operations (RDO)*, on the web site Global Security.Org, 8 September 2002; http://www.globalsecurity.org/military/ops/rdo.htm

3. Paul K. Davis, *Effects-Based Operations (EBO): A Grand Challenge for the Analytical Community* (Santa Monica, CA: RAND Corporation, 2001).
4. United States, Department of Defense, *Joint Vision 2020*; http://www.dtic.mil/jointvision/jvpub2.htm
5. "Operational Net States is aiming to transform its own military into a more special operations forces-like and jointly coherent force by 2015 in order to successfully conduct RDO and EBO anywhere in the world." LCol. W. F. Fleser, "Operational Net Assessment: Implications and Opportunities for SOF," *Special Warfare,* 15:4 (December 2002): 12.
6. Canada, Department of National Defence, *Canadian Forces Information Operations,* Department of National Defence publication B-GG-005-004/AF-010, April 1998, section 102, 5 March 2004 <http://www.dnd.ca/dcds/jointdoc/pages/keydocs_e.asp>.
7. Ibid., section 102.
8. *Joint Information Operations Planning Handbook.* U.S. Joint Forces Staff College, July 2002.
9. Canada, Department of National Defence, *Canadian Forces Information Operations,* publication B-GG-005-004/AF-010, April 1998, section 201.
10. Ibid., section 301.
11. North Atlantic Treaty Organization, Military Agency for Standardization, *NATO Glossary of Terms and Definitions,* AAP-6 (V), 7 August 2000.
12. Although specific capabilities of global SIGINT systems are hypothetical and are not described in the open literature, an interesting study of what such a system might look like can be found in *Draft Report on the Existence of a Global System for the Interception of Private and Commercial Communications*, European Parliament Temporary Committee on the ECHELON Interception System, PR\439868EN.doc PE 305.391, 28 May 2001.
13. CF Operations Policy for International Operations, Draft policy, dated July 2003.
14. In fact, the Communications Security Establishment (with some collaboration from the Canadian Forces Information Operations Group), is involved in providing assistance to other government departments in their CND efforts.
15. While not necessarily SOF doctrine, this is nevertheless a useful framework. The phases identified are based on the USAF Intelligence Planning Guide targetting process phases, which are *Objective and Guidance Derivation, Target Development, Weaponeering, Force Application, Execution Planning,* and *Combat Assessment*. They are taken from a US Air Force publication, *Air Force Pamphlet 14-210 Intelligence,* 1 February 1998. www.e-publishing.af.mil/pubfiles/af/14/afi14-117/afi14-117.pdf

16. For a very interesting read on the early stages of computer attacks, the reader is encouraged to consult Cliff Stole, *The Cuckoo's Egg: Tracking a Spy through the Maze of Computer Espionage* (New York: Doubleday, 1986).
17. Operation Security and Deception form part of Offensive Information Operations. See Canada, *Canadian Forces Information Operations,* Section 201.
18. Combat Power is defined as "The total means of destructive and/or disruptive force which a military [force] can apply against the opponent at a given time." See *NATO Glossary of Terms and Definitions.*

CHAPTER TWELVE

SPECIAL OPERATIONS AND POST-CONFLICT STABILITY

CIVIL AFFAIRS AND DIRECT ACTION

David Last and Michelle Malenfant[1]

One of the greatest challenges of the post-Cold War world has been the restoration of stability after protracted conflict. If we achieve this operational objective, we undermine the breeding grounds for extremism and violence, stem the destabilizing flow of refugees, and help to sustain global prosperity. But restoring stability is more a social, economic, and political problem than a military one. Is this a task for special operations? American doctrine includes Civil Affairs as a component of Special Operations Forces. European armed forces tend to view CA as a conventional capability, separate from their small special units charged with direct-action tasks. Today's conflicts raise an important question about structure and doctrine. What kinds of forces do we need to contribute effectively to post-conflict stability?

Special forces teams like the US Operational Detachments "Alpha" have a unique capacity to apply discriminating violence. Direct action can remove spoilers in a peace process. Mobilizing local militias can help to maintain order and even initiate community policing. The ODA can tread lightly in the local community. It is less likely to be perceived as an occupying force, but its capacity for direct action may help to protect international elements contributing to political, economic, and social stabilization. On the other hand, assessing needs, coordinating civic action, and generating cooperation with military forces responsible for security are jobs for civil-affairs units, when not actually jobs for civilians, and direct action against spoilers may incur reprisals against aid agencies and other soft targets. How to balance these conflicting needs in reconstruction?

This chapter explores the possibility that special forces' capacity for direct action can be combined with civil-affairs units' capacity to build relationships and coordinate civic action. If they can be effectively combined, then it may be appropriate to consider civil affairs as a form of special operation, in line with American doctrine. If they cannot, then keeping direct action and civil affairs separate may be more useful. The debate has been engaged for other capabilities. Public affairs efforts depend on trust and openness, while psychological operations may employ deception; should they be combined, or separated? They must be separated to prevent contamination of the public affairs function with the taint of PSYOPS "offensive fire". But they cannot operate in isolation.[2] On the basis of early reports of Provincial Reconstruction Teams in Afghanistan, we arrive at a similar conclusion for civil affairs and direct action. It is not enough to build relationships; there must be a capacity for coercive force, at arm's length from those wielding the soft power of democratization and development aid. We are still experimenting with how close this cooperation can be and how much force is necessary for safety. We should expect casualties and failures if we get it wrong; wielding force has consequences for vulnerable parts of an organization.

The chapter is in three parts. The first considers the nature of civil-affairs tasks in post-conflict stability operations, including something of the evolution of such tasks. This is followed by a description of the experience of PRTs in Afghanistan. Finally, we consider the advantages and disadvantages of combining civil-affairs and direct-action capabilities in a single organization.

POST-CONFLICT STABILITY OPERATIONS

Military forces alone cannot achieve stability; yet stability is often more central to the purpose of deploying military forces than is "war-fighting" or "war-winning". Security, governance, relief and development, and social-psychological reconciliation are the four dimensions that must be addressed in a connected way if international intervention is to provide useful support to long-term stability.[3] Some form of international presence provides the security guarantee that former combatants will no longer resort to force. Disarmament, demobilization, and reintegration (DDR) of large numbers of ex-combatants who may have no other skills must proceed hand in hand with reform of the indigenous security sector. The security sector includes not only military and police institutions but also the courts and prisons that are needed for police to serve society. Stabilization requires local soldiers and police to take over security functions from the international force (police first and eventually military). Courts and prisons must be local, and the body of law and government institutions to oversee security cannot be international for long. Paying for government and police salaries requires taxation, hence restoration of the economy; relief therefore can be only a stopgap measure until equitable economic development takes off. But for the economy to work, people must trust a common currency, must be free to move, and may have to deal with former enemies if common institutions are to function. This kind of trust is based on assurances of personal and community security, which the initial international presence must provide.

Stability operations should be seen in their historical context; they have been central to military purposes more often than not. Bland and Maloney have described the consistency of Canada's post-Cold War strategy of engaging in campaigns to support international stability, despite our failure to articulate it as policy.[4] In fact, Canada, Australia, and middle-ranked European powers have a long history of supporting the stability of international orders from which they benefit. In the nineteenth century, this entailed supporting the small wars of Empire.[5] Between the wars, it meant supporting the League of Nations, and during the Cold War, it meant supporting the UN while pursuing the objectives of the NATO alliance.[6] In each of these eras, different degrees of self-determination were permissible. Empires were expected to maintain order in their territories. League of Nations mandates formalized the arrangement, with a promise of eventual statehood. In general, territories with strategic or economic value, such as Cyprus, Namibia, or the Emirates, had less scope for autonomy. Territories that contravened the accepted order, like Cuba or Hungary, found little support for independence in international organizations. Although the UN was rich with the rhetoric of self-determination, it was acceptable for the U.S. to strangle Cuba and for the Soviet Union to invade Hungary.[7]

Neither nineteenth-century imperial policing nor Cold War counter-insurgency operations were aimed at self-determination. Unconventional warfare (UW) and foreign internal defence (FID) were conceived as special operations missions that were two sides of the same coin. UW would undermine hostile regimes, and FID would prop up friendly ones. The U.S. used civil affairs, UW, and FID in the global conflict between capitalism and communism from the 1960s to the 1980s.[8] The campaigns in Latin America were especially hotly contested and were subject to increasing public scrutiny as the Cold War wore into the 'eighties. In 1984, General Paul F. Gorman of US Southern Command established the Small Wars Operations Research Directorate (SWORD) and charged it with discovering the elements of successful counterinsurgency.[9] The SWORD papers identified principles of counter-insurgency, the most important of which was legitimacy.[10] Self-determination would contribute to legitimacy in counter-insurgency operations if the determination went the right way. CA and FID were therefore enlisted in democratization and development efforts at about the same time that the School of the Americas began to teach human rights and the primacy of civilian government – when the end of the Cold War was in sight.[11]

Stability operations in general can be seen as a continuation of the imperial policing tradition, in which there is a trade-off between legitimacy and force. The greater the local legitimacy of the intervention, the less force is required to restore order and maintain stability. UN transition missions, mandated to move states towards self-determination, can usually provide a fairly low-risk security guarantee with small numbers of combat-capable troops and police. The UN Transitional Executive Authority (UNTEA) and UN Security Force (UNSF) in West Irian in 1963 and the UN Transition Assistance Group (UNTAG) in Namibia in 1989 are both good examples of consensual civil-military cooperation to change the political status of a territory.[12] Interventions that have enjoyed less local legitimacy have been forced to deploy more force, but force has never been the key to stability. The UN has more social and economic tools for stability but lacks the capacity to wield force effectively.[13] A weak international presence might have to acquiesce to local power structures, organized crime, and drug-trafficking, with consequences for long-term stability.

Post-Cold War stability efforts in Somalia, Cambodia, Guatemala, Haiti, and the Balkans took the form of UN missions. Set up to save successive generations from the scourge of war (as the Charter explains), the UN combines military missions authorized by the Security Council to address war, with economic and social remedies managed by the organs of the General Assembly. The UN High Commission for Refugees, UN Development Plan, World Food Programme, and other organs of the UN make crucial long-term contributions to regional stability. But the UN framework for military action to provide security for these agencies hinges on legitimacy and consensus, which were limited in Cambodia and absent in Rwanda, Somalia, and the Balkans. The UN does not have the capacity to wage effective military operations against opposition and therefore authorizes regional bodies or coalitions to undertake stability operations when there is no agreement.[14] Competent military bodies like NATO do not have the political, social, and economic tools to support reconstruction, so typical stability operations involve three or four organizational pillars representing the different functions. The result can be complex and unwieldy. In Bosnia-Herzegovina, the Office of the High Representative tries to bring together the economic pillar of the European Union, the political pillar of the OSCE mission, NATO's military pillar, and various social dimensions (such as support for refugee-return) under the auspices of the UN Mission in Bosnia-Herzegovina (UNMIBH).[15] The large NATO Stabilisation Force (SFOR) provides for physical security but is not responsible for civil policing; UNMIBH provided the civilian police of the International Police Task Force until monitoring was taken over by the OSCE.[16]

The international community has struggled over the last decade with the problem of providing security and managing soft assets for development and stabilization. The same problems bedevilled efforts during the Cold War and even the colonial period. The international solution in the Balkans has been to make missions larger, bringing in more specialized agencies, sub-contracting to NGOs, and establishing elaborate procedures and structures for coordination.[17] But this can be costly and can lead to charges of neo-colonialism.[18] The national solution has sometimes gone in the opposite direction – contracting decision-making to a small "country team" led by an ambassador who coordinates all the instruments of national power deployed in a foreign country. This can be extended to a region such as Central America, within which the CIA, Special Forces, and USAID work together to achieve American policy objectives.[19] A country team can keep a lower profile than a big international mission but still risks accusations of interference. Both models inevitably include dispersed and vulnerable people, whose first lines of defence are the legitimacy of their task and the relationships that they establish with the local community.[20]

Elections play a crucial role in establishing legitimacy. They demonstrate to both international and local communities that intervention serves democracy and local interests, not those of the intervening powers. But they can also serve to legitimize the parties who are most entrenched in the conflict, hence the concern that early elections will merely leave intransigent ideologues or corrupt warlords in control of the political system. Parties with the greatest stake in elections will seek to manipulate or disrupt their outcome, thereby shaping the post-intervention environment in their favour. This is easy to do with threats and blandishments, and difficult for even a large military force to defend against. It was not until substantial NATO forces had deployed that Bosnia-Herzegovina was declared safe for elections, but even this did not set appropriate political conditions, because military forces could do nothing about human rights violations.[21] Similar problems were experienced in Afghanistan, where preparations for elections were complicated by violence deliberately targetting election workers.[22]

The critical challenge for stability operations is to repress violence while enabling the political, economic, and social dimensions of reconstruction. A large military force might not only be ineffective but could be seen as an occupying force, compromising the legitimacy of intervention and providing rich targets for those seeking to disrupt transition. A smart force that can respond to targetted attacks but that has a small social footprint might be more effective. Joint Commission Observers (JCOs) in the Balkans were small, armed teams living in the civilian community. They served liaison and intelligence functions during the transition from UN to NATO operations (1994 to 1996) and later served as observers until 2001.[23] Their strategic communications and special skills gave them a measure of personal safety as long as local authorities consented to their role. But they were not in a position to offer physical protection to local or international civilians.[24]

Small special teams like the JCOs are not big enough, and large military forces might create vulnerabilities, in addition to being more burdensome to the intervening powers. The PRT concept seeks the right combination of civil affairs and direct action to build community relationships while controlling violence through coercive action. Is this balance possible? Can the core civil-affairs functions be carried out in the absence of a pervasive security presence?

Civil military cooperation is designed to establish and maintain relations between military forces and civilians, including international organizations, non-governmental organizations, and the local authorities and populace in the operational area.[25] In American doctrine, the aim is primarily to facilitate the conduct of military operations by maximizing civilian support and minimizing interference. Lessening the impact of military operations on civilians is a secondary objective.[26] Although CIMIC and CA had their modern origins in the occupation of Germany and Japan, when military objectives were subordinated to political and economic goals,[27] the opposite priorities prevailed in the Cold War, when every military resource was focused on the military defeat of the enemy. Yet CA capabilities lend themselves to broader objectives. CIMIC is recognized as a command function, executed with the support of CA units and personnel.[28] CA specialists may have foreign language skills, cultural awareness, and formal education in psychology, medicine, law, governance, and social work. Frequently, they are involved directly with humanitarian and reconstruction efforts, distributing food, rebuilding schools and houses, and repairing bridges and roads.[29] Since none of these can be done without some degree of local cooperation, and since a security presence cannot ensure cooperation, CA tasks may sometimes be easier with a light security presence (presupposing cooperation) than with a heavy one.

US Civil Affairs doctrine is evolving rapidly with the challenges of Afghanistan and Iraq, but the core functions remain as described in the US Army manual on civil-affairs operations and set out in Table 12-1. They correspond broadly to the functions described in the Canadian CIMIC publication.[30] We can see these functions at the strategic level, too, in the structure of the Coalition Provisional Authority in Iraq.[31] This consistency suggests that the basic functions represent common experience and that in each case military force is secondary to the business of reconstruction and stabilization. However, military civil-affairs doctrine is focused on supporting military operations, and this leaves a broad spectrum of stabilization and reconstruction tasks that are of secondary concern to military commanders.

Given that there are adequate resources for political, social, and economic reconstruction, how much coercive power is sufficient to provide security? Answering this question requires an assessment of the kinds of coercive force that might threaten support for governance, relief and development, and reconciliation.

The US Army has three Special Operations Civil Affairs Battalions, each aligned with a regional theatre.[32] In addition to rapid deployment and higher standards of training and readiness, these battalions are distinguished from the reserve battalions by being prepared for at least five missions that are not within the normal scope of US Army Reserve Civil Affairs. These are FID and UW, CSAR, operations in austere environments in support of ODAs, and deployment by all means of infiltration. To the extent that civil affairs units are to be used in this sort of mission, they should train and operate with special forces. Beyond this, there are advantages and disadvantages to each of the alternatives described above.

The Coalition Provisional Authority in Baghdad prior to 30 June 2004 came close to providing full civil government by an occupying power. CIMIC,

TABLE 12-1
Civil-affairs Functions

Categories of Action	*US Civil Affairs Doctrine*[33]	*Additional Stabilization and Reconstruction Tasks*[34]
Political	• Support to Civil Administration (mainly conducted by reservists with special skills; includes civil assistance, civil administration in friendly territory, and civil administration in occupied territory)	• Develop civil society • Prepare and conduct elections
Economic	• Populace and Resource Control (manage dislocated civilians, NEO) • Humanitarian Assistance (disaster and refugee assistance – diminishes with increased hostilities) • Emergency Services (police, fire, ambulance, emergency preparation, work with AID, FEMA, and DART)	• Develop local enterprise • Build employment opportunities • Develop economic infrastructure
Social	• Military Civic Action (designed to win the support of the local population for the foreign national government)	• Inter-communal reconciliation • Cultural revitalization
Military/ Security	• Foreign Nation Support (identify and coordinate foreign nation resources, material, and labour to support military operations)	• Neighbourhood watch • Effective policing

and the normal operation of CA units, require legitimate local authorities with some powers, even if these are strictly limited to local affairs. Several circumstances can limit the authority of the local state. Governments may have limited capacity to rule (as in weak states like Liberia), or they may face competition from powerful local actors (as with the warlords in Somalia or Afghanistan), or they may face a state of anarchy and instability (as in Sierra Leone). In each of these cases, the military mission to "restore order" corresponds in practice to the need to support effective governance by establishing security and reinforcing the powers of legitimate government.

Psychological Operations can be employed to augment the influence of a small force, but caution is in order, as American doctrine makes clear. PSYOPS are defined as an "offensive fire"; they are directed at hostile and neutral audiences to influence attitudes and behaviour affecting the achievement of political and military objectives. Experience in war tells us that PSYOPS can be very effective at reducing the morale and combat potential of the enemy, encouraging surrenders and defections, or discouraging civilian support for a hostile government.[35] But these are negative rather than constructive accomplishments, and the use of PSYOPS to reinforce legitimacy has had many false starts. One poster released in Bosnia to encourage voting depicted a hand hovering over a chessboard, and the phrase, "it's your move". It was widely interpreted as evidence that the great powers were playing with Balkan pawns yet again, precisely reversing the message of empowerment intended.[36] To be effective, PSYOPS teams need to be very well connected to local culture and sensibilities and may need serious re-education to play a constructive role in managing public information, rather than an offensive one.

The heart of the argument for PRTs is that special operations forces can compensate for small numbers with good intelligence, a higher standard of training, and precise lethality. They can accomplish more than comparable numbers of conventional troops. They can live in austere conditions, dispensing with the security (and vulnerability) of a large encampment. They can use knowledge of local language and culture to elicit support from the communities within which they work. And because they are habitually employed in high-risk, low-profile missions, their casualties in remote battles are not as politically damaging as those of troops from conventional units.[37]

But special operations troops are neither disposable nor invincible. They lack the capacity to fight major land battles.[38] The kind of battle envisioned must be within their capabilities. When are special operations teams adequate to provide security for stabilization operations? How big do they need to be? Teams of a dozen or fewer formed the basis for Britain's fortified hamlet strategy in Malaya in the 1950s[39] and for America's Civilian Irregular Defence Group (CIDG) in Vietnam in the 1960s.[40] In these cases, the primary role was counter-insurgency, with little attention paid to the other dimensions of reconstruction.[41] A 1968 Brookings study recommended a security force in the tens of thousands to provide the framework for rehabilitation and development of Vietnam.[42] The JCOs deployed in Bosnia were adequate for liaison, monitoring, and some intelligence-gathering but were unsuited to supporting civilian engagement in the other dimensions of reconstruction. In the early phases of Operation Enduring Freedom, US Ranger companies and battalions deployed to isolated forward operating bases, relying on air support for backup. However, they were engaged primarily in seek-and-destroy missions against small, isolated groups of irregular troops in bad terrain.[43] They were generally not responsible for the security of civilians or the staff of international organizations that would later be engaged in reconstruction efforts.

Small teams combining direct action with civil affairs may help to provide a framework for civilian and NGO reconstruction efforts, but their success will ultimately hinge on the extent to which they can meet the security needs of both local and international players. PRTs in Afghanistan represent an interesting but slightly biased and risky experiment.

PROVINCIAL RECONSTRUCTION TEAMS

The bias in the PRT experiment is inherent in its origins. The concept originated not with the desire to achieve reconstruction and development objectives in the most secure regions but with the counter-terrorism task that continues to dominate Operation Enduring Freedom in the less-secure south and east. First proposed as "Joint Regional Teams" in November 2002, they were renamed PRTs in May 2003.[44] PRTs were established in February 2003 in Gardez, and the following month in Bamyan and Kunduz. Their focus was less on reconstruction than on garnering local support to undercut the remnants of the Taliban regime and on gathering human intelligence to help the hunt for al-Qaeda.[45] In this, the original American PRTs were the direct descendants of counter-insurgency techniques developed over half a century.

PRTs varied, but in 2003 generally consisted of a US Special Forces ODA (12 men) augmented by a civil-affairs team, engineering and medical sections, and assets devoted to strategic communications, psychological operations, intelligence gathering, and language support (local translators). At various times they worked with other American government agencies, particularly in the collection and dissemination of human intelligence. In the early stages, they consisted of just 60 to 90 people, mainly military. Some expanded up to several hundred, with most of the additional personnel being civilian, mainly employed by government agencies, although some NGOs on contract were included. They were quartered in compounds that had been secured initially by Ranger Companies and that can only be described as very austere. Few outside a small core stayed more than three months in location. They were sometimes co-located with elements of Afghan Militia Forces (AMF), which were generally sympathetic to the primary mission but not necessarily responsive to authorities in Kabul.

Under Operation Enduring Freedom, American PRTs conducted three sorts of activities. First, they attempted to map the community and its social and political structure: Where did power lie? Who was in charge? What were the key interests? Second, to garner support, they ran clinics, dug wells, and repaired buildings of local interest. These activities were generally at the behest of community leaders or chieftains whose good will was important to the mission. CA led these two activities, with PSYOPS, intelligence, and medical/engineering support as necessary. The ODA led security activities, initially by establishing contact with friendly local forces, then by conducting patrols (often with AMF), and offering some training (particularly in de-mining and patrolling skills) to local forces. ODAs often operated below strength, and they tended to seek security assurances from the AMF so they did not have to dissipate their strength on round-the-clock sentry duties.[46]

The American-led OEF was a counter-terrorist or counter-insurgency operation, but the UN Assistance Mission to Afghanistan (UNAMA) and NATO's International Stabilisation Assistance Force were focused on stability and reconstruction, initially only in the capital region. While OEF elements dealt with the *de facto* authority of local chieftains in tribal areas, UNAMA and ISAF dealt with the Afghan national government, whose writ scarcely extended outside Kabul. While international assets built up under NATO and the UN in Kabul, the U.S. resisted extending the mandate of ISAF and UNAMA beyond the capital for fear that it would interfere with combat operations. Yet the PRTs were too small and too poorly funded to take on significant development projects, and they had no mandate for local security.[47] Human rights reports continued to decry the abuses; drug-smugglers and violent local authorities thrived.[48] By the middle of 2003, the failure of Western countries to honour their pledges for development assistance, coupled with the evidence of continued lawlessness outside Kabul, led even conservative American analysts to call for more effort to "win the peace". The basic problem was that the mission was short of both combat troops and development resources.[49] This was the background to the expansion of the PRT concept.

New Zealand Defence Forces assumed leadership of the Bamyan Province Reconstruction Team in September 2003, providing an interesting model for Canadian special operations because of the contrast with the US experience.[50] In January 2004, Germany took over the PRT in Kunduz, making it the first NATO-operated PRT reporting back to ISAF in Kabul. Coalition forces continued to operate six additional PRTs in Parwan (U.S. and South Korea), Mazar-e-Sharif (U.K.), and the three American teams in Kandahar, Gardez, and Herat.[51] The PRTs led by New Zealand and Germany shifted the emphasis from counter-insurgency to reconstruction. Colonel Neville Reilly, the New Zealand PRT Commander, explained his role in extending the authority of the central government, working with the provincial governor and police chief, and encouraging local militia to disarm. The provincial governor's priorities were education and electricity supply.[52] New Zealand Defence Force press releases described the role of the PRT as:

> ...[establishing] relationships with the Afghan regional leadership to monitor and co-ordinate activities in order to strengthen the influence of the Islamic Transitional Government of Afghanistan (ITGA) and marginalize regional causes of instability. The [liaison] teams also facilitate aid efforts, monitor disarmament and assist in the reconstruction of Afghan institutions (education facilities etc.).[53]

The intriguing part of this mandate is to "marginalize regional causes of instability". How do they do that? The PRT consists of three liaison teams (LNO) supported by infantry, engineers (carpenters, plumbers, electricians), communications, logistics (drivers, cooks, supply technicians, medics, mechanics), and staff officers – a total of 91 predominantly army personnel. The

LNO teams consist of two officers and two NCOs, some of whom have gone through Special Forces selection and training. A UK development officer serves with the New Zealand PRT, following the Canadian practice of including a civilian "peace-building officer" with military deployments.[54] Although the 91 uniformed personnel are armed, fewer than half are combat specialists. A platoon of infantry provides local security for the camp, but the LNO teams are the key to the operation. These teams travel widely in the region and act as conduits for information. Their skills permit them to evaluate local forces, provide training, and command respect in a warrior culture. Some teams are qualified to call in air strikes or act as a foot on the ground for helicopter assault troops, giving the PRT a combat punch. However, the positive inducements of construction projects, aid money, and local assistance are calculated to win local support. Education, health care, and sanitation are basic needs; drug-traffickers and warlords do not provide them, but the PRT does. If there is intimidation or violence, the LNO teams can identify the source and escalate if necessary. They can quietly stake out smuggling routes and identify troublemakers, advise local officials on security measures, and manage human intelligence.

There are two differences between the 12-man ODA (the American model) and the four-man LNO teams (the British, New Zealand, and JCO model). The first lies in the distribution of skills. Both demand considerable cross-training in advanced skills such as weapons, fire control, explosives, communications, language skills, medical care, navigation, electronic warfare, and so on. But the degree of concentration is greater in four-man than in 12-man teams. The second is that the capacity for combat operations is less for four-man teams, and the emphasis on liaison, communication, and mobilization of indigenous resources is greater.

Security threats in Afghanistan include lawlessness and banditry: intertribal, inter-factional and intra-governmental conflicts with complex motives and strategies. Control over production and export of opium is a common motive, and "neo-Taliban" groups linked to the former Taliban and to al-Qaeda are growing concerns. If foreign troops are to lead in the hunt for disruptive elements, then the 12-man model, with significant backup, is preferable. But if the foreign role is merely supportive, as Colonel Reilly described it, then three four-man teams, with a higher proportion of officers, permit more simultaneous action and direction of other PRT assets.

DIRECT ACTION AND CIVIL AFFAIRS

The PRT is a useful model for response to the challenges of stability operations. We can see in them the combination of civil-affairs functions and direct-action capabilities in a single organization. The American model built around an ODA with capacity for direct action, and the British-New Zealand model built around liaison teams with some special capabilities offer two different patterns to consider. A third alternative is to separate civil-affairs and developmental action completely from any suggestion of coercive force. We can label these "military", "liaison", and "civilian" models for PRTs. The military model is built around a combat-focused special operations team. The liaison model is built around a group of liaison teams, which might call upon combat forces. The civilian model might include uniformed personnel, who might be armed but would perform only supporting roles and would be structured for self-defence, not combat.

The advantages of combining direct action and civil affairs centre on security and the utility of coercive force. In some cases stabilization may hinge on intimidating those who would perpetrate violence. NATO's IFOR achieved this with a massive military deployment – sixty thousand combat troops with sophisticated weapons and communications, air-supremacy, and a follow-on aid and development package that systematically rewarded cooperation and punished defection from the regime dictated by the international community. Civil-affairs operations were an integral part of this strategy.[55]

What are the options without massive military deployments? A small band of warriors, deployed in a community with a warrior culture, periodically fighting local battles to remove warlords and obstacles to peace, might come to be viewed as local protectors and guarantors of stability. But they may find themselves, as did American SOF in Haiti, drawn ever more tightly into local battles without being able to establish a framework for indigenous security and development.[56] The American ODA-based PRTs in Afghanistan, like the defensive bases in Vietnam, are a war-fighting counter-insurgency tool rather than a stabilization and reconstruction tool that enables development and aid agencies.[57]

The advantages of separating direct action from civil-affairs and relief-and-development activities centre on how locals interpret foreign military activity and on the importance of relationships and consent for the security of small, isolated teams. At a workshop in Ottawa in December 2003, several experienced international workers condemned the concept of PRTs, insisting that sufficient military forces should be deployed to provide for secure areas, within which international aid and development agencies could function safely as unencumbered civilians. The fear was that close association with military teams, which could be perceived to be part of a strategy of occupation and control, would turn the unprotected civilians into soft targets.[58] This seems to have been borne out by the unusual decision by *Médecins Sans Frontières* to withdraw from Afghanistan in July 2004, after a number of fatal attacks.[59] The conclusion seems to be that civilian development and aid agencies will resist being party to a counter-insurgency strategy but may not be able to justify the risk of deploying without a military security guarantee. Whether the liaison model provides sufficient distance to permit NGO collaboration remains to be seen.

These three models might be combined according to local circumstances. It might be reasonable for early PRTs to be combat-heavy, as the American models were. They might hand over to lighter PRTs following the liaison model, or to civilian teams at a later date. The problem with this linear conception of mission evolution is that people have long memories, and locals will not easily adjust as PRTs change characteristics every six months. Cultures that sanction inter-generational vengeance killings may not differentiate between the military PRT that killed a local resistance hero, and the softer liaison PRT that followed it six months later. This suggests that geographical rather than temporal experimentation may be more fruitful, and this appears to be what is in progress in Afghanistan.

CONCLUSION

If civil-affairs assets are used only to support prosecution of a military campaign, and if post-conflict stability is seen only through military lenses, then stability operations will look more and more like old-school imperial policing. We still have a lot to learn about methods for achieving post-conflict stability, but these are operations to which Canada may contribute much, by virtue of experience and national capacities.[60] The nature of Canadian involvement will continue to vary. But future operations may rely on a combination of covert and low-key tactics to control illicit violence, and open and visible activities to build working relations with the local populace. Direct-action capacity for the former, and civil-affairs and psychological-operations capacities for the latter will be part of every stability operation. The long-term commitment needed to support stability in places like Afghanistan and Iraq will generate demands for PRT-like structures from countries like New Zealand and Canada. Getting our combinations of direct action and civil affairs right will require some experimentation.

NOTES

1. The authors are grateful for the assistance of Larry Jenkins and Ulrich Scholz, whose comments and insights were helpful in arriving at our conclusions, and to Stefan Dordrechter and Karla Lyster for their research assistance. Views are those of the authors alone.
2. This was debated at the ABCA exercise, Focus 2000, resulting in revisions to the ABCA Handbook
3. Various treatments of these dimensions can be found in Michael Pugh, ed., *Regeneration of War-Torn Societies* (New York: St Martin's Press, 2000); David Last, "Picking up Peaces: Comparative Advantage in Post-Conflict Reconstruction" in *Over Here and Over There: Canada-U.S. Defence Cooperation in an Era of Interoperability,* ed., David G. Haglund, *Queen's Quarterly*, 2001; and John Hamre and Gordon Sullivan, "Toward Post-conflict Reconstruction," *The Washington Quarterly* 25:4

(Autumn 2002): 92. Hamre and Sullivan use the labels security, justice, social and economic development, and governance.

4. Douglas L. Bland and Sean M. Maloney, *Campaigns for International Security: Canada's Defence Policy at the Turn of the Century* (Montreal and Kingston: McGill-Queen's University Press, 2004), 23-27.
5. Norman Hillmer and J. L. Granatstein, *Empire to Umpire: Canada and the World to the 1990s* (Toronto: Copp Clark Professional, 1994).
6. Sean M. Maloney, *Canada and UN Peacekeeping, 1947-1974: Cold War by Other Means* (Toronto: Vanwell, 2003).
7. "Legitimate" is used here in a purely descriptive, rather than normative, sense. There were no systemic sanctions punishing the powers for their behaviour, as there had been none for colonizing powers in the nineteenth century.
8. John T. Fishel, *Civil Military Operations in the New World* (Westport, CT: Praeger, 1997), 3-16.
9. John T. Fishel, "War by Other Means? The Paradigm and its Application to Peace Operations," in *The Savage Wars of Peace: Toward a New Paradigm of Peace Operations,* ed. John T. Fishel (Boulder, CO: Westview Press, 1998), 5.
10. Discussions with John Fishel and Max Manwaring, 1996. See also the collected papers of the Manwaring project in *Uncomfortable Wars: Toward a New Paradigm of Low Intensity Conflict,* ed., Max G. Manwaring (Boulder, CO: Westview Press, 1991).
11. Interviews at US Army Command and General Staff College, Leavenworth, April 1995.
12. UN, *Blue Helmets* (New York: United Nations Department of Public Information, 1993). The Official UN history, *Blue Helmets* does not mention the subsequent resurgence of the independence movement in West Irian, which never really reconciled itself to Indonesian rule replacing Dutch colonial rule.
13. This consensus in military circles is most clearly articulated by John Hillen, *Blue Helmets: The Strategy of UN Peacekeeping* (New York: Brassey's, 2001).
14. Ibid.
15. Tomas Valasek, "Bosnia: Five Years Later," *The Defense Monitor,* Volume 29, Issue #10 (Washington, DC: Center for Defense Information, December 2000).
16. Mark Baskin, "Some Lessons for Security Sector Reform from Bosnia-Herzegovina and Kosovo," unpublished paper (Cornwallis, NS: Pearson Peacekeeping Centre, 2001).
17. On the general problem, see David Last, "Organizing for Effective Peacebuilding," in *Peacekeeping and Conflict Resolution*, ed. Tom Woodhouse and Oliver Ramsbotham (London: Frank Cass, 2000), 80-96; and Thomas G. Weiss, *Military-Civilian Interactions: Intervening in Humanitarian Crises* (Lanham, MD: Rowman and Littlefield, 1999).

18. International Crisis Group, *Bosnia's Nationalist Governments: Paddy Ashdown and the Paradoxes of State Building*, Balkans Report No. 146 (Sarajevo/Brussels: ICG, 23 July 2003), 19.
19. William W. Mendel and David G. Bradford, *Interagency Cooperation: A Regional Model for Overseas Cooperation,* McNair Paper 37 (Washington, DC: Institute for National Strategic Studies, 1995).
20. Roy Thomas, "The Role of Relationships in Providing Security for Unarmed UN Military Observers: Observations from Sector Sarajevo, October 1993 – July 1994," *The Liaison Journal*, Center for Excellence in Disaster Management and Humanitarian Assistance, Vol. 2, No. 3 (1998): 28-32.
21. 2nd Report of the High Representative for Implementation of the Bosnian Peace Agreement to the Secretary-General of the United Nations, Wednesday, 10 July 1996, especially paragraphs 79 and 80. http://www.ohr.int/other-doc/hr-reports/
22. Kim Barker, "Blast kills two Afghan women helping elections," *Chicago Tribune*, 27 June 2004.
23. Jon Anderson, "Joint Commission Observer Unit Finishes its Tour in Bosnia," *Stars and Stripes*, Sunday, 6 May 2001. British JCO teams were four-man SAS groups, while American teams were based on the ODA.
24. Interviews with JCO team members and local civilians, conducted in Prijedor and Gorni Vakuf, Bosnia-Herzegovina, January and March 1996.
25. Department of National Defence, *Civil Military Cooperation in Peace, Emergency, Crisis and War,* B-GG-005-004/AF-023 (Ottawa: DND, J3 DLLS 2-2, 1999), 3.
26. Department of the Army, *Civil Affairs Operations*, Field Manual No. 41-10 (Washington, DC, May 2000); see also US joint doctrine for civil affairs, noted below.
27. James Dobbins, John G. McGinn, Keith Crane, Seth G. Jones, Rollie Lal, Andrew Rathmell, Rachel Swanger, and Anga Timilsina, *America's Role in Nation-Building: From Germany to Iraq* (Santa Monica, CA: Rand Corporation, 2003), 8, 25.
28. Canada subscribes to the distinction between civil affairs units and the function of civil military cooperation, for which commanders are responsible. Canadian CIMIC manual.
29. United States, Department of Defense, *Joint Doctrine for Civil Affairs: Joint Pub 3-57.1* (14 April 2003); DND, *Civil Military Cooperation*, 1999, 1C-2, 2D-1, and Annex D to Chapter 5, *inter alia.*
30. DND, *Civil Military Cooperation*, 1999, Chapter 1.
31. Communication with author, June 2004.
32. Department of the Army, Field Manual 41-10, 3-31.
33. Ibid., 2-1 and elsewhere in Chapter Two.
34. Developed from Michael Pugh, editor, *Regeneration of War-Torn Societies* (New York: St Martin's Press, 2000).

35. DoD, *Doctrine for Joint Special Operations,* II-8. See also Canada, Department of National Defence, *CF Operations Manual,* B-GG-005-004/AF-000 (18 December 2000), Chapter 34.
36. Communication with author from Lieutenant Colonel Dana Eyre, 1998.
37. These advantages are discussed by Thomas K. Adams, *US Special Operations Forces in Action: The Challenge of Unconventional Warfare* (Portland, OR: Frank Cass, 1998), 2-25. See also Susan L. Marquis, *Unconventional Warfare: Rebuilding US Special Operations Forces* (Washington, DC: The Brookings Institution, 1997), 250-268.
38. Bernd Horn, "Special Men, Special Missions," in *Force of Choice: Perspectives on Special Operations*, eds., Bernd Horn, J. Paul de B. Taillon, and David Last (Montreal and Kingston: McGill-Queen's University Press, 2004), 14-15; and Department of National Defence, *The Asymmetric Threat Report* (31 August 2001), U-2.
39. John Coates, *Suppressing Insurgency: An analysis of the Malayan Emergency* (Boulder, CO: Westview, 1992).
40. Colonel (retired) Scott Crerar, "The Special Force Experience with the Civilian Irregular Defence Group (CIDG) and the Studies and Observation Group (SOG) in Vietnam," in *Force of Choice,* eds., Horn, Taillon, and Last.
41. The contrast can be seen in comparing Crerar's description of the CIDG and SOG to Metzner's description of the "pacification" program, which relied heavily on civil affairs. See Edward P. Metzner, *More than a Soldier's War: Pacification in Vietnam* (College Station, TX: Texas A&M University Press, 1995).
42. H. Field Haviland, Jr., Larry L. Fabian, Karl Mathiasen III, and Arthur M. Cox, *Vietnam After the War: Peacekeeping and Rehabilitation* (Washington, DC: The Brookings Institution, 1968).
43. Sean M. Maloney, *Enduring the Freedom: A Rogue Historian Visits Afghanistan* (Fairfax, VA: Potomac Books, 2005).
44. Barbara J. Stapleton, "The Provincial Reconstruction Team Plan in Afghanistan: A New Direction?" (Bonn: Agency Coordinating Body for Afghan Relief ACBAR, May 2003), 2.
45. Peace Operations Working Group of the Canadian Peacebuilding Coordinating Committee, "NGO/Government Dialogue on Provincial Reconstruction Teams (PRTs) in Afghanistan and the Militarization of Humanitarian Assistance, 4 December 2003, Final Report" (Ottawa: Canadian Peacebuilding Coordinating Committee, 2004), 2, 7.
46. Personal communication, April 2004. Some hearsay is involved in this account. See also *Provincial Reconstruction Teams: First Lessons Learned in Initial Implementation*, Coalition/Joint Civil-Military Operations Task Force (CJCMOTF), May 2003.
47. Ahmed Rashid, "The Mess in Afghanistan," *New York Review of Books*, 12 February 2004, 24-27.

48. Human Rights Watch, *Afghanistan's Bonn Agreement One Year Later: A Catalogue of Missed Opportunities*, Briefing Paper, 5 December 2002; Human Rights Watch, *All Our Hopes Are Crushed: Violence and Repression in Western Afghanistan,* Report, November 2002.
49. Council on Foreign Relations, "Afghanistan: Are We Losing the Peace?" Report by an Independent Task Force cosponsored by the Council on Foreign Relations and the Asia Society, June 2003.
50. Right Honourable Helen Clark, "NZDF to Lead Afghan Provincial Reconstruction Team," *Relief Web*, 22 September 2003.
51. "NATO takes over Provincial Reconstruction Teams," *Pakistan Tribune*, January 9, 2004.
52. Kevin Taylor, "Leader of NZ Afghanistan mission 'inspirational'," *New Zealand Herald,* 18 July 2003: 2.
53. Commander Sandra McKie, Defence Press Officer, New Zealand Defence Force, "Frequently Asked Questions Regarding the Deployment of the Provincial Reconstruction Team to Afghanistan," September 2003.
54. UK Foreign and Commonwealth Office Bulletin, "Provincial Reconstruction Teams," October 2003. On CIDA Peacebuilding Officers deployed with Canadian Peacekeeping forces, see Major Rohan Joseph Persaud Maxwell, *By Other Means: Peacebuilding During Military Operations,* unpublished thesis (Kingston: Royal Military College, June 2003)
55. *Evaluation of the Western Bosnia Rehabilitation Programme 1996-1998*, Centre for Defence Studies, King's College, London, 25 November 1999, 18-19.
56. Bon Shacochis, *The Immaculate Invasion* (New York: Viking, 1999), 284-285.
57. Crerar, "The Special Force Experience," 95-106.
58. Karla Lyster, rapporteur's notes (Ottawa: Carleton University, 4 December 2004). See also Peace Operations Working Group, "NGO/Government Dialogue"
59. Médecins Sans Frontières, "MSF Pulls out of Afghanistan," Kabul, 28 July 2004. http://www.msf.org/countries/page.cfm?articleid=8851DF09-F62D-47D4-A8D3EB1E876A1E0D
60. On experience, see Last, "Picking up Peaces"; on demographics, see Chapter Four of this volume.

CHAPTER THIRTEEN

ORBITAL ASSET OR OVERHEAD MENACE?

SPACE POWER AND SPECIAL OPERATIONS

Andrew B. Godefroy[1]

Special operations have always demanded the most sophisticated resources that a military force has to offer.[2] This demand has included space assets since the end of the 1950s, and space-based resources and products are now so integrated into Western forces for special operations that future missions are less and less likely to be executed without some type of space asset. From the simplest hand-held GPS receiver to the most sophisticated satellite imagery-analysis tool or target-designator, elite forces depend heavily on the advantages provided by highly sophisticated space-related technologies. These include early-warning, navigation, weather-forecasting, intelligence, surveillance, and reconnaissance devices. For most advanced militaries, space assets have not only influenced principles of warfare but have profoundly affected the way wars are prepared for and fought.[3]

At the same time, it would be reckless to assume that space power is always an asset to those who invest in this technology. Space power is a double-edged sword that special operations may find as much a hindrance as an advantage. While space-derived products, data, and intelligence were once the exclusive capability of only the most advanced military forces, their increasing diffusion into the commercial sector and to potential enemies during the past twenty years has greatly levelled the playing field. Adversaries not only have much greater space awareness; it is becoming more likely that they too may either employ counter-space measures to negate its advantage or even apply their own space power, albeit perhaps very limited.

SPACE POWER

When the Soviet Union successfully launched its first satellite, *Sputnik I*, into orbit in 1957, the idea of outer space as an enormously significant and potentially positive new frontier suddenly became a reality. At the very same instant, it also became a critical factor in strategy and policy as well as an unavoidable influence on the theory and practice of modern warfare. Today, the employment of space power for either deterrence or action is no longer theoretical opinion but rather a simple fact. By failing to adjust to this transformation, countries risk failure in warfare or success that comes only at great cost in life and materiel.[4]

Space power may be defined as the pursuit of national objectives through the medium of space and the use of space capabilities. It is important to note that this does not mean that space power may be thought of only in global or strategic terms, or that it consists of space-related intelligence or military space assets alone. Rather, it encompasses all of a nation's space assets – civilian and military, commercial and private, current as well as those planned for the future. Space power may be applied across the entire spectrum of conflict and during any phase of it, whether to shape a theatre or target before the initiation of hostilities or to achieve an objective after the fighting has begun. This chapter examines space power and the application of various space capabilities to special operations, particularly in the Canadian context.[5] As will be seen, space power can used not just respond to potential threats but to shape and mitigate them as space power and space capabilities are developed to meet the ever-expanding variety of conflicts that special forces may operate in.

Space capabilities or functions may be roughly summarized in eight categories: space launch, satellite communications, remote sensing, environmental monitoring, navigation and positioning, early warning, space control, and force application/ballistic missile defence (BMD).[6] Space launch is a necessary prerequisite for all aspects of space power. Lack of access to orbit severely limits the ability of a nation or actor to employ all other space capabilities. Satellite communications capability has reached most parts of the globe as cellphones replace landline signal-cable infrastructures. After space launch, remote sensing is perhaps the second-oldest space capability because surveillance and reconnaissance were among the first activities of both the US and Soviet space programs. The most important aspect of remote sensing, and perhaps the most dangerous, is its massively successful transition into the unclassified commercial market. Today, nearly anyone with a credit card and access to the Internet can have access to high-resolution satellite imagery of nearly any place on Earth. Environmental monitoring includes a host of space-based data-collection platforms that track everything from daily weather forecasts to annual changes to the Earth's atmosphere, terrain, polar caps, and oceans. As with remote sensing, there is an increasing diffusion of this capability from government into the commercial sector, although it remains largely funded and driven by government and civilian requirements.

By contrast, all three sectors are equally consumers of satellite navigation and positioning. While the space segment (satellites) and ground segment (satellite control stations) are controlled by the military, handheld navigation devices are readily available to anyone and can be employed just about anywhere in the world. More precise signals are available to select users (such as military special forces), but even the less precise set of signals will still allow someone to navigate to within a hundred meters or so of their intended target.

Of the eight categories only the last three are strictly defence-oriented, and only force application/BMD is a function largely outside the scope of deployed operations. Early-warning systems, originally designed to provide strategic defence against nuclear attacks, were migrated to more compact deployable systems in the late 1980s in response to the proliferation of Short Range Ballistic Missiles (SRBM) and related threats. Presently, deployed forces facing SRBM and tactical cruise-missile threats are able to deploy small-scale, yet highly efficient, integrated-tactical-warning and attack-assessment platforms (ITW/AA) within a theatre of operations. Space control is concerned with ensuring freedom of access to, and passage within, space while possibly denying the same freedom to an adversary. Usually driven by governments and national security policies, space control has traditionally been considered only in strategic terms. Space control may be critical to the success of a special operations mission in theatre, and counter-space missions or resisting space control may be an assignment of special forces or their adversaries. Finally, force application (e.g., the employment of space weapons or ballistic-missile defence) rests almost entirely at the strategic level and would not likely become a capability for special operations missions unless a country were faced with total war. Conversely, special forces may be assigned to seek and destroy force application/BMD targets. In both recent Gulf wars, Iraqi strategic-missile forces were critical targets that both US and British special forces units pursued actively.

With few exceptions, the space capabilities detailed above could be employed to support a variety of special operations.[7] Those associated with the provision of space-derived data are still the most germane to the current enhancement of equipment and personnel, although it is possible – if not very likely – that armed forces around the world will become increasingly dependent on all forms of space systems as space power comes to be institutionalized within all national military strategies and doctrines. At the beginning of this century, space power is as integral to war as air power was in the last century.

SPACE CAPABILITIES AND FORCES FOR SPECIAL OPERATIONS

Space assets are similar to special operations forces in terms of how politicians and military planners perceive them, as well as how they are funded, built, sustained, and employed. The two capabilities suffer similar criticism about their cost and utility in light of the modernization and transformation of other armed forces and technologies. One must ask, then, not only why we need forces for special operations but also why we need to support them with a space capability.

Special operations forces are designed to provide unique capabilities that cannot be effectively duplicated in other units of an armed force. Space assets do the same, although there are some land-based technologies that may appear to provide similar capabilities. Unmanned Aerial Vehicles (UAV) and imagery satellites are one such pair. But while a UAV may provide detailed overhead reconnaissance of a target just as an imagery satellite could, the UAV is constrained by weather conditions and limitations on its range, fuel, and coverage capabilities. It is also easier for its target to detect than a satellite. By contrast, the satellite never has to "de-ice its wings", can stay aloft considerably longer and cover exponentially larger areas simultaneously, and is much harder to detect and less susceptible to being interdicted or destroyed.[8] In essence, the UAV is a conventional means, while the imagery satellite acts in the role of special operations.

Given the unique capabilities that certain space assets may provide, it is logical to combine such a tool with forces that are uniquely suited to employ it. US SOF acquired space capabilities as early as the late 1960s, when the U.S. pursued the Initial Defence Communications Satellite Project (IDCSP) to provide better strategic communications for its forces in Vietnam. At the same time, US satellite imagery was coming into use in support of operational and tactical missions in Vietnam, and SOF received limited space-derived information and intelligence in support of their assigned missions during that conflict.

Space power remained a strategic asset for the U.S. throughout the 1970s and 1980s. Since SOF were also treated as a strategic asset, however, it is very likely that the two capabilities were integrated to project American power worldwide. Not surprisingly, details of space support to special operations in unclassified sources and literature is sparse, so we can only speculate as to how space assets may have been employed. Recent memoirs from SOF members serving during this period reveal little about space support, giving only generic hints about various space technologies used in support of missions. Overall, satellite imagery and satellite communications appear to have been the most applicable space assets.

The transition of space power from purely strategic activities to operational war-fighting in the 1990s revealed numerous impressive technologies and their impact on modern warfare. For example, the GPS constellation not only played a major role in the Second Gulf War (1990-1991) but has become a staple of nearly all modern allied targetting and offensive action since then. During the 2003 Iraq War, the U.S. demonstrated that it is capable of "tweaking" the constellation to ensure that the first satellites coming over the horizon receive the most recent frequency updates.[9] Although perhaps relatively transparent to deployed conventional forces in the theatre of operations, the ability to fine-tune GPS presented new opportunities for SOF to support unconventional-warfare, direct-action, and special-reconnaissance roles that have rapidly become the norm in places like Iraq and Afghanistan.

Other special-operations roles have also benefited from dynamic evolution of deployable space systems. Current mobile and handheld satellite communications play critical roles in supporting civil-affairs tasks, information operations, and psychological operations. Remote sensing, can assist with counter-proliferation missions, while GPS and Search and Rescue satellites support collateral tasks such as combat search and rescue and humanitarian assistance. Overall, the ability to put many space assets right into the end-user's hand has truly wedded space technologies to counter-terrorism and special operations in a way that many other modern technologies may not be.

WHEN SPACE IS THE ENEMY

Space gives forces conducting special operations a technological edge but can also cause problems. Increasing dependency on space support creates vulnerability, and space power can be employed as a weapon against forces engaged in special operations. Often at a disadvantage in terms of conventional firepower, adversaries are likely to exploit asymmetrical advantages using space assets whenever possible to even the odds against special forces.

Many tasks assigned in special operations depend heavily on extensive intelligence preparation of the battlefield and on accuracy in both planning and execution. Modern special operations have come to depend heavily on space assets to accomplish their tasks. This in itself is a vulnerability that adversaries will try to exploit. The most logical way to do so would be various forms of counter-space operations in order to degrade, or if possible, destroy friendly space assets. For example, recent conflicts in the Balkans, the Middle East, and Southwest Asia have demonstrated the importance of GPS to both special and conventional operations. A likely counter-space role for adversaries, then, would be to find ways of reducing or eliminating GPS capabilities. The loss of GPS capability, even for a very brief period, would seriously disrupt military efforts worldwide, effectively shutting down many special operations until the system was restored. To date, reported jamming techniques against GPS have had limited success, if any.[10] Since adversaries can affect neither the satellites nor the signal, they may choose the alternative of targetting GPS command and control stations on the ground. Adversaries might also view other ground segments as high-priority targets, given that they are a critical link in the chain of space power.

Space capabilities may also become an unexpected liability. In 2002 a British amateur satellite-tracking enthusiast was able to capture unencrypted US and British UAV video footage of operations in the Balkans that was being transmitted through a commercial satellite, *Telstar 11*.[11] Although NATO responses to media inquiries indicated a lack of concern, Richard Perle, then

Chairman of the Pentagon's Defense Policy Board, did report later that there was concern and that the transmissions would be encrypted in the future.[12] Fortunately, perhaps, it was a British citizen who discovered this satellite vulnerability and immediately reported the matter to authorities.[13] What if a Balkan adversary or criminal organization had found the leak first or monitored it during the execution of allied operations?

Another space-related incident occurred during the 2003 Iraq War, when the US Central Command temporarily banned all use of satellite phones operated by Gulf telecommunications company Thuraya after receiving intelligence that the company's satellite phone services had been compromised.[14] Thuraya satellite phones were extremely popular and were used across the entire Middle East theatre of operations by media, military, civilian agencies, non-government organizations, and civilians. Concerns were raised about security when it was realized that the phones were also equipped with a GPS-based user-location system. If Thuraya had been compromised (the company quickly issued a statement that it was never penetrated), enemy forces could have used the information to detect the approximate location of friendly units and direct attacks against them.[15] For example, if a US or British unit had an embedded journalist or a civilian-support component at their base of operations, Iraqi forces would have been able to locate that base and attack it.[16]

Adversaries may also take advantage of space power for their own activities. Third-party accessibility to space assets has increased tenfold over the last decade with the dynamic expansion of the commercial space market as well as increased remote accessibility through technologies such as satellite communications and the Internet. The latter could be extremely dangerous to friendly forces. Commercial products such as satellite cellphones and GPS receivers are in the hands of adversaries as well, and both are employed to good effect.

In addition to conducting counter-space operations against our special forces, adversaries will conduct their own intelligence preparation of the battlefield, now with the additional advantage of space-derived products. During the Vietnam War, North Vietnamese troops expended considerable effort to determine likely insertion and extraction points of US Military Assistance Command Vietnam SOG units along the Ho Chi Minh Trail, by using maps, aerial photos, radio-direction-finding techniques, and captured US materials. Their diligence paid handsome dividends, and American special operations against the Trail were often defeated.[17] Today, anyone surfing the Internet for an hour could easily collect meteorological and terrain data, highly detailed satellite imagery and maps, GPS navigation data, and details on friendly forces and use them within their immediate area of interest. Iraqi insurgents or al-Qaeda forces could use space assets to deny some freedom of manoeuvre to special forces deployed against them.[18]

More disturbing is the fact that adversaries may acquire more detailed or sensitive space products through political loyalty or simply by paying for them. For example, a commercial company might sell detailed space imagery without knowing its true customer. Of course, there are waiting periods for acquisition of products (usually 14 to 21 days), but this will not likely make a difference if the target is a static facility or garrison. Nor is there anything to stop adversaries or terrorists from purchasing a commercially available mobile ground-receiving station for their own use either. Current models are small enough to be towed behind a civilian SUV and are easy to conceal and employ. The right knowledge and equipment would make it possible to acquire downloads of imagery intended for other customers so long as the pirate ground-receiving station is located inside the area to which the satellite is broadcasting (the "downlink footprint").[19] Other space-derived information is equally vulnerable to theft because the technology is available to anyone who knows how to use it.[20]

Adversaries recognize the value of space power as well as its vulnerabilities. In addition to exploiting whatever resources are available to them, they will be wary of the advantage it may provide to friendly forces and will seek every opportunity to degrade or deny that advantage. For their part, special operations forces must recognize that space assets may become an overhead menace and plan for their own space-control activities during a mission.

CANADA'S DEFENCE SPACE PROGRAM

Although the fact has not been publicized, Canada has been an active participant in defence-related space activities since the end of the Second World War. Like its allies, Canada initiated a series of projects in the 1950s that focused on strategic defence, surveillance of space, and reconnaissance. For both political and technological reasons, however, all of these initiatives faltered during the following decade.[21] Nothing of the original Canadian defence space program survived into the 1970s, leaving the country to depend largely on the space assets of its allies and other third parties. Canada did not retreat from defence-space activities entirely, but from then on, the national space program focused almost entirely on the development of civilian and commercial applications and on international cooperation. Space and national security received little overt attention within defence policy for the next twenty years.

While it is very likely that Canada continued to receive strategic space intelligence from its allies throughout the 1970s and 1980s, it was not until 1987 that Canada officially re-affirmed its interest in a defence space policy or program.[22] This was spurred in part by the political debate then under way in Ottawa over the American Strategic Defence Initiative (SDI) and its potential impact on the 1986 renewal of the NORAD agreement. Among other concerns, the issue exposed the dangerous absence of knowledge or oversight within the Department of National Defence on matters related to defence space programs and ballistic missile defence. Canada had no defence space policy at the time, and few senior officers were well informed about the political, strategic, and technical aspects of the weaponization and militarization of space. Similarly, there existed no organization within DND that specifically monitored or dealt with such matters.[23] DND perceived the militarization and weaponization of space as essentially the same thing and generally opposed them, as did the government.

In 1987, DND responded with the hasty creation of the National Defence Headquarters Directorate of Space Doctrine and Operations, but the organization was disbanded just two years later. The expected peace dividend from the end of the Cold War, together with subsequent cutbacks in Canadian defence spending, ensured its early demise because many believed that the Canadian Forces did not need military space assets (beyond those intimately associated with space intelligence). When the New World Order presented a more dangerous and unpredictable security environment than anticipated, conflicts such as the Gulf War and the Balkans highlighted just how invaluable space support was to both war-fighting and stability operations. Arrangements were then made to institutionalize a Canadian post-Cold War defence strategy for space. Still, it was another seven years before that strategy resulted in the authorization of a new Directorate of Space Development (D Space D) within DND.[24]

Today, D Space D is responsible for the oversight and development of Canada's defence space program, including support for policy and strategy development, international cooperation on defence space, strategic space-intelligence initiatives, and occasionally, operational space-support.[25] With perhaps the exception of international cooperation on defence space, the main effort is on management and development of strategic-level technical space programs. Since other efforts such as the tactical exploitation of space receive fewer resources and support, very few of these initiatives actually come to fruition.[26]

The apparent neglect of support for defence space initiatives, however, cannot be laid at the feet of a seemingly uncaring Department of National Defence. Since the SDI debates of the mid-1980s, the issue of space and security has captured the attention of Canadian politicians, and the government's public opposition to the weaponization of space has become something of a centrepiece of Canadian foreign policy. This growing attention makes it increasingly difficult for DND to unilaterally articulate an aggressive defence space policy that provides a full spectrum of operational space support for its deployed forces. The Department of Foreign Affairs, for example, has confronted DND and other government departments, suggesting a growing correlation between the militarization of space and the possible weaponization of space. Citing the American experience in the 1990s, senior officials have argued that an increase in CF dependency and vulnerability with respect to space will likely lead to stronger justification, and possibly political support, for the development of defensive space systems and eventually offensive weapons.[27] The Director-General, International Security Bureau at DFAIT, has warned that encouraging militarization of space will make weaponization "a self-fulfilling prophecy".[28] It is clear that clashing agendas will stall any initiatives to provide new or enhanced space capabilities to deployed forces. This and the inherent expense of military space-applications make any plans for operational space support to special operations seem little more than a paper exercise.

SPACE POWER AND CANADIAN SPECIAL OPERATIONS

The situation does not look promising for Canadian Counter-Terrorism and Special Operations (CTSO) staff seeking to maximize the application of space technologies.[29] It can be assumed that most of the space assets currently employed have already been institutionalized and are probably related directly to the provision of intelligence. The general reluctance of other government departments to support any expenditure or resources on defence space activities in general is also evident. As a result, incorporating other existing or future space assets into special operations may prove difficult. It becomes critical, then, as this entire volume proposes, to determine exactly what options Canada might wish to exercise with respect to space capabilities and also what choices it must make to ensure some degree of success in building its space assets.

First, there are basic questions that must be answered. What does Canada already have by way of space capability for special operations, and what is it still looking for? In the absence of a clear answer to these questions, it may be more productive to discuss what special-operations staff might address when considering their own future use of space power.

Oversight, coordination, and integration for special operations and space must work at the highest levels. Canada's current defence space policy, last updated in 1998, remains very weak in defining guidelines or policy for operational space support and, more pointedly, support to CTSO staff.[30] The same may be stated for CF joint operations doctrine. It, too, is under revision, with both special-operations and space-support annexes still largely under construction. Policy and doctrine are meant to be dynamic and fluid documents that are continuously being revised. Documents in circulation, however, should be relevant enough to reflect current and near-future trends and *modus operandi*. The delays or lack of interest in modernizing DND space policy and CF joint space doctrine will retard the strengthening of the special operations-space relationship and may also affect evolution and funding.[31] The only advantage in the fact that these guidelines have not yet received a recent update is that CTSO staff still have an opportunity to have their own space-related interests identified and integrated into DND space policy and CF joint space operations doctrine before they are ratified. History has shown that top-level documents, once approved, may not be amended for at least five years, so the time to become involved in developing space policy and space doctrine is now.

Assuming that some relationship exists between special operations and defence space, or will be ratified in the near future, the next step would be to study the nature of that relationship. What do CTSO staff expect from space support? Are they simply looking for a space widget, or is there a desire for the institutionalization of a long-term space capability? We should also ask whether direct support for special operations should be left to a command organization such as D Space D, or to some other DND organization? What role might the CF Joint Operations Group play? Or would it be simpler to provide Canadian special operations forces with an internal or liaison capability instead? Finally, what mechanism will exist for CTSO staff to look ahead as space technologies and applications continue to evolve, and who will assess the impact of space on special operations?

Stronger working relationships between DND's CTSO staff and space organizations at all levels will not only influence policy and doctrinal issues but will also promote joint concepts and integration at the operational level. As well, identifying an Office of Primary Interest whose *true* primary responsibility is space support to special operations would certainly ensure that appropriate attention is given to lessons learned and to improvement of space systems and capabilities. At the same time, however, it is important not to leap to conclusions. Until definitive studies of operational space support for the CF have been completed, the best model or structure for this kind of support for special operations remains elusive. For decision-makers and operational planners, space support still requires proper definition.[32]

Since the current organizational culture within DND and funding restrictions will probably continue for the foreseeable future, a dramatic increase in CF space capabilities is unlikely. Rather, DND will probably continue to rely on the acquisition and delivery of space-derived information from third parties. This means a continued focus on the priority of maintaining defence space relationships with Canada's allies, deferring space-support roles and resources to the DND organizations that already supply space information and intelligence to various tasks and missions. It is also most likely, therefore, that organizations such as D Space D will not be assigned to provide operational space support in the near future.[33] As a result, beyond policy and doctrinal matters, CTSO staff would do well to plan for internal investments on advanced technologies for access to space resources and perhaps a small, specially trained cadre for space operations and support. For other relationships such as those mentioned above, active oversight and aggressive liaison must suffice until there is greater political and military support for DND space activities.

LOOKING AHEAD

The current era is one of conflict, with both space power and special operations enjoying positive political and military attention. In Canada, both the government and the public appear to remain somewhat uncertain about where defence-space programs and special-operations capabilities may lead the country. If the characteristics of the war on terror remain consistent over the next few years, these two assets will undoubtedly become required investments in the country's national security. For CTSO staff, knowing the advantages and dangers of space technologies will be one challenge; harnessing its power to protect Canada will be another. Obviously, many choices lie ahead.

NOTES

1. Copyright 2004 Andrew B. Godefroy, CD, PhD.
2. [Editor's note: as in other chapters in this volume, the capitalized term Special Operations Forces (SOF) is used only to refer to the range of capabilities described by this term in American doctrine.]
3. This is not to suggest that current and future special operations are being held captive by the advent of autonomous space technologies. As political scientist Seymour Melman once observed, "Men may be captives, but only of other men." For more on the classical debate surrounding autonomous technology and political and military decision-making, see Seymour Melman, *Pentagon Capitalism: The Political Economy of War* (New York: McGraw-Hill, 1970).
4. Colin S. Gray, "The Influence of Space Power Upon History," *Comparative Strategy*, 15 (1996): 293.
5. Space power is often examined in the political and strategic context of militarization or weaponization of space. This chapter recognizes these constructs but moves the analysis down a step, to focus on space capabilities that fall into one or other of these two roles.
6. These replace an earlier space-theory concept identifying four main categories/functions: space access, space support, force enhancement, and force application.
7. Using satellites to collect, analyze, or distribute space-derived data. These activities include imagery, communications, navigation, remote sensing, weather forecast, early warning, search and rescue, etc.
8. Assuming the satellite could be effectively targetted, it could be interdicted or destroyed by various ASAT weapons. Only a few of the major state powers currently have such a capability.
9. W. Scott, and C. Covault, "High Ground Over Iraq" and "Sweetening GPS: Squadron Boosted Accuracy 'Window' to Support Iraq Air Campaign,"*Aviation Week & Space Technology*, 9 June 2003: 44-48 and 48-49.
10. J. Singer, "US-Led Forces Destroy GPS Jamming Systems in Iraq," *Space News,* 25 March 2003.
11. P. Majendie, "Open Transmissions: British Satellite Enthusiast Watches NATO Spy Plane Video," *ABC News,* 13 June 2002.
12. Ibid.
13. The leak was first reported by British engineer John Locker.
14. The ban on Thuraya satellite phones in Iraq lasted from 2-16 April 2003.

15. AFP Qatar, "US Military Bans Use of Thuraya Satphones in Iraq," *Space Daily,* 4 April 2003.
16. The caveat being that Iraq may have gained actionable intelligence only. Conducting offensive operations on the basis of such intelligence is a separate challenge.
17. W. Rosenau, *Special Operations Forces and Elusive Enemy Ground Targets: Lessons from Vietnam and the Persian Gulf War (*Santa Monica, CA: RAND, 2001).
18. Web sites such as Federation of American Scientists (www.fas.org) and Global Security (www.globalsecurity.org), for example (and there are hundreds more), provide a wealth of open-source information including satellite imagery and detailed maps or relevant areas of conflict, US and allied Orders of Battle, as well as information on Allied operational concepts and doctrine. Weather forecasts are easily retrievable from US government web sites, as are updates and technical adjustments for GPS navigation systems. Adversary access to Open Source Intelligence should be a major concern for SOF planners.
19. Confidential source.
20. For example, captured US equipment (GPS receivers, satcom equipment, etc.) in Iraq may be employed to support adversary operations or to learn more about American operations and tactics.
21. Early in the Cold War, Canada initiated a series of defence space projects, including ballistic missile studies, surveillance of space systems, and anti-satellite weapons. For a detailed study of this subject see Andrew B. Godefroy, *Defence and Discovery: Science, National Security, and the Origins of the Canadian Rocket and Space Program, 1945-1974,* PhD Dissertation, Royal Military College of Canada, 2004.
22. See Canada, DND, *Space Policy Paper (*Ottawa: DND, July 1987, updated September 1992 and March 1998); see also DND, *Defence White Paper,* Ottawa: 1987, 1994.
23. Canada, DND, *A Canadian Military Space Strategy (*Ottawa: DND Chief of Review Services, 1989).
24. Ibid., 1. See also DND NDHQ Instruction DCDS 2/91 on the formation of the Space Defence Working Group. Defence space issues were part of the 1994 defence review and subsequent white paper; however, it was a series of internal DND working group efforts that eventually generated enough interest to have D Space D created.
25. The Assistant Deputy Minister Policy also takes a leading role in developing strategy related to space and missile-defence issues.
26. The nucleus of D Space D is regularly staffed with fewer than thirty military officers and civilians, including administrative support. Limited resources seriously retard adequate attention to all priorities and interests.

27. P. Meyer, "Arms Control Options In and From Space," in *Towards Fusion of Air and Space: Security Developments and Assessing Choices for Small and Middle Powers,* eds., D. Johnson and A. Levite (Santa Monica, CA: RAND, 2003), 82-85. See also D. Pugliese, "Federal Officials Clash Over Space Security," *National Post,* 22 March 2004: A6.
28. Meyer, "Arms Control Options In and From Space," 84.
29. [Editor's note: CTSO is a staff group in Canadian National Defence Headquarters, with responsibility for liaison and planning. The author uses it here in a generic sense to denote staff groups involved in planning and coordinating both counter-terrorism and special operations.]
30. DND, *Defence Space Policy* (unclassified) (Ottawa: DND, 1992, reissued 1998).
31. While some prefer the "old school" method of taking an informal approach to each and every mission or task, such policies will not ensure the survival of CF space capabilities or secure scarce funding for growth. As history has already shown, it was a failure to articulate a comprehensive, economically viable, and most importantly, relevant way ahead that was largely responsible for the near-dissolution of Canada's first defence space program at the end of the 1960s.
32. Confidential source. D Space D completed an ill-prepared and poorly directed stakeholder analysis on CF space support requirements in early 2004. A reluctance by the organization to take joint space support issues seriously, further exacerbated by internal lack of interest and conflict, in turn negated almost any opportunity to gain support for what was described by other DND organizations as an outdated and failing concept.
33. There is always the possibility, however, that experimental test beds or concepts may be fielded on a one-time case-by-case basis.

CHAPTER FOURTEEN

SPECIAL OPERATIONS FORCES AND TECHNOLOGY

TRADITION, INNOVATION, AND IMPLICATIONS FOR CANADA

Jason S. Ridler[1]

Like conventional forces, special forces are witnessing new challenges brought on by advanced technology. Discussion of a Revolution in Military Affairs, initiated by advanced information technologies, has caused Western militaries to reevaluate the complex relationship between armed forces and technology. Those engaged in special operations are defined by this relationship to a greater degree than their conventional counterparts. To achieve their goals and missions, they must compensate for quantitative deficiencies through qualitative excellence. This has required an attitude to technology that embraces change as a challenge to be met rather than a force to be resisted. It is this attitude that has contributed to the ascendance of US Special Operations Forces in the American-led war on terror, and to the bright future of special operations in general.

This chapter argues that forces engaging in special operations, such as US SOF and the U.K.'s SAS, derive their advantage from an innovative approach to technology. They find new opportunities as technology and operations change. In the 1970s, terrorism stimulated change in the SAS, and recently the RMA has presented opportunities for change in US SOF. National choices about technology, however, are closely linked to social and cultural variables and to national circumstances. It is these factors that will set the context within which Canada makes decisions about new technology to support special operations.

DOCTRINE, TECHNOLOGY, AND INNOVATION

Doctrine is a body of "fundamental principles by which military forces guide their actions in support of objectives."[2] Doctrine sets the parameters for the military's technological needs. Ideally, it should be reviewed regularly and rigorously to validate its assumptions. If necessary, assumptions should be changed, including those concerning technology. But as American military analyst Gordon McCormick observes, this task is difficult:

> Once established, traditional patterns of thought and action become comfortable and, hence, difficult to abandon, even when their continued utility has been called into question. As often as not, however, traditional formulas simply go unchallenged in the first place. What was once a successful way of doing things becomes, at some point, part of the conventional wisdom. The problem with such "conventions" is that they are not regularly subjected to re-evaluation. Continuing with the old ways becomes an article of faith, and faith... breeds a distrust of change.[3]

As the distillation of experience, tradition is a cornerstone of military effectiveness. But traditional thinking about doctrine and technology can innoculate against innovative approaches to both. Analyst Stephen Peter Rosen says that innovation of any kind is difficult for institutions in general and for the military in particular, yet failure to innovate can have dire consequences.[4] He illustrates McCormick's concerns by examining the US Army's failure to adopt a counter-insurgency (CI) role in the Vietnam era. Despite President Kennedy's personal interest and initiative, as well as the approval of senior military personnel, the adoption of CI training was thwarted by institutional belief that it was less important than the traditional war-fighting skills the U.S. needed to face the Soviet threat in Europe. This translated into nominal recognition of CI needs but no doctrinal, structural, or technical changes; institutional inertia blocked doctrinal and technical innovation.[5] A logical belief in the primacy of war-fighting may have compromised an effective refocusing of doctrine and technology for an army actively engaged in a difficult war that was very different from the one expected in Europe. This may have made defeat inevitable.

Forces intended for special operations, while not impervious to stagnation, are structured and oriented for the unconventional and so are more flexible and adaptable to change. Australian thinking about special operations consciously describes them as leading change for conventional forces: what is "special" today may become conventional tomorrow. Several other countries have adopted this approach to technology that distinguishes special forces from conventional.

Technology is one of the pillars that allow special forces like SOF to exercise strategic influence, traditionally deep behind enemy lines. Examining the Falklands War, British scholar Alastair Finlan observes,

> Special Forces have a reciprocal partnership with technology for their mission requirements are significantly different from conventional units and their needs often stimulate technological advances like the Lewes bomb in 1941...To a large degree, the success of these units, even, for that matter, their very existence, was (and still is) highly techno-dependant.[6]

Two critical factors define the relationship between special forces and technology. First, having the right technology is paramount to success. Second, the relationship between operational experience and technological development – that is, meeting new needs as they arise – must be maintained and supported. The U.S. appreciates this. Its Special Operations Command has its own R&D funds. While most of its budget is geared towards improving current systems, in 2000 it allocated $6.9 million of its $237.7-million budget towards development of its technological base.

> This program targets initiatives designed to advance technologies that meet critical SOF needs. These include reduced electronic signatures of SOF aircraft, lightweight power sources, and innovative weapons. Technology programs of other DoD and non-DoD organizations are reviewed to identify opportunities to cooperatively exploit emerging technologies and avoid duplication of effort. This approach of leveraging SOF funds maximizes the return on investment of SOF technology base dollars.[7]

Their forward-thinking approach and relatively small numbers allow SOF to embrace technological and doctrinal change more easily than American conventional forces by taking advantage of the technology developed by others for their own use. A brief historical example will illustrate the SOF approach to doctrine and technology before we turn to more contemporary challenges.

In the 1970s, as terrorism became an international concern, Britain's SAS was tasked with counter-terrorist duties. This role differed greatly from the traditional SAS role as specialized infantry fighting in Britain's receding empire, but the unit soon set a standard. General Sir Peter de la Billière, commander of the SAS from 1969 to 1974, recounted how SAS Captain Andy Massey had independently approached him with plans for introducing counter-terrorist (CT) capabilities. The headache of legal jurisdiction for such operations prompted the government to dismiss the initial proposal. After the Arab terrorist group Black September kidnapped and murdered Israeli athletes during the 1972 Olympic games, however, the government changed its mind. The SAS began their CT effort, code-named Operation Pagoda, and were given funds for new technologies to make organizational changes operationally effective.[8]

De la Billière claimed that the unit's small structure and continuous thinking about future challenges allowed the SAS to embrace this task quickly and effectively:

> It seemed vital that everyone, officers particularly, should be searching for change all the time – and indeed one of the Regiment's strengths lay in its habit of

> looking ahead, adjusting techniques to meet future demands (the creation of the Pagoda team was a perfect illustration).[9]

The new "techniques" involved the creation of the infamous "Kill House" and the introduction of stun grenades ("flash-bangs") for close-quarter combat. The unit adopted firearms more suitable for dynamic entry roles, replacing the traditional Sterling sub-machine gun with the US Ingram and introducing Remington shotguns for opening doors. They also introduced chemical protection equipment. Having met doctrinal requirements for new technology, they began intensive training in anti-terrorist missions, primarily hostage-rescue. Success was not achieved overnight. As historian Anthony Kemp noted, "[I]t took several years of patient experimentation to arrive at the present-day high-technology outfit worn by anti-terrorist squads worldwide."[10] But preparing for the future paid off when it counted. The SAS exercised these skills in April 1980, nullifying the terrorist seizure of the Iranian Embassy in London.

The secretive nature of special forces prevents close examination of technological development. The SAS's effective development of CT capability was supported by political, social, and cultural factors, not least Britain's strategic responsibilities and concerns. The contrast between the successful development of CT doctrine in the U.K. and the American failure to develop CI doctrine for Vietnam reinforces the importance of organizational culture. The SAS fostered an ethos of forward-thinking, seeing change as a challenge to innovate, acting quickly to incorporate new technology, and seizing opportunities presented by changing norms and new threats.

The "special operations" approach to technology is characterized by a willingness to think about the future and expend resources to experiment and develop new ways of doing things. It also implies financial support for uncertain and evolving technological needs. These features characterize SOF today, when technology seems poised to usurp some key functions associated with special operations or to provide dramatic new ways of accomplishing missions.[11]

RMA TECHNOLOGY AND SPECIAL FORCES

Many US analysts believe a Revolution in Military Affairs has been taking place since the Gulf War (1990-1991), primarily because of advanced information technology.[12] The most common definition of the RMA is that of Andrew Marshall, Director of the Office of Net Assessments in the US Office of the Secretary of Defense:

> A major change in the nature of warfare brought about by advances in military technology which, when combined with dramatic changes in military doctrine and organizational concepts, fundamentally alter the character and conduct of military operations.[13]

Most RMA analysts emphasize greater accuracy, lethality, stealth, and speed of decision-making in joint operations as the primary benefits for those militaries willing to risk technological, conceptual, and structural change.[14] The technologies most commonly associated with these benefits are precision-guided munitions (PGMs) and advanced intelligence, surveillance, and reconnaissance (ISR) assets, linked to sophisticated command and control systems.

Most RMA discussions relegate special operations forces to a supporting role, and their particular relationship with RMA technology has generated little open-source literature. It is instructive to consider the impact of ISR and PGM technologies on SOF and their success in the framework of the SOF approach to technology.

During the first Gulf War, SOF direct-action missions were initially carried out by advanced technology. Precision strikes from aircraft knocked out command and control nodes, destroying Iraq's technical infrastructure and communications capabilities. CENTCOM Commander General Norman Schwarzkopf championed air strikes instead of SOF teams in these missions because he believed they provided the same results for much less risk.[15] This changed on 18 January1991, when Iraq began firing Scud missiles at Saudi Arabia and Israel. Being mobile, the Scud launchers made a more difficult target for air strikes alone, so SOF and SAS were given the task of destroying or incapacitating them. Inserted into Iraqi territory by helicopter, they hunted and destroyed Scuds with explosives but also used man-portable GPS to provide terminal guidance for coordinated airstrikes.[16] Debate continues over the effectiveness of SOF in destroying Scuds by either demolition or airstrikes. Still, SOF is credited by some with deterring further strikes against Israel after January 26, preventing the widening of the conflict. But it was clear that technology was changing accepted SOF roles.

Operation Allied Force, the NATO air campaign over Kosovo, Serbia, and Montenegro in 1999, also raised questions about the advantages of high-tech ordnance over SOF. Strategic-airpower enthusiasts viewed NATO's air war against Serbia as proof that ground forces, including SOF, were not needed for decisive victory. Indeed, some analysts echoed General Schwarzkopf's opinion, seeing SOF's role in future operations as rather limited. USAF Colonel Charles Dunlap asked, "What is the role of the special operator when PGMs can strike high-value targets with relative impunity and effectively persuasive surveillance systems can produce battlefield intelligence without risking lives?"[17]

Nevertheless, SOF found a place within these new wars of accuracy, albeit a smaller one than some might have liked. After their experience in the Gulf, SOF and SAS trained for a role as "strategic targetters". American units took a Joint Fire Power course at Hurlburt Air Force Base in Florida, which included working with Air Force special operators.[18] Time has also cast a shadow of doubt over stories of war-winning airpower in Kosovo,[19] where SOF often provided target identification and terminal guidance.[20] The onset of the war on terror further vindicated the use of SOF. The Pentagon's "Northern Strategy" in Afghanistan called for the U.S. to support the indigenous forces of the Northern Alliance with PGMs against Taliban and al-Qaeda targets. SOF coordinated this effort on several fronts and increased the accuracy of the air campaign by "painting" targets with laser designators for PGMs to lock on to.[21] Beginning in 2001, Operation Enduring Freedom in Afghanistan confirmed accurate firepower as a cornerstone of Western warfare, with SOF as a key to that success.

How did SOF manage to survive being replaced by advanced RMA technology? Like the SAS in the 1970s, SOF found new opportunity in technological change. Their ability to innovate in response to the information revolution was helped by the fact that so many of the benefits promoted by RMA analysts reflect SOF approaches to war in general, as described in Table 14-1.

TABLE 14-1
US SOF adapt to the RMA

	The Promise of the RMA[22]	*Special Operations Forces*[23]
Technology	Application of precision force via precision-guided munitions	Direct-action missions, terminal guidance operations, precision-destruction operations
Doctrine	More rapidly mobile and flexible ground forces	Strategic asset defined by being readily deployable, mobile, and flexible towards change
Organization	Smaller, more modular units that can be easily combined and tailored to specific tasks	Quantitatively small by nature to allow for very specific missions, while still allowing for integration into conventional forces

Many analysts cite the 1991 Gulf War as the embryonic stage of the RMA. It can also be interpreted as an application of the doctrines espoused by T. E. Lawrence, an early proponent of modern unconventional warfare, who advocated destruction and disruption of enemy capabilities and infrastructure as an alternative to the risks of pitched battle.[24] Primarily, though, SOF preserved a critical role through their flexibility. They adapted to the task of Scud-hunting and, recognizing that a precedent was being set, considered their future role. They appreciated that it had changed *quantitatively* but found ways to provide a *qualitative* enhancement. This required new training – a joint approach to what might have been a solo operation in the past. It also forced SOF to look for new technological solutions, such as upgraded GPS systems and laser designators.

For modern Western militaries, there is no upper limit to desirable accuracy. The clearest picture is often obtained by the human observer, who can identify things in human terms, assess human costs, and be held accountable for human error. Current US Joint Doctrine for SOF reaffirms this: some information can be obtained only from human intelligence sources in target areas.[25] As commander of British forces in the Gulf War, de la Billière extolled the virtue of special operations forces for gaining information. "Once again," he reflected, "experience confirmed what the SAS had repeatedly demonstrated in Europe – that no amount of electronic surveillance is as effective as a pair of eyes on the ground."[26]

SOF's successful integration into new roles shaped by the RMA has not diminished their traditional attributes. SOF performed a variety of DA, strategic-reconnaissance, unconventional-warfare, CA, and PSYOPS missions during the Gulf War, in Kosovo, and throughout Operation Enduring Freedom in Afghanistan. Each demanded appropriate technology: horses, laptop computers, secure satellite links, and coordination with air support (from gunships to support helicopters) – all were needed to accomplish their goals.[27] The synergies of PGM and ISR have augmented SOF capabilities, not replaced them.

TECHNOLOGY, HUMAN ENVIRONMENT AND NATIONAL CIRCUMSTANCES

Technology is often viewed as a specific means to a specific end, but its impact and value are much greater. The late social critic Neil Postman noted that technology always changes the human environment: "In the year 1500, fifty years after the printing press was invented, we did not have old Europe plus the printing press. We had a new Europe."[28] Similarly, RMA proponents have framed their discussion around the information revolution's impact on the human environment. Alvin and Heidi Toffler integrated the Gulf War experience into their Wave theory, claiming that nations who view war in industrial terms will be handicapped when facing the "information" armies of tomorrow.[29] But technology also responds to pressure from the human environment: social, political, and economic contexts shape our decisions to create and use technology. The next section discusses how military technology can both change and be changed by the human environment, first by considering the value of PGMs to SOF missions beyond their initial strike, then by examining how national circumstances affect the making of decisions about technology.

Just the very presence of technology may have a psychological value that can affect operations. The 1993 U.S.-led intervention in Somalia offers one such example. The soldiers of Task Force Ranger noted that their MH-

60K Black Hawk helicopters, seemingly invulnerable to Somali small-arms fire, intimidated the angry crowds in Mogadishu, allowing the soldiers to conduct their mission with greater freedom of movement. This spell was broken when one helicopter was shot down by a rocket-propelled grenade. Fear of the Black Hawk was replaced by an emboldened spirit, creating a much more chaotic environment.[30]

Precision-strike capabilities offer special operations forces a similar tool of influence for a variety of missions without such a risk. Foreign internal defence missions require special forces operators to work alongside indigenous forces to maintain cohesion and increase military effectiveness. During Operation Enduring Freedom, this has been done in the complicated sociocultural environment of Afghanistan. Competing groups from the Northern Alliance, whose loyalty was mercurial and dependent on circumstances, were poorly armed and equipped by Western standards. Handing over caches of relatively inexpensive arms in exchange for cooperation would have been a risky bargain that ignored the lessons learned in Albania. Flooding the Albanian countryside with looted AK-47s after the collapse of the economy in the early 1990s contributed to the destabilization of the Balkans, which led to the 1999 NATO intervention and continues to be troublesome.[31] This may explain why the primary forms of support to Afghani soldiers during initial operations were ammunition (a limited resource), boots, clothing, blankets, and horse feed.[32] All helped solidify relations, but it was the ability of SOF to deliver PGM on strategic targets that won battles.

Advanced technologies have a particular impact on those who lack them. As Arthur C. Clarke noted, "Any sufficiently advanced technology is indistinguishable from magic."[33] While not a "supernatural power", SOF capability to direct regular and accurate strategic strikes gained credibility with the much more numerous Northern Alliance forces. From this perspective, a weapon used for DA missions can have dramatic application to CA and PSYOPS missions. In October 2001, thousands of leaflets warning civilians about the damage from incoming munitions often preceded air strikes to great effect. The accuracy of the bombing saved many civilian lives, securing not only vital infrastructure but also the gratitude of at least some of the Afghani people who were not injured in the attacks. There is no question that this was more effective than carpet-bombing cities like Kabul. Conversely, broadcasts about the lethality and precision available to the SOF on the ground, followed by deadly proof, provided PSYOPS units with antidotes to Taliban and al-Qaeda propaganda about the murderous West.[34] While delivery of PGM is a joint operation that requires sophisticated command and control, indigenous forces in Afghanistan associated it with the individual SOF soldiers they saw and dealt with regularly. PGM have a cascading value, enhancing a variety of missions at different ends of the conflict spectrum.

So far, we have observed how technology brings change to military affairs (PGM changed SOF roles) and their less obvious benefits as they change the military environment (secondary effects). But the human environment also affects technology. Authors such as Robert Pool and Kim Vicente have explored the complex way human values and systems of organization (social, political, and economic) have defined and shaped the creation and use of technology.[35] The same is true for military technology.

Historian John Lynn offers a conceptual model to help us understand future technological challenges. He identified three central characteristics that account for the similarity of "core" conventional army styles over the centuries. The first is similarity of political, social, and economic infrastructure, such as the state apparatus and systems of taxation and finance. The second characteristic is imitation of success, in which dominant armies are copied, from Carl Gustav's mobile artillery to the Prussian Grenadiers. The third characteristic is incorporation of new technology; failure in this can lead to disaster, as it did for India and China in the colonial era.

The variation in armies is accounted for by "periphery" factors that distinguish "core" military powers from others. Peripheral armies face financial limitations; they cannot afford the latest technology or the quantity or quality of assets amassed by the core players. Peripheral armies have different social, political, and economic institutions, which affect their values and perceptions. Finally, geographic realities shape peripheral armies, which may be landlocked or isolated, precluding certain kinds of development.[36]

Lynn sees technology as a core characteristic, not a revolutionary catalyst. Nations that fail to incorporate modern technologies have historically suffered serious consequences, both tactical and strategic. Effective use of leading technologies is integral to special operations. This core-periphery model illuminates some of the challenges facing nations that, like Canada, are charting special operations possibilities. Canada's government and military infrastructure are descendents of British tradition. JTF 2, tasked with counter-terrorism and other duties of national interest, is organized and armed along the lines of the SAS,[37] the archetypal CT force.[38] While it is obvious that levels of defence funding will affect Canada's future status as a core or peripheral state, the social structure of our armed forces and our willingness to undertake bold experiments may have a bigger impact. Chemical technology and professional jealousy provide just two examples of the dynamics that may affect the status of military forces like Canada's. Chemical technology highlights some of the issues we must address in our technological choices, and jealousy between conventional and special forces provides fertile ground for exploring social dynamics.

Chemical Technology

Drugs can be used as weapons, performance enhancers, and behaviour modifiers. Russian special forces used what is suspected to have been an opium derivative to subdue Chechen terrorists holding hostages in a Moscow theatre in October 2002. Over 100 of the 700 hostages were killed by the "knockout gas". Fully aware that use of any lethal chemical would violate the Geneva Conventions, Russia has maintained that the drug was based on the anesthetic Fentanyl.[39] Canada is highly unlikely to endorse lethal chemical weapons technology, but reliable non-lethal weapons might be added to the CT arsenal.

Chemicals might also be harnessed for performance enhancement and physiological manipulation. Andrew Marshall, the US government's leading futurist, has singled out drug enhancement as a key technology for future military consideration:

> People who are connected with neural pharmacology tell me that new classes of drugs will be available relatively shortly, certainly within the decade. These drugs are just like natural chemicals inside people, only with behavior-modifying and performance-enhancing characteristics. One of the people I talk to jokes that a future intelligence problem is going to be knowing what drugs the other guys are on.[40]

The prospect of fighting chemically enhanced soldiers raises the issue of performance-enhancing drugs for our own armed forces. For special operators, physical endurance, stamina, and brainpower are as essential as technology. Surviving in extreme and diverse environments with little logistical support defines most special missions. Nevertheless, increasing a soldier's ability to withstand fatigue by administering drugs is a thorny issue. US pilots involved in the friendly-fire incident that killed four Canadians in Afghanistan were taking amphetamines, an example of the risks of performance enhancement. Canada may prefer to pursue technologies that reduce the weight of a soldier's equipment. The US Army and Massachusetts Institute of Technology are actively pursuing nanotechnology to produce lighter combat gear with a variety of medical and protective functions. Collaboration on these initiatives would have benefits beyond the special-forces community.[41]

Behaviour-modification drugs are the darker side of pharmacological soldiering. Since the Cold War, some nations have invested in developing drugs that relieve the anxiety associated with combat stress without reducing the brain's ability to process information, make decisions, or sleep. This could make soldiers less fearful of death and less inhibited about killing. Special forces may find these appealing. Richard Gabriel, reporting on these developments in the 1980s, warned that such biochemical technologies could create an army of "sociopaths." Inheriting such soldiers at the end of a conflict may not be worth the cost.[42] Even perception of their use may tarnish the real accomplishments of blood and effort.

The use of drugs by adversaries should make us reflect on their utility, on repercussions from use, and on alternatives. Chemical soldiering calls into question human values like courage and sacrifice that have long been used to motivate soldiers. Replacing these with chemical efficiency may retard more than advance the cause of ethical soldiering as we understand it. But this will not prevent less ethical foes from exploiting something we find detestable, making it a concern for tomorrow's special operators.

Professional Jealousy

The tradition of war-fighting between professional armies led professional soldiers to reject police actions, small wars, and insurgency as proper objects of study. This inhibited many armies' responses to asymmetrical warfare, but special forces have so far avoided this fate. They are coming to be seen as the force of choice for diverse and unconventional missions. Successes in the war on terror have raised their stock amongst Western nations. This prominence has generated some resentment from conventional forces, which have also made impressive contributions to the war on terror.[43] Special and conventional forces have long been rivals. The heart of this rivalry is tied to animosity over "elite" forces in democratic nations. This is but one branch of a fundamental conflict in social affairs between talent and egalitarianism. As historians and philosophers Will and Ariel Durant noted over thirty years ago, "...freedom and equality are sworn and everlasting enemies, and when one prevails the other dies."[44] Can we champion the best in a society that cherishes equality?

Canada's effective employment of special forces is a relatively new "tradition", albeit one with historic roots.[45] Championing equality within the nation's social and political structure, including the military, has a longer history.[46] The stigma attached to "special" operations may translate into challenges to their demanding technical requirements. As Canadian Lieutenant-Colonel Bernd Horn has noted, conventional soldiers and fiscally minded policy-makers often see the technological needs of elite units as expensive, wasteful, and unfair, considering their size.[47] Without funds to purchase or develop necessary technologies, special units slide into irrelevance. Horn has argued that the speed of deployment and strategic reach of the now-disbanded Canadian Airborne Regiment were unappreciated by Canadian leaders, who preferred slow deployments that allowed time for alternate solutions.[48]

The war on terror may have changed the security environment sufficiently to give JTF 2 opportunities that the Canadian Airborne Regiment never had. The U.S. has dramatically increased its SOF capabilities, conducts independent SOF missions, and is removing CA and FID training missions from the SOF mandate to focus more on kinetic operations.[49] Canada's military, despite recent funding increases, is still facing fiscal crisis.[50] Land, sea, and air elements of the CF have longstanding claims for defence funds (the iconic saga of the Sea King helicopter would be humorous if lives were not at risk). And this is a period of conventional flux and special operations ascendancy.

As an alternative to massive restructuring for our conventional forces, an investment in manpower, firepower, and strategic transport for special forces may give Canada strategic relevance. If Canada pursues this strategy, it will require special forces that are both technologically and doctrinally compatible with the SOF, which are defined by the highest level of technological support. But failure to invest in the new technology needed to support special operations for Canada could condemn Canadian forces to peripheral status at a time when we desperately need to be taken seriously by our most important ally. There is an opportunity for a relatively big bang for a depreciated buck if policy-makers and professional colleagues can overcome their aversion to elite forces and acknowledge concrete operational achievements. This will require innovative thought and effective use of technology.

CONCLUSION

The West lives in an era defined by speed and consumption, and both have translated into rapid technological change. Against this backdrop the security environment presents a host of new threats. Successful special forces like the SOF and SAS have taken advantage of technological change to develop new roles and remain relevant. Risk and opportunity abound for militaries seeking new technology to face new enemies. The decisions made by countries like Canada with respect to military technology, the organizations that will wield it, and the doctrine that will guide its use, will both shape and be shaped by political, economic, and social context. We should beware of technological hazards like drugs, social hazards like professional jealousy, and political-economic hazards like chronic under-funding.

Creative thinking about doctrine, technology, and organization will allow special operations forces to remain viable. Canadian policy-makers must think dynamically about the technologies they choose to champion. The obvious material limitations faced by Canadian forces should not limit critical thinking. Rather, it should spur it on – Canada's forces must think more to live with less generous resources than our allies.[51] A tradition of innovation in doctrine and technology will permit special forces to negotiate the future and find a place for themselves in conflicts ahead.

NOTES

1. The author would like to thank Lieutenant-Colonel David Last, Ph.D., Dr. Mike Hennessy, and Dr. Sean Maloney of the Royal Military College of Canada and Dr. Alastair Finlan of the University of Wales for their support and advice during the project. All opinions, ideas, and errors, however, are the author's alone.
2. US Department of Defense, *Dictionary of Military and Associated Terms* (Washington, DC: DoD, 1993), 118.
3. Gordon McCormick, "The Dynamics of Doctrinal Change," *Orbis* 27 (Summer 1983): 268.

4. Stephen Peter Rosen, *Winning the Next War: Innovation and the Modern Military* (Ithaca and London: Cornell University Press, 1994), 1-53.
5. McCormick, 268.
6. Alastair Finlan, "British Special Forces in the Falkland War of 1982," *Small War and Insurgencies,* Vol. 13, No. 3 (Autumn 2002): 75-96.
7. United States Special Operations Forces, *Posture Statement 2000: Providing Unique Solutions to a Changing World* (2000), 99.
8. General Sir Peter de la Billière, *Looking for Trouble: SAS to Gulf Command* (London: Harper Collins, 1995), 280-82.
9. Ibid., 283-84.
10. Anthony Kemp, *The SAS Savage Wars of Peace, 1947 to the Present* (London: Penguin, 2001), 146.
11. Micro-robotic surveillance technology, for example, may make covert special-reconnaissance techniques obsolete or create demands for new skills for special operators.
12. The literature on the RMA has grown at an exponential rate since 1991, curbed only by the advent of the war on terror. It is now reflected largely in US discussions on "transformation". See Eliot Cohen, "A Revolution in Warfare," *Foreign Affairs,* Vol. 75, No. 2 (March/April 1996): 37-54; and Eric Sterner, "You Say You want a Revolution (in Military Affairs)?" *Comparative Strategy*, Vol. 18, No. 4 (October/December 1999): 297-308. For competing looks at Canada's response to the RMA, see Elinor Sloan, "Canada and the Revolution in Military Affairs: Current Responses and Future Opportunities," *Canadian Military Journal,* Vol. 1, No. 3 (Autumn 2000): 7-14; Sean Maloney and Scot Robertson, "The Revolution in Military Affairs: Possible Implications for Canada," *International Journal,* Vol. 54, No. 3 (Summer 1999): 443-462. Various defence web sites also cover the RMA; see *The RMA Debate: The RMA and Operations Other Than War* at http://www.comw.org/rma/fulltext/otherop.html.
13. Cohen, "A Revolution in Warfare": 38.
14. Sloan, "Canada and the Revolution in Military Affairs": 7-14.
15. *United States Special Operations Command: Tenth Anniversary History* (USSOCOM History and Research Office, 1997), 37-39.
16. US Department of Defense, "Question Five: The use of Special Operations Forces," in *Conduct of the Persian Gulf Conflict,* Interim Report to Congress (July 1991): 5-4; De la Billière, *Looking for Trouble*, 410-411.
17. Charles Dunlap, "Special Operations Forces After Kosovo," *Joint Force Quarterly* (Spring/Summer 2001): 8.
18. According to US Army Colonel Dave McKracken in a Pentagon " Special Briefing on Special Operations Forces Capabilities" (Wednesday, 12 December 2001).
19. Timothy Thomas, "Kosovo and the Current Myth of Information Superiority," *Parameters,* Vol. 30, No. 1(Spring 2000): 13-29; Martin Agüera, "Air Power Paradox: NATO's 'Misuse' of Military Force in Kosovo and

its Consequences," *Small Wars and Insurgencies,* Vol. 12, No. 3 (Autumn 2001): 121.
20. The role of SOF in Kosovo and Serbia is covered by Sean Maloney in Chapter Ten of this volume.
21. "Powell in the Middle," *Newsweek,* 1 October 2001: 26-29; Christian Caryl and John Barry, "Facing a Long Cold Winter," *Newsweek,* 12 November 2001: 22-29; Melinda Liu and Joshua Hammer, " 'Please Don't Forget Us'," *Newsweek,* 26 November 2001: 43-49; John Barry, "A New Breed of Soldier," *Newsweek,* 10 December 2001: 24-31; "Taliban fighters' surrender sought. Pentagon: No proof that Omar, bin Laden are together," *CNN.com,* 2 January 2002; Michael Hirsh, "Warlords and B-52s," *Newsweek*, 4 March 2002: 26-28; "Satellites and Horsemen," *The Economist*, 9 March 2002: 27.
22. These pillars of the RMA have been taken from Sloan, "Canada and the Revolution in Military Affairs," 7-14.
23. All missions and operational outlooks taken from United States, *Doctrine for Joint Special Operations, Joint Publication 3-05* (Washington, DC: Department of Defence, 17 April 1998), II-4-5.
24. See, in particular, T. E. Lawrence, *Seven Pillars of Wisdom,* reprint (London: Penguin, 2000), 193-202.
25. United States, *Doctrine for Joint Special Operations,* II-5.
26. De la Billière, *Looking for Trouble*, 411.
27. For a sampling of these roles, see John Barry and Michael Hirsh, "The Real Tip of the Spear," *Newsweek*, 8 October 2001: 37-40; "So Far, So Fairly Good," *The Economist*, 13 October 2001: 20-21; "A Puzzling Kind of War," *The Economist*, 20 October 2001: 16-18; "US paratroops raid Omar compound near Kandahar," *CNN.com,* 22 October 2001; "US Special Operations troops in commando raid," *CNN.com,* 22 October 2001; Evan Thomas and John Barry, "A Fight over the Next Front," *Newsweek,* 22 October 2001: 40-48; John Barry and Arian Camp-Flores, "Warriors of the Night," *Newsweek,* 29 October 2001: 23-29; Caryl and Barry, "Facing a Long Cold Winter"; Barry, "A New Breed of Soldier"; Evan Thomas and John Barry, "Evil in the Cross-Hairs," *Newsweek,* 24 November 2001: 10-20.
28. Neil Postman, *Technopoly: The Surrender of Culture to Technology* (New York: Vintage, 1993), 18.
29. Alvin and Heidi Toffler, *War and Anti-War: Survival at the Dawn of the 21st Century* (Boston: Little, Brown and Company, 1993).
30. Mark Bowden, *Black Hawk Down: A Story of Modern War* (New York: Signet, 2001), 95.
31. "Albania: Ready, Aim, Vote," *The Economist*, 17 April 1997; " Civil war threatens over Kosovo," *Globe and Mail*, 18 December 1997: A19.
32. Joshua Hammer and John Barry, "A Win in the Fog of War," *Newsweek*, 19 November 2001: 24-30.

33. This is the third of Clarke's three laws. See Arthur C. Clarke, *Profiles of the Future: An Inquiry into the Limits of the Possible* (New York: Harper & Row, 1962).
34. James F. Dunnigan, *The Perfect Soldier* (New York: Citadel Press, 2003), 233-237.
35. Robert Pool, *Beyond Engineering: How Society Shapes Technology* (New York: Oxford University Press, 1997); Kim Vicente, *The Human Factor: Revolutionizing the Way People Live with Technology* (Toronto: Alfred A. Knopf Canada, 2003). There is a branch of the history of technology dedicated to exploring the impact of contextual factors on technological development and application. See John Staudenmaier, *Technology's Storytellers: Reweaving the Human Fabric* (Cambridge and London: Society for the History of Technology and MIT Press, 1985), and "Rationality, Agency, Contingency: Recent Trends in the History of Technology," *Reviews in American History* 30 (2002):168-181.
36. John A. Lynn, "The Evolution of Army Style in the Modern West," *The International History Review* (August 1996): 508-512.
37. See David Pugliese, *Canada's Secret Commandos: The Unauthorized Biography of Joint Task Force Two* (Ottawa: Esprit de Corps Books, 2002), 14-40.
38. Several have either modelled themselves on or been inspired by the SAS. See Charles Beckwith, *Delta Force: The Army's Elite Counterterrorist Unit* (New York: Avon Books, 2000).
39. John Bowman, "Russian knock-out gas," *CBC News Online*, 28 October 2002, http://www.cbc.ca/news/features/knockoutgas.html
40. Douglas McGray, "The Marshall Plan," *Wired,* Vol. 11, No. 02 (February 2003).
41. See *MIT Institute for Soldier Nanotechnologies*, http://web.mit.edu/isn/
42. Richard Gabriel, *No More Heroes: Madness and Psychiatry in War* (Toronto: Collins Publisher, 1987), 137-151; see also David Grossman, *On Killing: The Psychological Cost of Learning to Kill in War and Society* (Boston: Little, Brown and Company, 1996), 46-51.
43. Warren Chin, "Operation 'Enduring Freedom': A Victory for a Conventional Force Fighting an Unconventional Army," *Small Wars and Insurgencies,* Vol. 14, No. 1 (Spring 2003): 57-76.
44. Will and Ariel Durant, *The Lessons of History* (New York: Simon & Schuster, 1968); 117.
45. See Bernd Horn, *Bastard Sons: An Examination of the Canadian Airborne Experience, 1942-1945* (St. Catharines, ON: Vanwell, 2001.
46. This chapter cannot deal with the highly charged issue of equality versus talent in detail, but for a critical look at the ramifications of equality's ascension over ability, see William Henry III, *In Defense of Elitism* (New York: Anchor, 1995).

47. Bernd Horn, "'Burn the Witch': A Case for Special Operations Forces," *The Army Doctrine and Training Bulletin,* Vol. 2, No. 3 (August 1999): 28.
48. Ibid.: 266.
49. Glenn Goodman Jr., "Expanded Role for Elite Commandos," *Armed Forces Journal* (February 2003): 34-38.
50. Chris Wattie, "'Bankrupt' Forces May Shut 5 Bases," *National Post*, 24 February 2004: A1, A5
51. Scot Robertson, "Challenge and Response: Innovation and Change in the Canadian Army," *The Army Doctrine and Training Bulletin,* Vol. 3, No. 3 (Winter 2000/Spring 2001): 69-74.

PART IV

DOCTRINES FOR SPECIAL OPERATIONS

CHAPTER FIFTEEN

SELECTION AND PREPARATION OF TEAM MEMBERS FOR SPECIAL OPERATIONS

Tom Dececchi and Bernadette Dececchi

Special operations may be complicated by the need for unique expertise to handle technology, speak obscure languages, or deal with advanced weapons. It is unlikely that the right computer programmer, Tagalog-speaker, or biological weapons scientist has serendipitously passed through all the special forces selection and years of training to be an integral part of the special forces team-in-waiting. We therefore need the means to select and prepare specialists and to integrate them effectively into small teams that might have to conduct difficult and dangerous operations. These teams might become an integral part of organizations like JTF 2 as it evolves to deal with new asymmetric threats. This chapter develops a model to assist human resources planners with this task.

The question of how to put together a team for a special operation is complicated by the fact that these operations cover such a range of possibilities. They may involve direct action in a hostile environment or covert action in a comparatively benign environment. The timelines for preparation may range from years (like America's build-up to the attack on Iraq) to months (like coalition operations against Iraq) to hours or days (as in hostage-rescue situations). This means that while we seek a "best solution", we may instead define a set of possible solutions defined by a number of factors. These include the type of threat, the level of technical complexity of the tasks involved in implementing a solution, the social-cultural complexity (including the degree of linguistic competence and cultural awareness that the team must possess), the availability of human resources, and the stress (both physical and psychological) that the team members might endure during the mission.

All these factors are functions of time. The level and nature of threat may vary with time. The technical complexity of the tasks may change over time as the threat affects our ability to break down tasks. Potential for specialization (in order to allow for easier training of members with diverse backgrounds) changes with the amount of time that is available. The availability of human resources internal to the group clearly depends on time: it is related to the number of missions running at any one time. The state of the resources internal to the task force at any point in time will also change. The level and type of stress that members are expected to face will change over time and depends on time because more time to prepare would help members to cope with the levels of stress, while more time during the mission may result in increased levels of stress. In some instances the ability to handle these stresses may be one of the most critical factors in deciding who may be able to take part in the mission.

Using this simplified model, we can identify some of the issues in terms of deciding who may take part in these missions. Sometimes an outside specialist is appropriate, and sometimes it makes more sense to give specialized training to an insider, who has already met the demanding standards of the organization. This is important because this model assumes that the cohesiveness of the unit deployed and the ability of its members to work together will be important factors in determining mission success. Also, because we will assume that in the situations where a special force might deploy there will be few external constraints on their actions, it will be important for the values of members to reflect what is acceptable in the CF and to Canadian civilian leadership.

We consider below some of the factors that may be used to develop parameters for these functions and give guidance on overcoming some of the problems presented.

SPECIAL OPERATIONS AND PROFESSIONALISM

Michael Ignatieff argues that warriors have always had an "an ethic of responsibility" and an ability to distinguish between "combatants and non combatants, legitimate and illegitimate targets, moral and immoral weaponry, civilized and barbarous usage in the treatment of prisoners and of the wounded".[1] Case studies of disparate groups such as the English warrior and the Sioux Indian show that they were heavily bound by social obligations, which corresponds to the concept of having an ethic of responsibility. Canadian officer Don Neil discusses the nature of professionalism: "The term professional is often applied to career soldiers throughout the Western world",[2] and the role of the officer has been labelled "the profession of arms" by analysts as diverse as Gwyn Dyer and General Sir John Hackett. In general terms, a profession boasts five elements that distinguish it from other occupations: a systematic theory (how it works), a system of authority (who reports to whom); community sanction (that it is both legal and acceptable to society), a culture;

and an ethical code. What distinguishes the military profession from other professions is the nature of its ethical code, the foundation of which is voluntary subordination of one's own interests to those of the state.

However, not all authors agree with this. Tom St. Denis, an officer with long service and some experience of combat, argues that there is a significant difference between a soldier and a warrior. [3] In today's military forces (particularly in Canada and the U.S.), the special forces are distinguished by individualism and non-conformity, by the desire to make decisions on their own, and by the aspiration to be more than the rank and file. This makes them an icon to some but can put them outside the realm of laws and states. This means that there is a potential for these elite forces to develop a rogue form of military ethos, more related to that of street gangs than to the professional forces of modern Western nations.

Doctrinal definitions of special forces and special operations situate them within the realm of professional military forces but with intimations of some of the warrior characteristics described by St. Denis. For the purposes of this chapter, Australian and NATO definitions provide useful guides. It is helpful to cite the Australian Defence Force (ADF) concept of Special Forces at some length to give an impression of the sort of operations on which outside experts might have to work.

> The role of Special Forces (SF) is to conduct operations beyond the range and capability of other ADF Force Elements (FE). SF are defined as "specially selected military personnel, trained in a broad range of basic and specialist skills, who are organized, equipped and trained to conduct Special Operations (SO)." Although SF usually operate at the strategic and operational level they may also be required to operate at a point of critical tactical significance or when no other ADF FE is capable of reacting within the required time and space. Army's commando capability is an integral part of the ADF SO capability…
>
> The Australian commando is a highly trained specialist capable of operating independently of conventional forces, in hostile environmental conditions, able to land on coasts or terrain impassable to conventional infantry, and operate without rest or logistic support during sustained operations for up to 72 hours. Specific to the commando is his basic combat skill, Close Quarter Battle (CQB) fighting, which is the basis of the commando's discriminate and surgical use of force.
>
> Each commando is trained in all unit weapons, basic parachute and small boat insertion skills, basic roping, and possesses two secondary skills from a suite of specializations including demolitions, medical, signals and climbing. The essential quality distinguishing the Commando Task Element (CTE) is 'esprit de commando' which incorporates strength of character, determination, enthusiasm and cheerfulness under harsh physical and environmental conditions, initiative self- reliance and comradeship. [4]

This description includes elements that might present barriers to casual employment of outside specialists: insertion by parachute and small boat, climbing, hostile environmental conditions, extended operations, and close-quarter fighting might deter many would-be assistants to the special operations cause. The appendix to this chapter reproduces extracts from an unclassified description of ADF selection criteria for Special Forces and Commandos, which elaborates on these issues.

The NATO definition of special operations is compatible with the Australian definitions of special forces, special operations, and commandos but focuses on the spectrum of conflict and the political circumstances under which special operations might be conducted:

> Special Operations are military activities conducted by specially designated, organized, trained and equipped forces using operational techniques and modes of employment not standard to conventional forces. These activities are conducted across the spectrum of military operations, independently or in coordination with operations of conventional forces to achieve military, political, economic and psychological objectives. Political-military considerations may require clandestine, covert or discreet techniques and the acceptance of a degree of physical and political risk not associated with conventional operations."[5]

Special forces are not rogue elements – not a kind of institutional Seven Samurai. They must be truly professional military personnel who accept and follow a military ethos based on core societal values, even though they may operate in difficult and dangerous situations that have little to do with societal norms. This is because their most important goal is to achieve national political objectives. But within this framework of military professionalism and self-sacrifice, we may need to deploy police, civil servants, or even civilians with special skills, in addition to selecting and preparing the right military personnel. This is our selection and preparation problem.

METHODS OF PERSONNEL SELECTION

The definition of special forces is at the core of the proposed selection and development model.[6] We are assuming that the individual members must be chosen because they have the ability to transform into modern warriors who will be able to operate in situations that would be difficult or impossible for the majority of the members of the CF but still maintain the military ethos of the CF and, by extension, support the core values of Canadian society. Therefore, we are *de facto* forced to consider selection criteria that are essentially based on characteristics of the individual rather than the tasks that comprise the job.

This is problematic in that although there are different approaches to the personnel selection process, the most commonly used processes can be described as involving some form of matching between a job description (the tasks that are involved in performing the job, the working conditions, and other aspects of the job), the job specification (what the job requires of the employees who do it, and the human factors involved), and the people who apply.[7] In this process, the details of the job and the tasks that are performed in "doing the job", and what this means in terms of a job specification, are defined in great detail and are derived from organizational analysis. The selected applicant is that individual who best matches these qualifications and therefore should be able to perform these tasks.

However, another method of personnel selection that has been gaining adherents involves looking at the competencies one wants in an incumbent (the knowledge, skills, abilities, or characteristics associated with high performance on a job).[8] One then selects the individuals who have these attributes. The literature indicates that this method works best in the selection of individuals for high-level professional or managerial jobs (or for jobs that require significant training and development). This is because it is often difficult or impossible to define *a priori* the exact nature of the tasks that they will be called upon to perform, even though one can define the general situations, and the expectations of the people occupying these positions. Thus, members will be selected on the basis of their inherent characteristics, not on their ability to perform certain sets of tasks.

If we look at traditional recruitment and selection as part of the overall process of human resource management, then, we see that we must adapt the model in Figure 15-1. What is now important is not the job specifications and

FIGURE 15-1
Traditional Recruitment and Selection in Context

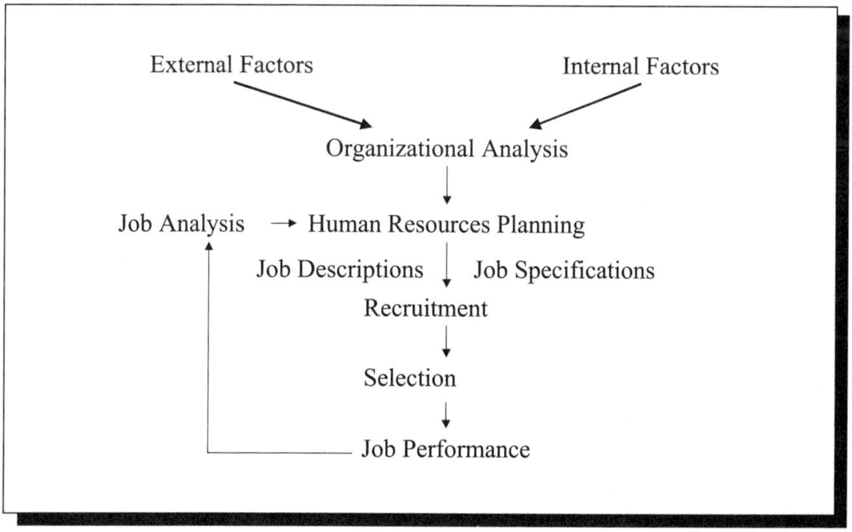

the job descriptions but a description of the competencies required for these positions because there is no set of tasks that define these jobs. But if this is true, then the question becomes how to develop a group. From which teams of individuals, who can perform complex tasks that may require many different types of expertise, can it be derived? How do we do this so that these teams can be assembled in the available time? What are the competencies that may be needed, and how can we identify them?

This approach seems compatible with the selection process outlined in the ADF Commando Capability Document, although the skill sets required of special-operations team members might be more diverse than those involved in Australian Commando units.[9] We should look at best practices, beginning with how other countries select their special forces, but the unique situation of Canada must be taken into account. For example, our two closest allies, the U.S. and the U.K., have military forces that are much larger than ours, as well as special-forces elements that draw on comparably larger pools. The CF budget is also smaller, and there is some evidence that special-forces units are significantly more costly to train and equip than are conventional units of comparable size.[10]

The CF will probably not be able to have members who are specialists in many diverse fields. This means that the selection criteria will be based on the competency model, where the competency is defined in terms of performing generic tasks associated with special operations. The Australian model for selection criteria is a good one for the CF to consider, but it also means that when we look at what other nations may include in their special forces, we will need to look at alternative ways of providing those skill sets. For example, civil affairs and psychological operations are included in some definitions of the scope of special operations, and might be provided through specially formed reserve units.

MODEL DEVELOPMENT

This model encompasses the different types of skill sets, as well as different methods for providing these skill sets as a function of time. At any point in time, potential team members will have certain skills and abilities as well as the basic competencies for which they were chosen. For example, if we select a physically fit Tagalog-speaking computer programmer, we can teach her to rappel out of a helicopter in a week; a military parachute course may take three weeks, but a civilian course might take just a few days.

Systems theory tells us that the world can be divided into two parts: that which is internal to the system and is under our control, which we can therefore change or modify; and that which is external to the system and is beyond our capacity to control at this time. This means that we can define the system as a black box. At any point in time, we can specify the inputs and the required outputs. Outputs imply that at that point in time the team would have a capacity to perform certain tasks if they are provided with certain resources. This means that, given the various abilities of individual members, the team would be able to perform tasks that require technical and social abilities and that require the team to operate under some level of stress.

We may assume that there will be some notice of missions, which allows for planning and for the development of human resources. However, because we are now looking at the situation over time, the situation itself will also change. That is to say, if we are required to act immediately when apprised of a potential threat, we will have certain resources, but if we have time to plan and train, we can add or develop additional resources. It will be possible to find a way around many of the constraints, but there are other considerations: the threats that we face will also change over time, and the changes must be considered in this equation. Similarly, we will now be facing a number of problems, some of which may be overlapping while others may be resolved before another one needs to be dealt with. The availability of our internal resources now becomes a function of time as well. The possible solution to a problem is, in effect, a series of solutions that are a function of time, and we can provide different solutions, depending on how much time we can be given.

FACTORS IN DEVELOPING HUMAN RESOURCES FOR SPECIAL OPERATIONS

At least five groups of factors are important in developing human resources for special operations. Not coincidentally, most have been addressed in the preceding chapters. We will consider threat, technology, social and cultural issues, competing tasks, and operational stress.

Threat can take an almost infinite variety of forms, and these forms will be associated with different types of special operations. For example, major events like the Pan American Games or Olympics may presage higher threat levels if heads of state choose to visit. G8 summits present obvious targets. Hostage-rescue and consequence-management tasks can be prepared for in advance, but the level of threat may change suddenly. Loss of fissile material, breach of security in biological or chemical facilities, or loss of weapons may indicate a sudden spike in threat. The period between September 11 and the coalition operations in Afghanistan was one of heightened threat and intense training, which demanded a rapid mustering of special-operations capabilities.

As the previous chapter demonstrated, technology is integral to special operations and is evident in everything from insertion techniques to special weapons and communications. How different are these from the techniques or backgrounds of the potential team members? Some forces, such as SOF and the ADF's Special Air Service Regiment (SASR), benefit from having units from which individuals regularly "step up" to the more specialized force. They learn parachuting with airborne units or submarine protocols with the navy before joining SEAL or DELTA teams, reducing the gap in new knowledge. The

SASR regularly recruits from Commando units. How much specialization or expertise is required beyond the level at which team members enter? Is there sufficient time for additional courses, or will members have to learn the new technology as they use it? There may be some kinds of technology that we cannot expect soldiers to use, either because of complexity or because of security classification or organizational issues. Canada's Communications Security Establishment, for example, guards certain kinds of sensors very carefully. It may be necessary to broaden the membership of a special team to include someone selected for technical expertise while relaxing some of the other criteria normally considered.

In developing technical expertise within a special operations team, there might be a trade-off between redundancies. Rather than every member performing every task, members might be prepared to perform overlapping sets of simplified tasks so that success does not depend on the survival or performance of a single individual. Careful planning would have to go into the technologies to be used and the ways in which the teams might be prepared to employ them within the time available.

Social and cultural issues have often been an afterthought or have been ignored completely in military training and organizational development. We have to think about the military culture and about the language and culture of the environment within which the military team will operate. Christian Leuprecht's chapter in this volume illustrates the depth of potential cultural and linguistic expertise available in the Canadian population, but bringing this expertise into the special operations community presents challenges for security clearance, cultural accommodation, and trust. Jason Ridler's chapter illustrates some of the perennial problems of institutional resistance to change, which these efforts are likely to stimulate. The selection and preparation problem goes beyond this. What level of linguistic competence or local knowledge is required? Are there political constraints or associations that would make candidates undesirable or even potentially dangerous to particular missions? What are the trade-offs between developing competencies within a core special-operator team and bringing in outside specialists, and what are the risks of using outsiders for a secure or sensitive mission?

It is unlikely that outside specialists will have a well-developed military ethos, although this, too, can be developed with time and preparation. We must therefore assess how important that military ethos is to a specific mission. Some would argue that the single most important characteristic for special operators is reliable behaviour without external constraint or supervision. This would mean that selection for reliability (if not military ethos) might be the most important criterion to preserve legitimacy in the eyes of military and political leadership.

Competing tasks or other assignments for a small cadre of special operators will affect what can be achieved in the timeframe being considered. Planners must consider not only the availability of members with special skill sets but also the risk of burnout. What is the relative priority of missions, and how is this likely to change over time? Being on constant stand-by without being employed may have more deleterious effects on a special organization than constant employment.

Much of the literature on the subject of stress suggests that it is necessary to develop members of special forces teams who have both the physical and psychological attributes necessary to perform under unusual situations. Highly stressful situations (especially if kept secret) may cause individuals to behave or perform unsatisfactorily. We have good measures for, and some experience of, selection and preparation of special operators, but use of outside experts in special teams brings new challenges. As outsiders, they are asked to function in a technologically and socially complex environment. What is the probability that experts will be able to complete these complex tasks in high-stress situations when they are not well prepared to face them? Should we select and train a computer programmer to rappel from a helicopter, or select and train a special operator to program a computer? Which is more likely to be a weak link in the special operations team? Discussions with SOF planners indicate that the preference is always for experienced operators, sometimes reaching back to find former operators who have since moved on to new specialties in demand (such as law or medicine); knowledge of special-operations culture and procedures is more important than expertise. Smaller countries like New Zealand and the U.K. are more willing to incorporate outside expertise and accept the risks that unknown stress may bring, because the special-operations community is not large enough to meet all contingencies.

If these are the main factors and trade-offs to consider, we can turn now to the different methods available for selecting, preparing, and developing expertise for special operations outside the special-operations community. We are concerned about technological expertise and social and cultural knowledge, as well as ability to fit into the special operations community and capacity to work in stressful situations. We need to understand how these factors are related to the time available to plan for and execute a particular type of mission, or the time available to prepare for foreseeable contingencies.

METHODS FOR SELECTING AND PREPARING EXPERTS

We have two basic methods of improving the capabilities or expertise of human resources. We can hire additional (or replacement) workers, or we can develop the human resources that we have. We argued above that selection should be based on a competency model for special-operations activities: if we select the right people, they will be able to develop the skills needed. Implicit in this model is the understanding that once an individual has been selected, the organization will provide the training and support to deal with specific situations.

What does this mean? If we select a fit and adventurous computer programmer, we have to train her to rappel, but if we select quick-thinking special operators, we may have to train them to program computers. The necessary support to deal with specific situations may mean providing training (not education) in specific skills. It may mean assigning team members technical support staff to act as tutors who can help them use a technology while they get used to it themselves; the programmer sits beside the special operator until the latter is confident. Or it may involve a more interactive support, in which designers develop aids or procedures to help non-specialists make use of the technology that they need for their jobs. We can find examples of all of these in the large SOF community, in which private industry plays a big role in preparing new technologies and the next generation of operators.

We can illustrate a systems approach to the development process in Figure 15-2, drawing on Canadian human resources experts Schwind, Das, and Wagar.[11]

FIGURE 15-2
A Systems Approach to Development

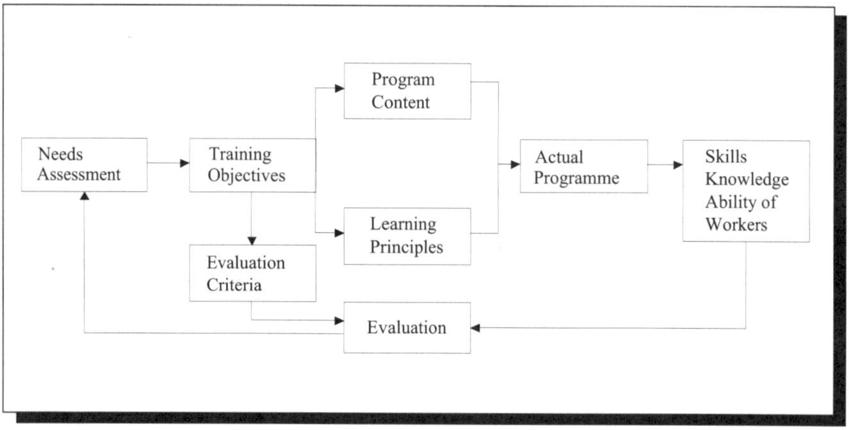

From this diagram it is easy to see that the process of developing an educational and training programme is similar to the process of developing a programme for selecting human resources. The first step is to conduct an analysis of what is needed. On the basis of this knowledge, we can begin to develop the various programmes to take individuals from where they are now to where they need to be.

When we hire individuals on the basis of competencies – who they are and their inherent skills and abilities – there is an implicit understanding that they will need training and professional development to become proficient in their positions. The "maturity", "physical", and "discipline" selection criteria for ADF Commandos (as indicated in the Appendix) are examples of attributes underlying selection, while specialist skills listed in paragraph 91 are examples of the sort of skill in which we might expect to train members.

We are postulating that there are two different types of skill sets that will be needed in special forces. The first are those skills that we know at least some of the members will need to possess, and we can train continuously to ensure that these skill sets are available. All the skills listed in the Appendix fit in this category. Other skills, however, will be mission-specific, perhaps arising from the new circumstances described in other chapters of this volume. Foreign languages or local knowledge, detailed knowledge of our own border, familiarity with new technology, or liaison to other organizations might all justify the employment of outside expertise on a special operation. The question then becomes how to develop the human resources so that they can meet these needs.

SUPPLYING AND DEVELOPING MISSION-SPECIFIC SKILLS

Six methods for supplying mission-specific skills that we might consider are contracting-out, partnerships, recruiting experts as team members, developing team members as experts, work simplification, and hiring experts for specific tasks. Partnerships and contracting-out are non-traditional means. Recruiting experts and developing expertise in the team rely on internal resources; work simplification can expand existing resources; and hiring temporary expertise is standard practice in the business world.

Christopher Spearin's chapter in this volume illustrates some of the potential for contracting-out special-operations tasks such as foreign training, hostage rescue, and close protection, but also indicates some of the risks involved. Contracting-out usually allows access to skills on short notice but does not permit the same degree of control over the operation that would be exercised were it conducted by government forces.

Partnerships may be the way of the future. Already it is apparent that Canada is unlikely to undertake operations without the participation of major allies, except for internal security operations. Defining our foreign roles ahead of time and preparing memoranda of understanding with other contributing countries would allow us to focus our efforts and acquire narrower skill sets more quickly, should they be needed.

Recruiting experts or specialists, then developing them as members of the special operations team may be a long process. It works well when physical standards and special attributes are not a barrier to performance. Civilian expertise, for example, can be easily incorporated into civil-affairs organizations. It may also be easy to incorporate experts from police SWAT or ERT teams, which have high entrance standards. Experts necessary for support (logistics, communications, medical, financial, and so on) could be found elsewhere in the military and may quickly develop the necessary professional ethos. If they undergo the same developmental activities over time, they should gain acceptance within the special operations community and be accepted as part of the team. Different physical standards for "assaulters" and "supporters" make it easier to accept and integrate outsiders. (A corollary benefit is that old assaulters can be retained for their expertise.) Building a large database of potential experts and starting early on the integration should allow this process to meet most specialist needs.

An alternative to recruiting experts is to develop expertise in special-forces team members who have already met the exacting standards. For example, qualified special operators might be sent to language school for a year or more or be sent to live overseas to develop local knowledge and contacts. This is the most costly and time-consuming of the options, and it presupposes some aptitude or prior knowledge on the part of the members chosen, but it might be necessary for the most demanding of the special operations tasks.

The fifth method is borrowed from private industry. Work simplification and training for specific tasks differ from individual training by focusing on the collective result. Typically this involves reducing the number of tasks assigned to each individual to simplify the training task and permit it to be completed in less time. For example, Canadian Tire might hire four unskilled workers to change oil, rotate tires, check fluids, and tighten belts, rather than hire one licensed mechanic. Larger organizations, like US Ranger companies or ADF Commando squads, find this kind of specialization easier than smaller special-forces organizations like an "Alpha team" of twelve or an SAS "brick" of four.

Today there are two additional means of work simplification. The first is to use "expert systems" or computer programs that have the ability to analyze situations and synthesize solutions based on the considered judgement or modelled behaviour of human experts. Medical and mechanical diagnostic tools are widely available, and specialist applications are being developed to support explosive ordnance disposal, chemical weapons detection, and other defence applications. The second involves the use of modern communications to access the expertise of distant human experts. Paramedics, for example, remain in contact with emergency room physicians while they are treating a patient at the scene; they become the eyes, ears, and hands of the physician. A further development of this is remote robotic technology, which permits the distant expert to manipulate tools himself. All three means of work simplification could significantly reduce the amount of training or professional development required by special operators for particular missions. They could enable the training of many individuals in small but overlapping skill sets, increasing redundancy and probability of success.

The last method is the riskiest. In the film, *The Rock*, Nicholas Cage plays a weapons expert who must defuse a biological warhead. The mission hinges on the survival and performance of this one specialist. Even if Nicholas Cage is willing, we can't always guarantee that Sean Connery will be available to keep him safe and get him to the target. Nevertheless, hiring experts off the street or borrowing them from other departments and sending them on missions as untrained members of special teams sometimes may be appropriate.

In addition to this suite of six methods to incorporate expertise, we should consider at least three approaches to professional development that would enhance specialized expertise over time. Training cadres, use of allied training programs, and computer-assisted learning (CAL) might all help to enhance special operations teams, depending on the time available.

First, we should consider using of a cadre of professionals in DND and other government departments to develop both long-term training strategies and short courses to develop specific skill sets rapidly. Developing a cadre of experienced people with an appropriate ethos should reduce the time and cost of preparing people with the right professional credentials. For this strategy to work, there should be some guidance about the sorts of missions that might be anticipated and the notice associated with each type of mission, perhaps in the form of a warning order: "Be prepared to field a local-security and direct-action team accompanying African relief specialists on 21 days' notice." This kind of warning would be valuable in conjunction with a work-simplification strategy, defining small new skill sets with reduced preparation times.

Second, we should consider renting space in the training programs of our allies. We have done this in the past with Marine Engineering and Technical Staff College education programs and should consider it for direct action, special reconnaissance, interrogation, and other special skills that have atrophied or never been developed in the CF. This assumes that such courses are available and open to Canadian participation. It also assumes that such courses would meet Canadian needs, although our training strategy might be to establish general skill sets that are applicable to a broader range of special operations than large forces have the luxury of preparing for.

Finally, might we develop computer-assisted learning tools that could be used by members at any time an in any location to develop specific skills? A bank of CAL tools might simplify individual training in two ways. It would make individual pre-mission training more easily accessible, and it might make some tasks in the field easier. This could work well with a work-simplification strategy and with a training strategy of developing general skill sets. CAL might provide a tropical medicine update to general medical-assistant knowledge, for example.

CONCLUSIONS

We have presented a model that describes how human resource planners might select skill sets for use in special operations. This model considers five factors that have a significant effect on demands for skills, and treats these factors as a function of time. Six methods of obtaining new skills offer alternatives to relying on internal resources. As we face new kinds of asymmetrical threats, it will be increasingly important to have diverse and flexible ways of incorporating external expertise into special operations teams.

NOTES

1. Michael Ignatieff, *The Warrior's Honour* (Toronto: Penguin Books, 1998).
2. D. Neil, "Ethics and the Military Corporation," *Canadian Military Journal,* Vol. 1, No. 1 (Spring 2000).
3. Tom St. Denis, "The Dangerous Appeal of the Warrior," *Canadian Military Journal*, Vol. 2, No. 2 (Summer 2001).
4. Australian Defence Forces, *Commando Capability* (Canberra: Australian Defence Forces, 2000), 97.
5. NATO, Allied Joint Doctrine *AJP-1A Combined SOF Concept 3200* (Brussels: NATO, March 1997), 1-A1.
6. [Editor's note: following the convention in the rest of this book, Special Forces capitalized refers to a specific doctrinal definition (the one used by the Australian Defence Forces in this case), while the term without capitals refers to the generic case.]
7. Hermann F. Schwind, Hari Das, and Terry F. Wagar, *Canadian Human Resource Management: A Strategic Approach,* (Toronto: McGraw Hill Ryerson, 2002).
8. Jean-Pascal Souque, *Focus on competencies: training and development practices, expenditures and trends*, Conference Board of Canada, Centre for Management Effectiveness (Ottawa : Conference Board of Canada, 1996).
9. Australian Defence Forces, *Commando Capability*, 97.
10. Lawrence McDonough, "A Special Operations Costing Model," Institute of Defence Resources Management Working Paper (Kingston: Department of Politics and Economics, Royal Military College of Canada, January 2004).
11. Schwind, *et al., Canadian Human Resource Management.*

APPENDIX
Selection Process in the ADF for Special Forces

38. Commandos provide a unique capability within the SF Group. The commando capability is a self contained, balanced and integrated force, capable of conducting Special Recovery Operations, Offensive Operations and Support Operations within a joint environment. ... The commando capability requires a high degree of interoperability with other SF units and complements those specialised capabilities resident within SASR. Although skill sets for Commando FE and SASR are similar, tasks and modus operandi differ markedly.

39. The commando capability in conjunction with SASR provides the ADF with the full range of SO capability options within the force-in-being. Full time commando elements constitute a high readiness capability principally for the conduct of special recovery, offensive and support operations. Commando elements may be used to supplement SASR's Special Reconnaissance capability when 'reconnaissance in force' techniques are more appropriate.

40. Selection of SF for a SO mission is determined by matching the availability and operational expertise of the FE with the operational requirement. SASR will generally be selected for low signature operations where discreet techniques are more suitable, while a CTE will be selected for larger scale operations where speed, surprise, manoeuvre and firepower is demanded.

ADF COMMANDO SELECTION AND TRAINING

88. Fundamental commando individual training consists of enhanced infantry and SF skills,with an emphasis on urban operations. Insertion and extraction skills are secondary to combat skills, although commandos are able to insert and extract using sea and air assets, as well as negotiating difficult terrain or obstacles, such as mountainous regions, bodies of water or cliffs. The three base level insertion/extraction skills maintained for operations are: parachuting, small craft operations and roping.

89. Personnel are selected for service with commando FE, individuals primarily categorised as commandos by the achievement of the initial cycle of training – the Commando Basic Training Course (CBTC), but also by their capacity to parachute, participate in small craft operations climbing and roping. Officers attend a Commando Officer Selection Course (COSC) *designed* to determine mental and physical aptitude for commando service, and Other Ranks complete a series of barrier tests prior to undertaking the CBTC.

90. Many positions within operational support companies and commando RHQ do not require commando training per se. With the exception of those administrative support positions that do not operationally deploy, service within commando companies and commando signal troops demands the successful completion of a CBTC, parachute course, roping course, amphibious operators course and a specialist skills course. Details of the CBTC and COSC are detailed at Annexes B and C respectively.

91. Specialist skills include communications, specialist weapons, medical and demolitions. Unlike conventional infantry units, within commando FE specialist skills are dispersed and held predominantly at platoon and section level in order to achieve maximum operational flexibility and access to firepower. Commandos trained in heavy weapons (SI'MG, mortars, anti-armoured and SAM systems) may be brigaded for training purposes but are allocated to heavy weapon platoons within commando companies for operations.

Selection. Members serving within commando FE are selected on the basis of certain mental and physical characteristics. Prerequisites for commando selection include:

a. **Maturity and Psychological Stability.** Individuals within commando FE undertake long, intensive and potentially dangerous courses with a minimum of supervision.

Within high risk SO there is significant scope for error, the consequences of which may present national or international repercussions. Individuals must demonstrate a sound intellect characterised by a high retention of instruction, initiative, and good judgement, in order to maintain a high state of equanimity and teamwork during stress.

b. **Physical**. Due to the nature, duration and environments in which commando operations are conducted; missions demand the highest levels of physical endurance and toughness. Individuals considering service with commando FE must prove high levels of fitness as well as operate comfortably in mentally intimidating environments; that is, at heights and on open seas.

c. **Discipline.** Commando operations and training require high levels of trust. Poor cohesion or ill discipline presented during potentially dangerous training or operations could prove fatal. A poor discipline record may indicate that applicants are deficient in the necessary self discipline and motivation demanded by commando service.

CHAPTER SIXTEEN

NATO DOCTRINE AND CANADIAN SPECIAL OPERATIONS

Benjamin Zyla

Canada's relationship with NATO goes back to the foundation of the Alliance in 1949. As a charter signatory to the Washington Treaty and a prominent advocate of postwar Atlanticism, Canada helped convince the U.S. to join the Atlantic partnership.[1] Even before the idea of a security arrangement outside the framework of the United Nations began in 1947, Canada nurtured good relations with Britain and France, her historical partners. Multilateralism has been a source of Canadian security and "defence against help" in the modern era. But Canada has long been reluctant to invest in defence. Contributing to special operations may play a decisive role in Canada's future with NATO as conventional forces rust out and threats evolve.

This chapter describes the common ground of NATO's Allied Joint Doctrine for special operations, as well as the practical military and political difficulties of launching and managing multinational operations. Both military and political difficulties stem from the end of the Soviet threat, which has dramatically changed NATO's role and weakened many of the ties that gave Europe and America common cause. But Canada's best option is to bolster the transatlantic relationship, supporting NATO's role in stability operations and encouraging non-US (both European and regional) contributions to the stability on which Canada's peace and prosperity depend.

NATO'S CONTRIBUTION

Today, politicians on both sides of the Atlantic celebrate NATO as the most successful alliance in history. Who can blame them? It brought peace and stability to a divided continent where two world wars originated. After the defeat of the Germans in 1945, the Cold War threatened stability. The Soviet Union tried to expand into Iran and Turkey in 1946 and to elbow the U.K. and the U.S. out of Greece in 1947. Under the guidance of Secretary of State Dean Acheson, the U.S. sought to reconstruct the industrial cores of Europe and Asia, bind them to the U.S., and ensure their future cohesion in the face of Soviet external threats and Communist internal threats. The Marshall Plan, implemented in 1948, and NATO were the primary means of accomplishing these aims.

Two forces tied North America and Europe together. The foremost was the geopolitical threat of Communist expansion in Europe; both continents had security interests in keeping the Russians behind the Elbe. The second was America's economic stake in Europe, which reinforced its strategic interest in European prosperity. After the end of the Second World War, Canada was committed to and engaged in not only NATO but also NORAD, the second pillar of Canadian security policy aimed at territorial defence. Alliances for stability remain central to Canadian security.

In 1989, the Soviet Union collapsed and with it the Communist threat that bridged the Atlantic. NATO's role as a defensive alliance came into question. But NATO survived, despite expectations that the Organization for Economic Co-operation and Development (OECD) would take over coordination of Europe's security.[2] Far from fading away, NATO reinvented itself and explored new roles, engaging former East-bloc countries through partnership-for-peace programs. Thus, NATO evolved from defensive alliance to organization for collective security.

As NATO redefined its role, the European Union developed policies that culminated in the Treaty of Maastricht. Incorporating the concept of the European Security and Defence Identity (ESDI), this can be seen as a milestone in European integration. Washington had encouraged European self-reliance and burden-sharing but was wary of European autonomy that might lead to competition. For both NATO and the ESDI, the new insecurities of the post-Cold War period suggested that if they did not address threats arising outside the NATO area, they would be irrelevant: out of area, or out of business.

NATO special-operations missions cannot be understood without reference to the changing security environment of NATO and of Europe in general. Since more than half of NATO's members are European countries that have managed to harmonize their economic and social policies, there is an obvious overlap of European and NATO assets and interests. Europe has grown together steadily and has implemented its own command and control structure through the Treaty of Nice. Surprisingly, Canada does not have an official response to the recent developments, partly because the U.S. is still actively involved in the Alliance and partly because Canada seems caught between its European heritage and North American geography. Some describe this inertia as a dangerous "free ride" that has contributed to Canada's diminishing influence in the world.[3] I argue that Canadian leaders have to make a strategic choice based on Canada's national interest: should Canada use NATO as its multilateral forum of choice for deployment of special operations? NATO's special operations doctrine and practice may be a useful alternative to unilateral operations or those led by the U.S. in support of stability.

NATO DOCTRINE FOR SPECIAL OPERATIONS FORCES

NATO's doctrine builds on national sources. International military staff assigned to NATO coordinate conferences and working groups attended by national delegations. NATO doctrine is based on common denominators and commonly understood definitions and practices. What makes some operations special? Since special operations are most effective if they have the protection of secrecy, much of the detail about tasks, mandates, and procedures for special operations is classified. National forces for special operations like US SOF, the U.K.'s SAS, Germany's *Kommando Spezialkräfte*, and Canada's JTF 2 each have unique structures and mandates. NATO Joint Special Operation Forces (JSOF) are a new and evolving concept.[4]

NATO publications define JSOF as military forces that are "specially designated, organised, trained and equipped".[5] They make use of "operational techniques and modes of employment [that] are not standard to conventional forces",[6] are highly flexible, and may be employed across a range of military operations. They can be deployed in peace-support, crisis, or conflict situations, independently or in support of conventional forces. How JSOF are deployed depends on each mission and thus cannot be generalized. Their goals, however, include achieving "military, political, economic and psychological objectives or a combination thereof".[7] Operations in secret may increase political risk, but the pay-off for success is higher than with conventional forces.

Most of the time, special forces are directed at high-value missions with critical objectives. Most forces for special operations can operate in theatre for only a limited period of time and "should not be substituted for other, more appropriate forces".[8] They are most suitable in peacetime because their missions require thorough planning. "We are not the fire department of NATO; our missions need planning time ahead."[9]

NATO doctrine mentions three principal tasks for JSOF: special surveillance and reconnaissance, military assistance, and direct action. This reflects a divergence between European and US models of special operations, which may now be converging as the U.S. makes changes to fight the war on terror: CA and PSYOPS have been removed from SOF doctrine; whether military assistance will come to be treated as a conventional operation remains to be seen.

The most prominent role for special forces is special surveillance and reconnaissance. Interviews with planning staff at NATO suggest that about four out of every five missions involve information-gathering or "intelligence collection assets".[10] Special Forces collect information on-site or complement information provided by other NATO members. Deployment of special forces in Bosnia (IFOR and SFOR) and Kosovo (KFOR), including the Joint Commission Observers (JCO), both provided political intelligence and enhanced force security. Their tasks included identifying threats to NATO forces, locating war criminals, mapping escape routes, and sketching houses. These missions mapped the capabilities, intentions, and activities of forces whose cooperation or hostility was conditional upon local interests that were affected.

Reconnaissance is an integral part of any special operation. Special operators in the Balkans talked to police officers, mayors, and residents to get a "local feeling" for the security environment and to gather ground information for future operations. Other tasks in such circumstances might include locating and targetting crucial bridges and water-pumping stations or more sensitive facilities, such as meteorological, geographic, and hydrographical targets in area-assessment operations. Special operators list and detect capabilities and intentions of the enemy, as well as social, cultural, and demographic data – detail that is impossible to collect through satellite images. The tasks are specific, detailed, and time-consuming. Although the information supports operational or strategic decision-making, it must be collected at a tactical, personal level because it is inaccessible to other sensors (although such sensors may be found at the tactical level). Quite often, special forces are deployed to locate targets prior to a larger air or sea campaign to target an adversary's command-and-control components or other lines of communication.

As operations in the Balkans progressed, NATO applied the concept of the Combined Joint Task Force (CJTF) to special forces for the first time in 1994, bringing multinational special assets together under a single command. The CJTF concept combines multi-national forces and organizes these forces in service components (land, air, sea). Non-NATO forces can be attached whenever it is deemed necessary or desirable to do so.

The second task for special forces is to provide military assistance to friendly or allied forces. Forces may be deployed in order to "protect a democratic society from subversion, lawlessness or insurgency".[11] In other words, NATO special forces may support friendly elements with "training and equipment".[12] A strict reading of Joint Doctrine could leave the impression that it includes both unconventional warfare (supporting an insurgency) and foreign internal defence (supporting a government against an insurgency). The emphasis on technical assistance to support engineering and security during humanitarian crises suggests a narrower interpretation, and interviews indicate that the European focus for military assistance is more likely to be on the deployment of JSOF for use of their non-combat skills, such as language ability, work in austere environments, and cultural accommodation.

The third task, direct action, relies on what are sometimes called "kinetic" or "hard" military skills. Direct actions are limited in scope and duration and are very precise. They may include direct-assault tactics or "stand-off attacks from maritime, ground or air platforms."[13] To reduce risk, there must be a plan for withdrawal from the hostile environment. Critical targets may be attacked directly by JSOF as a form of special warfare, "characterized by a unique set of objectives, weapons and forces".[14] For example, the task to locate, capture, and recover designated people and material of any kind would be assigned to JSOF. Careful reconnaissance and planning would reduce the need for hard power to a minimum, but the chief advantage of special forces is their adaptability in changing circumstances. This adaptability drives the loose force structure of JSOF, which is uniquely determined by each mission rather than permanently designed to oppose a hostile force with standard tactics. Reinforcement is not a routine operation for JSOF, and elements are designed for "small scale offensive actions" only.[15] NATO and US doctrine on direct action are becoming virtually identical.[16]

The variety of special force structures is matched by variety in weapons and equipment. Weapons from sniper rifles to precision-guided munitions provide precise lethality, and the PGMs could be delivered from maritime, air, or ground platforms. JSOF are typically deployed in small teams and are not capable of engaging larger units. Their success therefore depends largely on the synergy of "speed, stealth, surprise while covered by darkness".[17] Night-vision capabilities are an essential part of their equipment. They conduct operations distant from support bases, making state-of-the-art communications like secure satellite links essential. Sophisticated day-night, all-weather aviation is vital for infiltration and escape, while global reach into hostile territory may demand multinational cooperation.[18]

The size of special teams and the criteria for selection are national responsibilities, and joint doctrine cannot eliminate differences in national standards and cultures. This variety can be a source of strength. SOF teams have twelve members; Dutch special forces, eight; and SAS teams, four. The basic specialties found in a team usually include weapons (a team generally has a sniper), demolitions, medical, and communications skills (satellite, computer, and perhaps languages). JSOF teams may also incorporate civilian experts like police, lawyers, forensic experts, engineers, and language specialists. This practice requires more careful selection than does a larger force, which can provide secure transport and defended camps. A key asset for special operations is aviation for transport and support. The best of Europe's special forces have dedicated special-forces helicopters, which train exclusively with special-forces teams, while others rely on temporary assignment of conventional force assets.

NATO'S MILITARY DIFFICULTIES

The practical difficulties of working in a multinational environment are an open secret in Brussels, the butt of cartoons and jokes everywhere. NATO AJP 01 provides a standard doctrine for joint operations, but diplomatic language, massaged by committees, obscures real national differences in capability and conduct of operations. Since learning to work with more than twenty countries – let alone fight with them – can take a professional lifetime, this chapter can do no more than highlight examples. Intelligence, communications, equipment, logistical support, and interoperability are largely technical constraints that can be overcome with time and funding. Divergent special-forces cultures, however, are unlikely to be homogenized and may actually be sources of strength.

The foremost military problem may be intelligence. Every weapon system and plan requires specific types of information. The complexity increases as the information piles up, requiring many trained and experienced intelligence analysts, and sophisticated staff officers and commanders to filter and use the intelligence. If special forces are not deployed to gather intelligence, commanders rely on "national technical means" – primarily satellite images – for everything from city maps to weather conditions. Adding the textured information from well-placed special forces teams on the ground should improve matters, but if they are of variable quality, from various countries, with different mandates, they may add to confusion. In practice, the JSOF concept can reduce this problem and help make better use of limited national resources as part of a concentrated plan.

The second problem is that not only are special forces deployed to collect intelligence, but they also need intelligence to deploy. JSOF do not have their own intelligence assets, relying instead on their home states to pass on information that affects their situation. In theory, each nation should forward crucial intelligence immediately, but intelligence officers are often subject to national restrictions that limit the flow of information, particularly from human sources. This can delay operations and compromise the comparative advantage of special forces. The doctrine that "intelligence must be centrally controlled to avoid unwarranted duplication, ... and ensure the efficient, economic use of all resources"[19] has not yet overcome national barriers. JSOF often use personal contacts across national boundaries to maximize access to nationally controlled information, even when the details and sources may be obscured.

The third problem is that NATO sometimes struggles with diversity, in intelligence as in other military capabilities. The Dutch, Germans, and Canadians do not have access to their own military-grade satellite photography. For historical reasons, Germany has a limited intelligence establishment and relies heavily on its allies.[20] Much of Canada's privileged intelligence-sharing began to fade as arctic eavesdropping became less useful after the Cold War. The U.K. and U.S. dominate production and circulation of intelligence reports, and smaller countries have to evaluate whether they "give you the full picture of information or if they deliberately leave out some details and information that is shared with others".[21] There is suspicion that the U.K. and U.S. sometimes use their intelligence capability to control information flow and manipulate their allies.

Next to intelligence, the most essential capability for any special mission is probably secure communications. JSOF must be able to communicate with their home bases and with the NATO commander if they are to be useful as strategic assets. This often involves satellite communications. Not all contributing nations have secure, interoperable communications. Frequencies are limited, and smaller contributors like the Netherlands and Belgium rely on the U.K. to provide communications channels.[22] On top of these technical issues, there may be a language barrier. English is the language of choice for JSOF; new players such as Poland have to ensure not only that they have state-of-the-art equipment but also that operators can speak English with some fluency to participate in multinational special operations.

Logistical support to JSOF is difficult. Remote from NATO bases, JSOF in operations may need resupply as often as every ten days. Reliance on sophisticated equipment makes supply and maintenance critical to mission success. "There are thirty different types of batteries that need to be re-supplied eight to ten days into the operation," explains one experienced officer. The logistical problem increases in multinational operations: each nation has its own types of batteries, which are available only through the national supply chain. Stocking equipment in or close to hostile territory is risky and limits JSOF freedom of action. Insertion into a hostile area by helicopter makes every resupply operation hazardous.

Logistics is more than just resupply. It is the "science of planning and carrying out the movement and maintenance of forces. Sustaining a force to the necessary level and duration of operations to achieve its assigned objectives is the key objective of logistics."[23] In this larger sense, countries like the Netherlands, Germany, and Canada lack the transport, medical, maintenance, and even postal resources to carry out extended operations in distant lands. NATO infrastructure supported national assets for European operations in the Cold War but has not yet been developed for out-of-area JSOF operations to which Canada might contribute. Nevertheless, it may be easier for a multinational effort to meet these needs than it would be for any nation other than the U.S. to do so by itself.

Successful multinational operations hinge on interoperability, and this is an area that needs improvement. Although NATO doctrine demands standardization,[24] there seems to be a lack of commitment, especially when it comes to communications and information systems. Both technical and terminology standardization are desirable, but mere compatibility is the level commonly achieved in practice.[25] Maintaining this requires constant training and regular contact in multinational operations, implying long-term national commitment.

Many European countries follow the SAS model for tactics, equipment, and force culture. "Special forces commitments in Europe are very close and international," explains a former Dutch commander. They cooperate much more closely with each other than with the U.S., which is in a completely different league: having all their own assets, SOF do not need to share with conventional forces or other countries. The discrepancy was evident in Afghanistan, where Dutch, German, Canadian, and New Zealand special forces operated under the protection of, and often with the support of, US forces. Nevertheless, they were able to test interoperability and improved the prospects of future multinational operations. European special forces conduct multinational exercises annually, share techniques, and compare training within a community much smaller than their conventional counterparts. This cooperation extends beyond Europe. The German KSK and GSG 9, for example, share regularly with Israeli as well as British, French, and US special forces. Canada should consider increasing training with European special forces, both to benefit from the training and to enhance future multinational operations. While conventional forces rarely commingle below battalion level, special forces operate at the patrol or section level, which permits quite small elements to work together effectively.[26]

Military culture and personal attitudes of European special operators are distinct from their American counterparts. Europeans would agree that SOF are mission-oriented and tend to be entirely dependent on military assets, but this poses few problems because their military assets are comparatively unconstrained. European forces frequently have to improvise to overcome deficiencies, and they seem to struggle less when the situation changes quickly. Interviews with experienced German and Canadian officers suggested that the British approach to special operations is oriented towards soldier skills, rather than technological solutions. For example, there are imaginative alternatives to helicopter insertion that US SOF would not attempt: teams might take commercial aircraft, arrive as tourists or NGO workers, or walk in over difficult terrain. By contrast, US planners prefer to level the ground before insertion: "The hammer has to come first. This shows the diverse mentality of an operation and each nation has its own mentality."[27]

It is difficult to detect a hierarchy of preferred working relationships in the NATO special-operations community. There seem to be good relations between the Germans, Dutch, and Scandinavians, whose special forces have a common approach. "They understand each other almost blindly, and there is a lot of trust among those forces," says a Dutch Officer. The Nordic countries have a more open approach to special operations than the Italian and French forces, which are distinctly different. The U.S. has the greatest trust in the U.K.'s SAS and SBS and the least in French special forces. A German officer recounted the following story of operations in Yugoslavia to illustrate divergent military cultures. During the UNPROFOR period (before December 1995), a convoy was fired upon in Sarajevo. French special forces promised remedial action. Later that night they allegedly captured and killed the sniper, earning accolades in the French media. A Dutch officer explained, "It is accepted there, whereas this would be impossible in Holland or Germany" – tolerance for aggressive individual action seems to be greater in some forces.

NATO'S POLITICAL STRUGGLES

This is not the place to speculate on structural differences between North America and Europe. Nevertheless, it is noteworthy that recent Canadian governments have shown little interest in the effect of NATO's changing shape on Canada's relationship with Europe. Even Canadian officials in Brussels seem to lack a vision of Canada's role in the Alliance. The European Union's initiatives to establish common foreign and defence policy and to strengthen command and control are only one step in the evolution of an EU that offers important advantages to Canada, for the same reason that Canada turned to Europe in the 1970s under Trudeau. I would argue that it would be a mistake for Ottawa to turn away from Europe as these changes progress.

Canada's place is between Europe and the U.S., and force commitments are an instrument to keep its place. If Canadian diplomats in NATO are asked what Ottawa can bring to the table, the reply is, "Talk." Canada's achievements as a peacekeeper are old news, and they carry little weight. Canada's contribution to the war on terror has not made a big impression. But Canada can still be called upon to mediate between the U.S. and Europe, a role long practised in the Cold War. Of course, it has no formula to balance European aspirations with US global leadership and has only an imprecise desire to keep NATO as it is. Ottawa does not favour new European institutions that would divide resources or challenge US leadership, and therefore finds itself supporting the "3Ds" – no duplication, no decoupling, no discrimination – expounded by US Secretary of State Madeleine Albright in 1998 as conditions for an evolving policy on European security and defence. Canadian commitment to NATO is thus more a symbolic gesture than a military act: "We want to keep the seat at the table regardless of how many forces we commit."[28]

But Canada has a national interest at stake in NATO, and Paul Martin's government will have to evaluate the importance of its NATO contribution. The stake is not economic. Canada's economy depends largely on that of the U.S., which increasingly protects its territory through bilateral defence agreements.[29] British trade and international investment markets used to be important for Canada's prosperity, but Canada's economic centre of gravity is now clearly on the North American continent. The stake arises from our values and core national interests. Values such as promoting democracy, human rights, rule of law, multiculturalism, and civility are important, but secondary to interests. Historian Jack Granatstein lists four:

> (1) Canada must protect its territory, the security of its people, and its unity. (2) It must strive to protect and enhance its independence. (3) It must promote the economic growth of the nation to support the prosperity and welfare of its people. (4) It must work with like-minded states, in outside international forums, for the protection and enhancement of democracy and freedom.[30]

Canada's stake in Europe begins with its need to work with like-minded states to protect both its values and its independence from the principal threat to that independence, which is the U.S.

CANADA AND NATO EUROPE

NATO is not only a defence alliance but also a forum for the exchange of views and policies. It has always been so, particularly since the fall of the

Berlin Wall, when the threat of a Soviet attack subsided, making it pointless to maintain large numbers of tanks and troops on European soil. NATO is the most important of the international organizations in which Canada regularly meets its European allies and in which it is most likely to find common cause. It is therefore Canada's best gateway to Europe. During the Cold War, NATO helped Canada to balance US power and alleviate its pressures.

The new security environment that has become evident since September 11 has highlighted new roles for NATO. The Alliance is likely to take over the stability operations in Afghanistan after the U.S. concludes Operation Enduring Freedom. Force planners in SHAPE have already planned the force structure. This new type of role originated with the NATO Implementation Force (IFOR, replaced by SFOR) in Bosnia in 1995 and the Kosovo bombing, NATO's first out-of-area mission in 1998. Afghanistan can be seen as a continuation of this policy, and ISAF is unlikely to be its last. NATO can boast speedy response, coherent doctrine, and robust combat capability, while the UN produces compromise mandates, weak forces, and delayed response.

Taking on international stability operations implies three things for NATO and for Canada's role in the Alliance. First, it is likely to strengthen the transatlantic relationship. As a global leader, the U.S. must provide stability and security, and it desperately needs allies to share the costs of doing so. At the same time, stability operations are NATO's new *raison d'être*. Second, Canada is diplomatically positioned to revive its historical claim as a pre-eminent contributor to peace and stability, perhaps regaining some influence (if it is prepared to commit the resources to do so). Third, the long slide in contributions to conventional forces might be less important if Canada were to make a major new effort to develop special forces, which are singularly well-adapted to the new security operations.

If stability operations determine NATO's role in the near future, then the Alliance will need special forces in all their variants. JTF 2 already enjoys a good reputation amongst its European counterparts. Canada's special forces could be the means to secure Ottawa's interest in the Alliance and Europe through affordable contributions to stability operations.

CONCLUSION

Canada has a pragmatic approach to NATO. It seeks practical solutions rather than debating ideological or theoretical issues. Canadian staff in Brussels take operational planning seriously and have a reputation amongst their NATO colleagues as reliable professionals, but they are constrained by the lack of political will in Ottawa to either support military deployments or develop Canadian forces, which are inadequate for their numerous commitments.[31]

I have argued that the end of the Soviet threat removed a key motive for transatlantic solidarity in 1989. Canada has a vital national interest in stability, pursued with like-minded nations to resist US influence. It has no option but to remain engaged with NATO as part of its security strategy, but "...wartime alliances rarely survive the enemy's defeat,"[32] and Europe is developing its own foreign and defence policy and new security structures. The implication for Canada is that it must develop clear policies towards these efforts and must back those policies with resources or risk being forced back on an unequal bilateral relationship with the U.S. A Canadian contribution to European-backed stability operations serves both stability and Canada's independence from US policy.

NATO's future responsibilities will certainly include out-of-area operations. The scope and complexity of military operations will increase over the next decade, and many stability missions may demand "niche capabilities" – special forces with the capacity to work under austere conditions, conduct special reconnaissance, manage violence in remote areas, and adapt to chaotic circumstances with little support. Canadian special operators could make an important contribution to the Alliance and may be in high demand. Special operations could keep Canada alive in NATO. This would make them a vital policy tool, which might help Ottawa to steer the U.S. back towards an international order of multilateralism and support for international institutions.

Whatever Ottawa decides, special operations forces will play a crucial role in future military operations. They may seem expensive, but they are cheaper and more universally useful than conventional forces, as the Americans have learned. The Pentagon asked for an increase of almost a third in its spending on Special Forces to $6.7 billion in 2003.[33] The growing relevance of special operations should be a warning to force-planners and policy-makers alike.

NOTES

1. The U.S. showed no interest in such an alliance and had to be convinced by Canada and Britain to join. See David G. Haglund, ed., *What NATO for Canada?* Martello Papers No. 23 (Kingston, ON: Queen's University Centre for International Relations, 2002), 2.
2. The precursor to the OECD was the Organisation for European Economic Co-operation (OEEC), which administered aid under the Marshall Plan. Since the OECD replaced the OEEC in 1961, its mandate has been to build strong economies in its member countries, improve efficiency, hone market systems, expand free trade, and contribute to development in industrialized as well as developing countries.
3. Andrew Cohen, *While Canada Slept – How we lost our place in the world* (Toronto: Mclelland-Stewart, 2003).
4. NATO, Allied Joint Doctrine *AJP-1B Combined SOF Concept 3200* (Brussels: NATO, March 1997) and NATO Special Operation Policy (MC 437). [Editor's note: JSOF implies the use of national special forces within a joint framework. SOF is used to designate US SOF.]
5. *AJP 01 B*, section 0803, page 8-1.

6. Ibid.
7. Ibid.
8. *AJP 01 B*, section 0804, page 8-1.
9. Interview with a Dutch officer at NATO Headquarters in Brussels, 3 December 2003.
10. Interviews conducted at NATO Headquarters, 25 November to 5 December, 2003. Intelligence collections assets are described in *AJP 01 B*, section 0806(a), page 8-2.
11. *AJP 01 B*, section 0808, page 8-4.
12. Ibid.
13. *AJP 01 B*, section 0807, page 8-3.
14. Chairman of the Joint Chiefs of Staff, *Joint Publication 3-05: Doctrine for Joint Special Operations* (Washington, DC: Department of Defense, 2003), Chapter Two.
15. Interview with a Dutch officer at NATO Headquarters in Brussels, 3 December 2003.
16. Interestingly, a comparison of NATO doctrine *AJP 01*, section 0804, with pages 2-12 of *Joint Publication 3-05.20* shows that these two documents are identical on this point and on most other points as well.
17. Quoted from the US Special Forces Operations Doctrine by a Dutch officer interviewed at NATO Headquarters, December 2004.
18. *AJP 01 B*, section 0820, 8-8.
19. *AJP 01 B*, section 1203, 12-1.
20. Interview with a German officer at NATO Headquarters, 4 December 2003.
21. Two interviews with German officers at NATO Headquarters, 30 November 2003.
22. Interview with a Dutch officer on at NATO Headquarters, 3 December 2003; and *AJP 01 B*, section 1315, 13-4.
23. Conference of Defence Associations Institute, "A Nation at Risk: the decline of the Canadian Forces" (Ottawa, 2002), 31.
24. *AJP 01 B*, section 1307, 13-2.
25. Following the list in *AJP 01 B*, section 1307, 13-2.
26. Integration at patrol level is not advisable: "…that is when shit happens. You can integrate into a task force, but never on the patrol level," says a Dutch officer at NATO.
27. Interview with a German officer at NATO Headquarters, 4 December 2003.
28. Interview with a Canadian on the NATO International staff, conducted at NATO Headquarters, 26 November 2003.
29. Jack Granatstein, "The Importance of Being Less Earnest: Promoting Canada's National Interest through tighter Ties with the U.S," C. D. Howe Institute Benefactors Lecture, Toronto, 2003.
30. Ibid., 7.

31. Interview with Canadian staff at NATO Headquarters, 26 November 2003.
32. Stephen M. Walt, "NATO's Fragile Future," in *What NATO for Canada?*, ed., Haglund, 79.
33. Michael Fitzsimmons, "The Importance of Being Special: Planning for the Future of US Special Operations Forces," *Defence & Security Analysis,* Vol. 19, No. 3 (September 2003): 204.

CHAPTER SEVENTEEN

US SPECIAL OPERATIONS FORCES, TRANSFORMATION, AND IMPLICATIONS FOR CANADIAN DOCTRINE

James D. Kiras

Writing doctrine for a subject as contentious and sensitive as special operations is not an easy task for middle powers like Canada. After all, even within the U.S., sectors of the civilian and military population view special operations with suspicion and unease at best and, at worst, as "un-American".[1] The notion that Canada will employ special operations forces to conduct covert or clandestine missions in support of the national interest is at odds with its carefully cultivated image as an impartial and honest broker internationally. Further complicating Canadian efforts in drafting its own special operations doctrine is a dearth of samples to use as a starting point. Most countries prefer not to publish the details of how their special forces are organized and may even deny the existence of such forces. A readily available source of special operations doctrine is the U.S., but following that model too closely has political implications in a country that still struggles to define its relationship with its superpower neighbour.

Yet there are compelling reasons for Canada to understand the changes that are taking place across the US Department of Defense as a whole, and specifically within the SOF community.[2] The senior leadership is committed to transforming how DoD does everything from budget submissions and programmatic requests to special operations, even while fighting a war against a global, networked, irregular adversary. The U.S. will transform its military forces regardless of the pace of change of the armed forces of its allies. Some outside the U.S. feel that close allies, who are committed to the struggle against global threats such as terrorism and the proliferation of weapons of mass destruction, should benefit from the transformational initiatives.

This chapter surveys the roots of transformation and how the concept changed as a result of the September 11 terrorist attacks and the US response in Afghanistan. The performance of special forces in Afghanistan and Iraq has provided a model of the characteristics that transformed conventional forces will possess; the term "SOF-like" has been used to describe those characteristics. To stem confusion as the Canadian special operations community writes its own doctrine, the differences that separate special from conventional forces, which are not often clearly delineated, are explored in detail. SOF transformation will not occur at some undefined point in the future or involve futuristic technologies. The key is the closer integration of tasks into mutually reinforcing capability sets that are applied towards defined and achievable goals. The chapter concludes with an assessment of the impact of US transformation on the development of Canadian special operations doctrine and the choices that lie ahead for Canada.

The requirement and guidance to transform US forces have been articulated in studies that supported the writing of the 2001 Quadrennial Defense Review (QDR), the Review itself, and the Transformation Planning Guidance (TPG), and in statements by senior DoD officials. From the studies, one can derive the conceptual foundation of military transformation. The QDR, for example, outlines goals and risks associated with transformation.[3] A crucial concern was the inadequacy of US forces to deal with challenges of the post-Cold War era.[4] US Armed Forces were well equipped and prepared to fight a high-tempo war against a conventional adversary in Central Europe. The problem was that the "threat" or adversary upon which US force planning was predicated no longer existed. "Transformation", therefore, would address what individuals within the administration of George W. Bush perceived to be the most significant challenges to preserving US national security: missile defence, space superiority, information dominance, intelligence, and forward-basing and deploying forces.[5]

The terrorist attacks on the World Trade Center and Pentagon changed the character of the transformation debate. According to a senior DoD official, the new requirements to fight terrorism globally are on equal footing with both the requirements for transformation and the need to retain high-quality people and forces.[6] Although these goals continue to be important, they are overshadowed by the demands of the war being waged by the U.S. against global terrorism. Those concerned with the impact of the war on the US Armed Services question whether transformation can address the threat posed by al-Qaeda and other global terrorist groups: of what use is a military force against a globally dispersed, networked adversary? Can a military force defeat or deter actors who exploit the freedoms of open societies to use easily acquired technology for mass destruction, and who seek only destruction and martyrdom for themselves?[7]

President Bush unequivocally stated the resolve of the U.S. to respond to the threat of global terrorism: "But some governments will be timid in the face of terror. And make no mistake about it: If they do not act, America will."[8]

The question of *how* to respond militarily, however, was the subject of some debate. Most advocated combining ground troops with air strikes, to avoid the perceived mistakes in the Balkans in 1999.[9] Few considered using SOF, although then-Director of Central Intelligence George Tenant allegedly put the option forward.[10] Subsequent SOF activities in Afghanistan surprised even their most outspoken supporters.

US Special Operations Forces,[11] operating with coalition partners from countries as diverse as Australia, Canada, Norway, and Germany, demonstrated their strategic value in Afghanistan, Iraq, and elsewhere in three main ways: by providing a strategic "economy of force" option, by assisting indigenous combat forces, and by enabling and enhancing conventional platforms and systems.[12] SOF are a strategic "economy of force" option. This means that the military dividends yielded by a small SOF deployment are substantial, in comparison with the results from a much larger conventional force. During the first 100 days of the campaign in Afghanistan, for example, a US force of less than 3,000 troops, spearheaded by SOF, could boast impressive accomplishments. It helped to drive the Taliban from power, as Taliban leaders surrendered major cities to opposition forces, including Kandahar, Kabul, Kunduz, and Mazar-e-Sharif. At least 11 terrorist training camps and 39 Taliban command and control sites were destroyed, putting an end to foreign training in Afghanistan. Routes were blocked to prevent the escape of al-Qaeda and Taliban members. Many senior al-Qaeda and Taliban officials were either captured or killed. The Friendship Bridge between Afghanistan and Uzbekistan was reopened to transport humanitarian aid by land. Minefields and roads were cleared to ensure delivery of aid. Leaflet drops and radio broadcasts helped shape the battlefield.[13]

SOF were successful in breaking the Taliban control over most of Afghanistan, using both traditional and innovative approaches. Taliban and al-Qaeda forces dug into linear and static defensive positions, awaiting the eventual offensive led by the U.S. A substantial force had been fighting the Taliban in Afghanistan for some time. The United Front/Northern Alliance, led by Ahmed Shah Massoud until his assassination, numbered some 10,000 troops and fielded tanks, artillery, and armoured personnel carriers.[14] SOF used linguistic and cultural skills to contact and coordinate Northern Alliance forces and prepare them to take the offensive. The considerable impact of these skills should not be undervalued: although it is hyperbole to suggest that one SOF unit "turned the tide of the war", they did establish contact and work directly with the future leader of Afghanistan, Hamid Karzai.[15]

Other SOF characteristics are the flexibility, adaptability, and innovation of their personnel. These traits stem from the qualities of the operators, including training, independence, maturity, and operational experience. During the early stages of Operation Enduring Freedom, these SOF characteristics proved vital in providing effective targetting information to deal with rapidly changing conditions on the ground. In conjunction with information received from Northern Alliance forces, SOF provided targetting data to US aircraft loitering overhead.[16]

In previous conflicts, this had never been done on such a scale or with such accuracy. For example, GBU-31 Joint Direct Attack Munitions (JDAMs) allowed Vietnam-era B-52 bombers to provide close support, delivering munitions to within a few hundred meters of friendly troops.[17] Increasing the accuracy of precision munitions used against Taliban and al-Qaeda front lines was useful, but SOF demonstrated even greater strategic value after those lines cracked.

An offensive by United Front/Northern Alliance forces in the Mazar sector in early November culminated with the collapse and rout of Taliban forces. Two key elements in the rapid disintegration of the Taliban in the Northern Afghanistan were stronger cooperation between anti-Taliban forces and the concentrated, accurate air strikes against static defensive positions in urban areas and against mobile reinforcement columns.[18] SOF played a major role in enhancing the effectiveness of both. Mounted on horseback, pickup truck, or all-terrain vehicle, SOF used laptop computers, laser designators, GPS receivers, and satellite phones to call down aerial fire on the move.[19] In at least one case, the adaptive character and enabling value of SOF was clearly demonstrated: SOF-assisted horse cavalry successfully attacked and destroyed a force comprised of Taliban armoured fighting vehicles.[20] A single ODA,[21] with attached Air Force Special Tactics Squadron personnel, inflicted 2,200 enemy casualties and destroyed 29 tanks, 6 command posts, and other assets around Bagram.[22] Although Osama bin Laden and other senior al-Qaeda leaders remain at large and the war on global terrorism will continue for some time, there is little doubt that actions spearheaded by SOF have dealt a serious blow to al-Qaeda and deprived them of a state sanctuary.[23]

Although special forces had been used to great effect in previous campaigns, including British actions in Malaya and Borneo, they were often deployed in small numbers to draw minimum attention to the conflict.[24] During Operation Iraqi Freedom, however, more than 10,000 SOF personnel from the U.S., the U.K., Australia, and Poland demonstrated the effects that could be achieved by massed SOF. Their actions allowed small coalition forces, in conjunction with Kurdish *peshmurga* forces, to be deployed to tie down large Iraqi armoured and mechanized forces in the North.[25] SOF also logged an operational first: having conventional forces, including main battle tanks and elements of an airborne infantry brigade, placed under their control.[26] In addition, SOF denied the Ba'athist regime the use of Scud-launching areas in Western Iraq and seized a number of high-value assets to prevent their destruction, including oil refineries and pumping stations in the south and infrastructure like the Haditha dam. According to one analyst, SOF actions in Afghanistan and Iraq demonstrate that they "are becoming a critical new element of joint warfare in an era of asymmetric warfare."[27]

SOF AS A MODEL FOR TRANSFORMATION

Although the imperatives of transformation are clear, *how* to transform, and what transformed elements will look like, has been the subject of considerable debate.

An image of SOF personnel mounted on horseback, carrying modern military equipment, struck a chord with the senior leadership of the DoD. As the Secretary of Defense remarked, SOF "combined the most high-tech weapons with the most ancient of capabilities...and you used them in unprecedented ways...You brought a similar spirit of innovation to the battle in Iraq."[28] SOF embodied the spirit of transformation.

One result of the identification of SOF with transformation was the suggestion that conventional Services (the Army, Navy, and Air Force) should become "SOF-like" in their approach to future war-fighting. Arthur Cebrowski, head of the DoD's Office of Force Transformation, outlined "SOF-like" characteristics: "Ease of insertion, a depth of local knowledge, small unit agility are all very, very powerful attributes that the entire force should possess."[29]

It is not easy to distinguish what separates SOF from their parent Services. The qualities often used to describe SOF operators can be applied to many officers and enlisted personnel in the conventional forces in the conduct of their daily activities. And conventional personnel sometimes already possess valuable linguistic skills or cultural knowledge, or both.[30] Individual traits or specialized training and equipment are not what distinguish SOF from their Service counterparts. Neither are some of the core tasks that SOF perform: unconventional warfare, foreign internal defence, direct action, special reconnaissance, counter-terrorism, counter-proliferation of weapons of mass destruction, PSYOPS, and CA operations.[31] Some of these tasks are not unique to SOF;[32] for example, Marines have historically demonstrated the ability to conduct FID and DA missions with some success. Although the USSOCOM has been designated the lead military command for the ongoing war on terror, the Services and other government and defence agencies are playing crucial roles as part of the integrated response outlined in the National Strategy for Combating Terrorism (NSCT).[33] SOF capabilities can be better integrated to transform the force. The qualities that make SOF appear unique can be distilled and distributed throughout the conventional Services. Accomplishing that, however, would require significant change in how the conventional Services educate, train, and deploy. *What* SOF do is not as important as *how* SOF do it, reflecting specialized selection, training, and approaches to problem solving. At its root, being "SOF-like" requires a particular mindset that can be developed in the conventional forces.

WHAT DISTINGUISHES SOF FROM CONVENTIONAL FORCES?

It is important that those drafting special operations doctrine understand what separates SOF from conventional forces, especially as the latter strive to be more like SOF. Becoming "SOF-like" is more than just operating in small units, relaxing personal grooming standards, and drinking tea with the locals. Although conventional forces can perform some of the tasks associated with SOF, and individual Service personnel exhibit "SOF-like" qualities, SOF are differentiated from conventional forces by specific tasks that conventional forces cannot do well, if at all,[34] and by the unique conditions under which SOF perform their tasks. Some SOF tasks are beyond the scope of conventional units because of the unique skills required, operating environments, political sensitivities, and risks of failure. These include unconventional warfare, counter-terrorism, counter-proliferation, and some psychological operations.

Isolated or austere conditions with minimal support, strategically important missions, and no margin for error characterize the SOF environment. Hostage rescues illustrate the point. While other units might perform them, some SOF rehearse hostage rescues to the most exacting standards. They are the most likely to resolve a hostage situation quickly and with minimal collateral damage. Given the risk of failure inherent in most SOF tasks, higher risks associated with a lower level of training may be unacceptable to decision-makers.

SOF, however, cannot do it all. This includes such conventional-force specialties as massed long-range precision strikes, assaults against defences in depth, and sustained operations on the ground or at sea to demonstrate US resolve and commitment. There are also tasks that SOF have been called upon to perform for which they are not suited. Although SOF are capable of conducting tactical reconnaissance in support of conventional units, this is not the best use of their perishable skill sets and regional expertise. Conventional commanders have used SOF, rather than their own assets, precisely because of the different standards to which SOF operate under difficult conditions.

TRANSFORMING SOF: AN INTEGRATED CONSTRUCT

The response to calls for transformation in the Pentagon has often been framed in terms of platforms, systems, and emerging technologies. Others emphasized investments in the processing and sharing of information; they see future US military dominance as being based on processing information faster and more effectively, and striking targets more precisely, than an adversary can.[35] Some suggest that SOF transformation will be driven by individual platforms like the CV-22, exoskeletons for operators, or enhanced, secure communications and improved GPS receivers. Platforms and systems, however, often require long teething periods before they perform.

Within the SOF community, an alternative approach has been to articulate desired operational capabilities or attributes for development. These, however, are too vague to produce specific improvements. Examples include tailored and integrated operations, agile and unconventional logistics, force protection and survivability, ubiquitous access, and precision strike and effects.[36] The reality of SOF transformation – based on SOF capabilities and equipment, policy guidance, and the drivers and obstacles to transformation – is banal compared to the futuristic visions articulated by some. If transformation for SOF rests on the bedrock of dramatically improving their effectiveness and responsiveness, changes can be made in speed of response to crises, capacity to perform missions, and synergy of SOF capabilities.

Forces based in the continental U.S. suffer from the twin tyrannies of geography and technology. Geography and technology have sheltered the U.S. from the ravages of war for almost 150 years, yet they also present significant challenges when the nation needs to project military power quickly and efficiently. This is especially true if SOF are required to undertake preemptive actions against fleeting targets of opportunity. The dilemma can be resolved by basing SOF in the regions that they are expected to cover, rather than deploying them from the continental U.S. Moving forces forward, however, is expensive, requires support from potentially unstable host nations, and increases force protection requirements.

SOF are expanding to meet contingencies globally. "Growing the force" must be done with care for a number of reasons. The pool of available personnel is limited by the manpower of the conventional Services, and those numbers have been declining steadily since the end of the Cold War. Promotion, accession, and retention of talented personnel are also presenting challenges. Too little action and few opportunities for career advancement prompt personnel to leave, whereas too much action can lead to operator "burnout." Increasing the size of the force too quickly dilutes its overall quality and its capability to perform unique SOF missions.

Increasing the integration of SOF capabilities, in conjunction with sustainable growth of the force and forward basing, is one formula for transforming the force. Understanding SOF capabilities in the broadest sense is a first step towards better integration and assists in the drafting of doctrine. Traditional SOF tasks can be grouped into three sets of capabilities, illustrated in Figure 17-1, which shows SOF task sets and other forces – host-nation forces (including partisan movements), the forces of coalition partners, and conventional forces. There have been times when the commando and intelligence-gathering capabilities have appeared to work at cross-purposes. For example, during the North African campaign in the Second World War, the intelligence-gathering "road watch" missions of the Long Range Desert Group were made increasingly difficult by the success of SAS raids on Axis airfields, convoys, and supply dumps.[37] Similarly, raids by US Military Assistance Command Vietnam, Studies and Observation Group on the Ho Chi Minh Trail were largely compromised by failures of intelligence security.[38] Striking a balance between direct and indirect operations, especially if preemptive actions are undertaken, is more problematic in view of the political climate and the character of the adversary in the ongoing war on terrorism.

SOF possess other capabilities that further complicate the relation between commando and intelligence-gathering capabilities. Nation-building (CA) forces and those that conduct information operations (PSYOPS) are deployed to shape the environment and to prosecute and wage unconventional warfare. Although not mutually exclusive, the activities conducted in the three traditional capability sets (commando, influence and intelligence, and countering unconventional threats) were often performed separately due to differences in time, sensitivity, risk, geography, and importance.

FIGURE 17-1
Traditional SOF Capabilities and Mission Sets

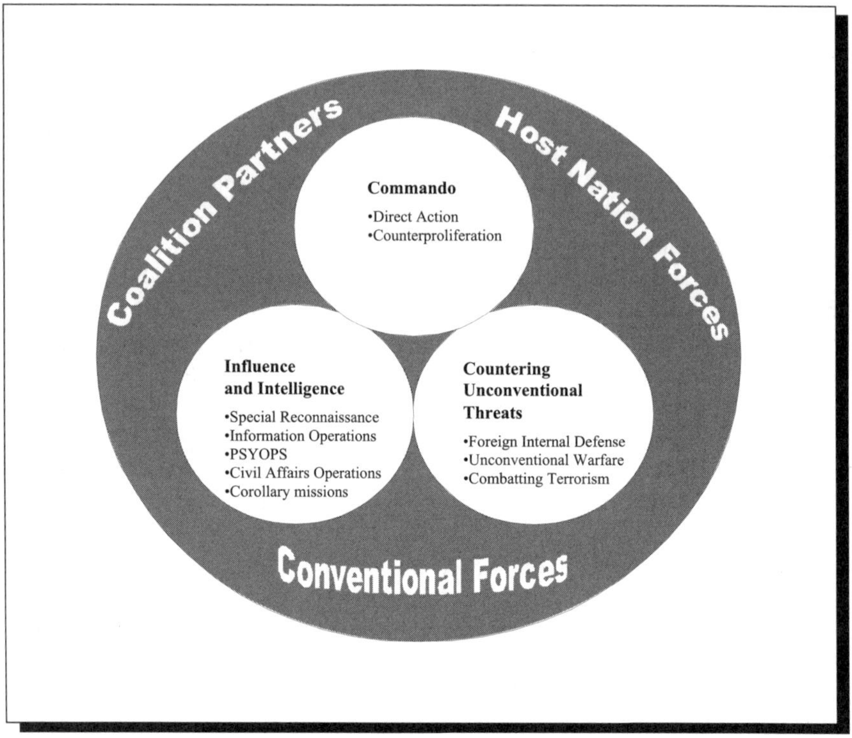

SOF forces have been able to transition from one mission set to another; tactically and operationally, they have shifted from special reconnaissance to direct-action missions and back. In other cases, the mission sets have been mutually exclusive: PSYOPS and CA have played little role in direct-action or counter-proliferation missions. In the course of their activities, SOF work with host-nation and coalition forces, as well as for conventional force commanders. The problem historically has been the integration of SOF capabilities into a coherent, *strategic* framework. Figure 17-2 suggests how these transformed capability sets differ from the existing framework to meet the challenges of the war on terrorism.

Within this construct, SOF capability sets work together in an integrated fashion with other government partners, coalition members, host nation forces, and conventional forces. Tasks performed under the capability sets address requirements specified in the National Security Strategy and correspond to three of the four goals outlined in the National Strategy for Combating Terrorism: defeating terrorists and their organizations; denying sponsorship,

FIGURE 17-2
Transformed SOF Capability Sets

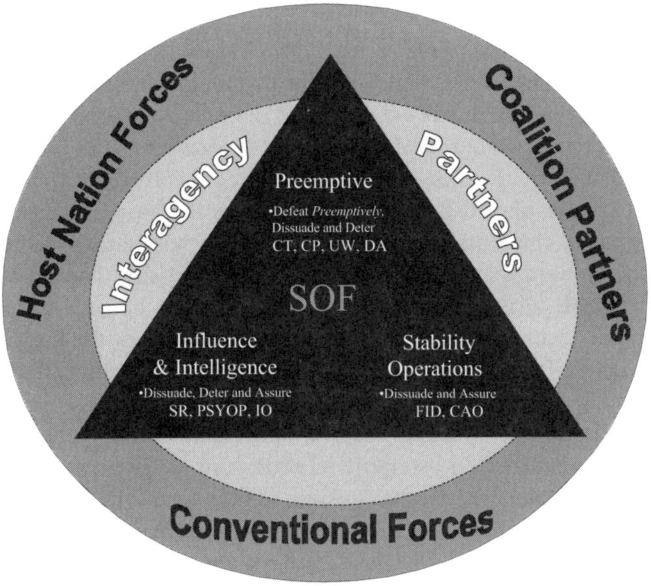

support, and sanctuary to terrorists; and, mitigating the underlying conditions that terrorists seek to exploit.[39] Rather than operating in isolation, SOF missions will be conducted with the goals of the NSCT in mind. For example, CA operations will not be conducted exclusively for the purposes of rebuilding infrastructure.

Missions designed to mitigate the underlying conditions, including building infrastructure and offsetting extremist messages through PSYOPS, may lead to the development of actionable information that will enable follow-on operations designed to defeat terrorist cells. Allowing countries to provide for the personal security of their citizens in the ungoverned and ungovernable regions of the globe, through stability operations programs, could compel terrorist cells to move, force them into conducting operations prematurely, or deny them support, thus enabling non-military host-nation or OGA activities or interdiction strikes. Such integrated efforts will be necessary as USSOCOM further solidifies its supported command responsibilities and conducts future operations in the war on terrorism, which is expected to last a decade or more.[40]

Chapter Twelve in this volume addresses some issues raised by integrating nation-building and direct action.

IMPLICATIONS FOR CANADIAN SPECIAL OPERATIONS DOCTRINE

SOF transformation may involve the closer integration of existing capabilities and tasks, although this is not reflected in the most recent version of Joint Publication 3.05, *Doctrine for Joint Special Operations*. SOF doctrine, however, was sufficiently flexible and well articulated that it required little revision to reflect the role played by specialized forces in the war on terror.[41] The Canadian special-operations community, however, has neither the breadth nor depth of the resources available to their US counterparts. The capabilities of JTF 2 are still maturing even as the force expands.[42] Indeed, those capabilities have been developing since the transfer and growth of the hostage-rescue mission from the Royal Canadian Mounted Police to the Ministry of National Defence over a decade ago.[43]

Tough choices lie ahead for those who draft Canadian special-operations doctrine. The command and support relationships will be easy to define and unlikely to cause controversy. The question of how Canadian special-operations forces will be used will prove to be the thorniest issue. The measure of merit for Canadian doctrine will be its balance between DA (which may require closer bilateral ties with the U.S.) and multilateral stability operations.

The difficulty facing the Canadian special operations community as it drafts new doctrine reflects the fundamental challenge of Canadian security. To what extent will Canada be involved in the war on terror? Closer ties with SOF counterparts in operations could pay political dividends for Canada. But the sensitive nature of special operations will preclude American sharing with half-hearted allies, and domestic constraints may limit Canadian enthusiasm. Will Canada be able to take advantage of the SOF transformation? Charting doctrine that reflects Canadian multilateralism and respect for sovereignty might be domestically palatable but may make Canadian special-operations capability irrelevant to its closest ally. If it is irrelevant to the Americans, it gains no political credit for Canada.

Working closely with SOF would also pay dividends for Canadian special-operations training, equipment, support, and doctrine. Allied special forces operating with US counterparts have benefited from American logistics, mobility, and combat elements that support SOF. Although nominally under US control, allied special forces have operated with considerable autonomy. In many cases, coalition partners have had distinct areas of operation; in others, they have worked directly with US forces. Polish special forces (GROM) learned and shared much in their close working relationship with SEALs during Operation Iraqi Freedom.[44] These benefits include combat experience, shared lessons learned, and perhaps most importantly, overcoming interoperability issues that arise during the friction of operations. Close working relationships between special operators from different countries often provide access to such resources as the latest equipment or precise information required during times of national crisis.[45] In hostile environments or forbidding terrain, allied operators can use interoperability with US forces to draw on SOF resources, like the AC-130 gun ships and aviation assets.[46] The details and outcome of the 1991 Gulf War SAS foot patrol known as "Bravo Two Zero" might have been different had team members possessed better equipment and interoperability with SOF.[47]

For small special units in their formative years, such as JTF 2 or the German *Kommando Spezialkraft* (KSK), operating together with larger, more experienced counterparts confers advantages beyond interoperability and access to technology. They can mature more quickly, avoiding "lessons in blood" taught by an adaptive terrorist adversary. Although forces such as GSG 9 conducted successful operations relatively soon after they were created, their achievement reflected intensive training for the highly focused hostage-rescue mission.[48] The current terrorist threat is different. Cells and individuals are operating in a loose network and are doing so in global settings from mountainous terrain to major urban centres.[49] Al-Qaeda members and affiliated groups use weapons that range from suicide belts and vehicle-borne improvised explosive devices to hijacked aircraft.[50] Given the range of environments and tactics, the closer that special forces work together in a coalition, the better they can deal with counter-terrorism scenarios.

The policy of the U.S. since September 11 has been to conduct the war on terror on its own terms. Although national interest plays a role, the U.S. faces a dilemma as the sole superpower. Within the UN or NATO, the U.S. is sometimes expected to provide resources and direction without dominating or exercising leadership. To circumvent debate and act quickly after September 11, the U.S. established and led a "coalition of the willing". SOF have been working closely with counterparts from the U.K., Australia, Poland, and other nations. Countries like Germany and Canada provided forces for special operations in Afghanistan but were reluctant to do so in Iraq in 2003.

Another option available to the Canadian special-operations community is to develop a doctrine that reflects Canadian foreign-policy goals and perceived values, founded on multilateral cooperation through established international or regional organizations. Such a doctrine might eschew robust counter-terrorism tasks, except in the case of *in extremis* domestic response. It would emphasize humanitarian and stability tasks in more permissive environments where international cooperation is more likely and the risks to forces are considerably lower. Canadian forces for special operations could conduct a range of tasks under a multilateral umbrella, including special reconnaissance, limited direct actions such as the seizure of international war criminals or rescue of international hostages, humanitarian de-mining, CA operations, humanitarian assistance, and force protection. In addition, JTF 2 members could continue to perform additional activities that suit more direct national interests, such as personal protection of visiting dignitaries overseas, securing Canadian embassy staff and grounds, and evacuation of Canadian citizens (NEO).

These "soft" special operations seem to conform to recent Canadian political preferences. They appear to limit the potential risk of failure and to preserve Canada's image as an honest broker and peacekeeper. Partners could count on Canadian expertise in communications and command and control systems and, perhaps, on Canadian leadership in humanitarian operations. Canadian leadership for "softer" multilateral special operations could relieve other special and conventional forces to conduct more combat-intensive missions.

There are costs and adverse consequences of soft doctrine. Canadian political leaders and policy-makers demand more of special operations, as we know from interviews and surveys.[51] The success of both peacekeeping and humanitarian operations is empirically linked to combat power. Doctrine based on humanitarian and multilateral principles would remove an important tool for controlling violence that affects Canadian interests and international stability. Soft doctrine would undermine confidence in Canadian special operators and exclude Canada from the most sensitive and strategically important missions. In the larger special-operations community, this would marginalize Canada and limit the political capital that could be gained from employing special forces. Compensating by willingness to deploy everywhere the UN deems necessary might quickly overstretch limited special capabilities and also increase risk.

Soft doctrine would expand collateral tasks that make retention of the best operators more difficult. In order to focus priorities for the war against terrorism, USSOCOM has removed collateral tasks from its doctrine.[52] SOF collateral tasks used to include coalition support, combat search and rescue, counter-drug operations, humanitarian de-mining, humanitarian assistance, and security assistance – tasks that can be completed successfully by conventional troops. Difficulties in recruiting and retaining special operators – rigorous physical and psychological selection means that less than ten percent of SOF applicants are successful[53] – have led both US Army Special Forces and Australian Special Operations Command to establish direct-entry selection and training.[54] Special operators are an expensive resource, difficult to develop and retain, and motivated by unorthodox and dangerous tasks. If they are used infrequently or employed for routine or low-profile collateral tasks, they may leave for lucrative and challenging commercial jobs. The need for options such as granting experienced SAS operators special permission to pursue short-term commercial opportunities, on condition that they return to service, suggests that it might be difficult to maintain or expand a formation like JTF 2 if it offers few challenges in return for demanding requirements.

CONCLUSION

The Canadian special-operations community can learn a great deal from the ongoing transformation of SOF to inform the development of their own doctrine, but such doctrine must suit Canadian policy and force structure. Unconventional warfare missions supporting regime change are not in JTF 2's future. International training assistance, CA, and PSYOPS are accepted and valuable missions but should be conducted by conventional forces. Too much focus on collateral missions that can be managed by less selective forces will undermine Canada's capacity to conduct the most difficult and dangerous missions, those from which the country will derive the greatest political benefit. Canadian special-operations doctrine should therefore focus on the more challenging missions of counter-terrorism, counter-proliferation, direct action, and special reconnaissance. This will keep Canadian special operators in the company of Australian and British allies and permit them to benefit from US technology, expertise, and support. Focusing on the most difficult and dangerous missions, and selecting the special men and women necessary to conduct them, will serve the country well.

NOTES

The views expressed in this chapter are those of the author alone and do not necessarily reflect those of his employers.

1. A useful historical corrective of this view that shows that the Founding Fathers conducted covert operations to further national ends is contained in Stephen F. Knott, *Secret and Sanctioned: Covert Operations and the American Presidency* (Oxford: Oxford University Press, 1996), 13-115.
2. [Editor's note: SOF refers to US Special Operations Forces. Where the author refers to forces not defined by US doctrine, the term is not capitalized.]
3. US Department of Defense, *Quadrennial Defense Review Report* (Washington, DC: Department of Defense, 2001), 30, 32-47, 57-58.
4. This conclusion has been a consistent theme emanating from US think tanks in the decade since the Cold War. The 2001 QDR Working Group at the Institute for National Security Studies, National Defense University, concluded, for example, that US forces would not face the following contingencies: global war against a near-peer, anti-U.S. alliance or ideology of military significance; and war in the open ocean or massed air-to-air engagements. Captain Sam Tangredi, USN, *All Possible Wars? Toward a Consensus View of the Future Security Environment, 2001-2025*, McNair Paper 63 (Washington, DC: NDU Press, 2000).
5. One of the most influential transformation studies was led by General Jim McCarthy, USAF (Retd). Study members included Admiral Stan Arthur, USN (Ret.); Dr. Paul Kaminski; Mr. Vic DeMarines; General Carl Mundy, USMC (Ret.); Dr. Ted Gold; Admiral Bill Studeman, USN (Ret.); Dr. Bill Graham; General Larry Welch, USAF (Ret.); and General Bill Hartzog, USA (Ret.). See "Press Briefing: Transformation Study," briefing slides, Institute for Defense Analyses, Alexandria, VA (12 June 2001.

The executive summary of the report, *Transforming Military Operational Capabilities*, is available online at http://www.defenselink.mil/news/Jun2001/d20010621transexec.pdf.

6. Dr. Stephen A. Cambone, Director, Program Analysis and Evaluation, Department of Defense, presentation entitled "Defense Program Overview," September 2002. See slide 4.
7. Steven Lambakis, James D. Kiras, and Kristin Kolet, *Understanding "Asymmetric" Threats to the U.S.* (Fairfax, VA: National Institute for Public Policy, 2002), 9-12.
8. President George W. Bush, "State of the Union Address," 29 January 2002. Transcript available online at http://www.whitehouse.gov/news/releases/2002/01/20020129-11.html.
9. It was generally agreed that exclusive reliance on precise air power has its limitations. See, for example, Mackubin Thomas Owens, "The Case for Ground Troops: Air power and special ops aren't enough to win this war," *The Wall Street Journal,* 31 October 2001. Less helpful critics suggested retaliation with nuclear weapons.
10. Prior to 11 September, Edward Luttwak suggested using SOF more aggressively. The main reason they had not been used against Osama bin Laden or Bosnian Serb targets, he postulated, was that the US Joint Chiefs of Staff were fearful of incurring casualties. "Pity US Special Forces: All Dressed Up and Nowhere to Go," *The International Herald Tribune,* 7 February 2001. An insight into how the campaign in Afghanistan was planned is contained in James Carney and John F. Dickerson, "Inside the War Room," *Time,* 31 December 2001-7 January 2002: 113-121.
11. Although this chapter refers exclusively to the activities of SOF in Afghanistan and is based on open-source material, the special operations forces of other countries (Australia, Canada, Denmark, France, Germany, New Zealand, Norway, and the U.K.) have played a considerable role in Operation Enduring Freedom. Given national sensitivities and varying secrecy policies, however, "the full extent of the involvement of the USA's allies in Afghanistan remains unclear." For a chart listing approximate numbers of foreign special forces involved in Enduring Freedom, see Kim Burger, "On the ground," *Jane's Defence Weekly,* 13 March 2002: 21.
12. James D. Kiras, "The Strategic Utility of Special Operations in the Conflict in Afghanistan," *Defence Review* (December 2001): 45-47.
13. Office of the President of the United States, *The Global War on Terrorism: The First 100 Days* (Washington, DC: The White House, 2002), 12-13.
14. Massoud, the charismatic leader who managed to keep together a loose coalition of anti-Taliban forces, was killed by two al-Qaeda suicide operatives posing as journalists on 9 September 2001. Ahmed Rashid, "Afghan resistance leader feared dead in blast," *The Daily Telegraph* (11 September 2001), and "Bin Laden seen as the prime suspect," *The Daily Telegraph* (12 September 2001). Estimates of Northern Alliance forces range from 6,000 to 15,000 armed fighters. See, for example, the estimates

(6,000-10,000) contained in Anthony Cordesman, "Human Rights and Military Operations in Afghanistan," 1 October 2001, available on the Middle East Policy Council website at http://www.mepc.org/articles/cordesman.html. Michael O'Hanlon suggests that the Northern Alliance had 15,000 men-in-arms: "A Flawed Masterpiece," *Foreign Affairs* 81:3 (May/June 2002): 49.

15. The specific SOF unit, as well as the personnel under Karzai's authority, repulsed a Taliban counteroffensive around the village of Tarin Kot, inflicting at least 300 casualties in the process. See Rowan Scarborough, "Karzai, A Team turned tide of war," *The Washington Times,* 22 January 2002.
16. Considerable criticism surrounded the use of airpower at the start of the campaign in Afghanistan because of the limited scale and intensity of the airstrikes; critics were prone to compare the effort to the air campaign in Kosovo in 1999. Preliminary sortie data are contained in O'Hanlon, "A Flawed Masterpiece," and Anthony Cordesman, *The Lessons of Afghanistan: Warfighting, Intelligence, Force Transformation, Counterproliferation, and Arms Control* (Washington, DC: Center for Strategic and International Studies, 2002), 4-5.
17. As one journalist aptly characterized the use of PGMs in Afghanistan, "In effect, close air support had been expanded from the exclusive realm of the attack helicopter or ground attack-fighter to include heavy bombers dropping munitions up to 5,000 lbs." See Anthony Davis, "How the Afghan war was won," *Jane's Intelligence Review*, Vol. 14, No. 2 (February 2002): 7-8.
18. Davis also identifies a third factor in the Taliban's collapse: a lack of defence-in-depth beyond the initial line of resistance. Ibid., p. 9.
19. See, for example, details contained in Thom Shankar, "Conduct Of War Is Redefined By Success Of Special Forces," *The New York Times,* 21 January 2002; and Jan Cielski, "Ten US troops killed 1,300 Taliban," *The National Post,* 9 January 2002.
20. Charles M. Sennott and Ellen Barry, "The fast fall of the Taliban," *The Boston Globe,* 21 November 2001; and Roland Watson, "Cavalry charge tanks," *The Times,* 8 November 2001.
21. The core unit of the US Army Special Forces is the Operational Detachment Alpha, better known as an "A Team." An ODA is comprised of twelve personnel: an officer, a senior enlisted man (a Warrant Officer), and ten sergeants (from E-6 to E-8, or Staff to Master Sergeant in rank). In addition to language proficiency, the personnel within the ODA are cross-trained in skills from medical and communications to weapons and cross-cultural. A primary task of an ODA is to train and advise foreign military counterparts to conduct foreign internal defence (counterinsurgency) or unconventional warfare (insurgency).
22. Details of this specific ODA's activities can be found in Dana Priest, "'Team 555' Shaped a New Way of War: Special Forces and Smart Bombs Turned Tide and Routed Taliban," *The Washington Post,* 3 April 2002;

and transcript of remarks given by Mr. Robert Andrews, Principal Deputy Assistant Secretary of Defense for Special Operations and Low Intensity Conflict, Office of the Secretary of Defense, at the National Defense Industry Association SO/LIC Symposium, Crystal City, VA, 7 February 2002.

23. In addition to the failure to catch the senior Taliban and al-Qaeda leadership because not enough ground forces were deployed quickly enough to block off escape routes, Michael O'Hanlon suggests that another shortcoming of Operation Enduring Freedom has been the inability to resolve expeditiously the legal status of captured fighters. See "A Flawed Masterpiece," 56-57.
24. The US commitment of SOF to Vietnam was larger but less effective. See the assessment by Richard H. Shultz, Jr., *The Secret War Against Hanoi: Kennedy's and Johnson's Use of Spies, Saboteurs, and Covert Warriors in North Vietnam* (New York: Harper Collins, 1999), 277, 309-318. For details on SAS operations in Malaya and Borneo, see Tim Jones, *Postwar Counterinsurgency and the SAS, 1945-1952: A Special Type of Warfare* (London: Frank Cass, 2001).
25. For an overview of SOF activities in Combined Joint Special Operations Task Force-North, see Williamson Murray and Robert H. Scales, Jr., *The Iraq War: A Military History* (Cambridge, MA: Belknap Press, 2003), 185-195.
26. Ibid., 189.
27. Anthony H. Cordesman, *The Iraq War: Strategy, Tactics, and Military* Lessons (Westport, CT: Praeger, 2003), 365.
28. "SOCOM Change of Command," Remarks as delivered by Secretary of Defense Donald H. Rumsfeld, MacDill AFB, Tampa, FL, 2 September 2003; http://www.defenselink.mil/speeches/2003/sp20030902-secdef0422.html.
29. Arthur Cebrowski, Director, Office of Force Transformation, Speech to the Heritage Foundation, 13 May 2003, 8.
30. Sgt. Danny L. Patterson, "US Marine remembers his roots...Russian native returns for visit," Story Identification Number: 200372315120, US Marine Corps News Release, 12 July 2003; http://www.usmc.mil/marinelink/mcn2000.nsf/lookupstoryref/200372315120.
31. SOF core tasks and operational priorities to meet the requirements of the 2002 National Security Strategy are surveyed in USSOCOM, *US Special Operations Posture Statement, 2003-2004* (Tampa, FL: USSOCOM, 2003), 27-31.
32. Although they are core to USSOCOM responsibilities, US Code, Title 10, Subtitle A, Part I, Chapter 6, Section 167, "Unified combatant command for special operations forces"; http://www4.law.cornell.edu/uscode/10/167.html.
33. Secretary Rumsfeld announced USSOCOM's responsibility in the war on terrorism in a press briefing given on 7 January 2003. The National

Strategy for Combating Terrorism established a "4D's" strategy to meet the scourge of international terrorism: Defeat terrorists and their organizations; Deny sponsorship, support, and sanctuary to terrorists; Diminish the underlying conditions that terrorists seek to exploit; and Defend US citizens and interests at home and abroad. These goals, along with objectives to meet them, are located in Office of the President of the United States of America, *National Strategy for Combating Terrorism* (Washington: The White House, February 2003), 15-28.

34. Colin S. Gray, *Explorations in Strategy* (Westport, CT: Praeger, 1996), 153.
35. See, for example, Secretary of the Navy Gordon England on network-centric warfare in "Precision Weapons, Networks Trump Navy's Need For New Ships, England Says," *Aerospace Daily,* 17 October 2002.
36. The other SOF attributes developed by USSOCOM's Future Concepts Working Group include SOF Warrior; Regional Expertise, Presence, and Influence; and C4ISR Dominance. Briefing, SOF Future Concepts Working Group to SOF Education Council, 17 October 2002. See also General Peter J. Schoomaker, "Special Operations Forces: The Way Ahead," and Lieutenant Colonel Scott Moore, "Special Forces: The Way Ahead," in *Force of Choice: Perspectives on Special Operations* eds., Bernd Horn, J. Paul de B. Taillon, and David Last (Montreal and Kingston: McGill-Queen's University Press, 2004), 161-198.
37. John W. Gordon, *The Other Desert War: British Special Forces in North Africa, 1940-1943* (Westport, CT: Greenwood, 1987), 144.
38. North Vietnamese agents working within the intelligence structure compromised both intelligence-gathering and raiding activities of MACV-SOG. Another contributing factor along the Ho Chi Minh Trail was the American use of overt insertion methods by helicopter, whose presence provided warning to North Vietnamese counter-SOF teams. A concise summary of North Vietnamese adaptation to SOF tactics is contained in Shultz, Jr., *The Secret War Against Hanoi*, 222-235 and John Plaster, *SOG: The Secret Wars of America's Commandos in Vietnam* (New York: Simon & Schuster, 1997), 80-89.
39. Office of the President of the United States, *The National Strategy for Combating Terrorism*, 15-24.
40. The Unified Command Plan, or UCP, outlines the areas of responsibility for the Geographic Combatant Commands (GCCs). Each GCC has a commander who is the supported authority for their region, with others providing support to them. USSOCOM has been given the global responsibility, as the supported command, to prosecute the global war on terrorism.
41. See, for example, the list of revisions contained in Chairman of the Joint Chiefs of Staff, *Joint Publication 3-05: Doctrine for Joint Special Operations* (Washington, DC: The Joint Staff, 2003), iii.
42. Although doubling the size of a unit with fewer than 300 operators may not seem difficult, other factors enter into consideration, such as the length

of time over which such expansion will occur, the terms of the mandate for expansion, and the size of the overall force – the pool from which selection will be made. The difficulties of the conventional services in recruiting and retaining quality personnel are magnified for SOF; artificial and inflexible timelines for expansion will almost invariably lead to acceptance of recruits who are below standards. David Pugliese, Juliet O'Neill, and Tim Naumetz, "Beef up special forces, DND told," *The Ottawa Citizen,* 6 October 2001. The recommendation that JTF 2 grow to over 1,000 personnel in order to "contribute meaningfully to international efforts against terrorism" risks breaking the existing force; policy-makers would do well to review the historical record of their coalition partners before undertaking such a rash course of action. Interim Report of the Standing Committee on National Defence and Veterans Affairs, *State of Readiness of the Canadian Forces: Response to the Terrorist Threat, List of Recommendations* (Ottawa, ON: Public Works Canada, November 2001).

43. The response capability of the RCMP for domestic hostage-rescue and terrorism was embodied in the Special Emergency Response Team, or SERT. The Department of National Defence assumed control of the mission in early 1992.
44. GROM was created in 1991. For details on the unit, its activities, and its exchanges with other SOF, see Samuel Katz, "GROM: The Advent of Polish Thunder," *Jane's Intelligence Review,* Vol. 10, No. 8 (August 1998): 13-17.
45. According to Ken Conner, the relationship between SOF operators and their SAS counterparts led to training and the provision of Stinger missiles to combat the threat of low-flying Argentine aircraft during the Falklands War. *Ghost Force: The Secret History of the SAS* (London: Weidenfield & Nicolson, 1998), 250-252.
46. SOF specific platforms include fixed wing AC-130H/U Gunships, the MC-130E/H Combat Talon infiltration/exfiltration aircraft, and EC-130E Commando Solo psychological/information broadcasting aircraft; rotary wing MH-60K Blackhawk, the MH-47E Chinook, the MH-53J/M Pave Low III/IV, and A/MH-6 Mission Enhancement Little Bird helicopters; maritime surface craft include Mark V Special Operations Craft; submersibles including Advanced SEAL Delivery System and Swimmer Delivery Vehicles; and, on the ground, Light Strike Vehicles and Ground Mobility Vehicles.
47. The inability of the patrol to notify higher headquarters of the requirement for extraction, or maintain communications, was a critical point of failure during this mission. Andy McNab, *Bravo Two Zero* (London: Corgi, 1994), 125-127, 131-134.
48. The development of GSG 9, in response to the embarrassing 1972 "Munich Olympics Massacre," is covered in Rolf Tophoven, *GSG 9: German Response to Terrorism* (Koblenz: Bernard & Graefe Verlag, 1985), and

explained by its founder, General (retired) Ulrich Wegener, "The Evolution of Grenzshcutzgruppe (GSG) 9 and the Lessons of 'Operation Magic Fire' in Mogadishu," in *Force of Choice*, 107-118. Details of the successful 18 October 1977 rescue operation conducted by GSG 9 in Mogadishu, Somalia, are contained in J. Paul de B. Taillon, *Hijacking and Hostages: Government Responses to Terrorism* (Westport, CT: Praeger, 2002), 125-137.

49. A peerless open-source description of al-Qaeda activities in different countries is contained in Rohan Gunaratna, *Inside Al Qaeda: Global Network of Terror* (New York: Columbia University Press, 2002), 95-220.
50. Audrey Kurth Cronin provides a clinical survey of terrorist means in *Terrorists and Suicide Attacks,* CRS Report RL32058 (Washington, DC: Congressional Research Service, 2003).
51. Chapters Seven and Eight of this volume.
52. See Joint Chiefs of Staff, *Joint Publication 3-05*, iii.
53. Terry White provides a survey of SOF selection programmes in *Swords of Lightning: Special Forces and the Changing Face of Warfare* (London: Brassey's, 1992), 28-62.
54. Minister Assisting the Minister for Defence, "Media Release: New Scheme to Boost Special Forces," Minister for Employment Services MN57/03, 20 October 2003.

CHAPTER EIGHTEEN

CHOICE OF FORCE

SPECIAL OPERATIONS FOR CANADA?

David Last, Tim Lannan, and Jamie Green

These two volumes on special operations are intended to help Canadians think about the sort of special operations their forces should be able to conduct.[1] For some countries at some times, special forces have been the force of choice. But we have to look beyond the glamour of today's images to tomorrow's political choices. Will our special forces give politicians the choices they need? What have special operations forces accomplished for us in the past? What sort of operations will challenge us in the future? What do civilian leaders expect of those charged with special operations? What new challenges face us today as we try to develop the forces we need for tomorrow? And finally, consider the cover of this volume. Does Canada want fit young soldiers for dangerous missions abroad, a domestic counter-terrorist force, a repository of special skills for consequence management at home, or mature and worldly security experts with a human touch? These are some of the choices facing our policy makers.

WHAT HAVE THEY DONE FOR US LATELY?

Special operations have been a major source of innovation to deal with the real violence that occurred against the backdrop of conventional stagnation and nuclear deterrence. East and West did not lob nukes at each other. Armoured columns did not clash on the German plains. Most of the enormous Western investment in conventional and nuclear weaponry served its purpose by remaining unused. But special forces *were* used, and they evolved dramatically.

The first volume of the series, *Force of Choice: Perspectives on Special Operations*, touched on the historical record of special operations. Special operations are defined fundamentally by special people, carefully selected and highly trained for difficult and dangerous missions. Although born of allied weakness in the most difficult days of the Second World War, they have become the force of choice for the most powerful and technologically advanced states in their fights against terrorism and insurgency, which are the weapons of the weak.[2] National leaders confronting failure search for new ways of fighting, whether in 1940 or in 2003, and special operations forces provided innovative alternatives. Conventional forces reduced the risks associated with new ways of operating (often by preparing for the last war), but special forces experimented more boldly.

Five paradigms have characterized the evolution of Western special forces. The first is support to conventional forces in interstate war. Navy SEAL advocate William McRaven's vision of special operations as a basis for grand strategy draws largely on Second World War cases in which small forces helped prepare the way for conventional victory, but there were few opportunities during the Cold War for daring raids like those on Eban Emael, St Nazaire, and Alexandria. These strategic raids remain the model for direct-action missions.[3] The second paradigm is insurgency (or unconventional warfare) and counter-insurgency (or foreign internal defence), which characterized the wars of decolonization and the Cold War rivalry of the major powers.[4] The third paradigm to emerge in the nineteen-seventies was domestic hostage-rescue and counter-terrorist operations, which were internationalized and militarized in the 'eighties. Without this internationalization, counter-terrorist forces might have evolved as a branch of domestic police operations.[5] Internationalization allowed special forces like the SAS and Delta to develop new roles, supporting conventional forces in oil wars and stabilization operations from the nineteen-nineties to the present.[6] This brings us to the fifth paradigm, which might be characterized as special reconnaissance, targetting, and liaison – perhaps a rebirth of the first paradigm. But throughout their evolution, special operations required a clear vision of national interest and leadership at the highest levels, if they were to be used at all.

Canada has not participated in much of this evolution since the Second World War, and we should ask why. In that war Canada developed the innovative First Special Service Force with the U.S. and contributed many individuals to allied special operations. Our subsequent efforts focused on high-quality conventional forces, safely barracked in Germany. Canadian contributions to the broader stability effort were masked as peacekeeping.[7] In the nineteen-sixties, Québec's quiet revolution produced a serious threat to national security – Québecois nationalism. Foreign deployments carried risks of national discord with echoes of earlier crises brought on by imperial wars. As francophone society became more engaged in national decision-making, it became more important to tacitly steer policy away from contentious issues. Canada would not participate in UW or FID. PSYOPS had implications at home. Even CA was easier to contemplate as a benign secondary duty. Not until the McDonald Commission had exorcised the misdeeds of the barn-burning RCMP, and political intelligence had been safely isolated from policing by segregating CSIS, was it safe to start up a national counter-terrorist unit (with the emphasis firmly on hostage rescue – the most benign of its possible missions).[8] Other countries had more violent and long-lived nationalist movements, class warfare, student violence, and police death squads to stimulate counter-terrorist units; Canada did not. Ottawa found better solutions.

Our modest heritage of special operations and their stunted growth during the Cold War are important indicators of Canada's place in the world and its security priorities.[9] Domestic security comes first, and foreign commitments such as UW and FID are to be avoided. Whether Canada can afford to continue like this depends on our future. The weapon of the weak may be particularly useful in some scenarios. Skills formerly applied to UW and FID may be the basis for building stability. Direct action and strategic reconnaissance might support the rule of international law and derail future wars.

WHAT DOES THE FUTURE HOLD FOR CANADA?

Alternative future security environments in the first chapter of this book suggest that major interstate wars represent only a small part of the spectrum of threat in the future, as it has been in the past. Major wars feature in only two of the eleven scenarios, but protracted, low-level violence within states characterizes all but one of the remainder. Criminal violence that undermines the political authority of states is also a common theme.[10] Protracted politically and economically motivated conflicts are widespread today, and fear of them may constitute the greatest threat to liberal democracy, as America's response to September 11 seems to indicate.[11]

Violence within Canada is plausible in several of the future scenarios. It might be urban, class-based, separatist, or indigenous, and it would test the changes to emergency legislation since the October Crisis, but it seems likely that both resources and legislation will prove adequate for most domestic disorders. More alarmingly, the U.S. is already one of the most crime- and violence-prone states in the West, as well as one of the most heavily armed. It is close to major Canadian urban centres, and jurisdiction matters could complicate response. As Mexico worries America, America should concern Canada under several of the future scenarios generated by Proteus.[12]

Canada's future probably depends more on what happens to the U.S. and the world order that it sponsors than on anything that occurs uniquely within Canada. Neither Canadian force-development scenarios nor future scenarios developed by others foresee direct attacks on Canada. Direct military attacks on the U.S. or its allies by other states are unlikely, but intrastate violence close to home and asymmetric or idiosyncratic attack by non-state actors are possible. The concept of asymmetry has generated a lot of thinking about new threats and vulnerabilities that may affect Canadian security in the future. Asymmetric attack involves unmatched capabilities – chemical, biological, or radiological attacks on population centres by non-state actors, for example. Idiosyncratic attack, on the other hand, capitalizes on limited awareness of, or preparation for, attack. The September 11 attacks were both asymmetric (in using commercial airliners) and idiosyncratic (in exploiting unanticipated suicide hijackers).[13]

The potential for both asymmetry and idiosyncrasy is evident in the preceding chapters. Managing our border with the U.S., benefiting from demographic diversity, using information effectively, and dealing with commercial security companies are just some of the factors that will shape our conduct of security operations. Some combination of military, paramilitary, and police forces, combined with civilian resources, will have to characterize the security response to the ugly pictures of the future.

The low-intensity internal conflicts of "Home Brew," "Amazon-Dot-Plague," and "Enemy Within" might be addressed by a force that is black and blue – combining special operations with sophisticated policing. Irregular warfare that transcends national and regional boundaries is the most frequently predicted scenario ("Militant Shangri-la," "Yankee Going Home," "Cast Adrift," "Trouble Elsewhere," and "Argy Bharji"). Indeed, it might be said to characterize the world we live in now. For this world, black and green (combat-oriented) special forces can help to deal with the transnational aspects of the threat, while black and blue, within frameworks of international police cooperation, may be more effective at stemming the tide of domestic threat.

Finally, the two scenarios for global war ("Everybody's Brawling," and "Asian War") suggest circumstances in which special warriors again serve mainly to support the efforts of conventional forces. Black and combat-oriented green special forces would work closely with conventional forces, and there would be demand for troops like the US Rangers or Australian commandos to fill in gaps.[14] But conventional forces in 2020 might look very different from those of today, and our best hope for developing the sophisticated teamwork and technology for the big wars might be to invest heavily today in the future-leaning special forces that will get us through low-intensity conflict and irregular warfare. Certainly America's military transformation and drive towards "SOF-like" forces seems to be heading that way.

These scenarios imply a range of new tasks. We expect to have to deal with disaffected groups with access to weapons of mass destruction attempting to attack population centres. Consequence management will be important. Is managing CBR consequences a special operation? Is Canada's nascent NBC Response Team part of the special forces community? Civil-affairs capabilities will be necessary to work with both domestic and international civil agencies in both hostile and benign circumstances. Is CA conventional or special? In the first volume of this series, Last suggested that there was a distinction between units that needed public trust and cooperation to work (such as those engaged in civil affairs or consequence management) and units that needed secrecy to avoid vulnerability. But these might converge in the future. First responders, including CBR response teams, might be deliberately targetted as part of a terrorist strategy. Should they be veiled in secrecy to preserve their capacity to respond? Does low visibility by itself confer membership in the special forces community because the uniform and parade square become liabilities and a different sort of soldier is needed? Other future tasks may include psychological and information operations, direct action against hostile non-state actors, population containment, and so on. Who does these things?

We should be cautious here of a phenomenon sometimes found in the special-forces community. The "not-my-job" syndrome comes in two parts. The first part says, "Only we are special" (because we do the most push-ups, have the highest standards, and so on). This is a variant of conventional regimental narcissism and can be healthy if suitably contained. But it may tend to isolate the most innovative parts of the military organization. The second part says, "Because we are special, we only do our type of work". Taken to its logical conclusion, the not-my-job syndrome leaves evolving tasks untended, as each tribe focuses on its jealously guarded expertise: gunners fire guns; tankers drive tanks, and special forces kick down doors. Who will pick up the new tasks, which may or may not be special but are definitely not traditional or conventional? It is partly to allow readers to develop their own ideas about what is "special" that we have avoided using the American label, SOF, to apply to all these other things that might be deemed special.

If there is a common theme in these scenarios it is that multi-agency teams of special forces and police will be needed to handle a variety of low-intensity and transnational conflicts. Commanders and staff will have to have a sophisticated understanding of the international environment, good international contacts, and knowledge of the local microcosm that shapes specific operations. Good use of our demographic advantage will help us to interact with the global community, but choices about where and how we get involved will be political. This brings us to what our political leaders expect.

WHAT DO OUR LEADERS EXPECT?

Mullen's survey of senators and members of parliament who have been involved with defence issues gives us an important insight into political priorities. Helping Canadians by managing the consequences of mass attack or helping them by rescuing hostages at home or abroad are both important tasks. Typical conventional missions are more important to these political leaders than special operations (in contrast to the views of bureaucratic policy-makers and opinion-leaders). They prefer multilateral authority for assertive international missions but are prepared to go it alone to rescue Canadians abroad.

The idea of national support for a rules-based international order is attractive. Canada might contribute to a safe international community by legally sanctioned seizures of predatory warlords or those who violate international humanitarian law. Or we might conduct covert inspections of dubious nuclear and chemical facilities and mount raids to destroy those that violate international agreements. But today these are fantasies. Powerful states are reluctant to allow regimes that might bind them, as the US responses to the International Criminal Court and the Anti-Ballistic Missile Treaty suggest. Breau's chapter makes clear the limitations of international law. Coalition action is a more plausible scenario than world police.

The most powerful states can flout the law, but most gain by living within it. International law is still overwhelmingly supportive of the sovereign rights of states. Unilateral intervention to preempt attack, arrest war criminals, or destroy weapons facilities is generally not acceptable. The law is evolving, however, and Responsibility to Protect, if legitimized by international institutions, may permit special operations in support of a broadly defined international community. This leaves the door open for the future if Canada has the capacity to contribute, but it does not suggest that Canada will be leading the charge to breach sovereignty in the name of protecting the weak or upholding the law. We are more likely to join a UN posse or the NATO Response Force than an American one.[15] Whether "international community" is a euphemism for "western states" depends on our ability to build a consensus on key values like democracy and human rights. This in turn will hinge not only on American leadership but also on the ability of America's allies to shape its policies and help it to lead.[16]

Our exploratory elite survey suggests that senior bureaucrats and media opinion-leaders prioritize helping Canadians and humanitarian action. Managing the consequences of CBR attacks at home is the highest priority, and rescuing hostages is more important than any aggressive action. Reliable, traditional partners are best. The fact that elites rate special operations as more important than many conventional force tasks suggests they are more sensitive than politicians to the limitations of conventional forces in the new security environment. The pattern of responses also raises the dilemma of prevention: is there evidence that preemptive or aggressive actions can reduce domestic risk, or do they increase it?

National security decision-making in Ottawa occurs in a marketplace, which revolves mainly around the prime minister and Cabinet. New cabinet structures under Paul Martin may permit greater strategic vision and preparation of options, but response to crises will be inevitably reactive, and there is scope for many agencies to be involved in the initial response. Since September 11, more departments have become involved in defining security and responding to threats. Intelligence support for decision-making seems well articulated, though protected from the public and not always heeded by decision-makers. A sense of national interest is well developed in the policy marketplace, particularly with respect to domestic constituencies. It generally does not support adventurous overseas operations.

These insights about the expectations and perceptions of politicians and mandarins raise important questions for doctrine. We do not expect political leaders to demand unilateral aggressive direct action overseas, and so we would expect any international activity to be undertaken in collaboration with allies. Interoperability is therefore the starting point for international action. Work with our traditional allies – America, Britain, Australia – seems to be strongly supported by political leaders, and these are countries with well-developed special forces. But should we focus on doing what they do or on doing what they do not do as well as we can? Our demographic advantage raises the larger policy question – should we be everywhere America is, or everywhere it is *not*? American policy-makers would prefer to have the legitimacy of respected liberal states lining up with it as it goes abroad, but there are many places where it needs stability and where its presence is an irritant.

If unilateral action is unlikely abroad, it is essential for sovereignty at home. Domestic legislation permits military and police collaboration in counter-terrorism, border security, and consequence management. The doctrinal questions concern the way in which these organizations evolve and are structured. Do they co-exist with conventional formations? Should new units be given unique chains of command or reporting channels, to protect them from public scrutiny, to permit seamless command and control, or to develop new partnerships? Ridler's description of technical innovation in the SAS suggests that a separate identity and culture helps special units to evolve to meet new challenges, while conventional ones may be constrained by ties to the larger military establishment.

Whatever else our leaders expect, they surely demand that military forces remain capable of meeting evolving challenges to Canadian security, even when they may not articulate those challenges in defence policy.

WHAT CHALLENGES WILL DRIVE CHANGE?

Change at home, change abroad, the new economy, and the evolution of human ecology are some of the challenges articulated by the authors in both of these volumes. Hataley demonstrates that the Canada-U.S. border is not just a space but also a meeting of institutions, which are vital to Canada's economy and security. "Mexicanization" of the border could be hugely damaging, and committing Canadian special forces to task forces in which the U.S. places its trust may help to keep the border traffic flowing.

Leuprecht demonstrates that Canada has a comparative advantage in conducting stability operations in a global community because our multicultural society is generally well disposed towards government and accepts its good intentions. Retaining and developing this advantage hinges on domestic security as much as on use of survey and census tools to help locate and mobilize ethnic communities. Our domestic, no less than our international, security may therefore hinge on precisely the kind of multiethnic policies that have been criticized by some as undermining military effectiveness.[17]

Maloney's study of Afghanistan and Kosovo demonstrates that special operations are an integral part of strategy before, during, and after overt combat.

They form an interface with local forces and are most effective when accompanied by compatible forces that bridge the gap between small special teams and large conventional units and formations. US Rangers, airborne units, reconnaissance companies, alpine and light infantry formations with high standards of fitness and training all serve this bridging function, but the critical roles of liaison, targetting, special reconnaissance and direct action are filled by special forces. CA and PSYOPS became increasingly important in post-conflict stability operations, but "special activities" such as assassinations, abductions, and covert intelligence may have been used by some of Canada's allies. Will Canada participate in this sort of war? Can it afford not to? A dispassionate look at these operations – perhaps not very different from some of the small wars of empire in the last century – is needed to match doctrine and law to practice.

Schwarz-Morgan challenges the assumption of stable mental and intellectual models. If we draw parallels between Cecil Rhodes's adventurers and today's private military companies, or between special forces in Afghanistan now and imperial police a hundred years ago, our implicit assumption is that individual minds worked in the same way then as now. Perhaps they do not. The forces exerted on an infant's mind have changed great deal in the last century and even the last decade. Since the mind is the most important battlefield, we need to pay more attention to how we select for and defend mental stability in our thinking soldiers, how we seek predictable outcomes in a virtual environment, and how that essential stability might be attacked or undermined.

If human ecology is changing, so are our social and economic structures. Globalization, transnational companies, and privatization are affecting what used to be nationally dominated structures.[18] Private military companies may be able to perform some special operations functions, such as bodyguard and technical security or training tasks. But they also compete for a small pool of highly trained labour and make it more difficult to sustain small special forces kept in reserve, when their members are motivated by action. The doctrinal challenge here is to find a balance between training specialists who will leave for the private sector when underemployed, and having too few specialists, forcing reliance on a mercenary private sector. When door-kicking is only one of many necessary skills, keeping the right kinds of specialists on hand requires new kinds of organizations and career patterns and new ways of building durable and effective teams.[19]

The small-team concept epitomized by PRTs offers a new way of approaching post-conflict stability operations when a large presence means vulnerability. But should these teams be structured primarily for special combat or for liaison? Are civil affairs a special operation? The answer has obvious implications for training and selection. We conclude that civil affairs are more usefully seen as distinct from direct action and most other special operations. Blurring the distinction between stability operations and counter-insurgency tends to lead to escalating imperial policing, rather than moderating violence.

Our conclusion about the structure of stabilization teams based on the PRT experience raises questions about who is "special" and what we have to do to keep them that way. This is a contentious subject. In the first volume, anthropologist Anna Simons described the unavoidable dynamics of group cohesion, concluding that affirmative action or admission of women and gays would inevitably weaken team bonds with disastrous results.[20] But those visioning the future argued for more diversity as an operational necessity for the future,[21] and both Leuprecht and our knowledge of PRTs suggest a constructive role for knowledge of local language and culture. Doctrine needs to address how people with the right language, phenotype, and local knowledge can be integrated into teams without compromising our capacity to be highly selective according to other criteria; strength and speed are not the only things that matter in "special" operations.

The availability of information and new means of collecting and disseminating it are salient challenges in developing the next generation of special operations. Leblanc and Knight describe the role of information operations in supporting special operations through the complete operational cycle, from selecting an objective to planning, execution, and assessment. The message is that information itself may be the substance of the mission, and Canada's Information Operations Group (CFIOG) is a strategic resource for the next generation of special operations. Godefroy's discussion of space illustrates that technological advances present both opportunities and risks. Combined with open markets, they may make information available to enemies. Even when they are available only to us, new technologies may create vulnerabilities to disruption or deceit or dangerous false confidence.

Given the evolution of special operations in the past, the possible scenarios of the future, and the special operations we might expect Canadian political authorities to demand, how do the most important challenges affect future special operations for Canada? Instability abroad and complex high-risk policing at home seem to be the two central challenges for now, with major wars of uncertain character a distant future prospect.

Our NATO allies have tended to concentrate on direct-action, small-unit capabilities in their special operations communities, while eschewing PSYOPS and treating CA as a conventional asset. When they undertake support to foreign training, they tend to do so with conventional troops, combining training assistance with foreign aid and diplomatic support to security sector reform. Canada has done the same with modest contributions to security assistance in Haiti (police) and Sierra Leone (military). Stability operations are therefore largely conventional, with support from special operations mainly in the form of liaison. This is a generalization; Maloney mentions training by NATO special operations units in Macedonia: "The absence of more serious attacks is attributable to Macedonian security forces who received additional training and equipment from NATO member special operations forces."[22] But it is likely that this training could have been conducted equally well or perhaps more effectively by a regular training cadre, such as the British Short Term Training Team in Sierra Leone, who certainly faced no less chaotic an environment.

The U.S., in contrast to NATO's evolving practice, has historically included CA, PSYOPS, and foreign training missions in the US SOF mandate, making support to stability (and destabilization) a special operation. As Kiras explains, transformation and the war on terror are pushing the US towards the European model, principally to devote more resources to direct action and counter-terrorism tasks.[23] As we consider the challenges of stabilization operations abroad, and the nature of border and domestic security at home, we should ask whether security training and development might be more appropriately managed within the framework of police and conventional forces. The central problem is one of rule of law, civilian control, and reform of the security sector, including eliminating irregular and rogue forces. In the nineteen-seventies, the UN pushed an agenda linking development, disarmament and security (to little avail),[24] while the U.S. and U.S.S.R. pushed at each other's allies with UW and FID. Today, most of Canada's allies seem ready to link diplomacy, development, and defence (3D) in their stabilization efforts. The vehicle for this is cooperation among foreign ministries, aid agencies, and defence departments; PRTs are just one manifestation.[25]

Stability operations that reduce the potential for future rogue regimes, failed states, and terrorist havens are the main challenge driving the evolution of special operations for use abroad. Both the U.S. and other allies seem to be moving in the direction of regularizing 3D contributions to stability, in which special operations forces like the SAS and Australian commandos work alongside development officials, diplomats, and conventional military training teams. Doctrine will therefore have to establish the vehicles through which cooperative planning, deployment, and resource allocation will occur for stability operations. In Canada, these vehicles would logically reside outside DND, probably in central agencies like the Privy Council Office.

The main challenge driving the evolution of special operations for domestic use is the emergence of complex, high-risk policing. Since JTF 2 was established, both the RCMP as a national force and provincial and municipal police forces in urban centres have increased their capacity to deal with hostage-taking, armed stand-offs, and explosives. There are relatively few domestic policing scenarios in which the national counter-terrorist unit has a comparative advantage, both because of the capability of urban police and because of the time it takes to deploy JTF 2 anywhere in the country. Nevertheless, there remains a range of tasks for which JTF 2 is the force of choice. These are characterized by size (requiring coordination of multiple teams), technology (involving mobile platforms, complex targets, or CBR weapons), and jurisdiction (involving national interests or international coordination). These factors suggest that staying large enough for any contingency, retaining a technological edge, and rehearsing command and control arrangements at the national and international level are central to the future employability of

Canadian special operations forces in domestic operations. Interdepartmental liaison and evolving relationships with provincial and municipal authorities are crucial elements in doctrine for domestic special operations. The extent to which individual units, formations, or staff officers can communicate across national boundaries, involve foreign authorities, or plan for contingencies involving other states should also be explicit. Informal links helped General Wegener make a success of the Mogadishu operation, but how far can commanders go without political approval, and how much must be prepared in advance against such contingencies?[26]

The challenge of a big future war of uncertain characteristics is an old one for writers of military doctrine. During the Cold War, it was solved by examining the opponent's doctrine. Before that, doctrine simply extrapolated from the last war. Neither option seems entirely germane for special-operations doctrine for the future. Balancing historical experience with creative experimentation in contemporary operations seems the best way to prepare for future wars.

THINKING ABOUT CANADIAN DOCTRINE

We know how special operations have evolved, we can guess what the future holds for Canada, and we have some idea about the tasks that will be demanded by political leaders. In this light, we should consider the scope of special-operations doctrine, and the environments that we should anticipate.

Since this research began, the term CANSOF (Canadian Special Operations Forces) has emerged to designate units and organizations of the Canadian special operations community. Although there is no doctrinal solution yet, four existing elements of CANSOF are noteworthy. First in seniority is JTF 2, which has had the mandate for counter-terrorism and domestic hostage-rescue since 1992. While the priority remains domestic counter-terrorism, JTF 2 is also expected to project forces abroad for other strategically important tasks. The Canadian Forces Joint NBC Defence (CFJNBCD) Company is the second element. It became operational in December 2002 and represents a national capability to respond to CBR and nuclear incidents. The First Canadian Air Division (1 CAD) provides dedicated helicopter support to CANSOF operations. Finally, a directorate within NDHQ is responsible for all CANSOF force employment issues. The Director is the senior advisor to the CDS on all CT and special operations questions.

What should be the scope of Canadian special operations doctrine? If we begin by defining special operations in terms of contemporary American SOF, we can narrow its scope to exclude most of what Canadian forces do today. But if we think of special operations as a laboratory for the future use of armed force in all its variations, then every branch of the Canadian Forces will be engaged in them. We may be much closer than the American juggernaut to "SOF-like" conventional forces, capable of casting convention to the winds to innovate and overcome. The CF have had to do so for at least two decades to accomplish accelerating operations with shrinking and aging resources. Doctrine for the most SOF-like elements today (like JTF 2, CFIOG, and the CFJNBCD Company) might be focused on leading the more conventional elements into more effective combat teams for tomorrow. If the scope of special-operations doctrine encompasses any innovative and experimental use of technology, organization, or human skills to achieve new operational effects, then it applies across the forces and perhaps into other branches of government. Does this help, or hinder, the evolution of special operations? Narrowing the scope contributes to the "not-my-job" syndrome, which could prevent the full use of already small Canadian military resources. Special-operations doctrine should therefore be a tool for every person in uniform and for many who are not. When the over-weight and over-forty logistician, the 19-year-old Tagalog-speaking reservist, and the RCMP superintendent see themselves as innovative warriors on the same team as the JTF 2 assaulter, we will start to make progress toward useful doctrine for special operations.

What about the types of operations that might be encompassed within special-operations doctrine? American doctrine encompasses nine core tasks, including direct action, UW and FID, and counter-proliferation. Transformation is reducing the role of civil affairs and psychological operations, and NATO practice already leaves these largely to specialized, but not special, conventional forces.[27] But it is not immediately obvious that tasks like unconventional warfare and counter-proliferation are central to Canadian security or political priorities; doctrine that articulated these tasks for Canadian forces might languish, marginalized by other priorities. This deduction can be derived even from the American definition of Special Operations, if only we apply it to Canadian circumstances. What are the "military, diplomatic, informational, and economic objectives..."[28] in which the Canadian government is prepared to invest? Doctrine for stabilization operations abroad, and above all for the management of consequences of WMD attack or of domestic disaster at home, might be very important for senior leaders in DND, in other departments, and in central agencies. The importance of an open border for the Canadian economy and the need to engage multicultural domestic constituencies constructively in the management of international conflicts threatening to spill into Canada suggest two more areas of high priority for future special operations.

Canadian special operations are unlikely to be as ubiquitous as American or even British special operations. Nevertheless, both our political and elite surveys indicate relatively strong support for an expeditionary capability. Not only would inability to deploy overseas violate government expectations, but it would also damage the long-term viability of any force held in reserve to conduct special operations. The private market in special operations makes it risky to leave highly trained assets on the shelf if they can be used abroad.[29] The logic sounds circuitous, but it may be sensible to maintain a domestic capacity, frequently deployed overseas on discretionary missions, in order to preserve the non-discretionary domestic response that is essential for sovereignty.

The distinction between kinetic and non-kinetic operations is central to the character of special operations. Candy for kids (CIMIC) and chemical clean-ups are non-kinetic; they can be done with older and slower soldiers. Kicking doors and killing warlords are kinetic; they demand the fittest young killers. Seen in isolation, it makes sense for large forces like those of America, Britain, and France to separate these functions, and relegate the non-kinetic tasks to conventional forces, with lower selection standards. For a smaller force (say, one with only three regular brigades) this is not an obvious choice. A small force has to preserve talent, and when aging knees are no longer up to kicking doors, two decades of experience can be recycled for use in non-kinetic operations. Equally important, phenotype, language, specialized knowledge, and unique experience may be essential for kinetic operations but not available amongst fit young killers. A central problem for special operations doctrine is therefore the appropriate combination of personnel across the kinetic/non-kinetic divide for a mix of missions. Team-building models may be more important than terrain models for future commandos.[30]

GETTING STARTED

We should finish this book at the beginning. In answer to the question, "what special operations for Canada?", it is tempting to jump to a conclusion. Some readers, no doubt, hope for advocacy of an expanded JTF 2, a resurrected Special Service Brigade, or battalions of computer hackers. Organizational solutions can be supported with descriptions of exciting new operations like counter-proliferation and anti-terrorism against a background of insipient big-power rivalry and evil rogue regimes. On the way to the next big war, will we encounter even more exotic special operations, such as cyber-terror, private corporate war, and ethnic infiltration?

The beginning of the next generation of special operations for Canada is more prosaic. It is the path of the shrewd but maligned political soldier, like Maurice Pope in the 1940s, carefully working the corridors of Ottawa and Washington.[31] It is the path of the carefully prepared seduction of other departments and agencies whose work is vital to national security. Lest old age and caution triumph over youth and zeal, it is also the path of freeing the next generation of leaders: from risk-averse training, from pedestrian professional development, and from tribal loyalties to yesterday's technology. Neither regimental narcissism nor the egotism of the "Special" will lead us to useful doctrine for Canada.

The "sizzle" of special operations is their execution. The "steak" is their systematic support, imaginative evolution, and intelligent integration with the real strategic needs of the country. This starts with an understanding of

Canadian politics, from which our policies are derived and on which our doctrine must be built. We will not find the future of Canadian special operations in the doctrine and practice of our allies, although we must learn from their experiences. Canada's special operations will emerge from our leaders' expectations of a safe society in a stable world.

NOTES

1. The first volume is *Force of Choice: Perspectives on Special Operations,* eds. Bernd Horn, J. Paul de B. Taillon, and David Last (Montreal and Kingston: McGill-Queen's University Press, 2004).
2. Lieutenant-Colonel Bernd Horn, "Special Men, Special Missions: The Utility of Special Operations Forces – a summation," in *Force of Choice*, eds. Horn *et al.*, 12
3. Captain (N) William H. McRaven,"Special Operations: The Perfect Grand Strategy?" in *Force of Choice,* eds. Horn *et al.* and *SPECOPS* (Novato, CA: Presidio, 1995).
4. Colonel (ret.) Scott Crerar, "The Special Force Experience with the Civilian Irregular Defence Group (CIDG) and the Studies and Observation Group (SOG) in Vietnam," in *Force of Choice*, eds. Horn *et al.*
5. Lieutenant-Colonel J. Paul de B. Taillon, " Learning Lessons in Special Operations," and General (ret.) Ulrich Wegener, "The Evolution of Grenzschutzgruppe (GSG) 9 and the Lessons of 'Operation Magic Fire' in Mogadishu," in *Force of Choice*, eds. Horn *et al.*
6. Alan Bell, "Successes and Failures of Special Forces Operations During the Falklands War," and General Peter J. Schoomaker, "Special Operations Forces: The Way Ahead," in *Force of Choice*, eds. Horn *et al.*
7. Sean M. Maloney, *Canada and UN Peacekeeping: Cold War by Other Means 1945-1970* (St. Catharines, ON: Vanwell, 2002).
8. Since September 11, we may have left this surety behind. See Parliament of Canada, *Proceedings of the Special Senate Committee on Bill C-36* (formerly the Subject Matter of Bill C-36), Issue 10 – Evidence, Ottawa, Monday, 10 December 2001. Senator Murray noted that the bill failed to provide for adequate oversight and reporting on the actions of the RCMP, which are given new powers by the anti-terrorism legislation but are not subject to the parliamentary oversight provided by the Security and Intelligence Review Committee, the Security and Intelligence Review Committee for CSIS.
9. See Horn, "Special Men, Special Missions," and Chapter One of this volume.
10. See Chapter One of this volume.
11. This has been a theme in US Congressional hearings in the aftermath of the hastily passed *Patriot Act.* For academic context, see Richard Crockatt, *America Embattled: 9/11, Anti Americanism and the Global Order*

(London: Routledge, 2003). For a more polemical treatment, see Gore Vidal, *Dreaming War: Blood for Oil and the Cheney-Bush Junta* (New York: Nation Books, 2002).

12. See Chapter One of this volume.
13. Montgomery Meigs, "Unorthodox Thoughts about Asymmetric Warfare," *Parameters*, Summer 2003.
14. Major Tony Balasevicius, "A Ranger Capability For The Canadian Army: Can It Lead The Way?" forthcoming in *Army Training and Doctrine Bulletin*, 2004.
15. Canada has agreed to participate in Rotation 6 of the NATO Response Force.
16. Crockatt, *America Embattled.*
17. This has been a recurring complaint in some bodies. See, for example, J. L. Granatstein, "Military Education," Conference of Defence Associations, Graduate Student Symposium, 13-14 Nov 1998. http://www.cda-cdai.ca/symposia/1998/98granats.htm
18. Robert B. Reich, *The Work of Nations: Preparing ourselves for 21st Century Capitalism* (New York: Alfred A. Knopf, 1991).
19. Bernadette and Tom Dececchi, Chapter Fifteen in this volume.
20. Anna Simons, "The Evolution of the SOF Soldier: An Anthropological Perspective," in *Force of Choice*, eds. Horn *et al.*
21. Schoomaker, "Special Operations Forces: The Way Ahead"; Lieutenant-Colonel Scott Moore, "Special Operations Forces: Visioning for the Future," in *Force of Choice*, eds. Horn *et al.*
22. Sean M. Maloney, *Operation KINETIC: The Canadians in Kosovo 1999-2000* (forthcoming: 2006).
23. James Kiras, Chapter Seventeen in this volume.
24. United Nations, *Disarmament Study Series 8: Relationship between Disarmament and International Security* A/36/597 (New York: UN Department for Public Information, 1982); United Nations, *Study on the Relationship between Disarmament and Development: Report of the Secretary General* A/36/356 (New York: United Nations, 1981).
25. Ann Fitz-Gerald, *Addressing the Security-Development Nexus: Implications for Joined-up Government*, (Montreal: Institute for Research on Public Policy, 2004).
26. Wegener, "The Evolution of GSG 9".
27. As recently as December 2003 the nine core SOF tasks were direct action, special reconnaissance, foreign internal defence, unconventional warfare, counter-terrorism, psychological operations, civil affairs, operations, counter-proliferation of weapons of mass destruction, and information operations, US Joint Chiefs, *Joint Publication 3-05: Joint Special Operations Doctrine* (Washington, DC: Department of Defense, 2003), viii. On transformation and its direction, see James Kiras Chapter Seventeen in this volume. On NATO, see Ben Zyla, Chapter Sixteen in this volume. NATO is currently reviewing MC437, *NATO Special*

Operations Policy and intends to reconcile the disparity between US doctrine's nine core tasks and NATO's three.

28. *JP 3-05*, I-1.
29. See Christopher Spearin, Chapter Five in this volume.
30. See Dececchi and Dececchi, Chapter Fifteen in this volume
31. Desmond Morton, "Military Leadership and Change in the 1990's," XIII Annual CDA Institute Seminar, Ottawa, January 1997. http://www.cda-cdai.ca/library/morton.htm

GLOSSARY

3D	Diplomacy, Development, Defence (U.K.)
ABCA	America, Britain, Canada, Australia, and New Zealand
ACOTA	Africa Contingency Operations Training Association (U.S.)
ACRI	Africa Crisis Response Initiative (U.S.)
ADM	Assistant Deputy Minister (Canada)
AFSOC	Air Force Special Operations Command
AJP	Allied Joint Publication (NATO)
AMF	Afghan Militia Forces (U.S.)
BMD	Ballistic Missile Defence
BSE	bovine spongiform encephalopathy
C2W	Command and Control Warfare (U.S.)
CA	Civic Action (U.S.) or Civil Affairs (NATO, Canada, U.S.)
CBP	Bureau of Customs and Border Protection (U.S.)
CBR	Chemical, Biological, and Radiological
CD	Counter-Drug
CF	Canadian Forces
CFIOG	Canadian Forces Information Operations Group
CIA	Central Intelligence Agency (U.S.)
CIC	Citizenship and Immigration Canada
CIDA	Canadian International Development Agency
CIDG	Civilian Irregular Defense Group (U.S.)
CIMIC	Civil-Military Cooperation (U.S., NATO)
CJTF	Combined Joint Task Force (U.S., NATO)
CNA	Computer Network Attack (Canada, U.S.)
CND	Computer Network Defence (Canada, U.S.)
CNE	Computer Network Exploitation (Canada, U.S.)
CNO	Computer Network Operations (Canada, U.S.)
CNT	Counter Narco-Terrorism (U.S.)
COG	Coordination and Operations Group (Canada)

COS	Commandement des Opérations Spéciales (France)
COSC	Commando Officer Selection Course (Australia)
CP	Counter-Proliferation (U.S.)
CPC	Clerk of the Privy Council (Canada)
CPWMD	Counter-Proliferation of Weapons of Mass Destruction (U.S.)
CSAR	Combat Search and Rescue (U.S., NATO)
CSE	Communications Security Establishment (Canada)
CSIS	Canadian Security and Intelligence Service
CSIS	Center for Strategic and International Studies (US NGO)
CT	Counter-Terrorism (U.S.)
CTCMA	Counter-Terrorism and Consequence Management Arrangements (Canada)
CTE	Commando Task Element (Australia)
CTSO	Counter-Terrorism and Special Operations (Canada)
D Space D	Directorate of Space Development (Canada)
DA	Direct Action (U.S.)
DART	Disaster Assistance Response Team (Canada, U.S.)
DCPC	Deputy Clerk of the Privy Council (Canada)
DDR	Disarmament, Demobilisation and Reintegration (UN)
DFA	Department of Foreign Affairs (Canada)
DFAIT	Department of Foreign Affairs and International Trade (Canada); see also FAC
DLSC	Directorate of Land Strategic Concepts
DM	Deputy Minister (Canada)
DND	Department of National Defence (Canada)
DSC	Defence Systems Limited (U.K.)
DSS	Diplomatic Security Service (U.S.)
EBO	Effects-based operations (U.S., Canada)
EO	Executive Outcomes (South Africa)
ERT	Police Emergency Response Team (Canada, U.S.)
EU	European Union
FAC	Foreign Affairs Canada (formerly DFAIT)
FAR	Field Anomaly Relaxation
FE	Field Elements (Australia)
FEMA	Federal Emergency Management Authority (U.S.)
FID	Foreign Internal Defense (U.S.)
FJS	*Fallskarmsjagerkola* (Sweden)
FOB	Forward Operating Base (U.S., NATO)
FSO	Foreign Service Officer (Canada)
FSSF	Devil's Brigade, First Special Service Force (Canada-U.S.)
GEOCC	Government Emergency Operations Coordination Centre (Canada)
GPS	Global Positioning System
GROM	*Grupa Reagowania Operacyjno Mobilnego* (Poland)
GSG	Gurkha Security Guards (U.K.)

GSG 9	*Grenzschutzgruppe* 9 (Germany)
HUMINT	Human Intelligence (U.S.)
HV	*Hrvatski Vojnik*, Croatian Army
IAC	Intelligence Advisory Committee (Canada)
IAEA	International Atomic Energy Agency
IAS	Intelligence Advisory Secretariat (Canada)
ICC	International Criminal Court
ICJ	International Court of Justice
ICSI	Interdepartmental Committee on Security and Intelligence (Canada)
IDCSP	Initial Defence Communications Satellite Project (U.S.)
INS	Immigration and Naturalization Service (U.S.)
IO	Information Operations
IPAG	Interdepartmental Policy Advisory Group (Canada)
IPB	Intelligence Preparation of the Battlefield (U.S.)
IPG	Interdepartmental Policy Group (Canada)
IPTF	International Police Task Force (UN)
ISAF	International Security Assistance Force (NATO operations in Afghanistan)
ITAR	International Traffic in Arms Regulations (U.S.)
ITGA	Islamic Transitional Government of Afghanistan (NZ)
ITW/AA	Integrated Tactical Warning/Attack Assessment platform (U.S.)
JCO	Joint Commission Observers (U.K., NATO)
JCS	Joint Chiefs of Staff (U.S.)
JIATF	Joint Interagency Task Force (U.S.)
JSOC	Joint Special Operations Command (U.S.)
JSOF	Joint Special Operations Forces (NATO)
JSOTF	Joint Special Operations Task Force (U.S.)
JTF 2	Joint Task Force 2 (Canada)
KDOM	Kosovo Diplomatic Observer Mission
KFOR	Kosovo Force (NATO)
KLA	Kosovo Liberation Army
KSK	*Kommando Spezialkräfte* (Germany)
KVCC	Kosovo Verification Coordination Centre
KVM	Kosovo Verification Mission
LNO	Liaison Officer or Liaison Officer Teams (NZ)
MACVSOG	Military Assistance Command Vietnam Studies and Observation Group (U.S.)
MC	Memorandum to Cabinet (Canada)
MMSI	Ministers' Meeting on Security and Intelligence (Canada)
MONUC	*Mission Observateur Nations Unies au Congo*
MPRI	Military Professional Resources International
NALT	Northern Alliance Liaison Team (U.S.)
NATO	North Atlantic Treaty Organisation
NBCRT	Nuclear, Biological and Chemical Reaction Team (Canada)

NCACC	National Conventional Arms Control Committee (U.S.)
NCTP	National Counter-Terrorism Plan (Canada)
NEO	Non-combatant Evacuation Operations (U.S.)
NGO	Non-Governmental organizations
NOC	National Operations Centre (Canada)
NORAD	North American Aerospace Defense
NSA	National Security Agency (U.S.)
NSC	National Support Centre (Canada)
NSC	National Security Council (U.S.)
NVAT	Network Vulnerability Assessment Teams (Canada)
OAF	Operation Allied Force, the NATO air campaign in Kosovo/ Serbia, 1999
OAS	Organization of American States
OCIPEP	Office of Critcal Infrastructure Protection and Emergency Preparedness (Canada)
ODA	Operational Detachment "Alpha" (U.S.)
ODTC	Office of Defense Trade Controls (U.S. Department of State)
OECD	Organisation for Economic Cooperation and Development
OEF	Operation Enduring Freedom (U.S.)
OPI	Office of Primary Interest
OPSEC	Operational Security (Canada, U.S.)
OSCE	Organization for Security and Cooperation in Europe
PAG	Public Affairs Group (Canada)
PCO	Privy Council Office (Canada)
PGM	Precision-guided missile
PMC	Private military company
PMO	Prime Minister's Office (Canada)
PRT	Provincial Reconstruction Team (U.S., NATO, Afghanistan)
PSAT	Ad Hoc Committee on Public Security and Anti-Terrorism (Canada)
PSC	Private security company
PSYOPS	Psychological Operations (U.S.)
RCMP	Royal Canadian Mounted Police
RDO	Rapid Decisive Operations (U.S.)
RPIMa	*Régiment de Parachutistes d'Infantrie de Marine* (France)
RUF	Revolutionary United Front (Sierra Leone)
S16	Section 16 Committee (Canada)
SAR	Search and Rescue
SARS	Severe acute respiratory syndrome
SAS	Special Air Service (U.K., Australia)
SASR	Special Air Service Regiment(Australia)
SBS	Special Boat Service (U.K.)
SCONDSA	Standing Committee on National Defence and Security Affairs
SCONDVA	Standing Committee on National Defence and Veteran's Affairs
SDI	Strategic Defence Initiative

SEAL	Sea-Air-Land (US) Naval Special Forces
September 11	Attack on the World Trade Center and Pentagon, 11 September 2001
SF	Special Forces
SFOR	Stabilisation Force (NATO)
SG	Solicitor General (Canada)
SIGINT	Signals Intelligence (Canada)
SIMG	Standard Infantry Machine Gun (Australia)
SIS	Special Intelligence Services (U.K.)
SO	Special Operations
SOE	Special Operations Executive (U.S.)
SOF	Special Operations Forces (U.S.)
SOG	Special Operations Group (U.S.)
SPHEP	Security, Public Health and Emergency Preparedness (Canada)
SR	Special Reconnaissance (U.S.)
SSE	Sensitive Site Exploitation (U.S.)
SSG	Special Protection Forces (Sweden)
SWORD	Small Wars Operations Research Directorate (U.S.)
TAG	Technical Advisory Group (Canada)
TF	Task Force
UAV	Unmanned Aerial Vehicle
UCK	Kosovo Liberation Army
UNAMA	UN Assistance Mission to Afghanistan
UNCIVPOL	UN Civil Police
UNDP	UN Development Program
UNHCR	UN High Commission for Refugees
UNITA	Union for the Total Independence of Angola
UNMIBH	UN Mission in Bosnia-Herzegovina
UNMIK	United Nations Mission in Kosovo
UNSF	UN Security Force (West Irian, 1963)
UNTAG	UN Transition Assistance Group (Namibia, 1989)
UNTEA	UN Transitional Executive Authority (West Irian, 1963)
USAID	United States Agency for International Development
UW	Unconventional Warfare (U.S.)
VJ	*Vojnik Jugoslavien*, Yugoslav Army
WFP	World Food Program (UN)
WMD	Weapons of Mass Destruction (U.S.)
WWW	World Wide Web

CONTRIBUTORS

Susan Breau, PhD is the Dorset Fellow in Public International Law at the British International Institute of International and Comparative Law. She taught international law at Queen's University Belfast and currently is a visiting fellow at the London School of Economics.

Bernadette Dececchi is a doctoral candidate in the Department of Education at the Ontario Institute of Advanced Studies in Education. Her research focuses on non-commissioned members' experiences in military education.

Tom Dececchi, PhD teaches in the department of Business Administration and in the Graduate Program in Defence Management and Policy at the Royal Military College of Canada.

Andrew B. Godefroy, PhD served with both the Directorate of Space Development and the Canadian Forces Joint Operations Group from 1999-2004, during which time he was involved with strategic space analysis as well as operational definition and development of Canadian Forces experimental operational space-support concepts and procedures.

Jamie Green is an air force officer cadet at the Royal Military College of Canada studying politics and researching contemporary conflict.

T. S. (Todd) Hataley is currently a PhD candidate at Queen's University, with a research focus on the management of international boundaries.

Michael A. Hennessy, PhD is an Associate Professor of History and War Studies and Chairman of the History Department of the Royal Military College of Canada.

Bernd Horn, PhD is a Canadian infantry officer who is currently the Director of the Canadian Forces Leadership Institute and an adjunct associate professor of history at RMC.

James D. Kiras, PhD is assistant professor of comparative military studies in the School of Advanced Air and Space Studies at the US Air War College. From 2001 he worked on special operations policy issues for the US Department of Defense, and he is currently a senior fellow with the Strategic Studies Group at the Joint Special Operation University, Hurlburt Field.

Scott Knight, PhD is a former Canadian Air Force pilot and professor in the Electrical and Computer Engineering department at the Royal Military College of Canada.

Tim Lannan, MA is a Canadian officer with experience of special operations, currently working with the Asymmetrical Threat Working Group and staff responsible for counter-terrorism and special operations.

David Last, PhD is a Canadian artillery officer who teaches political science and war studies at the Royal Military College of Canada and currently serves as the Registrar.

Sylvain P. Leblanc is Canadian Signals officer, doctoral candidate, and professor in the Business Administration Department of the Royal Military College of Canada.

Christian Leuprecht, PhD is a Social Sciences Research Council of Canada postdoctoral fellow in the Department of Political Science and Economics at the Royal Military College of Canada

Michelle Malenfant, MA is a Canadian reserve intelligence officer who studied international relations at Dalhousie and has worked with the Canadian International Development Agency and the Office of Public Diplomacy at NATO Headquarters.

Sean M. Maloney, PhD is a Canadian historian who travels widely in operational theatres. His recent books include *Canada and UN Peacekeeping*,

Glen Milne is an adjunct professor at Carleton University, Ottawa, and a consultant providing facilitation, strategy, policy, and training to government, non-profit and business organizations.

Stephanie Mullen is completing her PhD at Carleton University on women in the Canadian Commons and Senate. She teaches politics at Queen's University in Kingston.

Jason S. Ridler, MA is a doctoral candidate in War Studies at the Royal Military College and has developed and taught courses on technology and war for officer professional education. He has also published works of horror, crime, and science fiction.

Nicole Schwarz-Morgan, PhD teaches politics and philosophy at the Royal Military College and is researching the impact of technology on the human brain focusing on dysfunctions of children and young adults. She is an associated researcher with the Laboratoire d'Analyse de l'Information Stratégique et de Veille Technologique, École Militaire de St-Cyr, Coëtquidan (France).

Christopher Spearin, PhD is an Assistant Professor of National Security Studies at the Canadian Forces College, Toronto, where he teaches in the Command and Staff Course, the Advanced Military Studies Course, and the National Security Studies Course.

Hugh Thorburn, PhD is professor *emeritus* at Queen's University in Kingston, teaches politics, and has edited eight editions of *Party Politics in Canada*.

Benjamin Zyla is a doctoral candidate in War Studies at the Royal Military College with degrees from Germany and Canada. He teaches politics at RMC and is conducting research on foreign policy and security.

Queen's Policy Studies
Recent Publications

The Queen's Policy Studies Series is dedicated to the exploration of major policy issues that confront governments in Canada and other western nations. McGill-Queen's University Press is the exclusive world representative and distributor of books in the series.

School of Policy Studies

Force of Choice: Perspectives on Special Operations, Bernd Horn, J. Paul de B. Taillon, and David Last (eds.), 2004 Paper ISBN 1-55339-042-3 Cloth 1-55339-043-1

New Missions, Old Problems, Douglas L. Bland, David Last, Franklin Pinch, and Alan Okros (eds.), 2004 Paper ISBN 1-55339-034-2 Cloth 1-55339-035-0

The North American Democratic Peace: Absence of War and Security Institution-Buiding in Canada-US Relations, 1867-1958, Stéphane Roussel, 2004
Paper ISBN 0-88911-937-6 Cloth 0-88911-932-2

Implementing Primary Care Reform: Barriers and Facilitators, Ruth Wilson, S.E.D. Shortt and John Dorland (eds.), 2004 Paper ISBN 1-55339-040-7 Cloth 1-55339-041-5

Social and Cultural Change, David Last, Franklin Pinch, Douglas L. Bland, and Alan Okros (eds.), 2004 Paper ISBN 1-55339-032-6 Cloth 1-55339-033-4

Clusters in a Cold Climate: Innovation Dynamics in a Diverse Economy, David A. Wolfe and Matthew Lucas (eds.), 2004 Paper ISBN 1-55339-038-5 Cloth 1-55339-039-3

Canada Without Armed Forces? Douglas L. Bland (ed.), 2004
Paper ISBN 1-55339-036-9 Cloth 1-55339-037-7

Campaigns for International Security: Canada's Defence Policy at the Turn of the Century, Douglas L. Bland and Sean M. Maloney, 2004
Paper ISBN 0-88911-962-7 Cloth 0-88911-964-3

Understanding Innovation in Canadian Industry, Fred Gault (ed.), 2003
Paper ISBN 1-55339-030-X Cloth ISBN 1-55339-031-8

Delicate Dances: Public Policy and the Nonprofit Sector, Kathy L. Brock (ed.), 2003
Paper ISBN 0-88911-953-8 Cloth ISBN 0-88911-955-4

Beyond the National Divide: Regional Dimensions of Industrial Relations, Mark Thompson, Joseph B. Rose and Anthony E. Smith (eds.), 2003
Paper ISBN 0-88911-963-5 Cloth ISBN 0-88911-965-1

The Nonprofit Sector in Interesting Times: Case Studies in a Changing Sector, Kathy L. Brock and Keith G. Banting (eds.), 2003
Paper ISBN 0-88911-941-4 Cloth ISBN 0-88911-943-0

Clusters Old and New: The Transition to a Knowledge Economy in Canada's Regions, David A. Wolfe (ed.), 2003 Paper ISBN 0-88911-959-7 Cloth ISBN 0-88911-961-9

The e-Connected World: Risks and Opportunities, Stephen Coleman (ed.), 2003
Paper ISBN 0-88911-945-7 Cloth ISBN 0-88911-947-3

Knowledge, Clusters and Regional Innovation: Economic Development in Canada, J. Adam Holbrook and David A. Wolfe (eds.), 2002
Paper ISBN 0-88911-919-8 Cloth ISBN 0-88911-917-1

Lessons of Everyday Law/Le droit du quotidien, Roderick Alexander Macdonald, 2002
Paper ISBN 0-88911-915-5 Cloth ISBN 0-88911-913-9

Improving Connections Between Governments and Nonprofit and Voluntary Organizations: Public Policy and the Third Sector, Kathy L. Brock (ed.), 2002
Paper ISBN 0-88911-899-X Cloth ISBN 0-88911-907-4

Institute of Intergovernmental Relations

Canada: The State of the Federation 2003, vol. 17, *Reconfiguring Aboriginal-State Relations,* Michael Murphy (ed.), 2005 Paper ISBN 1-55339-010-5 Cloth ISBN 1-55339-011-3

Canada: The State of the Federation 2002, vol. 16, *Reconsidering the Institutions of Canadian Federalism,* J. Peter Meekison, Hamish Telford and Harvey Lazar (eds.), 2004
Paper ISBN 1-55339-009-1 Cloth ISBN 1-55339-008-3

Federalism and Labour Market Policy: Comparing Different Governance and Employment Strategies, Alain Noël (ed.), 2004
Paper ISBN 1-55339-006-7 Cloth ISBN 1-55339-007-5

The Impact of Global and Regional Integration on Federal Systems: A Comparative Analysis, Harvey Lazar, Hamish Telford and Ronald L. Watts (eds.), 2003
Paper ISBN 1-55339-002-4 Cloth ISBN 1-55339-003-2

Canada: The State of the Federation 2001, vol. 15, *Canadian Political Culture(s) in Transition,* Hamish Telford and Harvey Lazar (eds.), 2002
Paper ISBN 0-88911-863-9 Cloth ISBN 0-88911-851-5

Federalism, Democracy and Disability Policy in Canada, Alan Puttee (ed.), 2002
Paper ISBN 0-88911-855-8 Cloth ISBN 1-55339-001-6, ISBN 0-88911-845-0 (set)

Comparaison des régimes fédéraux, 2e éd., Ronald L. Watts, 2002
ISBN 1-55339-005-9

John Deutsch Institute for the Study of Economic Policy

Higher Education in Canada, Charles M. Beach, Robin W. Boadway and R. Marvin McInnis (eds.), 2005 Paper ISBN 1-55339-070-9 Cloth ISBN 1-55339-069-5

The 2003 Federal Budget: Conflicting Tensions, Charles M. Beach and Thomas A. Wilson (eds.), 2004 Paper ISBN 0-88911-958-9 Cloth ISBN 0-88911-956-2

Canadian Immigration Policy for the 21st Century, Charles M. Beach, Alan G. Green and Jeffrey G. Reitz (eds.), 2003 Paper ISBN 0-88911-954-6 Cloth ISBN 0-88911-952-X

Framing Financial Structure in an Information Environment, Thomas J. Courchene and Edwin H. Neave (eds.), Policy Forum Series no. 38, 2003
Paper ISBN 0-88911-950-3 Cloth ISBN 0-88911-948-1

Towards Evidence-Based Policy for Canadian Education/Vers des politiques canadiennes d'éducation fondées sur la recherche, Patrice de Broucker and/et Arthur Sweetman (eds./dirs.), 2002 Paper ISBN 0-88911-946-5 Cloth ISBN 0-88911-944-9

Money, Markets and Mobility: Celebrating the Ideas of Robert A. Mundell, Nobel Laureate in Economic Sciences, Thomas J. Courchene (ed.), 2002
Paper ISBN 0-88911-820-5 Cloth ISBN 0-88911-818-3

Available from: McGill-Queen's University Press
c/o Georgetown Terminal Warehouses
34 Armstrong Avenue
Georgetown, Ontario L7G 4R9
Tel: (877) 864-8477 / Fax: (877) 864-4272
E-mail: orders@gtwcanada.com